AN INTRODUCTION TO INDIAN PHILOSOPHY

An Introduction to Indian Philosophy offers a profound yet accessible survey of the development of India's philosophical tradition. Beginning with the formation of Brāhmaṇical, Jaina, Materialist and Buddhist traditions, Bina Gupta guides the reader through the classical schools of Indian thought, culminating in a look at how these traditions inform Indian philosophy and society in modern times. Offering translations from source texts and clear explanations of philosophical terms, this text provides a rigorous overview of Indian philosophical contributions to epistemology, metaphysics, philosophy of language and ethics. This is a must-read for anyone seeking a reliable and illuminating introduction to Indian philosophy.

Bina Gupta is Curators' Distinguished Research Professor, Professor of Philosophy and Director of South Asian Studies Program at the University of Missouri.

Chapter 2 : The Vedas

AN INTRODUCTION TO INDIAN PHILOSOPHY

Perspectives on Reality, Knowledge, and Freedom

Bina Gupta

NEW YORK AND LONDON

First published 2012
by Routledge
711 Third Avenue, New York, NY 10017

Simultaneously published in the UK
by Routledge
2 Park Square, Milton Park, Abingdon, Oxon OX14 4RN

Routledge is an imprint of the Taylor & Francis Group, an informa business

© 2012 Taylor & Francis

The right of Bina Gupta to be identified as author of this work has been asserted by her in accordance with sections 77 and 78 of the Copyright, Designs and Patents Act 1988.

All rights reserved. No part of this book may be reprinted or reproduced or utilised in any form or by any electronic, mechanical, or other means, now known or hereafter invented, including photocopying and recording, or in any information storage or retrieval system, without permission in writing from the publishers.

Trademark notice: Product or corporate names may be trademarks or registered trademarks, and are used only for identification and explanation without intent to infringe.

Library of Congress Cataloging-in-Publication Data
Gupta, Bina, 1947–
An introduction to Indian philosophy : perspectives on reality, knowledge, and freedom / Bina Gupta.
p. cm.
Includes bibliographical references and index.
1. Philosophy, Indic. I. Title.
B131.G87 2011
181'.4—dc22
2011005933

ISBN13: 978–0–415–80002–0 (hbk)
ISBN13: 978–0–415–80003–7 (pbk)
ISBN13: 978–0–203–80612–8 (ebk)

Typeset in Baskerville
by Swales & Willis Ltd, Exeter, Devon

To
Claudio
Who is the light of our daughter's life
And
Whom Madan and I cherish as our own son

CONTENTS

PREFACE

This book has grown out of an upper division Indian philosophy course and a graduate seminar on Advaita Vedānta that I regularly teach at the University of Missouri-Columbia. So, one could say that the present work has been in the making for over three decades.

Indian philosophy represents one of the most ancient traditions of human culture, yet Western philosophers generally ignore it. This neglect may stem from a presumption common among them that philosophy, as a systematic inquiry, properly understood, is exclusively a Western phenomenon—and hence absent within non-Western cultures. Thus I was not surprised when over a decade or so ago, I found the philosophy faculty at my university arguing that a course titled "Introduction to Philosophy" should only include Western philosophy as its content, thereby implying by the omission of a qualifying adjective that there is, or can be, no philosophy other than its Western incarnation. This book is conceived with the thought that the true understanding of the other requires respect for the other, not appropriating the other into oneself. Its novelty consists in highlighting—contrary to the dominant Western view—the fact that Indian philosophy is also truly philosophy, not merely spiritual, religious, and esoteric, while at the same time having its own distinctively unique approaches to things. This book clearly demonstrates that there exists an amazing variety of epistemological, metaphysical, ethical, and religious conceptions in Indian philosophy. These conceptions developed within a period, roughly, of 1,500 years, and contain very sophisticated arguments and counter-arguments that were advanced by the defenders of each thesis and its opponents. One of the goals of this book is to dispel these myths and bring out the theoretical, discursive rigor of Indian philosophy.

"Indian Philosophy" refers to the philosophical concepts, theories, and schools that developed in the Indian sub-continent. In ancient days, most of the philosophical works were written in the Sanskrit language, while in modern times, philosophical works are written, not only in English, but also in many modern Indian languages. The Sanskrit words for "philosophy" are "*ānvikṣīkī*" (examination of things by the means of true cognition) and "*darśana*" ("standpoint" or "system"). The classical *darśanas* of Indian philosophy have been the focus of my attention in this work. Given the space limitations, it was not possible to include Islamic or Sikh traditions, though these religious and philosophical traditions have thrived in Indian culture for many centuries and have made important intellectual contributions.

Those who are familiar with Indian philosophy know well that Indian philosophy is rich and variegated; it represents the accumulation of an enormous body of material reflecting the philosophical activity of 3,000 years. It is a multifaceted tapestry and cannot be identified by one of its strands. Thus, the task of providing an introduction to such a vast topic as Indian philosophy is daunting, both by virtue of its magnitude and the competence needed to carry it out. Any author venturing to write such a book needs to be conversant not only with the general philosophical issues, history of Indian philosophy, the Buddhist thought, but must also possess necessary linguistic skills, i.e., expertise in the Sanskrit language, a combination which is not easy to come by.

There are two standard approaches Indian philosophy: the topical and the historical. The topical approach expounds Indian philosophy under such headings as "Theory of Knowledge," "Metaphysics," "Ethics," "Social and Political Philosophy," and brings together the various views held by different philosophers and/or philosophical systems irrespective of the historical order in which these views appeared, took shape, and developed. J. N. Mohanty's *Classical Indian Philosophy* follows this approach. The historical approach, on the other hand, arranges the various systems in the order in which they appeared; thus, an account of the Vedic and the Upaniṣadic thought precedes the introduction of the Buddhist philosophy. Hiriyanna's *Outlines of Indian Philosophy* follows this approach. A historian, irrespective of how valuable his/her work may be, is likely to be bogged down with philosophical questions, and may not be sensitive to the ways the philosophical questions and issues outlive their introduction and may have a life of their own. In this book on Indian philosophy the issues, arguments counter-arguments, objections, responses to the objections, and so on, contribute the main driving force, though an historical order of exposition prevails.

No philosophy or philosophical system exists in a vacuum; a philosophy neither originates nor develops bereft of some under-girding context. It is a product of the contemporaneous and preceding cultures and exerts a decisive formative influence on the social and cultural achievements of ages that follow. A system of philosophy must be evaluated in light of its own aim and historical setting, by comparison with the systems immediately preceding and following it, by its antecedents as well as the results, and by the developments to which it leads. Keeping this in view, the systems are introduced in a historical order, but the exposition of each system focuses on certain key questions and issues. The approach therefore may be called historical-cum-philosophical. It demonstrates that there has been through the centuries a remarkable development, emergence of new interpretations of the ancient texts, new ways of arguing for the old theses, and sometimes a totally novel point of view.

The source material of Indian philosophy particularly demands such a combination. The basic Sanskrit texts are presented in argument-counter-arguments, objection-reply forms, and I would like the Western students to learn to appreciate the rhetoric that bears testimony to the vibrant Indian intellectual life. Such a mode of presentation is also needed to dispel, as stated earlier, from the minds of the Western readers certain persistent myths about Indian philosophy, and to bring home to them the truth of Indian philosophy, namely that it has been a genuinely philosophical and intellectual, highly sophisticated, rigorous discipline. The attempt is made to (1) understand a particular philosophical system in its integrity, to enter into its fundamental doctrines with an open mind in order to grasp its philosophy as a whole; (2) subject each philosophical school has been subject to philosophical criticisms, first of an internal sort, in order to reveal fundamental inconsistencies between the different assumptions of the philosophy, and secondly, an external sort which discloses the limitations of a given philosophy when judged by reference to phases of human experience and knowledge to which it fails to do justice.

The book will serve two additional basic purposes: it will (1) help students understand the different ways in which basic philosophic issues have been considered in India, and (2) introduce the students to an understanding of the Indian mind.

This book, while staying close to Sanskrit sources, (1) expounds various positions rather freely and in some details which are relevant for the contemporary students' interests, and (2) for each part, adds some selected texts in lucid English translation without jeopardizing the integrity of original Sanskrit texts. Wherever necessary, I have added comments in parentheses to make translations easier to understand. It is my hope that these translations will give the student some taste of the literary style and philosophical rhetoric of the source material, without being too bogged down with the philosophical questions.

Regarding the content of this book, after an introduction that sets the stage for what is to come in the subsequent chapters, I begin with the Vedas and the Upaniṣads, the foundational texts of the tradition, where one finds the first philosophical questions and some decisive answers. I discuss the three *nāstika* and the six *āstika* systems. The encounter with the Buddhist critique led to the rise and the strengthening of the Vedic *darśanas*, each with its epistemological bases, logical theory, metaphysics, and ethics. A systematic exposition of the *darśanas* gradually takes precedence over the historical and we have the six *āstika darśanas* expounded in a manner that skips over centuries of development. All this leads to the section in which four schools of Buddhism and Vedānta become the focus of my attention, because as we stand today in the twenty first century, it is these two that have earned a global interest. There have been numerous attempts to interpret and reinterpret them in novel ways. In my interpretations, I have tried to be as faithful to the Indian tradition as was possible for me, in order to enable my readers to have an accurate and authentic understanding of the various philosophical conceptions that are found on the Indian philosophical scene.

Regarding the audience, it is my hope that this book will introduce undergraduate students, possibly beginning graduate students, to classical Indian philosophy. Its primary audience will be philosophy students who have already been introduced to Western philosophy but not yet to Indian philosophy. Therefore, it is safe to assume that these students will have familiarity with such philosophical terminologies as "theory of knowledge," "metaphysics," reality," and "appearance." They, however, will have no acquaintance with such Indian philosophical terms as "*ātman*," "*brahman*," "*pramāṇas*," "*dharma*," "*mokṣa*," etc. Though I have explained these technical terms suitably, I have used these Sanskrit terms throughout the book in order to make students familiar with basic Indian philosophical vocabulary. I have tried to make use of them as much as was needed in my view to represent the schools in the manner they were expounded in Sanskrit works and I have tried my best to avoid making them difficult. How far I have been successful I will let my readers judge.

Writing this book has been a difficult enterprise. I recognize that some of the material discussed in this book is very complex. This complexity is confounded by the problems involved in translating complex philosophical concepts from Sanskrit to English. I apologize for any difficulty the students may encounter in following my exegesis and interpretation. If this work challenges the students to further investigate the issues raised herein, I will have succeeded in my effort.

It is both a duty and a pleasure to express my sincere thanks to those friends, scholars, and students who have contributed to this work in various ways. It is not possible to list them all individually. I extend my heartfelt gratitude to such scholars as Sibjiban Bhattacharyya, B. K. Matilal, J. N. Mohanty, and Karl Potter, whose books and papers have played a significant role in shaping my views on the issues under consideration. I want to thank Mr. Kim Sang, Director, Asian Affairs Center at the University of Missouri–Columbia, for providing me all sorts of assistance with my research projects. Finally, I would like to thank my husband, Madan, and daughter, Swati, for believing in me, supporting me, and being there for me when I needed them.

Bina Gupta
Columbia, Missouri
December 25, 2010

ABBREVIATIONS

AV	*Atharva Veda*
BG	*Bhagavad Gītā*
BGBh	*Bhagavad Gītābhāṣya*
BP	*Bhāṣā-Parriccheda with Siddhānta-Muktavalī*, Advaita Ashrama edition
BS	*Brahmasūtra*
BSBh	*Brahmasūtrabhāṣya*
BU	*Bṛhadāraṇyaka Upaniṣad*
CU	*Chāndogya Upaniṣad*
KUBh	*Kena Upaniṣadbhāṣya*
MAU	*Māṇḍukya Upaniṣad*
MMK	*Mūlamadhyamakakārikā*
MU	*Muṇḍaka Upaniṣad*
NB	*Nyāya Bhāṣya*
NS	*Nyāya Sūtras*
RV	*Ṛg Veda*
SB	*Śatpatha Brāhmaṇa*
SDS	*Sarvadarśanasaṁgraha*, Chowkhamba Sanskrit Series edition.
SK	*Sāṁkhya-kārikā*
Śvetā	*Śvetāśvatara Upaniṣad*
TPS	*Tattvopaplavsiṃha*
TSD	*Tarka-Saṃgraha of Annaṃbhaṭṭa with Dīpīka*, Progressive Publishers edition
TSDNB	*Tarka-Saṃgraha of Annaṃbhaṭṭa with Dīpīka*, Bombay Sanskrit and Prakrit Series edition
TU	*Taittirīya Upaniṣad*
TUBh	*Taittirīya Upaniṣadbhāṣya*
VP	*Vedānta Paribhāṣā*

Part I

1

INTRODUCTION

I Preliminary Considerations

In my classes on Indian philosophy in American universities, I am often asked: what is Indian philosophy? How is Indian philosophy different from Western philosophy? I find it difficult to answer these questions because I am being asked not only "what is philosophy" but also what makes Indian philosophy "Indian." In dealing with such general questions, one must always bear in mind that the frequently used designation "Indian philosophy" is as much a construction concealing in its fold many internal distinctions as is the designation "Western philosophy." One cannot but point out—which would be obvious to my readers—that the difference between Western analytic philosophy, as it took shape from Russell and Wittgenstein onwards, is substantially different from the Western post-Kantian philosophy which developed from Kant to Hegel. Thus, the designations "Indian" and "Western" do not bring together any common essence among systems of thinking coming under them, excepting features which may indeed be contingently related to philosophical thinking, namely, geographical points of origin.

It seems to me that history and geography are not of much help in this search for essential features of a philosophical tradition. It is indeed anachronistic to give a geographical adjective to a mode of thinking, unless one agrees with Nietzsche's statement that Indian philosophy has something to do with the Indian food and climate, and German Idealism with the German love of beer. There must be some way of characterizing a philosophical tradition other than identifying such contingent features as the geographical and historical milieu in which it was born, some way of identifying it by its concepts and logic, the problems, the methods, and other issues that are internal to the tradition under consideration.

Prior to the Colonial period, philosophers of India did not concern themselves with the question of the differences between Indian and Western philosophy. Most of these philosophers wrote in Sanskrit, some in their local languages, and never sought to distinguish what they were doing from what was being done outside the pan-Indic culture. The task of distinguishing Indian thought from the Western modes of thinking became gradually important to Indian philosophers in the Colonial period. Almost every Indian philosopher worth the name, writing in English (because that was the only Western language in which they wrote), expressed some opinion about it, although these opinions differed considerably. It is worth noting, however, that no Western philosopher—unless he/she was also an Indologist, e.g., Paul Deussen (1845–1919), Halbfass (1940–2000), or had acquired some acquaintance with Indian thought under the guidance of an Indologist, e.g., Schopenhauer (1788–1860), and Hegel (1770–1831)—thought it necessary to delimit what is called "Western philosophy" from non-Western philosophies. It is difficult to ascertain the reason for this asymmetry; perhaps, it is a political rather than a philosophical question. Likewise, the Indian philosophers of the classical period, e.g., Śaṃkara (788–820 CE), Vācaspati (900–980), or Raghunāth Śiromaṇi (1477–1557) did not deem it necessary to distinguish their domain of thinking from the Western or the Chinese thought. However, since the question has been raised, philosophers like me—trained both in Western thought and traditional Indian philosophy, writing on Indian philosophy, and hoping to contribute to the development of Indian thought while maintaining her continuity with the tradition—must provide a satisfactory answer. This predicament is not only mine, but also characterizes such thinkers as Sarvepalli Radhakrishnan (1888–1975), Bimal Matilal (1935–1991), and J. N. Mohanty (1928–present). It is incumbent on my part to concede that, though reared in the Western academia, I carry in my baggage the entire tradition of Indian thought.

There are two kinds of positions taken by my predecessors on the issue of how Indian philosophy is different from Western philosophy. One position, more prevalent in the generations of thinkers ending with Radhakrishnan as its high priest, may be articulated thus: in spite of superficial similarities, Indian and Western modes of thinking are fundamentally different, and this difference may be expressed in such binary oppositions as intellectual–intuition, discursive/logical–spiritual, and theoretical–practical. This way of looking at the contrast is rejected by such philosophers as Matilal and Mohanty, who tend to see affinities between the Indian and the Western modes of thinking, and argue that both traditions have developed their own logic, epistemology, and metaphysics, and so the binary oppositions listed above fail to capture the exact differences between the two traditions. These thinkers, especially Matilal, under the influence of modern Western philosophy overemphasize the analytic nature of Indian philosophy; Matilal selects and juxtaposes the Navya-Nyāya (the new Nyāya school) and the modern Western philosophy of language. Mohanty has also done a similar juxtaposition by selecting the theories of consciousness in Indian philosophy and modern Western phenomenological theories of intentionality from Brentano, Husserl, and Sartre. I stand in continuity with the second group of Indian thinkers and am greatly influenced by their writings. Matilal and Mohanty make a good case for bridging the distance between Indian and Western philosophies. My goal in this work however is not to bridge the distance between the two, but rather to focus primarily on Indian thought in its own terms as it presents itself to the participants in its discourse from ancient times up until the beginning of the Colonial period. The question is: How was the Indian world of thinking circumscribed? If we can give an adequate representation of this world in the broadest outline, it would enable us to compare and contrast the pictures that emerge. I will attempt a total circumspection of the structure of Indian thought, in the hope that it would not only make differences between Indian and Western philosophies evident, but also recognize affinities brought out by the thinkers of the last generation.

II Philosophy and Cultural Context

All human activity, philosophical or otherwise, takes its distinctive shape within a cultural setting and tends to bear the mark of that culture. In reviewing the concept and the scope of "philosophy" in the Western context, we see that it has changed considerably over the 2,500 years of its existence. As is well known, the word "philosophy" etymologically means "love of wisdom" (from the Greek "*philia*" meaning "love or desire," and "*sophia*" meaning "wisdom"). Philosophy thus originally signified any general practical concern, encompassing in its scope what today are generally known as the natural and social sciences. As late as the eighteenth century, physics was still called "natural philosophy." Eventually, science broke away from philosophy and became an independent discipline in its own right. The separation forced philosophers to redefine the nature, goals, method, and boundaries of their own inquiry.

One tradition within speculative philosophy has always focused its attention on metaphysics. Philosophy in this context is considered to be an inquiry into the nature of ultimate reality. The business of metaphysics, it is argued, is to answer the most fundamental questions possible about the universe: its composition, the "stuff" of which it is composed, and the role of individuals within the world. The Platonic theory that over and above the world of particulars there exists a realm of forms, the theory that God created the universe, and that the soul is immortal, all furnish examples of metaphysical speculations. Until fairly recently, a majority of philosophers believed that speculative theorizing was one of the most important tasks of a philosopher. Most Western philosophers today no longer believe that the role of philosophy is to "discover" the real nature of the world; it is rather, first and foremost, to provide a clarification of the basic concepts and propositions in and through which philosophic inquiry proceeds. These philosophers are only interested in the linguistic study of logical analysis of propositions, concepts, and terms. Their contention is that philosophy's primary function is to analyze statements, to identify their precise meaning, and to study the nature of concepts *per se* to ensure that they are used correctly and consistently. This conception of philosophy as conceptual analysis is widespread among philosophers, especially in Great Britain and America, and such a linguistic analysis is considered to be the *sine qua non* of any proper philosophical enterprise. The point that I am trying to make is as follows: the presuppositions behind Western philosophy, which give it its unique character and flavor, are the product of a particular history and a set of discrete cultural traditions. Both the content and forms of inquiry distinctive of Western philosophic inquiry have been shaped to some indeterminate extent by—for want of a better term—the "meta-philosophical" assumptions, presuppositions, and values which, historically, have given philosophy its own unique and distinctive character.

Likewise, the context of Indian philosophy is particular to a specific set of cultural conditions, and its lineage is likewise different from the complex set of social, cultural, intellectual, and sociopolitical forces that have formed Western philosophy. The Indian tradition represents the accumulation of an enormous body of material reflecting the philosophical activity of 2,500 years. It goes back to the rich and the large Vedic corpus, the earliest and the most basic texts of Hinduism.[1] The earliest extant texts of the Hindus are the Vedas, a title which does not refer to a particular book, but rather to a literary corpus extending over two thousand years. The Indian philosophical tradition, in its rudiments, began in the hymns of the *Ṛg Veda* (which we will study in the next chapter), the earliest of the four Vedas composed most probably around 2000 BCE.[2] This rootedness has given rise to the widespread belief—not only among educated Western intelligentsia but also among the Indian scholars—that Indian philosophy is indistinguishable from the Hindu religion. The reason for this belief is obvious: it is possible that whoever were the first translators/interpreters of the Vedic literature saw there what they found to be a religious point of view consisting of beliefs, rituals, and practices, having an eschatological concern, and came to the unavoidable conclusion that, given that all Indian philosophical thinking goes back to the Vedic roots, the entire Indian philosophy must be religious in its motive, inspiration, and conceptualization. But to draw this conclusion from the literary and the philosophical evidence available is uncalled for. There are several mistakes in this argument, which will be obvious to my readers as we proceed in this work; however, I will draw the attention of my students to two such mistakes: (1) It results from an unthinking application of the Western word "religion," or its synonym, that covers up the distinctive character of Vedic religion. The very word "religion" being Western in origin, when applied to the Indian context, prejudges the issue. The entire attempt to impose the Western concept of "religion" over Vedic thought is a mistake. It completely distorts the significance of the Vedic hymns, the Vedic deities, and the entire worldview that articulates a certain relationship between human beings, nature, and the celestial beings in poetic forms. (2) The second mistake consists in not recognizing that if philosophy is borne out of pre-philosophical literature, then philosophy must also be of the same nature as that out of which it arises. Thus, the conceptual and logical sophistications of the Indian philosophical "schools" are totally overlooked out of either prejudice, or ignorance, or both.

Indian philosophy is rich and variegated. It is a multi-faceted tapestry and cannot be identified with one of its strands. Therefore, any simplification is an oversimplification. The problem is further compounded when we realize that in the Indian tradition there is no term corresponding to the Western term "philosophy." The term *"darśana"* used in the Indian tradition for "philosophy" is a rough approximation and lends itself to a variety of meanings not connoted by its Western counterpart. *"Darśana,"* derived from the Sanskrit root *"dṛś,"* means "to see" or a "way of seeing." "Seeing" as the end result of *darśana* is "seeing within"—the Indian seer sees the truth and makes it a part of his understanding. "Seeing within" should not, of course, be understood in a subjectivist sense; it signifies "seeing" or "insight" using the intellectual means with, the help of which insight is gained. Indian philosophy is not merely a search for knowledge of the ultimate reality but also a critical analysis of the data provided by perception. Leaving aside *darśana*, another term used to describe Indian philosophy is *"ānvīkṣikī,"* which has been defined as "a critical examination of the data provided by perception and scripture."[3] Inference is called *nyāya* because it consists in critically analyzing the data previously received by perception as well as by the authority derived from the foundational texts (Vedas). In case of a conflict between two, the testimony of the foundational texts was probed into, analyzed, in order to determine how far it could be reconciled with the canons of logical reasoning.

Darśana also means a "standpoint" or "perspective" (Cf. *dithi*, the Pāli word for "a point of view"). And it is in this second sense that Indians allowed the possibility of more than one *darśana*. There are nine *darśanas* or "schools" or "viewpoints" of Indian philosophy: Cārvāka, Buddhist Philosophy, Jaina, Sāṁkhya, Yoga, Nyāya, Vaiśeṣika, Mīmāṁsā, and Vedānta. Traditionally these schools are grouped under two headings: *nāstika*, and *āstika*, which in common parlance, signify "atheist" and "theist" respectively. However, in the Sanskrit philosophical commentaries and schools of Indian philosophy these terms mean "the one that denies the authority of the Vedas" and "the one that accepts the authority of the Vedas" respectively. Accordingly, the first three schools are generally called *"nāstika,"* and the last six *"āstika."* It is customary to couple the six *āstika darśanas* in pairs: Sāṁkhya-Yoga, Vaiśeṣika-Nyāya, and Vedānta-Mīmāṁsā; the former in each pair is viewed as providing a theoretical framework and the latter primarily a method of physical and spiritual training. However, in viewing the evolution of these schools such a coupling together does not make much sense: for example, it is misleading to characterize the Nyāya school as a method of physical and spiritual training. Neither the six *āstika darśanas* nor their basic framework is found in the Hindu foundational literature (Vedas). As a matter of fact, each *darśana* has grown and developed far beyond what was anticipated by the early scholars.

Philosophy in the Indian tradition was not simply an intellectual luxury, a merely conceptual hair splitting, a mere attempt to win an argument, or defeating an opponent, although all these excesses characterized many works of Indian philosophy. Underlying these excesses, there was an awareness of a thorough process of thinking towards a distant goal on the horizon for the individual person or for humankind as a whole. These *darśanas* had a certain acceptance of the relations between the theoretical and the spiritual, and a certain conception of being from within the bounds of a tradition. In order to comprehend the philosophies of these *darśanas*, it is imperative that one understands the context in which these philosophies are embedded. To this end, I will focus on several presuppositions of Indian philosophies.

III Presuppositions of Indian Philosophy

I will discuss three presuppositions, which are: (1) *karma* and rebirth, (2) *mokṣa*, and (3) *dharma*. In the language of R. G. Collingwood, we may call them "absolute presuppositions"[4] and the rest of the philosophy may be regarded as a rational and critical elaboration of these presuppositions. The resulting philosophies do not justify these presuppositions; they rather draw out what follows from them.

Karma/Rebirth: it is almost universally admitted that a common presupposition of pan-Indic thought is encapsulated in the words "*karma*/rebirth." The word "*karma*" is derived from the verbal root "*kṛ*," meaning "act," "bring about," "do," etc. Originally, "*karman*" referred to correct performance of ritualistic activity with a view to receiving the desired results. It was believed that if a ritual is duly performed, nobody, not even divinities, could stop the desired results. On the other hand, any mistake in the performance of rituals, say, a word mispronounced, will give rise to undesired results. Thus, a correct action was a right action and no moral value was attached to such an action. Eventually *karma* acquired larger meaning and came to signify any correct action having ethical implications. Depending on the context, it could mean (a) any act, irrespective of its nature; (b) a moral act, especially in the accepted ritualistic sense; and (c) accumulated results, i.e., unfructified fruits of all actions. Underlying these senses is the idea that a person by doing, by acting, creates something and shapes his/her destiny.

Karma is based on the single principle that no cause goes without producing its effects, and there is no effect that does not have an appropriate cause. Freed from any theological understanding, that is, independently of postulating any God or supreme being as the creator and destroyer of the world including animals and humans, the idea is to posit a necessary relation between actions in this life, previous births, and rebirth in the next. Since many of our actions seem to go unrewarded in the present life, and many evil actions go unpunished, it seems reasonable to suppose that such consequences, if they do not arise in this life, must arise in the next. *Karma* carries the belief that differences in the fortunes and the misfortunes of individual lives, to the extent they are not adequately explicable by known circumstances in this life, must be due to unknown (*adṛṣṭa*) causes which can only be actions done in their former lives. These two concepts of *karma* and rebirth are interlinked and together form a complex structure. Belief in *karma* is also shared both by the Buddhist and the

Jaina thinkers despite the differences in their metaphysical and religious beliefs. It has entered the American vocabulary and is expressed as "what goes around comes around."

The doctrine of *karma* forms the basis of a plethora of ethical, metaphysical, psychological, and religious Indian doctrines. A commonly stated account of *karma* in terms of "as you sow so shall you reap" or "as you act, so you enjoy or suffer" are attempts to connect the underlying thought to our ordinary ethical and soteriological thinking and, precisely for this reason, does not capture the underlying thought in its totality. A necessary sequence of lives, worlds (insofar as each experiencer has his/her own world), destinies, and redemptions is posited in order to eliminate all traces of contingency, arbitrariness, or good/bad luck from the underlying order. It is not a causal order in the ordinary sense, because the causal order obtains within a world and is not the result of the moral nature of God as the creator or attributing moral nature to the God (e.g., when one says "the God is good"), which presupposes that the God's will, despite its omnipotence, conforms to this underlying order. As a consequence, though religious thinkers in India formulated their concepts of divinity to conform to this underlying order, the very fact that the atheistic thinking, e.g., Buddhism, and non-theistic thinking, e.g., Advaita Vedānta (non-dualistic Vedānta), recognized this absolute presupposition only shows that theology, like morality, is only a faint attempt to throw light on this presupposition and does not completely illuminate it.

Though we understand the ideas of "*karma*" and "rebirth" and in some way wish to accept it, nevertheless our understanding and acceptance never rise up to the level of clarity that we expect of our thoughts. In this context, Heidegger's insight—Being as distinguished from beings can never be brought to pure presence or complete illumination, that all unconcealment goes with concealment, presence with absence, light with darkness—makes me wonder whether it is possible to achieve clarity in the case of an absolute presupposition. All our attempts to capture the idea of *karma*/rebirth by employing the categories of causality, moral goodness, reward/punishment, and the logical idea of God as the dispenser of justice, are faint attempts to illuminate *karma* and rebirth, because the chosen categories are from the areas of experiences in mundaneity with which the thinker is familiar, areas *karma* and rebirth however cover past, present, and future experiences.

Most Indian thinkers seek to establish *karma* on logical grounds. The two familiar arguments are that in the absence of such an order, there would arise the twin fallacies of phenomena that are not caused and that which do not produce any effect. This idea of necessary causality requires, better yet, demands, that every event has a cause and that every event must produce its effects. It is worth noting in this context that the idea of causal necessity that is applied is modeled after empirical and natural order best exemplified in scientific laws and philosophically captured in Kant's Second Analogy of Experience.[5] The resulting understanding of *karma*/rebirth then becomes a super science, a science that not only comprehends the natural order and the human order but also all possible worlds, each world corresponding to one birth. The order that is being posited in the *karma*/rebirth is not a natural order, and what is called a "theory," if it is a theory, is neither a scientific theory nor a super science. Many Hindu and the Buddhist enthusiasts wish to see it as a scientific theory, though it does not share any features of a scientific theory. Then, there are those who regard it a "convenient fiction,"[6] which would imply that the entire pan-Indian culture, both the Vedic and the Buddhist, is based upon a fiction. Again, where must we position ourselves as critics in order to hold such a view of these ultimate presuppositions? As thinkers, we have no ground to stand upon from which we can pass such a judgment.

A plausible philosophical move would be to say that *karma*/rebirth encapsulates Indic peoples' understanding of a transcendental ground of the human life and the world. It is not an empirical or scientific theory, it belongs to a different order, neither natural nor supernatural (the supernatural being understood as another natural). The transcendental, usually construed as the domain of subjectivity, selectively isolates an area of human experience and grounds the totality of the empirical in it. Many thinkers have rejected this conception of ground and prefer that the ultimate ground be ontological, some principle of being. *Karma* and rebirth encapsulate a fundamental understanding of that ontological ground, of our relationship to the world, which cannot be adequately accounted by the metaphysic of nature or metaphysic of subjectivity. Both the Advaitins and the Buddhists postulate beginningless ignorance (*avidyā*) and argue that this principle accounts for our inescapable experience of obscurity, darkness, and failure to completely understand this ontological ground. And yet, both the Hindus and the Buddhist philosophers have sought to throw light on it in different ways and have assured us that though we do not quite understand it, wise individuals do, because they have a direct experience of this ontological ground. It is worth noting that in Advaita Vedānta, this beginningless *avidyā* is not simply non-knowledge, i.e., not knowing; it is also a positive entity, the source of all creativity, indeed, of entire mundaneity. In Indian thought *karma* rebirth, no matter how shielded from us, no matter how inviolable in its operations (even gods cannot escape it), gives to humans the possibility of escaping from its clutches, becoming truly free, and realizing one's essence, which is *mokṣa*.

Mokṣa: *Mokṣa* is the next absolute presupposition, functioning not as a determining ground but as the *telos* as it were beckoning humans to escape the ontological ground of *karma* and to come home to its transcendental essence. "*Mokṣa*" is derived from the Sanskrit root "*muc*," which means "to release" or "to free." Accordingly, it signifies "freedom," "release," i.e., freedom from bondage, freedom from contingency. *Mokṣa*—notwithstanding the differences regarding its nature and the path that leads to it—means spiritual freedom, freedom from the cycles of bondage, freedom from the mundane existence, and the realization of the state of bliss. It is the highest value—value in its most perfect form—a state of excellence, the highest good, which cannot be transcended and, when attained, leaves nothing else to be desired.

From the Indian standpoint, all human beings, in fact all living beings, are of dual nature, they are, in the words of Foucault, "empirical-transcendental doublets."[7] In one aspect, as being in the world, i.e., mundane, he transcends this-worldly nature into a series of other lives posited by the *karma*/rebirth order, in the other aspect, i.e., as transcendental self, he is a pure, free, non-worldly spirit as though inserted into the mundane context from which he aspires to achieve and return home. These two kinds of transcendences are different: transcendence into other lives and other worlds with which this life and world are connected by unspent traces conceived as forces is very different from the transcendence of all mundaneity into the pure spirit to be accomplished in *mokṣa*. The first transcendence we do not quite understand, although we try to make it intelligible in various ways using such natural categories as necessity, such moral categories as desert and punishment, and theological categories as divine goodness. The later, viz., *mokṣa*, is a possibility that stands before us on the horizon as pure light, self-shining, and whose pure light seems to blind us, because we are accustomed to seeing things in a mingling of light and darkness.

The conceptual problem really concerns how the empirical-transcendental doublet is made possible. How do I, who in essence is pure freedom, become or appear as my empirical being? In other words, how the transcendental appears as empirical? The origin of the empirical, its ontological ground, is not in the transcendental, but rather in the dark ground of being, viz., in the order of *karma*/rebirth. Thus, we have an ultimate dualism between *karma*/rebirth and the transcendental, which is both my essence and serves as the *telos* of my empirical being. The conceptual situation in which the human existence is caught may be analogous to, but not identical with (and I introduce it for the benefit of my students familiar with Western philosophers), the dualism with which Kantian philosophy leaves us, between the unknown and the unknowable thing in itself and the pure self which reflection uncovers and to which moral thinking adds content as pure willing.

There is no need to belabor the point that the two dualisms, the Indian and the Kantian, are not the same but they are somehow analogous. The dualism between *karma*/rebirth and *mokṣa* is forced upon us as we try to understand the human situation but it soon dawns upon us that *mokṣa* is freedom from the clutches of *karma*/rebirth. In *mokṣa*, one is awakened to one's true being.

All schools of Indian philosophy, with the exception of Cārvāka, accept *mokṣa*. Saying this does not amount to asserting that all the schools of Indian philosophy ended with the same conception of *mokṣa*. Each school developed its own conception of *mokṣa* and also demonstrated the possibility of *mokṣa* so conceived. "*Anirmokṣa*" (impossibility of *mokṣa*) then becomes a material or non-formal fallacy (*hetvābhāsās*), which, for a philosophical position, is more serious than a formal logical fallacy, belonging to the domain of logical argumentations. Thus, we have a general conception of *mokṣa* as freedom or as release, but the specific understanding of *mokṣa* in each system is determined by the conceptual categories available in that system. The general conception of *mokṣa* as freedom serves as an ultimate presupposition and the specific understanding becomes a philosophical doctrine.

Dharma: so far we have seen that there are two ultimate orders: the first pointing backward to the order of *karma* and rebirth, and the second pointing forward to the possibility of freedom as the *telos* which beckons upon us. Human life is not truly human if it is not conscious of these two opposite directions. *Dharma* promises to mediate between these two and announces itself as grounded in the tradition handed over from the past and promises to help accomplish the goal sought after in future. The term "*dharma*" is derived from the Sanskrit root *dhṛ*, meaning "to sustain," "to support," "to uphold," "to nourish," etc. It is the most basic and pervasive concept, and embraces a variety of related meanings. It signifies the harmonious course of things; at times, it refers to a necessary attribute (the *dharma* of water is to flow, of the sun to shine); at other times, to religion; and, still at other times, it refers to duty in its normative aspect. *Dharma* in the last sense—setting aside the many different understandings and interpretations—means the rules and laws which individuals should follow. In short, *dharma* is the Hindu counterpart of Western "moral duty."

Dharma as a system of rules governs every aspect of human life in the human's relationship to himself, to his family, to his community, to the state, to the cosmos, and so on. Accordingly, we have family-*dharma*, royal-*dharma*, *dharma* pertaining to various stages of an individual's life, caste-*dharma*, ordinary *dharma*, and so on. Besides the social differentiation of *dharma*, there are also *dharma*s that cannot be brought under the social rubric, e.g., an individual has a duty to himself (e.g., purity), to others irrespective of *varṇa* (e.g., charity), to gods (e.g., sacrifice), and nature (e.g., protecting the plants). These rules have different strengths, and hold good with differing binding force, permitting exceptions at times, and, in their totality, form a world by themselves. But how does one determine the essence of each domain? Who legislates them, if at all they are legislated? Alternately, do they flow from the essential nature of each domain as the *dharma* of water is to flow and fire to burn? It is here that philosophy can get down to work instead of simply invoking a *dharma śāstras* (*dharma*-treatises). But the work is endless, and *dharmas* provide an endless field of philosophical research.

Now, with this enormously complex notion of *dharma*, it is only inevitable that there would be situations in one's life when these *dharmas* under whose powers one lives one's life come into conflict with each other. It is these duties that generate moral dilemmas and determine the tragedies of the epics, leading to deeper spiritual vision and to the need for *mokṣa* or spiritual freedom to override what seems to be the inviolable claim of *dharma*. The origin of *dharma* does not lie in the command of God, but rather in immemorial tradition and customary usages. *Dharma* is the embodiment of truth in life, eternal and "uncreated," as is life itself. The relation of *dharma* to God is thus somewhat nebulous and constitutes a perennial issue for commentary and disputation in Hindu literature exemplified, for example, in the great Hindu epic, *Mahābhārata*.

Dharmas also promise consequences and goals to be reached in the future. If you wish to attain such and such goal, then you should follow such and such line of actions. This hypothetical imperative, to use Kantian language, always refers to future goals to be reached. The conceptual world of *dharma*, therefore, talks about rules of actions received from time immemorial, and ascending orders of human existence to be reached by performing these rules. Human existence is thus caught up in the pursuit of goals in this world or in the next, thereby giving rise to theories of morality and theological doctrines. The philosophical systems find here a fertile field for conceptualization.

But *dharma* in the long run cannot bring to a human being the ultimate freedom or *mokṣa* which is his constant secret aspiration. *Dharma* is still caught up in the order of *karma*/rebirth and within that order promises to humans better and happier lives. *Dharmas* are only stepping stones always pointing beyond themselves, never reaching a resting place, because each world, no matter how much happier and better, is still within the clutches of the dark ontological ground of *karma*/rebirth and contains the same distant *telos* of *mokṣa* on the horizon. It is this human situation which comprehends human's pursuit of knowledge, morality, and religion, but aiming at something still higher which includes both human history as a development of the race and of the individual which all take place as though *a priori* delimited by the ground of *karma*/rebirth and the goal of freedom from it. In between lies the space of thinking, of the philosophy of the *darśanas*.

IV Important Features of the *Darśanas*

Before proceeding further, let me briefly review some of the important features of the eight *darśanas* (excluding the Cārvākas) so that the readers may gain an overview of their philosophies before diving into a detailed study of some of these issues.

1 Each *darśana* has a *pramāṇa* theory. The technical word "*pramāṇa*" has been variously translated as "proofs," "means of acquiring knowledge," "means of true or valid cognition," or even "ways of knowing." The Indian materialists admit perception to be the only means, the Buddhists accept perception and inference, the Nyāya admits four by adding *upamāna* (comparison) and *śabda* (verbal testimony) to the Buddhist two, and Advaita Vedānta accepts six and adds *arthāpatti* (postulation) and *anupalabdhi* to the Nyāya list.
2 In the Western epistemologies, e.g., in Kant, there is a continuing tension between the causal question of how cognition comes into being and the logical question of its validity, a tension not found in Indian epistemologies. The *pramāṇas* are both instruments by which cognitions arise, as well as the ways of justifying a cognitive claim.

3 The *pramāṇa*s are advanced not merely to validate empirical cognitive claims, such as "it rained yesterday, or it will rain tomorrow," but also to validate such philosophical claims as "the world has a creator," or that "all substance is permanent." In most Western philosophies, philosophical and empirical statements are sharply differentiated, and the grounding of the empirical epistemic claims follows a pattern that is different from what the grounding of philosophical claims requires. In Indian epistemologies, philosophical-epistemic claims are treated on a par with the empirical-epistemic claims insofar as the methods of validation are concerned. Even the Advaita Vedānta school uses the *pramāṇas* to validate its basic thesis that reality is One, universal consciousness, although there is a gradation of the *pramāṇas* with regard to their relative strength.

4 Another feature of the theory of *pramāṇas*, irrespective of the system one has in mind, is the primacy of perception. This feature has two aspects: every other mode of knowing—inference (*anumāna*) or even verbal testimony (*śabda)*—presupposes and is founded on perception. One must *see* the smoke on the yonder hill in order to be able to infer that there must be fire. One must *hear* the words, in order to grasp their meanings. Perception, however, is not limited to sensory perception. According to many schools, perhaps with the exceptions of the Buddhists, one also perceives universals and relations.

5 Every knowledge is a manifestation of an object to and by consciousness, so that consciousness—irrespective of the theory of consciousness upheld—plays the evidencing role. The *darśanas* disagreed regarding the self-manifestedness of consciousness, but that it is the only source of manifestation of an object was beyond dispute. The above thesis led to an epistemological realism in the *darśanas*, which will become obvious as we proceed in our investigation.

6 Though correspondence and coherence (*samavāda*) were widely used as a criterion of truth, all *darśanas* held in common a pragmatist account of truth. The two concepts when available tended to merge together: Truth leads to successful practice (*arthakriyākāritva*) pointing to a close relation between theory and practice. This relation has often been noticed but misconstrued as implying that Indian philosophy lacks theoretical thinking; it is practically motivated by the ultimate goal of freedom from the chain of rebirth/*karma*. The truth however lies deeper. Suffice it to note here that in this respect, Indian thinking is a close ally of the Greeks, especially Socratic thinking, which assumed that philosophical thinking paves the way for the cultivation of wisdom.

7 The ultimate goal, not alone of philosophy but also of ethical life, serves as a spiritual transformation of existence. This presence of a spiritual goal for all philosophical thinking has been well recognized but at the same time misconstrued. Spirituality in this context does not exclude theoretical thinking, but demands that one searches for the *truth* in order to reach this goal. Saying that Indian philosophy is spiritual calls up the picture of a

philosopher meditating in the *yogic* postures. This picture is misleading insofar as much of philosophical thinking transpired in the form of objections and replies *ad nauseum.*

8 At the same time it must be recognized that the practice of *yoga* was a pervasive component of the Indian culture—the Hindus, the Buddhists and the Jainas, so that many philosophers while excelling in theoretic thinking did as a matter of fact practice *yoga.* A consequence was the development of the various types of *yoga* as well as various differing concepts of the spiritual goal sought after, consistently with a *darśana's* theoretical position.

9 What was common to all the *darśanas,* then is the acceptances of the following soteriological structure:

Avidyā → *karma*/rebirth → (*saṁsāra*) bondage → *mokṣa.*

Each term in this chain was differently conceived in light of the *darśana's* theoretical system, and the practical goal and the path to reach the goal suitably made the system's own representation of it.

10 Within the fragments of their work, Indian philosophers did practice what Western thinkers call "theory." However, they neither conceptualized the idea of a "pure theory" nor glorified it by making it autonomous; they made it a stage in a process, which is motivated by the spiritual goal of self-knowledge. Basic to the metaphysical theories of the classical schools of Indian philosophy was the distinction between self and not-self, and the goal of the removal of suffering by self-knowledge.

11 At the same time, parallel to the spiritual pursuit, there is a strong naturalistic component of each *darśana.* The Sāṁkhya, Nyāya, and Vaiśeṣika had a strong naturalistic strand which was however joined to a spiritual strand insofar as it recognized that the true self—even the individual self—is not a product of nature, and that the pursuit of *mokṣa* is the highest goal. Thus, there are two independent strands of thought: the naturalistic and the spiritualistic. The two eventually merged, each retaining its own identity while influencing the other. It may be a more authentic characterization of Indian philosophical thought to say that *a reconciliation of the two seeming opposites, "nature" and "spirit," is what it aimed at*—analogously to the opposition between theory and practice.

12 Ethics in the Hindu context parallels Hegel's concept of *Sittlichkeit,* i.e., the actual order of norms, duties, and virtues that a society cherishes. Whereas in classical Western moral philosophy the task of ethics is to legitimize and ground our moral beliefs on the basis of fundamental principles (e.g., Kant's principle of universalizability without contradiction, Mill's principle of utility, etc.), the Hindu ethical philosophies do not give a supreme principle of morality to legitimize all ethical choices, but rather cover a large spectrum of issues encompassing within its fold a theory of virtues, a theory of rules, the ideal of doing one's duty for duty's sake, actual norms, customs, and social practices that an individual in society cherishes.

I hope the above overview lays down and circumscribes a boundary within which the philosophies (*darśanas*) found their fields of work. Once this field was opened up by *the Vedas* and circumscribed by *karma* and rebirth, *mokṣa*, and *dharma*, philosophy could now reflect upon not merely these mysteries and presuppositions, but also explore the nature of human existence that they helped to delimit and define reality, truth, and values.

This space, which I have just described as the space for thinking or philosophy, for knowing, was first opened up, disclosed, and given to the people of this India by what came to be known as the Vedas (*śrutis*). But to exactly understand the nature of this "origin," one must clearly understand what is meant by "opened up," "disclosed," or "given to the people." Schleiermacher, a German interpreter of the sacred texts, held that hermeneutics is the art of avoiding misinterpretations,[8] and in the case of the *śrutis*, misinterpretations abound. To say that *śrutis* "opened up" or "disclosed" means they gave people a new way of looking at things. The three presuppositions listed above define a new way of looking at things. How this disclosure took place cannot be made precise by using the model of Moses receiving the "Ten Commandments" from God. It surely was not a revelation in the standard Judaic-Christian sense of the term. One could, using Kant, say that "a light broke upon all students of nature."[9]

With this in mind, let us discuss the Vedas, the foundational texts of Indian tradition.

Part II

THE FOUNDATIONS

VEDAS: Indian tradition
name of literature of the religious e
speculative thinking of the Hindus.

2

THE VEDAS

The Indian philosophical tradition in its rudiments began in the Vedas, the earliest extant texts of the Hindus. The Vedas are not the name of a particular book, but of the literature spanning over two thousand years, which record the religious and speculative thinking of the Hindus. These texts were collected over several centuries by several generations of poets, philosophers, and *brahmins* (priests) and were not systematized as a collection until around 800 BCE. Thus it is not surprising that these texts vary significantly not only in form but also in content.

The Vedas, the foundational texts of the Hindus, are written in old Sanskrit; their expressions are highly symbolic and not easily translatable. Deriving from the verbal root √*vid*, meaning "to know." Accordingly, the Vedas etymologically mean "knowledge" (*Wissenschaft*) and, by implication, "the sources of knowledge." The Vedic corpus may be regarded as a body of texts incorporating all knowledge, sacred as well as profane that the community at one time possessed and prized. These texts not only discuss the nature of the deities to be worshipped, religious hymns to be chanted in praise of gods and goddesses, the rituals to be performed to please the deities and avoid their wrath, sacrificial rituals to be performed, but also knowledge on mundane topics like agriculture, social organization and practices, medicine, astronomy, music, as well as such philosophical topics as the source of all things, the origin of the world, and the nature of the relationship between the world and the one principle. When one takes all these into account, one realizes that it is not only Indian philosophy, but all subsequent developments of the sciences as well, that is grounded in the Vedas, making it easier to understand why the Indians look upon the Vedas as having unquestionable validity.

Given that the Vedas were transmitted orally from teacher to disciple for a considerable period of time, they are called "*śrutis*" (from *śru*, "to hear"). Evidently this designation says what it means: the Vedic texts were recited, remembered, and orally transmitted from teacher to the student for a long time. Given that they were not written down until much later, it is difficult to assess correctly the difference between the original form of the Vedas and what we find today.

The tradition distinguishes *śruti* from *smṛti* (what is remembered). The Vedas are taken to be self-authenticating and in case of conflict between *śruti* and *smṛti, śruti* prevails. The Vedas are "*apauruṣeya*," i.e., "not created by a human being"; they are eternal, authorless, without any beginning, which should not be taken to mean that the "*śrutis*" were "revelations," as many Indian and Western writers claim. Such a translation hides a deep prejudice deriving from the Judaic-Christian tradition, i.e., it attempts to understand the Vedic worldview with concepts appropriate to the Judaic-Christian tradition. The Vedas are not God's word; at no time did God interrupt the course of history to reveal the Vedas. The sacred, even infallible, status of this literature most probably is not due to its revealed character (as is often misleadingly attributed), but rather to the fact that it is the source of the Hindu culture and civilization: everything begins there, including philosophy.

The Vedic literature is usually grouped in two primary phases: the verse literature (*saṃhitas*), and the expository literature in prose (the *saṃhitas*, the *āraṇyakas*, and the *Upaniṣads*). *Saṃhitas* include within its fold the collections generally known as the four Vedas: the *Ṛg Veda* (RV), *the Sāma Veda*, the *Yajur Veda*, and the *Atharva Veda* (AV).

Of these collections, the *Ṛg Veda* is the oldest of the four Vedas. The term "*Ṛg*" is derived from the root √*ṛc*, which means "a hymn," "to praise," and "to shine," and the term "*veda*," a cognate of the English term "wisdom," gives the collection its name: "the sacred wisdom consisting of stanzas of praise." Each verse of the hymns of the *hotars* (an ancient order of Aryan priests) was called a *ṛc*, or a praise, stanza. These hymns were probably recited by the *hotars* priests who invoked Vedic divinities during the detailed and complicated ritualistic sacrifices performed in those days.

The purpose of *Yajur* and *Sāma Veda*, compiled after the *Ṛg Veda*, is essentially liturgic. The *Yajur* may be regarded as the first manual of the Vedic rituals. It explains the duties of a priest responsible for the performance of a sacrifice, formulas to be to be used in a sacrifice, preparation for the utensils used, physical site and the altar where the ritual is performed, and the meaning and the purpose of the sacrifice, etc. The *Sāma Veda* is a collection of melodies that were chanted at different sacrifices, the *Ṛg Vedic* stanzas set to music. In the *Atharva Veda*, we find the beginning of Indian medicine. There are hymns addressed to different powers for the sake of alleviating diseases, death, etc. Additionally, this collection also contains many highly speculative hymns, which, at times, are monotheistic and, at other times, monistic in nature.

The general characterization of the four groups given above should not be overemphasized because the themes of different natures appear at places where one would expect them to appear, but they also appear at places one would not expect them to appear. To each of these Vedas were assigned a number of texts grouped together as Upaniṣads, where philosophical questions in a more pointed sense arose for the first time; accordingly, the entire Vedic corpus may be divided into two parts: the portion concerned with actions and the portion concerned with knowledge. The Upaniṣads belong to the latter section, which we will study in the next chapter.

Whereas the four Vedas are in verse, the texts known as the *brāhmaṇas* (relating to *brahmins* or the priests) are in prose. The *brāhmaṇas* are professional literature in which one priest speaks to another priest. The *brahmin* professionals devoted their entire lives to the performance of the rites and traveled from estate to estate to compete for various positions patronized by kings. Rituals at times brought together *brahmins* from different regions for weeks, for a year, leading to a never-ending discussion about the nature of the sacrifices, guidance regarding the sacrifice to be performed befitting the occasion, and so on. The underlying idea behind the rituals points to the fact that rites sustain the universe, that there is a correspondence between the microcosms and the macrocosms. Whereas the *brāhmaṇas* were primarily concerned with the relationship between the rite and the cosmos, the *āraṇyakas* ("forest treatises") go a step further and remind the person that the true wisdom consists not in the performance of the sacrifice, but rather in grasping the spiritual significance of the reality that underlies these rituals and sacrifices, thereby pointing to a three-way parallelism between microcosms, the macrocosms, and the rituals.

In order to make students conversant with the Vedic worldview, I will first discuss the *Ṛg Vedic* religion, and conclude with a discussion of the central philosophical concerns of the Vedas.

I The Vedic Deities (*Devas*) and the Principles of Interpretation

Ṛg Vedic Devas

The *Ṛg Veda* contains 1028 hymns organized in ten books. Interpretation and reconstruction of the *Ṛg Veda*, like the other three Vedas, is fraught with peril. In many places, a difficult idea is expressed in a simple language; at other places a simple idea is obscured by a very difficult language. It is replete with half-formed myths, crude allegories, paradoxes, and tropes. These difficulties notwithstanding, the collection remains the source of the later practices and philosophies of the Hindus.

In the *Ṛg* Vedic hymns a plurality of *devas* (the shining ones) or deities have been addressed and invoked. From a functional point of view, these deities may be grouped under three headings: (1) the deities of the natural world, e.g., *Sūrya* (Sun), *Uṣas* (dawn), *Vāyu* (wind), etc., (2) the deities that represent the principals of human relations, e.g., *Indra* and *Varuṇa*, and (3) the deities of the ritual world, e.g., *Agni* and *Soma*.

(1) The Vedic deities were often personified natural forces. Many hymns are addressed to the deities of the natural world, e.g., *Sūrya* (Sun), *Uṣas* (dawn), *Vāyu* (wind), and so on, though the degree of personification varies significantly. The Vedic seers were interested in nature, in establishing a correlation between

human activities and nature. An attempt was made to read natural phenomena in terms of their own behavior; a flood meant that the river was angry, spring signified peace and prosperity and the fact that the deities were pleased. They projected their own emotions upon nature.

(2) *Indra* is the most addressed deity in the *Ṛg Veda*; in fact, a quarter of the *Ṛg Veda* is dedicated to him. His *vajra* (the thunderbolt), horses, and chariots receive enough attention in the hymns. He drinks *soma* (the defied drink of immortality) and bestows fertility upon women, at times by sleeping with them. He is addressed at once as the war-*deva* and the weather-*deva*. However, his most famous deed is the unloosening of the water with his thunderbolt. He slew the demon *Vṛta* who prevented the monsoon from breaking. *Vṛta* had dammed the water inside a mountain that resulted in a massive drought that caused much human death and suffering. *Indra* is also represented as a benevolent power and a mediator. At times, he is referred to as an *asura* (demon), although most of the hymns emphasize his heroic deeds.

Another *deva*, *Varuṇa*, is most important from an ethical point of view: he oversees moral behavior. *Varuṇa* is a celestial *deva par excellence*, a universal monarch. Guilty human beings confess to *Varuṇa*. He is an enemy of falsehood and the punisher of sin. He resides in a thousand-column golden mansion and surveys the deeds of human beings. His eye is the Sun who is also his spy. The Sun sees everything and reports to *Varuṇa*. In addition to the Sun, *Varuṇa* has a number of other spies whose sole duty is to report on the evil doings of human beings. *Varuṇa* is a just and inscrutable *deva* who inspires the sense of guilt and the feeling of awe. Human beings are destined to sin, and only *Varuṇa* can release them.

(3) *Ṛg Vedic* hymns allude to numerous complicated and detailed rituals in which the *devas* are invoked to attend the sacrifice. Thus it is not surprising that there is a tremendous interest in *Agni* and *Soma*, the two deities essentially associated with all sorts of rituals. In fact, *Agni* is the second most addressed *deva* in the Vedic hymns.

Agni is indispensable in the performance of sacrifices. He symbolizes the renewal and interconnectedness of all things and events. On the one hand, *Agni* is greater than the heaven and the earth, on the other hand, he is a householder—he is the household fire, which even today is the center of domestic rituals. Fire serves as the medium and transforms the material gifts of the sacrifice into the spiritual substance from which the deities draw their strength and of which they can partake. In *Agni*, both the divine and the human world coalesce. *Agni* acts as the mediator between the deities and human beings. The meeting point is the sacrificial altar where *Agni* as fire consumes the oblation in the name of the deities, and in so doing transmits his virtues to human beings he represents. *Soma* is the divinized plant of immortality. The juice of the *soma* plant is ritually extracted in the famous soma sacrifice, a very important feature of many Vedic rituals. This juice—filtered in a woven sieve—is identified with the sky and the pouring of the juice, water, and milk is identified with all sorts of cosmic processes. Thus, both *Agni* and *Soma* are very close to human beings.

Many other deities have been mentioned in the *Ṛg Veda*: *Mitrā* (the *deva* of compacts and vows and is associated with *Vṛta*), *Viṣṇu* (known for his three strides that measured the universe), and *Yama* (the *deva* of death), to name only a few. Surprisingly, the deities that became important in later Hinduism, e.g., *Viṣṇu* and *Śiva*, play an insignificant role in the *Ṛg Vedic* hymns.

Principles of Interpretation

The Vedic hymns have given rise to various interpretations. Here I will briefly recall three influential interpretations as well as the principles that underlie these interpretations.

In the first place, there is the Sanskrit commentary of Sayāṇa.[1] This commentary not only captures but has also influenced the way in which the Sanskrit Vedic scholarship came to understand the Vedas. This interpretation takes the Vedic deities to be real gods with supernatural powers, and the hymns as prayers in which these deities are praised so that they may confer material and other worldly benefits on human beings and communities. This understanding, which may be called both ritualistic and polytheistic, has exerted tremendous influence on the writings of both Indian and Western scholars.

Sāyaṇa's interpretation captures neither the original intent nor the spiritual significance of the hymns. It is indeed true that there are multitudes of divinities in the Vedas. However, a careful reading of the hymns reveals that the conceptual apparatus that goes with polytheism is not found in the *Ṛg Vedic* hymns. In polytheism, gods are fully personalized entities having a precise function and power, and there is an organized system of gods with a clear ranking. In Greek polytheism, for example, many gods are hierarchically arranged in a patriarchal family with Zeus as the head. The gods have a very clearly defined function and symbolism. Their place in the hierarchy is determined by their relationship to Zeus. We find goddesses of wisdom and sex, of marriage, of beauty, of war, etc., and their power is limited insofar as they must answer to Zeus, who has the power to modify the results of their actions. Gods are fully personalized entities and are divided into watertight compartments. The Vedic divinities, on the other hand, are not fully personalized entities; they are not divided into watertight compartments. In the Vedic pantheon there is no organized system of the *devas* with specific power and rank. The *Ṛg Vedic* hymns extol a particular divinity and even exaggerate its importance at the expense of the other deities. They glorify the *devas* using the terms or epithets generally applicable to other *devas* (power, wisdom, brilliance) and often attribute to her or him mythical traits and actions that characterize other *devas*. In these hymns the interconnections among the deities are glorified, their distinctions implicitly rejected. For example, *Indra* is assisted not only by the storm *deva*, but also by *Viṣṇu* in the breaking of the monsoon. *Indra* was the recipient of the *soma* sacrifice aimed at promoting rain and fertility. It was believed that the *soma* juice was highly intoxicating and it was the source of inspiration of the *devas* to inspire them to do good deeds. Indeed, it is the copious imbibing of *soma* that gives *Indra* the power to overcome his enemies. As *Indra* assumes a position of greater supremacy in the pantheon, *Soma* becomes associated with his activities and is at times praised as a mighty warrior. At other times, *Varuṇa* and *Indra* are portrayed in opposition to each other, but still at other times, they complement each other. There is no counterpart of the Greek Zeus in the Vedic hymns. I am adopting here a perspective that follows the Advaitic hermeneutic perspective rather than the literal meaning that the Western Indologists uphold following the literal translations.

A slightly modified reading of Sāyaṇa's interpretation is found in the chapter on *Ṛg Veda* in Radhakrishnan's book on *Indian Philosophy*.[2] Taking a developmental point of view, Radhakrishnan maintains that (1) in the Vedic hymns there is a transition from a naturalistic polytheism through a henotheism to a spiritualistic monism which we find in the Upaniṣads, and (2) from the religious attitude of prayer—meant to elicit benefits and avoid calamities—there emerges a dominantly philosophical enquiry, an inquiry into the one being, *ekam sat*, the *brahman*, subsequently identified with the inner self or the *ātman*.

Radhakrishnan's reading is attractive insofar as it accommodates the Western ritualistic interpretation and synthesizes it with the traditional interpretation of Sāyaṇa. The Radhakrishnan reading, however, does not accurately represent the Vedic worldview. Indeed, many *devas* are worshipped, but the *devas* are not gods; *deva* (cognate with Latin *deus*), derived from the noun *div* (sky), suggests a place of shining radiance. To call "*devas*" "gods" is not appropriate. *Īśvara* (God), a fully personalized concept, is not found in the Vedas, and the Vedic concern with the cosmos is to be understood not naturalistically, but in a sense that is prior, not posterior, to the nature–spirit divide. One must not lose sight of the fact that if it is naturalism, this naturalism is not materialism, and the spiritualism that is achieved is not a-cosmic, which finds a vibrant spirit in all natural forces and powers. Thus we need to look upon the Upaniṣads not as a movement of thought beyond the Vedic religion, but as very ancient commentaries, that provide varied interpretations of the hymns. The best account of the spiritualistic understanding of the Vedic deities is given in the third interpretation.

Śrī Aurobindo provides the third line of interpretation.[3] On Aurobindo's reading, given the Vedic etymologies, the Vedic deities or rather their names, at the same time, have a set of different meanings, which confer on the stories of the sacrifices at least three different meanings: the external-ritualistic, the psychological, and the spiritual. He argues that the Vedic words, especially the names of the deities such as "*Agni*," "*Indra*," "*Varuṇa*," "*Mitra*," etc., have a host of interconnected meanings. The Vedic Sanskrit words, derived from their verbal roots, have the multivalence of meanings. To impose a universal meaning on them is to lose sight of this important mutivalency. For example, the word "*agni*" means both the "natural element fire," "a supernatural deity" symbolized by the fire, and an "inner spiritual will" which aspires after the highest knowledge. All these meanings stem from the multivocity of the verbal root from which the word "*agni*" is derived.

If we follow this line of interpretation, we can say that the Vedic thinking had not yet clearly separated thought from poetry and nature for them was still spiritual; there was no Cartesian split between matter and mind. The Vedic rituals are social acts, rule-governed and supposed to bring about social good. They also symbolize deep spiritual action, discipline, *yoga*, penance, austerity, intended to bring about transformation of the inner being. These movements are inevitably blended.

Thus, it would be a serious mistake to think that the Vedic religion at best was polytheism and at worst nature worship. The worship of *devas* was not simple nature worship; it was part of a complicated system of rituals which could only be performed by priests. Gradually, sacrifices became more and more detailed and complicated. Initially, the goal was to satisfy and please the *devas*, however, eventually sacrifices became an end in themselves. It would perhaps be better to say that whereas the Vedic hymns express an intuitive experience and appreciation of the world, from the Upaniṣads begins a gradual emergence of intellectual, better yet, of clear philosophical thinking. Again, it would be equally hasty to ascribe to the Vedic texts a religion, which postulates a distinction between man and God or gods, or to take the hymns as expressions of deity worship. It would be more appropriate to find in them a mode of thinking, a mode of experiencing the world that was prior to religion and philosophy unprejudiced by the subsequent distinction between nature and spirit.

In the later *Ṛg Vedic* hymns there is a tendency away from a series of more or less separate deities toward the notion of a single principle. What is remarkable about these texts is that they do not end with a definite answer; they raise many more questions, and at times end with such agnostic conclusion as "who knows, perhaps, no one, not even the *devas*." They move between a wonderful poetic response to nature and an inquisitive mind that asks questions without being committed to any dogmatic answer. We find on the one hand, first-rate poetry and on the other, the beginnings of human questionings about the truth of the world around us. If, as Heidegger often remarked, original thinking is poetic and that "thinking" (*Denken*) is also "thanking" (*Danken*),[4] then the Vedic hymns show the emergence of that original thinking, not yet frozen into conceptual abstractions.

The overall point of view points to the sacredness of the manifest nature, the recognition that behind the manifest nature there is an unmanifest spiritual principle, and that the ideal life is to be in conformity with the deeper vision of the unity of all things which, at the same time, preserves a stratified and hierarchical, orderly nature of social organization. We also find in these hymns indications of the belief in the imperishability of a soul, and a belief in the efficacy of one's actions across death and rebirth.

Thus, there are central philosophical concerns and questions that the Vedic seers were trying to come to grips with. I will discuss these questions and concerns under two headings: (i) the conception of the true order and the essence of humanity, and (ii) cosmology.

II Central Philosophical Concerns

The Conception of the True Order and the Essence of Humanity

The Vedic seers held that the universe is governed by "order," or "way" or "truth," called "*ṛta*," an abstract principle that ensures justice and order in the universe.

No term in English really captures what is meant by this concept in the Vedic context. Etymologically, "*ṛta*," is derived from the verbal root √*ṛ*, meaning to "go," "move," etc.; it signifies "the course of things," that which enables the world to run smoothly. It is at once the ordered universe and the order that pervades it. It represents the law, unity, and rightness that underlie the orderliness of the universe.

Ṛta enables natural events to move rhythmically: days follow nights; there are succession of the seasons, the cycles of birth, growth, decay, and so on. *Ṛta* provides balance, and guides the emergence, dissolution, and reemergence of cosmic existence. It represents a powerful power that not only regulates the physical but also the ethical world; it sustains and unites all beings. Not only natural phenomena but also truth and justice are subject to *ṛta*. *Varuṇa* is the custodian of *ṛta*, the Vedic counterpart of the later notion of *dharma*. It is the moral law that regulates the conduct of human beings. When human beings observe *ṛta*, there is peace and order. In social affairs, *ṛta* is propriety and makes possible harmonious actions among human beings. *Ṛta* is truth in human speech. *Satya* as "agreement with reality," and *anṛta* as "negation of *ṛta*," eventually became confined to truth and falsity of speech respectively, and appeared in moral contexts to represent virtue and vice generally. In human dealings, *ṛta* is justice, and in worship *ṛta* assures correct performance of ritual, which results in harmony between human beings and the deities, human beings and nature, and among human beings in general. In short, *ṛta* is the right course of things, the right structure of things. Going against the structure would be *anṛta*. Basically the idea permeating the *Ṛg Veda* is that nature in all its diversity and multiplicity is not chaos, but rather governed by a basic cosmic law.

There are no hymns addressed to *ṛta*, there are many references to it emphasizing the natural (the way things are) and the moral (the way they should be). Even divinities derive their strength from *ṛta*, e.g., "from fervor *ṛta* and truth were born";[5] "*ṛta* is the movement of the Sun,[6] and "*ṛta* is also the way of Heaven and Earth;[7] "*ṛta* removes transgressions;[8] "*ṛta* is the right path for humans."[9] In short, the natural course is the proper course. Human beings should follow *ṛta* and avoid *unṛta*.

The Vedic hymns raise numerous philosophically important questions: What is the essence of human beings? Who am I? What happens at death? Does anything survive after death? Given that when the breath goes out, life ceases to exist, at many places the essence of human beings is taken to be breath, or such an airy substance as wind. However, most discussions focus on *ātman* (usually translated as "soul") as the essence, a subtle essence, which exists in the human body. It denotes a dimension of human being that is distinct from the physical body. In other words, soul denotes the non-physical or immaterial dimension that survives death. AV X.8.44 and X.2.23 also reiterate the same point when they explain *ātman* as the essence of human beings.

The Vedic seers believed in three horizontal levels (*triloka*): the earthly level, the atmospheric level (where the birds and the gods' chariots flew), and *svarga* (the abode of the gods and the blessed dead ones). On death, the *ātman* leaves the body and goes to heaven, the level above the atmosphere. During the Vedic era, human beings prayed for a long earthly life. Praying for a span of one hundred years was the norm. People generally believed that the correct performance of rituals would ensure them a place in the heaven. *Śatpatha Brāhmaṇa* (SB) also reinforces the idea of the separation of the soul and the body; at another place declares that those who do not perform sacrifices are born again; at still another place, assures us that the due performance of sacrifices ensures material comforts in another world and that doers of bad deeds are punished. Thus, though the discussions of the destiny of human beings are scattered, there is no doubt that the principle of *ṛta* and the ideas of reward and punishment later evolved into the notions of *dharma* and *karma* respectively, two basic presuppositions of Indian philosophy discussed in the previous chapter.

Cosmology

The questions regarding the world-breath corresponding to the life-breath of the human being led to several speculations regarding the source of the world and the process of creation. Several questions were asked: What is the source of things? What is the nature of that deeper principle which underlies manifest nature? What is the relation between that one principle and the diversity of empirical phenomena?

Regarding the ultimate source of things, one finds various speculations. The Vedic divinities could not be said to be the source of the world because they were associated with the natural world; for example, the deities of rain and wind resided in the atmospheric level, *Soma* on the earthly level, and *Agni* on all three levels. Even the divinities that were not associated with the natural world, e.g., *Indra* and *Varuṇa*, were taken to reside in some spatial location or the other and so could not be said to be the source of the world. Thus, in the later hymns we find a transition from the personal to the impersonal power or principle to explain the origin of things.

To explain the nature of the one and its relation to the empirical world and the process of creation, I will focus on three hymns: RV X.90 and 129, and *Atharva Veda* XIX.53.

In X.90, we see the first streak of the monistic thought. The universe is derived from the various parts of the *Puruṣa*, the "Primeval Man." *Puruṣa* is at once the entire existence and an androgynous being. *Puruṣa* is the sacrificial victim and the deity of the sacrifice. In this hymn the gods perform the sacrifice, the *Puruṣa* becomes the oblation, and from the dismemberment of the *Puruṣa were created* all animals, the four castes, and the cosmic powers, e.g., the moon, the sun, the wind, breath, etc., The hymn expresses *Puruṣa* as both immanent and transcendent: immanent because it pervades the entire existence, transcendent because it is not exhausted by the existence of the universe.

The hymn in no uncertain terms declares that the *Puruṣa* precedes and goes beyond the creation, which became very important for later Indian philosophical speculations. It has given rise to countless speculations and serves as the paradigm for many sorts of creations, e.g., it is recited in the rites performed after the birth of a son, in the ceremonies performed when the foundation stone of a temple is laid, and so on. *Puruṣa* typifies Hindu cosmogonic divinities, e.g., *Prajāpati* (the lord of all creatures), which repeatedly appears in AV. There are various hymns addressed to the Support, on which everything rests. The notion of Support resembles the *Puruṣa* of RV.

It should come as no surprise that the Vedic poet was intent on finding an answer to the question "what is it that is the warp and woof of everything else?" The famous "Hymn to Creation" (X.129) articulates the Vedic seer's attempt to go beyond "being" and "non-being" to a primordial being, their unifying ground. The hymn opens in the time before creation, when there was nothing: neither being (existent) nor non-being (non-existent), no mid-space, no trace of air or heaven; even the moon and the sun did not exist so that one could differentiate between the day and night, days and month. The One, which was enveloped by emptiness, came into being by its own fervor, desire (the primal seed of mind) arose giving rise to thought; thus, existence somehow arose out of non-existence. At this juncture, the poet realizes that he has gone too far; to claim that existence arises out of non-existence goes against the verdict of experience. Thus, after presumably describing the origin of things, the last two verses ask whether anyone truly knows what is really the origin of the existents. Even the deities cannot answer this question, because they were created along with the world. Thus, the poet concludes that the origin of the existents is inexplicable; it is an enigma, a riddle. It is worth noting that creation in the Indian context is never creation *ex nihilo*; it signifies the ordering of already existing matter into intelligible form. In other words, the cosmos is evolved out of its own substance.

The hymn from the *Atharva Veda* included in this text articulates time as the one ontological reality; it is the creator, preserver, and the destroyer of the universe. The Sanskrit term "*kāla*," derived from the root √*kal*, means "to collect," "to count." Time, in these hymns, collects or gathers past, present, and future. Time is compared to a perfectly trained horse upon which a jar filled with water to the brim is placed; time runs like a horse without spilling even a single drop. Everything—earth, heaven, Sun, wind, breath, etc.— originates in time. It is not an exaggeration to say that time is both the *Prajāpati* and the *brahman* of the AV.[10]

To sum up: The Vedas—devoted to *devas*, natural phenomena, sacrifices, the ultimate source of things—remain important sources of the Hindu practices and philosophies even today. A scattered discussion of such concepts as "reward and punishment," "birth and rebirth," "identity and difference," and "spirit and nature," is found throughout the Vedic texts. In the later *Ṛg-Vedic* hymns, there is a tendency to move away from a series of more or less separate deities or powers of nature, toward the notion of a single principle. All these idea finds a fuller exposition, development, and conceptualization in the final part of the Vedic corpus known as "Upaniṣads," which I will discuss next.

Summary

3
THE UPANIṢADS

Anyone acquainted with the story of the unfolding of Indian philosophy is aware of the fact that the Upaniṣads, the foundational texts, are multifaceted, versatile, and address a plethora of logical, epistemological, grammatical, linguistic, hermeneutical, psychological, physiological, and phenomenological theories. The Upaniṣads, formally part of the Vedas, set forth the nature of ultimate reality, self, foundation of the world, rebirth, immortality, to name only a few. They are generally taken to signify the esoteric teachings imparted orally by the *Gurus* (spiritual teachers) to their disciples. Such teachings were not meant for common persons. The Upaniṣads clearly command "no one who has not taken a vow think on this."[1] Eventually, such expressions as "*paramam guhyam*" (the greatest secret)[2] came to be used for the Upaniṣads. Thus the Upaniṣads gradually came to signify the highest knowledge which was received from the teacher, a sort of secret instruction, which could only be imparted to those students who were qualified to receive it. The prefix "*upa*," denotes "nearness"; *ni*, means "down," or "totality"; and *sad*, "to sit," "to attain," or "to loosen." Etymologically, a disciple humbly approaches the teacher, to gain esoteric knowledge of the totality to break away from the bondage of the world. In this oral erudition, the *guru* and the pupils engaged in discussions and debates that added to the erudition and eventually became incorporated as part of the textual tradition.

First a few remarks about the texts themselves. The principal Upaniṣads were composed sometime between 600 and 300 BCE. There is no agreement regarding the number of the Upaniṣads composed. It is generally believed that there are over two hundred Upaniṣads; the tradition maintains that one hundred and eight are extant. Of these, eleven are said to be the major Upaniṣads; they are: *Bṛhadāraṇyaka* (BU), *Chāndogya* (CU), *Taittrīyā* (TU), *Īśā*, *Kena*, *Kaṭha*, *Praśna*, *Muṇḍaka* (MU), *Māṇḍukya* (MAU), *Śvetāśvatara* (*Śvetā)*, and *Maitrī*. Of these eleven, CU and BU are the longest. The order of their composition and antiquity is difficult to ascertain; philological scholars have been trying different hypotheses and applying different methods to determine their antiquity. These texts were not compiled in the same period. Given that they were composed by different individuals, living at different times and in different parts of North India, their methods of presentation, and the larger cultural contexts in which these teachings were inserted, were different. Additionally, the individuals who put the Upaniṣads into their final written form may have incorporated their own teachings in the Upaniṣads.

Under the patronage of Dara Shikoh, the son of Śāha Jahān, the Emperor of Delhi, in 1656, the Upaniṣads were first put into written form; fifty Upaniṣads were translated into Persian. In 1801–1802, Anquetil Duperron translated these texts from Persian into Latin. Schopenhauer, after studying the Upaniṣads in Latin, stated: "With the exception of the original text, it is the most profitable and sublime reading that is possible in this world; it has been the consolation of my life and will be that of my death."[3] Since then, the Upaniṣads have been translated into all the major languages of the world.

It is not easy to summarize the teachings of the Upaniṣads. These are open-ended texts and lend themselves to a variety of interpretations. Additionally, these texts use symbols, narratives, metaphors, and concrete images to convey their thoughts further compounding the interpretive problems. However, there is a broad theme that runs through these texts and this theme has been reiterated in many different ways using different paradigms. Each Upaniṣadic teaching stresses the coherence and final unity of all things. To that end, the Upaniṣads identify a single fundamental principle which underlies everything and explicates everything. Behind the spatial and temporal flux, there is a subtle partless, timeless, unchanging reality, called "*brahman*." This fundamental principle is also the core of each individual and this core has been designated as the "*ātman*," the "self," the life-force independent of physical body.

Etymologically the word "*brahman*" is derived from the verbal root *bṛh*, meaning, "to grow," or "the great"; thus, the word "*brahman*" came to mean "the greatest" and "the root of all things"; "*ātman*" meant "breath," and came to signify the essence of the individual person. The central teaching of the Upaniṣads revolves around the thesis that the *brahman* and *ātman* are identical. To the Upaniṣadic seers the *ātman* and the *brahman* signify the same reality, one within, and the other without. I will begin with the discussion of the *brahman* in the Upaniṣads

I *Brahman*

We saw in the previous chapter that towards the end of the RV many questions about the origin and the nature of being were being asked. It was asked: Does being emerge from non-being or from prior being? The former alternative was set aside as absurd and the latter was not quite rejected but was seen as leading to further questions about the origin of being. If one being lies at the beginning, then we need to know who or what that being is. For sure, this being is not the god of religion, and it is given a new designation as "*brahman*," the most perfect being, the greatest, from which all things arise and into which they all return. In the Vedic hymns the term "*brahman*," refers to the power contained in the words recited as well as the mysterious power present in the utterances of the

Vedic hymns. The primary goal in the Vedas is to search for the power connecting the microcosm with the macrocosm, though the idea of *brahman* as the ground of all things is not entirely absent.

The word "*brahman*," though found in the Vedas, comes to prominence in the Upaniṣads. Who is this *brahman*? This fundamental question is formulated in many different ways in the Upaniṣads, which are replete with such questions as: What is the one being that underlies many beings? What is that by knowing which all else becomes known? What is that by knowing which one overcomes suffering? What is that from which everything arises? There is also the standard metaphysical enquiry: What was there at the beginning? What is that from which all things arise and into which they all enter after dissolution? The answer in all cases is *brahman*.

The Vedic sense of power continues in the Upaniṣads: *Kaṭha Upaniṣad*, for example, points out that the various *devas* carry out their respective jobs because of the fear of the *brahman*;[4] *Kena Upaniṣad* informs us that the various *devas* have no power outside the power of *brahman*, and so on.[5] The *brahman* of the Upaniṣ ads, however, is much more than a power; it is the cause of the origination, sustenance, and destruction of the world.[6] In the BU, when Yājñavalkya is questioned about the number of gods, he initially says that 3306 gods were simply manifestations of thirty-three gods, and then successively reduces the number to six, three, two and a half, and then one. This god is none other than the *brahman*, and all other gods of the Vedas, the senses, and the mind are said to be the various powers of the *brahman*.[7] This *brahman* is not only the source of everything, but also the core of each individual being called "*ātman*."

In MU, Śaunaka (a householder), with a great deal of respect and humility, asks Angirā (a wise man): what is that by knowing which all else becomes known?[8] The text that immediately follows does not answer this question but rather seems to move on to other matters including the classification of knowledge into higher and lower and the order of creation (or emanation) of the world by (or from) *brahman*. MU concludes with the statement: "all this is *brahman*," that "*brahman* is this one world." It appears as if with the affirmation that the *brahman* is everything, it follows that to know *brahman* is to know everything.

But what is the nature of the *brahman* apart from its being everywhere and everything? Bhṛgu puts this question to his wise father Varuṇa.[9] Varuṇa informs his son that the *brahman* is that from which things are born, in which they live after being born, and into which they return upon departing. Bhṛgu leaves in his quest for the real. He initially thinks that the *brahman* is food. All beings arise from food, after being born live in it, and return to it at the end. This is the first answer. If this is so, then one should increase food. Further reflections reveal to him that the *brahman* is neither food, nor the vital breath, nor *manas*, nor intellectual awareness; it is bliss (*ānanda*), that all beings arise out of bliss, continue to live in bliss, and return at the end into bliss.

The entire *Iśa Upaniṣad* uses paradoxes and antinomies to explain the nature of the *brahman*. For example, whereas V.4 describes the One as "unmoving, yet swifter than the mind," V.5 articulates the *brahman* as that "moving and not moving," "far and near"; it is inside this world; it is also outside. *Kaṭha* reiterates that the *brahman* is subtler than the subtle, greater than the great; seated at one place, it travels far; although sleeping it wanders around; it is present as bodiless in all bodies, present as eternal in all non-eternal things.[10] The *Śvetā* makes the same point when it asserts that the *brahman* is smaller than the smallest; greater than the greatest.[11]

One cannot but ask how to interpret these patently self-contradictory statements? Clearly, if they are literally true, then our logic fails. It is more plausible to suggest that our ordinary categories (space, time, motion, rest, one and many, etc.) do not apply to the *brahman*; application of these categories generates contradictions. The *brahman* is all-encompassing, nothing is excluded from it. It is unmoving insofar as it is eternal; it is swifter than the mind because it is inconceivable. The *brahman* signifies the totality of things; it is both the unmanifested beyond and the manifest phenomena, implying it is both one and many.

In another dialogue, which occurs in the BU, there is a clear break from the ritualistic tradition of identifying the *brahman* with the self residing in various deities. The text occurs in the course of a conversation between Bālāki (a *brahmin*) and the king of Kāśī, Ajātaśatru.[12] In this dialogue, Bālāki, a *brahmin*, successively argues that the *brahman* is the person in the sun, in the moon, in the lightning in the sky, in the air, and in the fire. The king rejects all these accounts. I presume that these answers prevailed among *brahmins* in the ritualistic tradition. The king then took Bālāki by his hands to a person who was fast asleep, and asks: "Where does the person inside this man go when he is asleep, when he wakes up wherefrom does he return? Where is he, what is he doing, when the person is asleep but dreaming?" The king finally informs Bālāki that during sleep when the senses are restrained, the empirical person rests in the space within the heart. In dreams, the mind and the senses are not restrained and a person is able to move as he pleases, he becomes a king or a *brahmin* as it were. In deep sleep, however, a person knows nothing; in this state, one rests like a youth or a king or a *brahmin* who has reached the maximum of bliss.[13] The different centers of life are there, but their truth is *ātman*, the truth of truth.[14]

It is quite clear from the above conversations that the Upaniṣadic seers reject attempts to identify the highest being with any one natural or naturalistically identifiable entity as not satisfying the description, and in so doing set aside all objective and cosmological thinking about the *brahman*. The answers generally end up with the affirmation that the *brahman* is none other than the inner self of all beings, especially of humans, called "*ātman*." Thus, a turn from the cosmological to the psychological mode is affected. However, one is still not clear what is the precise nature of the innermost essence of human beings, the *ātman*. Let us discuss what the Upaniṣadic seers have to say about this essence.

II *Ātman*

Many Upaniṣads analyze the states of consciousness (waking, dreaming, and dreamless sleep) to arrive at the knowledge of *ātman*. Among the paradigms used, the paradigm of hierarchy, in which one moves from the grossest to the subtlest, explains the nature of the *ātman* very clearly. The most succinct, systematic, and formal analysis of the states of consciousness occurs in the MAU; however, the two earliest and significant precursors to the MAU's analysis are found in the BU and CU.

In the BU, the analysis of the states of consciousness occurs twice; apart from the Ajātaśatru and Bālāki dialogue discussed above, there is a conversation between the Sage Yājñavalkya[15] and King Janaka, in which the King desires to know the source of illumination that makes it possible for human beings to function in this world. Yājñavalkya successively informs the king that it is the light of the Sun, the light of the moon, the fire, and the speech. The King is not satisfied with these answers and rejects them. Yājñavalkya then goes on to describe three states of consciousness: waking, dreaming, and dreamless sleep. In the waking state a person moves and functions on account of external physical light, but in the dream state a person passes from the dream consciousness to waking consciousness and then returns to dream consciousness as a fish swims from one bank of the river to another. In deep sleep, however, there are no dreams, no desires, and no pleasure; the self in this state is free from pain, does not lack anything, does not know anything; there are no desires, no dreams.[16] The self sees by its own light, it is the ultimate seer; there is no other for the self to see. There is a perfect quietude (*samprasanna*), there is nothing wanting or lacking; it is bliss. The self is its own light; it is self-effulgent, it is self-luminous. In this state, though the self does not see with the eyes, it is still the seer. The character of seeing is intrinsic to the self; the self can never lose this characteristic just as fire cannot lose the characteristic of burning.

Indra, Virocana, and *Prajāpati* dialogue in the CU reiterates that "pleasures and pain do not touch the bodiless self."[17] *Indra* representing the gods and *Virocana* representing the demons, after undergoing the necessary preparations with austerity and penance, go to *Prajāpati* and ask him to instruct them about the knowledge of the immortal self,[18] which is free from sin, old age, death, hunger, thirst, etc., and knowing which, one is not afraid of anything. Prajāpati asks them to wear their best clothes and jewelry and look into a pool of water, which reflects his adorned image. Prajāpati tells them that the true self is nothing but the self seen in a reflection: that the self is the same as the body. Virocana leaves with the mistaken notion that the *ātman* is the same as the body and informs the demons accordingly. Indra, however is not satisfied and returns to Prajāpati for further instructions, but Indra rejects Prajāpati's subsequent answers that the *ātman* is the self seen in the dream and the dreamless states. Finally, Prajāpati reveals to Indra the true nature of the self, that as the support of the body, it is unchangeable essence of the empirical self. It is the highest light (*parama jyotiḥ*), the light of lights.

The above analyses of the states of consciousness found in BU and CU point to the self that is at once beyond the three stages (waking, dreaming, and dreamless sleep) and also endures identically through them. This self is experienced not in deep sleep but in the fourth, the transcendental stage. MAU calls this state "*turīya*." At the outset, MAU declares that the self has four feet (or quarters). The waking state is said to be outward-directed; it is conscious of external objects, consciousness is tied to external objects or in a modern jargon, its intentionality is outward-directed. In the dreaming state, the self is inward-directed. There are no outer objects, but inner objects produced by inner desires and impressions are there. Intentionality is still there, but the intentional objects are inner. In the deep sleep state, however, the experiences that characterize waking and dreaming experiences disappear. In this state the self is called "*prājñaḥ*," pure consciousness. Since there is no individuated, object-directed consciousness, the pure consciousness in this state, is called "*prājñah-ghana*," or "consciousness enmassed or densely packed" into which all objects and object-consciousness are dissolved. Finally, the fourth state, is described as "the lord of all" (not in the sense of God), but as the truth of all, as that which underlies all the others and comprehends them within it. It is called luminous, because it has for its object only consciousness that is the light itself. It enjoys consciousness in itself unrelated to any objects whatsoever. It is also called the source of all, the inner controller, the beginning and the end of all objects—the real self or *ātman*.

Note that there are two ways of construing the doctrine of the four states of consciousness. The first three may be regarded as empirical pointers to the transcendent, the fourth. Alternately, the fourth may be regarded as what comprehends and makes possible the other three. The first is suggested in the BU and CU, and the second in the MAU. Irrespective of whether one explicitly admits the fourth state, the point that is being made is as follows: in what lies beyond the three states, the self becomes non-dual; it becomes one with the *brahman*. Thus, it is not surprising that at many places in the Upanisads, the two terms the "*brahman*" and the "*ātman*" are used synonymously. The CU asks: "What is *ātman*? What is *brahman*?"[19] When the inquiry pertains to the source of the universe, the word "*ātman*" is used, and in other cases when the inquiry is regarding the true self of a human being the word "*brahman*" is used. For example, in the dialogue between Bālāki and Ajātaśatru discussed above, the conversation begins with the *brahman* ends with the *ātman* as the world-soul from which gods, divinities, and all beings are derived.

III *Brahman* and *Ātman*

Four Upaniṣadic sayings, known as the "Four Great Sayings," have generally been regarded as expressing the quintessence of the Upaniṣads. These sentences in different ways reiterate that the *brahman*, the first principle, is discovered within the *ātman*, or conversely, the *ātman*, the essence of the individual self, lies in the first principle, the *brahman*, the root of all existence.

For my present purposes, I will elaborate on only one of these four, viz., "*tat tvam asi*," which contains one of the clearest discussions of the identity thesis. The dialogue occurs in the CU[20] between Śvetaketu and Uddālaka. In this conversation, Uddālaka identifies the being (*sat*), the ground of all existence, and the source of all human beings, with the self of Śvetaketu. This identity thesis has been repeated nine times in this conversation. To give students a flavor of the style and content, I have translated a portion of the conversation at the end of this chapter.

The context is as follows: Uddālaka sends his son Śvetaketu to study with a teacher. Śvetaketu studies with the teacher for twelve years and returns home very proud of his knowledge and learning. Noticing his son's arrogance, Uddālaka asks his son: "Do you understand the implications of that teaching by which the unheard becomes heard, the unperceived becomes perceived, the unknown becomes known?" Śvetaketu informs his father that he does not know the answer. Using the example of things made of clay and gold, Uddālaka explains to his son that knowing a lump of clay amounts to knowing all things made of clay and knowing a nugget of gold amounts to knowing all things made of gold, because things made of clay differ only in form but the essence is the clay and things made of gold differ only in form, the essence is gold; likewise, the self of Śvetaketu is not different from the being or the essence, the ground of entire existence. Śvetaketu does not quite understand what his father was trying to tell him, and so asks his father for further instructions. Uddālaka points out that in the beginning, there was only being, and that being had a desire to become many. Thus, he, out of himself, projected the universe, and after projecting the universe entered into every being. That being alone is the essence of all things; all beings have this essence as their support.[21] Śvetaketu is still not sure about what his father is trying to convey to him, so he requests further instruction. Uddālaka asks Śvetaketu to bring a fruit from the *nyagrodha* tree and instructs him to cut it open. Śvetaketu does so and finds seeds in the fruit; but he does not find anything in the seeds. The father explains to the son that the entire tree comes from the invisible essence that exists within the seeds: "Believe me, my child, that which is the subtle essence, this whole world has that for its self. That is the true self. That thou art, Śvetaketu."[22] This being, the source of everything, is the self of Śvetaketu, which is not different from *ātman* or consciousness. This pure consciousness, the being that is the ground of all existence, also underlies empirical consciousness.

The thesis of the identity of the *ātman* and *brahman* has been an influential landmark in the history of Indian thought. Two different concepts, two different goals, two objects of inquiry are pursued, and in the final analysis, are found to be the same. The inquiry regarding the *brahman* is perhaps more connected with the Vedic discourses: What is that one being which is called by different names? What is that ultimate stuff or power which is at the root of all things? and so on. The Upaniṣads pursue the Vedic question, and reject such answers as that the *brahman* is the primal fire, water, the sun in the heaven. Regarding the *ātman*, such answers as that it is body, or the life-principle, or the *manas*, or the *buddhi* were rejected. Finally, *ātman* is understood as the indwelling spirit in all things which is *brahman*.

The different texts and teachers emphasize different aspects of this identity. Many texts in the Upaniṣads proceed step-by-step ascending from co-relation to a final identity. Thus, to the idea of *ātman* as body there corresponds the concept of "*brahman*" as material nature. To the concept of *ātman* as the life-principle within there corresponds the concept of the *brahman* as indwelling life-principle within all beings. While there is such a correlation between how one understands the nature of the individual self and the nature of cosmic reality, the gap between them is eventually closed, and one passes from co-relation to identity when both the terms are understood in their true nature. Thus, with regard to both, *ātman* and *brahman*, there are many kinds of discourses, some affirming the final truth with regard to each while others exhibit a graded movement as in the doctrine of five sheaths (*kośas*), which like onion skins have to be peeled off until the inner most core comes to light. MAU's analysis takes us through the four states of the self: the waking, the dreaming, the dreamless, and the fourth that transcends all three, in which the inner nature of the self is manifested. Again, one can notice a difference in the teachings of Ajātaśatru in BU and Uddālaka in CU. There are differences in emphases from which different philosophical positions might be derived. Ajātaśatru identifies the self of deep sleep with maximum bliss, Yājñavalkya argues that the true self, though not an object of thought, is experienced in the state of deep sleep, because in this state consciousness alone is present without any object.[23] Self by nature is free, pure, and eternal. It remains unaffected by pleasure and pain. It is perfect serenity and bliss. Uddālaka begins with *sat* or being, Yājñavalkya and Prajāpati, on the other hand, begin with an analysis of the states of experience.

One way to understand identity is to read it as the identity of the objective and subjective reality. The distinction between the subjective and the objective, the inner world of the spirit and the outer world that one perceives, seems to have been there even in antiquity, and one could argue that the distinction determines the two different directions in which search was going on, and perhaps we could suggest that the identity thesis overcomes this distinction. In this context, it is worth noting that the distinction between subject and object was not clearly formulated in the Upaniṣadic texts. *Sat* or being underlies both subject and object; thus, the two concepts "*brahman*" and "*ātman*" may be construed as laying down two paths both leading to the same goal which may be said to be either *ātman* or *brahman* or identification of the two, better yet, *ātman-brahman*, which is neither subjective nor objective, but both rolled in one. This identity thesis (we now know particularly from Frege) between two terms is significant, and not a mere tautology; the two terms have different meanings but an identical referent. Affirmation of such an identity, I imagine, must have shaken the intellectual world of that time resulting in various systematizations in the Vedāntic systems. I might add that this metaphysical achievement predates by almost 2000 years the philosophy of Hegel, in which reality was taken to be the spirit, beyond the subject/object distinction.

Leaving aside "*tat tvam asi*," there are three additional sentences which are said to express the quintessence of the Upaniṣads: *prajñānaṃ brahma*, "*brahma* is intelligence";[24] *ahaṃ brahmāsmi*, "I am *brahma*";[25] and "*ayam ātmā brahma*," "this *ātmā* is *brahma*."[26] These sentences in different ways reiterate that the *brahman* and the *ātman* are identical. The point that is being made is that the reality encompasses everything; it signifies the totality of things. It is both the unmanifested beyond and the manifest phenomena, implying it is both one and many; it is also the self, the seer, and the thinker. Thus, it is not an exaggeration to say that each Upaniṣadic teaching stresses the coherence and final unity of all things; everything is *brahman*.

IV The *Brahman* and the World

The Upaniṣads conceive this *brahman* both positively and negatively. The "Four Great Sayings" given above describe *brahman* in positive terms. Additional positive sentences are found in most of the Upaniṣads; for example, the *brahman* is that which consists of mind, whose body is life, whose form is light, whose conception is truth, whose soul is space, containing all works, desires, odors, and tastes, and encompassing the whole world, the speechless and the calm.[27] I am *brahman*,[28] all this is the *brahman*,[29] and so on. Again, one also finds such negative statements, such as the *brahman* is neither gross, nor subtle, nor short, nor long, nor red, nor adhesive, without shadow, darkness, air, space, attachment, taste, smell, eyes, ears, speech, mind, light, breath, mouth, and measure, and without inside and outside.[30] The negative sentences are best typified by "*neti, neti*," "not this, not this."[31] Accordingly, the *brahman* in the Upaniṣads is said to be both *saguṇa* (with qualities) and *nirguṇa* (without qualities). The positive sentences assert that everything, this object in front of me, the object at a distance, all are *brahman*; the negative sentences in effect deny that any of these things is the *brahman*. Thus, the question arose regarding how to reconcile these contradictory statements if the Upaniṣads are not to be guilty of self-contradiction.

One group of thinkers privilege the affirmative over the negative, the others follow the reverse route. The former group argues that the negative sentences say that none of this by itself is the *brahman*, that negation presupposes a prior affirmation which is then to be denied, and this is exactly what happens. The second group holds that the affirmative sentences affirm the final truth, i.e., all that we see, the totality of all things, has its being within the *brahman*, but none separately. The first group accords priority to the negative sentences by maintaining that the negation, the *brahman* is "not this," "not this," is the final truth, while the affirmations are provisional affirmations that everything is the *brahman*. There is no need to choose between the two; it is enough for our purposes to underscore the fact that the great commentators of Vedānta, which we will study later in the chapter on Vedānta, follow different interpretations of the same Upaniṣadic sentences. Ultimately one has to choose which line of interpretation is logically stronger before deciding which interpretation is more plausible.

Corresponding to the two views of the *brahman* as *saguṇa* and *nirguṇa*, there are two answers regarding the question of the cause of the world. According to the former, the world is a real emanation of the *brahman*; according to the latter, the world is simply an appearance of the *brahman*. *Śvetā* at the outset asks such questions as: Is *brahman* the cause of the world?[32] Wherefrom have we all come, who has kept us alive, and at the end where do we go? Time, the nature of things, destiny, chance, the elements of being, or the *ātman* of the nature of knowledge (the all-knowing, thinking self) have been rejected as being the cause of the world. No reason is given for rejecting these possibilities. The *Śvetā* proceeds to develop a rather theistic conception of the *brahman*, with *māyā* as its creative power that creates the world in accordance with the *karmas* (*dharma* and *adharma*) of the finite souls.

The major trend of thought in the Upaniṣads, however, remains a theory of emanation, not of creation. The two metaphors that dominate are: (1) a spider producing its web, and (2) a lump of salt dissolved in a bucket of water. Let me elaborate. Just as a spider creates its web, without requiring any other cause, from within, and also swallows it up, so does the world emanate out of the *brahman*, and goes back into it. Uddālaka, the father, asked his son Śvetaketu to place a lump of salt in the water and return to him in the morning. When Śvetaketu came in the morning, the father asked Śvetaketu to go and get the lump of salt from the bucket of water. The son could not do so, because the salt had dissolved. The father then informed the son that as we are able to perceive salt by other means, touch and sight, similarly, we can perceive the *brahman*, the immanent being of everything in the world, by other means. Most Upaniṣadic seers agree that the *brahman* is the cause of the world and that the world is not manifested out of any external matter; it rather is a manifestation of an aspect of the *brahman*. Several Upaniṣads articulate the *brahman* as the creator, sustainer, and destroyer of the world and articulate the *brahman* both as the material and the efficient cause of the world.

From the standpoint of the *nirguṇa brahman*, the world is an appearance of the *brahman*, and the principle of *māyā* accounts for this appearance. The teachings of Yājñavalkya in BU, for example, imply that duality is not real; he notes "duality as it were,"[33] meaning that duality is illusory. The world as an appearance, the sensually perceived world, is due to *māyā*, which in the Upaniṣads denotes the empirical world, i.e., the world characterized by space, time, cause-effect, and so on.

Irrespective of whether the Upaniṣadic seers construe the *brahman* as cosmic or acosmic, they generally agreed that empirical knowledge cannot be trusted to give us the higher knowledge, the knowledge of the *brahman*. Accordingly, the Upaniṣads make a distinction between the higher knowledge and lower knowledge. In MU, the wise man Angira told Śaunaka that those who know the *brahman* say that there are two kinds of knowledge, the lower and the higher.[34] The lower consists of the four Vedas, grammar, rituals, astrology, etc. Knowledge of anything that changes, and eventually perishes, is lower knowledge. The higher knowledge (than which there is nothing higher) is knowledge of the unchanging immutable, immortal, *ātman/brahman*. The highest knowledge is the knowledge of omnipresent self. Each of the lower objects could be worshipped as if it were *brahman*, but only the *ātman* is *brahman*. The true *object* of the higher knowledge is the unseen, unperceivable, omnipresent subtle *brahman*, inapprehensible to the senses, imperishable, omnipresent, subtle *brahman* who is the cause of all things.[35] From this *brahman* arises *hiraṇyagarbha*, name, form, and food.[36] Scattered throughout the Upaniṣads is the idea that this *brahman-ātman* is the highest knowledge, the knowledge of which leaves nothing else to be known. It brings about the highest good, puts an end to all suffering, and brings about immortality.

The Upaniṣads repeatedly reiterate that the knowledge of the *brahman* is the highest knowledge. However, can we literally speak of the knowledge of the *brahman*? There are texts that strongly emphasize the ineffability and unknowability of the *brahman*, e.g., "the self cannot be reached by the spiritual learning, nor by intellect";[37] "one who knows does not know (it), one who does not know, knows,"[38] "Words return from it without reaching it."[39] One could argue that the *brahman* is like the Kantian thing-in-itself, unknown and unknowable. Nothing could be further from the truth. The above quoted texts only suggest that our ordinary epistemic means do not yield the knowledge of the *brahman*, the only means to *mokṣa*. "One who knows *brahman* becomes *brahman*."[40]

Kena Upaniṣad raises what may be called a more strictly philosophical question, namely, what makes knowledge possible? Or, literally, who is spurred by whom? Because of whom? The eyes see it; the ears hear it, etc. The idea is that the senses including *manas* and *buddhi* by themselves cannot perform other appropriate functions unless they are guided by the *ātman*. So, in the long run, it is the *ātman*, which makes it possible for them to discharge their proper functions.

The sense organs and other cognitive faculties perform their appointed jobs owing to the inspiration, intention, or command of something other than them. And yet, this something else, the *ātman*, is not seen by the eyes, expressed by words, or reached by the mind. How is it then that though in itself incapable of being known, it makes knowledge possible? Verse 1.5 improves upon the last formulation: this *ātman* is other than what is known and also other than what is unknown. An object is either known, or unknown, or in part known, while remaining unknown in other aspects. But the subject, the knower, is neither known nor unknown. It is not seen by the eyes, and yet because of it the eyes see; it is not comprehended by the *manas* (mind) while the *manas* is manifested by it, the speech organ cannot articulate it but the speech organ and the sounds produced by it are manifested by it. This precisely is the *ātman* or the *brahman.*

The point that is being made is well established philosophically: the subject, the self, the *ātman*, is the ground of the possibility of knowledge of objects, but in itself is not a possible object.

It is not the case then that I know *ātman-brahman*; it is not the case that I do not know *ātman-brahman.* A paradox no doubt but the paradox has to be confronted in its full implications. "One for whom *brahman* is said to be unknown, truly knows it: one who knows it does not indeed know it."[41] This is the paradox of transcendental philosophy. The *ātman* manifests all objects because it is self-manifesting.

The *brahman-ātman* is not accessible through empirical modes of knowing. Hence, the question: how is it known? This particular question has been answered in many different ways in different Upaniṣads. MU states that when the "*buddhi* is purified of all faults, one becomes fit for acquiring that knowledge."[42] Being self-manifesting, *brahman* shows itself to one whose heart is pure, who has practiced austerity, and has "burnt away" all his faults.

The *Kaṭha* introduces the metaphor of a chariot: the body is like a chariot on which the *ātman* rides, the *buddhi* or intellect is the driver of the chariot, the *manas* or the mind is the rein, the sense organs are the horses and the sensory objects are what the horses travel over. The complex of self, i.e., the sense-organs and mind, is what the wise call the "enjoyer." When the *buddhi*, under the influence of an unsettled mind becomes non-discriminating, the horses become uncontrollable. On the contrary, a settled mind knows the path, and the charioteer *buddhi* is discriminating, the mind is controlled, making it possible to reach the sacred goal.[43]

But all these faculties, as functioning within the body, have their efficacy only with regard to empirical knowledge, i.e., the lower knowledge. Thus we find in the *Kaṭha* a clear affirmation: "The self is not reached by Vedic hymns, nor by intellect, nor by hearing the scriptures. He whom the self chooses, reaches him, the self manifests his own nature for him."[44] This last sentence as formulated here suggests a theistic conception of god. But on the Śaṃkara's reading, true being, self-manifesting consciousness is revealed only to those who are true aspirants, those who seek to know the true self whole-heartedly.

One of the texts, the *Iśa Upaniṣad*, in which knowledge (*vidyā*) and its opposite ignorance (*avidyā*) are discussed, says that the *avidyā* leads to darkness, but *vidyā* leads to still greater darkness. It is by knowing *vidyā* as *vidyā* and *avidyā* as *avidyā* that one overcomes death and attains immortality. These two verses have given rise to various interpretations. It is not necessary to examine these interpretations. Suffice it to note that many commentators understand by *avidyā* knowledge of the plurality of things and take *vidyā* in this context simply to be textual knowledge of the Vedas.

Though most schools of Indian philosophy accept *mokṣa* as the highest knowledge, they differ regarding the process that leads to it and what in fact happens upon attaining *mokṣa*. Some schools regard knowledge, others devotion, and still others a combination of the two, to be indispensable for reaching this knowledge. Some schools believe that upon attaining the highest knowledge, the empirical individual (*jīva*) becomes identical with the supreme self, others believe that it becomes a part of the supreme self. On one account, *mokṣa* is reached all at once; on another, it is reached step-by-step. The latter account makes moral life and religious practices preliminary and preparatory steps towards the final goal. These differences are a function of the ontological and epistemological presuppositions of the school, and we will study some of these issues in the chapters to follow.

Before closing this chapter, let me note the following: inquiry into the nature of knowing precedes that into the nature of being in the order of knowledge, although in the order of the way things are, being precedes knowing. The Upaniṣadic affirmation that the knower of *brahman* becomes *brahman* formulates the paradox, leaving it open for at least two interpretations. In a straightforward sense, it simply means that knowing results in a realization of being. But it lends itself to being understood the other way around as well; that is, one who becomes *brahman*, alone is the knower of *brahman*. Knowledge is identity with the *brahman*.

APPENDIX I

TRANSLATIONS OF THE SELECTED TEXTS[1]

The *Ṛg* and *Atharva Vedas*

I *Ṛg Veda* (RV)

X.90 Hymn to Puruṣa

1 The *Puruṣa* has a thousand heads, a thousand eyes, and a thousand feet. He pervades the universe everywhere, and remains beyond the breadth of ten fingers.

2 Whatever has happened, in addition, whatever will be: all is this *Puruṣa.* He acquired the right to be immortal; he becomes greater by his (sacrificial) food.

3 Such is his glory, but he is greater than all this. All creatures are one-fourth of him; three-fourths are (the world of) the immortal in heaven.

4 The *Puruṣa* went up with three-fourths of his nature, one-fourth remained here. From this (one-fourth), he then spread himself over all that is animate as well as all that is inanimate.

5 *Virāt* (the brilliant or the shining one) was born out of him; from *Virāt* was born *Puruṣa* again. As soon as he was born, he spread eastward and westward over the earth.

6 When gods prepared the sacrifice . . . the spring became the ghee (clarified butter) for it, the autumn the sacred gift, and the summer the fire-wood.

12 [When they divided the *Puruṣa*] . . . the *brahman* was his mouth, out of his two arms were the king (*rājanya*) made, his thighs became the *vaiśya,* from his feet was the *śudra* born.

13 The moon was born from his mind, from his eyes the sun, from his mouth *Indra* and *Agni,* and from his breath *Vāyu* (wind) was born.

14 From his navel came mid-air, from his head, the sky, from his feet, the earth, the regions from his ear, thus the worlds were formed.

16 With the sacrifice, the deities sacrificed the sacrifice. The mighty ones attained the heights of heaven, the place where the ancient gods dwell.

X.129 Hymn to Creation

1 The non-being there was not, nor was there being at that time; there existed neither the air nor the sky beyond. What covered them? From where and in whose protection? And was there unfathomable water?

2 Death did not exist nor deathlessness then. There was no sign of night or of day.

Breathless that One breathed through its self-nature. There was nothing else beyond that.

3 There was darkness, hidden in darkness, in the beginning. All this was an unillumined ocean. That Creative Force (thing) covered by the emptiness. That One was born by the power of heat.

4 From thought there developed desire in the beginning, which existed as the primal offspring. Searching in their hearts through wisdom, the poets found the connection of the being in the non-being.

5 Their cord was stretched across: What was there below (it) and what was there above? There were begetters—powerful beings! (There was) fertile power below and potency above.

6 Who really knows? Who can here proclaim it? From where was it born, whence this creation? The gods are later than the creation of this (world). So then who does know from what it came to be (into being)?

7 This creation, from where it came into being, whether it was created or whether it was not created—he who is its overseer in the highest heaven, he only knows—or, may be, he does not know.

II *Atharva Veda* (AV)

*X.7.7–8 and X.8.13 Hymns to Support (***Puruṣa and Prajāpati** *of the* **Ṛg Veda***)*

X.7.7

Oh, wise man, tell me who of all is the all-pervading God, supported by whom all the worlds were firmly established by Prajāpati?

X.7.8

How far did God enter within the whole universe, created by the all-pervading God, having all the forms? What part did he leave unpenetrated?

X.8.13

The God Prajāpati resides within the soul. Himself unseen, he manifests himself in various shapes. With one half of his being, he produced the entire universe. How can we know of the other half?

X.8.43–44 Hymns to Ātman *or Soul as the Supreme One*

X.8.43

Men having knowledge of the *brahman* know God, the Lord of the soul, within the nine-door[1] lotus flower and enclosed within three bonds.[2]

X.8.44

Desireless, powerful, immortal, self-existent, who is satisfied with the delight that is his nature, lacking nothing—he is free from fear of death who knows this *ātman*, which is powerful, undecaying (remains young).

XIX 3 Hymn to Time

1 Just as a horse with seven-roped reins carries a chariot, similarly an unageing, omnipresent, all-potent deity who has thousand-fold powers of vigilance—indestructible and the Almighty— has as his wheels the entire world. . . .

2 Time carries along seven wheels: seven are its centerpieces and immortality is its axle. The same time, revealing all these worlds, moves as the primeval deity.

3 A filled jar has been placed upon Time. The entire universe is there in the omnipotent and the omnipresent god. We on the earth see him in different ways. He illuminates all these worlds. They call him Time; he pervades the entire vast sky.

4 He alone brought together worlds (beings); it alone encompassed them. Though their father, he became their son. There is therefore no other higher majesty.

5 Time created these heavenly spheres, also these terrestrial spheres. All that was created before is stationed in Time in various forms. All that will be created in future and all that moves on, will be created in Time.

6 Time produced the very existence of creation and its wealth. The sun shines in Time. All creation finds its existence in Time alone. The eyes can see only due to Time.

7 The mind, the vital breath and the named—all are well placed in Time. All subjects enjoy themselves at the very approach of Time.

8 Time is the Lord of all. He is the protection of the king or the Sun. In Time are fully established the austerity, the grandeur, the vast universe, and the Vedic lore.

9 The universe is firmly established in him, stirred by him and created by him. The same Time, being *brahman*, the mighty one, sustains the universe, his greatest sacrifice.

1 The nine doors are: two eyes, two ears, two nostrils, mouth, anus, and penis. The lotus is the body. Throughout this work, apart from translating the original texts, if necessary in the interest of clarity, I have included the comments in the parentheses. I have followed this format in all the appendices included in this book.

2 The three bonds are *sattva, rajas*, and *tamas*.

10 Time created all creatures. He created *Hiraṇyagarbha* (the Lord of all beings) at first, the source of all creation. The self-existent, the self-effulgent, and the heating energy, all were simply Time's own self, revealed to us.

The Upaniṣads

Investigations about the *Brahman*

I *The* Taittrīyā Upaniṣad

III.1.1–6

1 Bhṛgu, the son of Varuṇa, came to his father, and said, "Sir, teach me about the *brahman*." He replied, "It is food, life, sight, hearing, mind, and speech." He said further, "It is that from which all these beings arise, that by which, after being born, they are sustained, that in which, when departing, they enter. Know him, that is the *brahman*."

He (Varuṇa) performed austerity. Having performed it [he (Varuṇa) received the wisdom.]

2 He learnt that food is the *brahman*. It is from food that all these beings are born, it is from food that after being born they live, and when departing they return into it.

After having learnt this, he again approached his father, Varuṇa, and said to him "Teach me the *brahman*."

Varuṇa said to him, "Seek to know the *brahman* through austerity, the *brahman* is austerity."

He (Bhṛgu) performed austerity. Having performed austerity [he, Varuṇa, received the wisdom].

3 He learnt that life is the *brahman*, that it is from life that all beings are born, that from life after being born they live, and when departing they return into it.

After having learnt this, he again approached his father, Varuṇa, and said to him "Teach me the *brahman*."

Varuṇa said to him, "Seek to know the *brahman* through austerity, the *brahman* is austerity."

He (Bhṛgu) performed austerity. Having performed austerity [he, Bhṛgu, received the wisdom].

4 He learnt that mind is the *brahman*. From mind indeed arise all these beings, being born they live by the mind, and, when departing, they enter into the mind.

Having known this, he (Bhṛgu) again approached his father Varuṇa, and said "Teach me the *brahman*."

To him (Bhṛgu), he (Varuṇa) said, "Seek to know the *brahman* through austerity, the *brahman* is austerity."

He (Bhṛgu) performed austerity. Having performed austerity [he, Bhṛgu, received the wisdom].

5 He learnt that intellect is the *brahman*, from intellect indeed all these beings arise, being born they live by the intellect, and when departing they enter into the intellect.

Having known this, he (Bhṛgu) again approached his father Varuṇa, and said "Teach me the *brahman*."

To him (Bhṛgu), he (Varuṇa) said "Seek to know the *brahman* through austerity, the *brahman* is austerity."

He (Bhṛgu) performed austerity. Having performed austerity [he, Bhṛgu, received the wisdom].

6 He learnt that bliss is the *brahman*, from bliss indeed all these beings arise, being born they live by bliss, and when departing they enter into bliss.

This wisdom taught by Bhṛgu and Varuṇa is established in the highest heaven. One who knows this, becomes well-established. He becomes the possessor of food, and eats food. He becomes great with his offspring and cattle, his fame becomes great with the wisdom-of-the *brahman*.

II Bṛhadāraṇyaka Upaniṣad

II.1.1–20

1 There lived one (conceited) Bālāki of the Gārgya clan, who was merely an expositor. He went to Ajātaśatru of Kāsī, and told him "I will tell you about the *brahman*." Ajātaśatru said, "I will give you one thousand cows for this favor." . . .

2 The Gārgya (i.e., Bālāki) said, "The person in the yonder sun, I worship him as the *brahman*." Ajātaśatru said, "Do not speak to me about him. I worship him as surpassing all beings, as their head and their king. One who worships him surpasses all beings, becomes the head and the king of all beings."

[In 3–13, Bālāki and Ajātaśatru exchange the same pattern of conversation with regard to the person in the moon, in the lightning, in the air, in the fire, in the water, in a mirror, in the heavens, the person in a shadow, and the person in the self.]

14 (Finally) Ajātaśatru said, "Is that all?" Gārgya said, "That is all." Ajātaśatru said, "With all this, it (the *brahman*) is not known." Gārgya said, "Allow me to be your pupil."

15 Ajātaśatru said "This is indeed contrary to practice that a *brahmin* should come to a *kṣatrīya* expecting the latter to teach him about the *brahman*. However, I will impart this knowledge to you clearly." He took him (Bālāki) by hand, rose and together approached a person who was asleep. They call him with the names "Great, white-robed, shining, Soma." The person did not wake up. He (Ajātaśatru) woke him up by pressing him with his hands. He then woke up.

16 Ajātaśatru said, "When this person fell asleep—this person who is full of intellect—where was it, and from where did it come back." This Gārgya did not know.

17 Ajātaśatru said, "When this one (being) fell asleep, this person who is full of intelligence restrains by his intelligence the intelligence of the sense-organs,

rests in the space within the heart. He is said to be asleep when he takes in those senses. When the breath, the speech, the eye, the ear, and all these sense organs are restrained, then the mind is restrained."

18 As in dream he wanders, these are his worlds. He becomes, it seems, a great king or a great *brāhmaṇa*. He assumes states, high and low. Just as a great king, along with his people, moves about in his country according to his desire, so in a dream, along with his sense organs, he wanders about in his own body according to his desire.

19 When he falls soundly asleep, and knows nothing, he—after coming through the seventy two thousand channels which extend from the heart to the pericardium, he rests in the pericardium. Just as a young man or a great king or a great *brāhmaṇa* rests after having reached the height of bliss, so he now rests.

20 From this self all breaths, worlds, divinities, and all beings emerge, just as a spider moves along the thread and as particles of fire come from the fire. The secret meaning of self is that it is the truth of truth. The life breaths are truth; the self is their truth.

III Chāndogya Upaniṣad

The Nature of the Ātman (Indra Prajāpati Dialogue)

VIII.7.1–4

1 The self which is free from all sin, free from old age, death, grief, hunger and thirst, who desires the truth, wills the truth, he should be known. One who knows that self reaches all the worlds and all desire. Prajāpati said this.

2 Both the gods and the demons heard it. They said, "We seek that self, by seeking which one reaches all the worlds, and also all desires." From the gods, Indra went to him, Virocana from the demons. The two approached Prajāpati, with fuel in hand.

3 The two lived there (with Prajāpati) for thirty-two years the life of discipline of "aspirant of *Brahmā*." Then, he (Prajāpati) said to them, "Desiring what, have you been living (this life of austerity)?" This the two (Indra and Virocana) said. "The self which is free from evil, old age, death, sorry, hunger, and thirst, who desires the truth, who thinks of the truth, he (that self) should be sought, he should be understood. He who knows that self, reaches all the worlds and all his desires. That is said to be your word, Sir, we are living [this life of discipline] desiring (to know) him (that self)."

4 Prajāpati said to them (Indra and Virocana): "The self is the person that is seen in the eye. That is the immortal, the fearless (self), that is the *brahman*." They asked, "But, Sir, who is the person that is seen in water and in a mirror?" He (Prajāpati) replied, "He is the same that is seen in all these."

VIII.8.1–3

1 (The two looked at themselves in a bowl of water, and told Prajāpati) "Oh, divine Sir, we see the self, (we see) a picture (of ourselves) up to the hair and nails."

2 (As requested by Prajāpati, the two put on their best attire, and looked into the bowl of water.) "What do you see?" asked Prajāpati.

3 The two said: "Oh, divine Sir, we see ourselves dressed up in the best clothes . . . ." Prajāpati said: "That is the self, the immortal, the fearless, the *brahman*." The two of them left with a heart full of tranquility.

VIII.9.1–3

1 (Prajāpati saw them go back, and said) "They return without knowing the self. Whoever follows this teaching (i.e., that the body is the self) will perish, whether he is a god or a demon. The self is blind when the body is blind, lame when the body is lame, perishes as soon as the body perishes. I see no good in it."

2 Indra returned, fuel in hand . . . he said, "If the body is well-adorned, the self is, well-dressed if the body is, blind if the body is blind, lame if the body is so, lame when the body is lame. This self perishes as soon as the body does. I do not like it."

3 Prajāpati agreed, and said "I will explain this further, after you live with me for thirty-two years." So did Indra. To him, then, he (Prajāpati) said.

VIII.10.1–2, 4

1 He (Prajāpati) said, "He who wanders about freely in a dream, is the self, the immortal, the fearless, the *brahman*." Indra returned with a quiet heart. But not yet reaching the gods, he saw the problem (in it). When the body is blind, the self is not blind, if the body is lame, the self is not so, it does not suffer from the defects of the body.

2 "This self is not killed when the body is killed, not one-eyed if the body is so, yet it is as though he is killed, as though he is undressed. He experiences, as it were, something is unpleasant; he even weeps as it were. So I do not see any merit in this."

4 (Prajāpati agreed) and said "Live with me for an additional thirty-two years, then I will explain it further." He (Indra) lived with him (Prajāpati) for another thirty-two years. To him, then, he (Prajāpati) said.

VIII.11.1–3

1 "When a person is asleep, whole and tranquil, and does not know any dream, that is the self, the immortal, the fearless, the *brahman*." Indra went away with a peaceful heart. But even before reaching the gods, he saw this problem. This self does not know himself as "I am he," nor does he know the things (around him). He appears to have been annihilated. I do not find any merit in it.

2–3 Again, he (Indra) returned, fuel in hand. Then he lived with Prajāpati for five more years which amounted to one hundred and one years in all . . . so do people say, Indra lived with Prajāpati for one hundred and one years, the disciplined life of a seeker after sacred knowledge. To him (Indra), then he (Prajāpati) said.

VIII.12.1

1 (Finally, Prajāpati said to Indra) "Oh, Indra, this body is truly mortal. It is bound by death. Yet, it is the seat of the self which is deathless and bodiless. The embodied self is subject to pleasure and pain. There is no escape from pleasure and pain for the embodied. But they do not touch the one who is bodiless."

The Brahman–Ātman *Identity Thesis*
(Śvetaketu–Uddālaka Dialogue)

VI.1.3–5 and 7–8

(Uddālaka asked his son, do you know that) "by which the unheard becomes heard, the unperceivable becomes perceived, and the unknowable becomes known?" Respected sir, how can there be such a teaching? "Just as by knowing one lump of clay all that is made of clay is known, the differences being only a name arising from speech, reality being only clay. Just as by knowing a nugget of gold all that is made of gold is known, the differences being only a name arising from speech, reality being only gold . . ." (Śvetaketu replies) "Respected sir, I did not know this, for if they (my teachers) had known it, why would not they tell me so? Please tell me. . . ."

VI.8.7

(The Uddālaka said:) That which is the essence of all things, the world has it for its self. That is the truth, the self, that art thou (Śvetaketu). Please teach me further. Uddālaka said, "So be it, Oh! dear."

VI.10. 1–3

Just as the rivers from the eastern flow east, from the western towards the west. They move from sea to sea, and merge into the sea and become the sea itself and do not know "I am this river," "I am that river," In the same manner, "all human beings, though they come from one being, do not know that they have come from one being . . . That which is the essence of all things, the world has it for its self. That is the truth, the self, that art thou" (Śvetaketu). Please teach me further. Uddālaka said, "So be it, Oh! dear."

VI.13. 1–3

"Put this lump of salt in water, and come to me next morning," (the teacher said). Then the student did so. The teacher said: "Please bring here the salt you put in water last evening." The student looked for it, and did not find it, since it was dissolved. He (the teacher) said, "take a sip of this water from this end. (Tell me) how does it taste." "Salty," (said the student). "Take a sip from the other end (and tell me) how is it." "Salty," (said the student). "Throw it away, and then come to me," (said the teacher). He (the student) did so. Then he said, "My dear, you do not see pure being, (but) it is indeed here." "That which the entire world has as its subtle essence is its self. That is the truth. That is the self. That art thou, Śvetaketu." (the teacher said).

Part III

NON-VEDIC SYSTEMS

4

THE CĀRVĀKA *DARŚANA* AND THE *ŚRAMAṆAS*

Many scholars, for example, Radhakrishnan, hold that in the Indian context "the materialistic school of thought was as vigorous and comprehensive as materialistic philosophy in the modern world."[1] There is no need to enter into a discussion of this claim in this chapter. For our purposes it is sufficient to note that originally there were two trends in Indian thought: the materialistic and the spiritualistic. Of these two trends, the latter, which came to fruition in the Vedas and the Upaniṣads, we shall have ample reasons to get acquainted with in the chapters to follow; the former, however, is generally a neglected story, though the germs of the materialistic philosophy are found in the Upaniṣadic literature, e.g., in the Uddālaka conception that mind is created out of the finest essence of food,[2] in the Indra Prajāpati dialogue that the self is identical with the body,[3] in the early Buddhist literature,[4] and in the repudiation of the afterlife in the *Kaṭha Upaniṣad*[5] and *Maitrī Upaniṣad.*[6] The materialism, more truly the naturalistic tendencies, left a permanent mark on Indian thought. It influenced and greatly shaped such powerful systems as Nyāya, Vaiśeṣika, and Sāṁkhya—although these systems sought to combine both the naturalistic and the spiritualistic tendencies.

In this chapter, I will discuss the Cārvākas (the *lokāyatas*) and the *śramaṇas.* These are ancient systems that antedate or were contemporaneous with the rise of Buddhism and provided a formidable challenge to the Vedic ritualism and the *brāhmaṇic* hierarchy. The Buddhist texts, especially the *Pāli Nikāyas,* are excellent sources of our knowledge of the *śramaṇas.*

I The Cārvākas (*Lokāyatas*)

In the history of Indian philosophy materialism is generally associated with the Cārvāka school. The original meaning of the word "Cārvāka" is shrouded in mystery. On one view, Bṛhaspati was the founder of this school. Bṛhaspati is equated with the teacher of gods who propounded materialism among the demons in order to ruin them.[7] On another view, there was a sage named "Cārvāka," the disciple of Bṛhaspati, who promulgated materialism. On still another view, "Cārvāka" is not a proper name. The term "Cārvāka" describes a materialist who taught the doctrine of "eat ("*carv*" meaning "eat" or "chew"), drink, and be merry." Alternately, the name "Cārvāka" may also mean the words that are pleasant to hear (*cāru* = nice and *vāk* = word). Irrespective of the meaning of the word "Cārvāka," there is no denying that the Cārvāka school in Indian thought has been taken to be synonymous with the Lokāyata school[8] and its followers have been known as "*lokāyatikas*."

The word "*lokāyata*" has been variously translated as that which is "prevalent in the common world," "the basis of the foolish and the profane world," a "commoner" or "a person of low and unrefined taste," etc.[9] In the second act of the allegorical play *Prabodahcandrodayam*, teachings of materialism are summed up as follows:

> *Lokāyata* is the only *śāstra*; perception is the only source of knowledge; earth, water, fire, and air are the only elements; *artha* and *kāma* are the only two goals of human life; consciousness (in the body) is produced by earth, water, fire, and air. Mind is only a product of matter. There is no other world. Only death is *mokṣa*. On our view, Vācaspati (Bṛhaspati), after composing this important *śāstra*, in accordance with our likings (inclinations), dedicated it to the Cārvākas, who spread it through his students and students of the students.[10]

The *Lokāyatas* seem to have been around during the time of the rise of Buddhism and were known and condemned as being the "abusers of the Vedas," "negativists," "deniers of the after-world." Their teachings seem to have two aspects: on the one hand, they indulged in destructive arguments, and, on the other hand, were clearly connected with the practice of statecraft and politics. It seems their original interest was practical: denial of the authority of the Vedas, of "another world," i.e., of life after death, denial of morality ("no good or bad"), rejection of the idea of God, of reward and punishment and so on. The art of sophistry and negative disputation gradually came to be a system of philosophy with its own metaphysics and epistemology. This transformation is said to be the work of one Cārvāka, which, in the Indian tradition, has been taken to stand for a "materialist."

As materialism developed from being a general denial of all morality to being a well-argued philosophy with its logic, epistemology, and ethics, the Cārvākas, or at least the new brand of them known as the "well-educated Cārvākas," came to be recognized as philosophies and continued through the ages to be included among the classical *darśanas*. Their negativist rhetoric of deriding the Vedic beliefs changed into a philosophical style. It is quite possible that the negative portrayal of the Cārvāka school has been exaggerated, because no *lokāyata* texts with the exception of the *Tattvopaplavasiṁha* ("the lion that throws overboard all categories") have survived.[11] Tucci, however, argues that, from the fact that no *lokāyata* text is extant, one cannot conclude that no *lokāyata* text ever existed.[12] S. N. Dasgupta echoes similar sentiments when he notes that a commentary on *Lokāyata śāstra* by Bhaguri existed in ancient times,[13] though it is difficult to say anything about the author of *Lokāyata śāstra*. Regarding the *Tattvopaplavasiṁha* (TPS), its editors hold that this text more precisely belongs to a "particular division"[14] of the Cārvāka school and that this work carries the skeptical tendencies of the Cārvāka school "to its logical end."[15] In reviewing the philosophical doctrines of the Cārvāka school, we must keep in mind that the primary sources of our information are the writings of those opponents of Cārvākas who have sought to refute or ridicule it. It is unfortunate that we have no choice but to rely on such accounts.

My exposition in the following will primarily be based upon such doxographic writings as Madhva's *Sarvadarśanasaṁgraha* (SDS),[16] which portrays the Cārvākas as hedonists, and materialists, and calls this school "the crest-gem of the atheistic school."[17] In the opening paragraph, Madhva states:

> The efforts of the Chārvāka are indeed hard to be eradicated, for the majority of living beings hold by the current refrain—
>
> While life is yours, live joyously;
> None can escape Death's searching eye;
> When once this frame of ours they burn;
> How shall it e'er again return?[18]

It is worth noting that Madhva at the outset of his work presents Cārvāka in a very unfavorable light and sets up an adversarial tone *vis-à-vis* the *brāhmaṇical* tradition. The passage highlights and brings to the forefront the opposition between Cārvāka and other schools of Indian philosophy. For example, the *brāhmaṇical* schools accept the four goals of life, after-life, the soul that survives the body, and the eradication of pain by *mokṣa*. The Cārvākas, on the other hand, propound a crude or unrefined form of hedonism, reject after-life, soul, and *mokṣa*. With this in mind, let us discuss what Madhva has to say about Cārvāka epistemology and metaphysics. His account may be summed up in the following words:

1 Perception is the only valid source of knowledge;
2 Neither inference nor scriptures is a valid source of knowledge;
3 The self is the body;
4 Consciousness arises from the combination of the natural elements which constitute the body; and
5 No dormant consciousness in the fetus; consciousness does not continue after death.

The Cārvākas argue that perception is the only means of knowing the truth: whatever is available to sense-perception is true; whatever is not, is doubtful. They reject inference (*anumāna*) because there is no sufficient ground for ascertaining the truth of invariable, universal relation called "*vyāpti*." Inference proceeds from the known to the unknown and there is no guarantee that what is true of the perceived cases will also hold good of the unperceived ones. Let me give an illustrative example: "on perceiving smoke on a hill, one infers that there is fire." This inference is based on the *vyāpti*: "wherever there is smoke, there is fire." The Cārvākas ask: how does one determine the validity of universal major premise, i.e., the universal relation of co-existence between the major term (e.g., "fire") and the middle term (e.g., "smoke")? In response, they point out that such a universal relation can never be ascertained with certainty.[19] One cannot know it by perception because the possible future concomitance is not something with which the senses can come into contact. Moreover, the contact between the senses and the object gives us knowledge of the particular object that is in contact with our senses, and this contact cannot produce the universal connection between the fire and the smoke. Thus, perception can determine what is here and now, but it cannot provide us with the necessary connection required for a valid inference.

Nor can *vyāpti* be determined by inference because *anumāna* itself is dependent upon a *vyāpti*. To say that we can determine *vyāpti* by *anumāna* is to open the doors to infinite regress. Madhva notes: Inference cannot "be the means of the knowledge of the universal proposition, since in the case of this inference we should also require another inference to establish it, and so on, and hence would arise the fallacy of an *ad infinitum* retrogression."[20]

Śabda (verbal testimony) and *upamāna* (comparison) also cannot help us in determining the universal relation because knowledge generated by *śabda* and *upamāna* presupposes inference. Accordingly, Madhava concludes: "Hence by the impossibility of knowing the universality of a proposition it becomes impossible to establish inference, ..."[21] We can only determine with a higher degree of probability, never with certainty, what is to be true in all cases. Thus, depending as it does on the apprehension of a *vyāpti*, *anumāna* is not a *pramāṇa* (means of true cognition).

The Cārvāka critique extends to include *śabda* as a *pramāṇa*, because its validity is ascertained by inference. Additionally, the Vedic testimony has no cognitive value; they are regarded by the Cārvākas as nothing more than idle utterances of the *brahmins* who sought to serve their own interests. All their words about "merit" and "demerit," life after death, and sacrifices, are completely useless from the cognitive point of view. In short, *śabda* also fails to deliver certain knowledge.

By rejecting *anumāna*, Cārvākas place themselves in a precarious situation, because any proof they give to prove the validity of their own position would require some sort of inference. How can Cārvākas prove that perception is the only *pramāṇa*? at this juncture, Cārvākas realize that there are only two alternatives open to them: either accept the validity of inference as a means of true cognition or refuse to recognize even perception as a source of true cognition. both these positions have in fact been taken, the first by Purandara and the second by Jayarāśi Bhāṭṭa.

Purandara, a seventh-century Cārvāka, concedes that although inference may be used to strengthen perceptual beliefs, it has absolutely no power to yield any knowledge of what lies beyond the limits of sensory perception, for example, existence of life after death.[22] Perhaps the rationale behind maintaining the distinction between the usefulness of inference in our everyday experience and in ascertaining truths beyond perceptual experience lies in the fact that an inductive generalization is made by observing a large number of cases of agreement in presence and agreement in absence, and since agreement in presence cannot be observed in the transcendental world even if such a world existed, no inductive generalization relating to such a world can be made.

Jayarāśi Bhāṭṭa argues that there is no valid ground for accepting perception as the only source of true cognition, because perception itself cannot be regarded as the means for ascertaining the validity of perception. Accordingly, Jayarāśi demonstrates the invalidity of all the *pramāṇas* accepted by Indian philosophical schools. He employs dialectical arguments and challenges the validity of the theories of knowledge put forward by Nyāya, Mīmāmṣā, Sāṁkhya, and Buddhism. Jayarāśi starts with his opponent's concepts, suggests various alternative definitions, and shows that while some of these definitions are inapplicable, others lead to contradictions. Let us briefly review his arguments to examine the status of perception as a *pramāṇa*. Jayarāśi begins with the Nyāya definition of perception: "perception is a cognition which arises from a contact between sense and object, cannot be designated [by words], is non-erroneous, [and] has the nature of non-determination."[23] Jayarāśi attacks the term "non-erroneous" that occurs in the Nyāya definition of perception. The non-erroneousness is, of course, not known by perception, because perception always involves perception of an object and the non-erroneousness of perception is not an object. Neither can it be known through *anumāna* because such an *anumāna* in itself would have to be based on perception, which will make it a case of *petitio*. Thus, as the non-erroneousness of perception cannot be established, either by perception or by *anumāna*, perception cannot be regarded as a *pramāṇa*. He further argues that there is no valid ground for accepting the existence of material elements, because if perception is the only valid source of knowledge, how can one be certain that perception reveals the true nature of objects? Accordingly, he not only argues for the invalidity of all the *pramāṇas* but also the consequent invalidity of all metaphysical principles and categories. Thus, the title *Tattvopaplavsiṃha* is appropriate as the main thesis of the book demonstrates the impossibility of establishing the truth of any view of reality.

Leaving Jayarāśi aside, the Cārvākas accept perception as the only *pramāṇa* and use this logical epistemological theory to support their materialism. Everything arises out of a combination of the four elements and dissolution consists in their separation. Their core metaphysical doctrines may be stated as follows:

1 Earth, water, fire, and air are the only realities;
2 Consciousness arises from these elements in the same way as the intoxicating

nature of a drink arises from the combination of elements each of which separately does not have that power to intoxicate; and

3 The so-called self or *puruṣa* is nothing but the body possessed of consciousness.

Regarding #1, note that the Cārvākas do not include *ākāśa* or "ether" in their list of the elements, since it is not cognizable by sense-perception. Accordingly, they argue that the entire material world is composed of the four perceptible elements. In other words, all living organisms, including plants and animals, are composed of these four elements.

With regard to #2, the Cārvākas point out consciousness is perceived to exist in the body, therefore, it must be a property of the body. In response to the question, how can four non-conscious elements when combined produce consciousness, the Cārvākas point out that just as when betal leaf, lime, and nut are combined red color originates which is not there originally, similarly, four material elements combined in a special way give rise to a conscious body, though none of the constituents possess consciousness. In short, consciousness is a by-product or epiphenomenon of matter. A familiar objection regarding the impossibility of accounting for memory is addressed by Cārvākas thus: memory is due to the persistence of traces (*saṃskāras*) of this life's previous experiences in the present body.

The Cārvākas use #3 to reject both the Hindu belief in an eternal self and the Buddhist thesis that self is nothing but a series of impermanent states in rapid succession. When a person dies, nothing survives. What people generally mean by soul is body with consciousness. Whereas we do not perceive any disembodied soul, we do directly perceive self as identical with the body in our daily experiences. Such judgments as "I am lame," "I am fat," "I am thin," bear testimony to the fact that the self is not different from the body.

It is worth noting that the Cārvāka position with regard to the self underwent some changes. Other schools of philosophy, especially the Naiyāyikas, severely criticized the Cārvāka position that consciousness is generated by the four elements, and that the self is not different from the conscious body. The Naiyāyikas argue that if none of the elements have the property of consciousness, their being together cannot produce consciousness. Moreover in the state of swoon or coma there is no consciousness, but the self continues to exist. There is no evidence that with the death of the body, the self also ceases to be. The Cārvāka, in its epistemology, depends upon perception, but no perceptual evidence establishes that with death, the self also becomes extinct. Nor can the Cārvāka use inference or any other form of reasoning to substantiate his position for he has already rejected inference as a *pramāṇa*. Indeed the Cārvāka critique of inference itself makes use of inference, and in so doing becomes guilty of self-contradiction. Additionally, how can Cārvākas reject *śabda* as a *pramāṇa*, when they depend upon the words of his predecessors, materialist teachers, and so on.[24]

In the face of such criticisms, the Cārvākas modify #3, i.e., that self is nothing but the body possessed of consciousness, into 3^1 3^2 and 3^3 as follows:

3^1 It is the functioning sense organs that constitute the self. But realizing that since there are many sense organs, some of which may be deficient (for example, eyes being blind), it would amount to saying that the self of a person must be many, and at times in conflict with each other.

They again modify their position as follows:

3^2 The self is the body with the *prāṇa* (life-force) in it, which is due to the intersection of the body with the environment outside. This allows them to speak of one self in each body as well as of many instruments of experiencing, e.g., the visual, tactual, auditory, and taste sense organs. The life-force, the *prāṇa*, when inside a body, becomes "conscious," but when it leaves the body, like the air outside, it becomes unconscious. But, then, this would amount to saying that there are different kinds of life-breath, and that each of these constitutes a distinct self. Additionally the breath, being exhaled out every moment, could not be called the self.

The Cārvākas again change their position as follows:

3^3 The self is the *manas*, that is to say that consciousness is located in the *manas* (which experiences pleasure and pain, and whose properties are desire, jealousy, etc.), which is one in each body. But *manas* being subtle, i.e., lacking as it does gross dimension, cannot be perceived, which would make pleasure, pain, etc.—that belong to it—imperceptible. Additionally, if the self is the *manas*, it could not have the sense of "I."

All these criticisms lead the philosophers to posit a self as distinct from the body, the sense organs, life force, and the *manas*. Thus, it is not surprising that Sadānanda in his *Vedāntasāra* points out that there were four schools of Cārvāka: one school takes self to be identical with the body; another takes self to be the vital breath; still another takes self to be identical with the sense-faculties, and the fourth takes the self to be identical with the mind.[25] The distinction is based on the different conceptions of the self where each succeeding view is more refined than the preceding one. However, all schools agree that self is a by-product or function of the matter. There is no transcendental being or god. There is no heaven or hell; the life ends in death. Consciousness originates with a specific concatenation of the four physical elements known as the living body and disappears when these four elements disassociate.

II The *Śramaṇas*

The voice of the Cārvākas was the voice of protest against excessive Vedic ritualism, superstitions, and exploitation by the *brāhmiṇs*. It is worth noting that the Cārvākas were not the only group of people to voice their protest against *brāhmaṇism*. By the sixth century BCE, another class of philosophers exercised a tremendous influence on the Indian tradition. As the Vedic culture originating in the Eastern valley began to spread eastward along the Gangetic plains, there arose a reaction against many of its excesses. This reaction was as much religious as it was social and political. It was a time of great upheaval and turmoil in India. The old structures of tribunal republics had begun to break down, and new kingdoms had begun to take shape. There was a great deal of uncertainty: old ways were being replaced by the new. Many wandering ascetics and mendicants, with different philosophical and religious ideas, were establishing their authority and superiority. These people did not belong to a specific class, though they provided a formidable challenge to the authority of the *brāhmins*. In general, they rejected the Vedic proliferation of deities and ritualism, the Upaniṣadic conception of the *ātman* and the *brahman*, the doctrine of rebirth and *karma*, the efficacy of action, the domination of the priestly class, and the distinction between good and bad. They lived the life of wandering mendicants and argued that heaven and hell were invented by deceitful *brāhmiṇs* to exploit people in order to earn their livelihood.

And, of no lesser importance, there was the reaction of the local self-governing republican communities against the monarchical systems which the *brāhmaṇism* of the Vedas and the Upaniṣads had glorified. Regarding the nature of the universe, their views varied considerably, however; they believed that the universe is not created by any supernatural power or god. They subscribed to a sort of naturalistic conception of the universe insofar as they believed that within nature there are different reals: matter, life, mind, etc.; there is nothing beyond nature. These wanderers were known as the "*śramaṇas*" (recluses).

Much controversy surrounds the *śramaṇas* of Indian tradition. We do not know their social origin. We however, know that they abandoned their family lives and offered alternative ways of knowing the truth. In general they appealed to experience as the source of knowledge and in so doing aligned themselves with the empiricists. This group of wanderers rejected *Brāhmaṇism*, but otherwise differed a great deal among themselves.

The reference the *śramaṇa* (from "*śram*" meaning "to exert") or "who practices religious exertions" is found as early as the BU, where it occurs alongside *tāpasa* (from "*tapa*" meaning "to warm") or who practices religious austerities implying that the *śramaṇas*, like the *tāpasas*, belonged to a class of religious ascetics.[26] Numerous references to *śramaṇas* are found throughout the Buddhist texts, both earlier and the later. It is difficult to ascertain with certainty whether the "*śramaṇas*" of the BU refer to the *śramaṇas* found in the Buddhist literature.

The oldest Buddhist records, i.e., the *Pali Nikāyas*, mention that the Buddha met some of them to discuss their views. Each of these *śramaṇas* had many lay followers and ascetics. A Buddhist text *Sāmaññaphala Sutta* ("Fruits of the life of a *śramaṇa*") provides a description of the six *śramaṇas* of the pre-Buddhist India in the course of a dialogue between Ajātaśatru, the king of Magadha, and the Buddha.[27] In this text, six *śramaṇas* are listed in the following order: Pūraṇa Kassapa, Makkhali Gośāla, Ajita Keśa-Kambala, Pakudha Kaccāyana, Niganṭha Nātaputta, and Sañjay Belaṭṭhiputta.

Pūraṇa Kassapa was an antinomian who denied all moral distinctions between good and bad. He held that theft, murder, and robbery are not bad and the acts of charity and sacrifice are not good. He argues: "In generosity, in self mastery, in control of the senses, in speaking the truth, there is neither merit nor increase of merit."[28] It is known as no-action theory (*akriyāvāda*). The soul does not act; thus, no merit accrues to a person from sacrifices, just as no demerit arises from the so-called bad actions. There is no cause and condition for knowledge and insight. Barua brings his views under *adhicca-samuppāda,* i.e., the theory of "fortuitous origin." He also points out that some Jaina writers identify Pūraṇa Kassapa's doctrine regarding the passivity of the soul with the Sāṃkhya view.[29] The *Pāli* epithet "*pūraṇa*" means "complete" or "perfect"; accordingly, his followers believed that Kassapa had attained perfect knowledge or wisdom.

Makkhali Gośāla, the leader of the Ājīvika sect, was a contemporary of Mahāvīra, the twenty-fourth perfect soul of Jainism. Pāṇini[30] holds that Makkhali or *maskarin* wandered here and there carrying a *maskara* (bamboo staff) about him. Makkhali taught that neither purity nor sufferings of men has any cause, and that one's actions have no efficacy, power, or energy. There are no moral obligations. He denied *karma* and agreed with *Pūraṇa* that good deeds have no bearing on transmigration which is governed by "*niyati*" (fate), a rigid cosmic principle. "The attainment of any given condition, of any character does not depend either on one's own acts, or on the acts of another, or on human effort. All beings are without force and power and energy of their own. They are bent this way and that by their fate . . . that they experience ease or pain"[31]

One often hears that *Ājīvikas* followed severe ascetic practices. They gave up household life, covered their bodies with a kind of mat, and carried a bunch of peacock feathers. They abstained from taking ghee and sweets, and practiced begging. It is difficult to determine why *Ājīvikas* prescribed moral observances, but at the same time also denied their value. Makkhali himself observed religious practices not as a means to attaining *mokṣa,* but rather to gain a livelihood.

Ajita Keśa-kambala is taken to be the earliest representative of materialism in India. He was called "*Keśa-kambala*," because he wore a blanket of hair on his body. He, in addition to denying moral distinctions and "merit" and "demerit," taught that there is neither the world nor the other world. He says:

> There are in the world no recluses or *brāhmaṇa* who have reached the highest point, who walk perfectly, and who having understood and

> realized, by themselves alone, both this world and the next, makes their wisdom known to others. A human being is built up of four elements. When he dies the earth in him returns to and relapses to the earth, the fluid to the water, the heart to the fire, the windy to the air, and his faculties (the five senses and the mind) pass into space.[32]

In short, a human being consists of four elements, viz., earth, water, fire, and air, so that life after death these elements return to the original elements.

As a corollary to his metaphysics of radical materialism, in terms of ethical teachings, Ajit held that there is no merit in offering sacrifices, there is no life after death, and no one passes from this life to the next. Good deeds do not give rise to any result (*phala*). No ascetic has reached perfection by purifying the mind, following the right path, and has experienced this world and the next world.

Pakudha Kaccāyana, argued that there are seven things which are neither made nor "caused to be made." The four elements, i.e., earth, water, fire, and air, are the root of all things. These elements do not change qualitatively, meaning thereby that they are permanent. In addition to these unchangeable entities, there are three more elements, viz., pleasure, pain, and soul. The four elements unite as well as separate without human intervention, i.e., without any volitional activity. Pleasure and pain, on the other hand, are the two elements of change and bring the four elements together along the lines of Vaiśeṣika *adṛṣṭa*. Barua points that out that Pakudha Kaccāyana is the Empedocles of India insofar as both argue for the four elements as the root of all things with two principles of change: love or pleasure and hatred or pain.[33] Finally, the soul is the living principle, *prāṇa* (vital breath) or what we understand by "*jīvātmā*"; there is nothing transcendent. He is taken to be the forerunner of the Hindu Vaiśeṣika school.

Nigaṇṭha Nātaputta is another *śramaṇa* discussed in this text. "*Nigaṇṭha*" means "a man free from bonds"; he is self-restrained and has washed away all evils. A *nigaṇṭha* "lives restrained as regards all evils, all evil he has washed away; and he lives suffused with the sense of evil held at bay. Such is his fourfold restraint."[34]

Sañjay Belaṭṭhiputta, denies the possibility of certain knowledge: "If you ask me whether there is another world—well, if I thought there were, I would say so. But I don't think, it is thus or thus. And I don't think it is otherwise. And I don't deny it. And I don't say there neither is, nor is not, another world."[35] It is quite possible that Sañjay was the first to formulate the four-fold logic of existence, non-existence, both, and neither.

These *śramaṇas* with the exception of Nigaṇṭha Nātaputta directly or indirectly deny the moral basis of *karma* and *mokṣa*. Ajita Keśa-kambali (*keśa* = hair, *kambala* = blanket) propounded materialism, and may very well have been the forerunner of Cārvāka in India. Gośāla is taken to be the founder of the school known as *Ājīvikas*.[36] Sañjay, agnostic, may be the teacher of Sāriputta, one of the famous disciples of the Buddha. Niganṭha Nātaputta or Mahāvīra is associated with Jainism. Basham, in his work entitled *History and the Doctrine of the Ājīvikas* discusses the six *śramaṇas* and argues that (1) Ajita Keśakambali, Niganṭha Nātaputta, and Sañjay Belaṭṭhiputta "have little relevance to the study of *Ājīvikas*"; (2) Niganṭha with Vardhamāna Mahāvīra are the same person," and (3) of the remaining three, viz., Pūraṇa Kassapa, Makkhali Gosāla, and Pakudha Kaccāyana, Makkhali and Pūraṇa are associated with later *Ājīvikas and* Pakudha with the Dravidian *Ājīvikas*[37] Jayatilleke, on the other hand notes, that in order to do justice to the doctrine of the skeptics, he will use *Ājīvikas* to denote those *śramaṇas* "who were neither Jainas, Materialists, or Sceptics."[38]

The Jaina tradition portrays Gośāla, an ascetic, as a person of low family born in a cow-shed (*go-śala*). Apparently, Gośāla once approached Mahāvīra and expressed his desire to become Mahāvīra's disciple; Mahāvīra, however, refused to accept him. Imitating Mahāvira, Gośala became a naked man and declared himself to be a "*jīna*," "a victor," a *tīrthaṇkara* (a person who has mastered all passions and attained omniscience). Mahāvīra exposed Gośāla's true nature for who he was, that he was a fake and declared that he, Mahāvīra, was the only true *jīna*, not Gośala. He is said to have codified the *Ājīvika* six factors of life: gain/loss, joy/sorrow, and life/death. It is difficult to say with absolute certainty whether the Jaina account of Gośala is correct, but there is no doubt that the Buddhists took the *Ājīvikas* to be their main rival, because they practiced extreme self-mortification and rejected the Buddha's Middle Way. In Pāli *Nikāyas*, one frequently comes across such compounds as *śramaṇa-brāhmaṇa* which refer to two different groups of holy ascetics, the former denoting ascetics of all affiliations and the latter denoting only the upholders of the Vedic tradition. It is worth noting that the *brāhmaṇas* were never referred to as *śramaṇas* and the *Buddha* was referred to as *mahā* (great) *śramaṇa*.

The rise of the *śramaṇas* marks the end of the Vedic period, the beginning of the Upaniṣadic era, and a conflict between the *śramaṇas* and the *brāhmaṇic* philosophies. They became a powerful force in then India; it was a voice to get rid of the oppression of the past and welcome different perspectives. The emergence of the rise of Buddhism and Jainism provides an eloquent testimony to their influence, and I will discuss these schools next.

5

THE JAINA *DARŚANA*

As I have noted on earlier occasions, there are two very ancient streams of Indian thought: spiritualistic and naturalistic. The naturalistic stream finds systemization in two major systems, namely, the Vaiśeṣika and the Jaina. Both developed naturalistic theories of the external world, but combined it with a non-naturalistic theory of the human soul, which may be called "spiritualistic eschatology." This combination of naturalism and non-naturalism is a uniquely interesting feature of Indian thought. The two additional systems in which naturalism survives in some form are Buddhism and the Sāṃkhya. In this chapter, we will turn our attention to Jainism.

The extensive Jaina literature is believed to have been based on the teachings of Mahāvīra (literally the "great hero"), a senior contemporary of Gautama Buddha. The term "Jainism" is derived from the Sanskrit root *ji*, "to conquer," meaning the one who has conquered his desires and passions and has become a perfect soul. Not much is known about Mahāvīra's life. His given name was Vardhamāna. He was the son of Siddhārtha, a *kṣatriya* chieftain of the Licchavis, born at a place near modern Patna in Bihar, married a woman named Yaśodā at an early age, had a daughter, and at the age of twenty-eight left home to become a mendicant. He led a very austere life for twelve years and wandered naked in the Gangetic plains. He met Buddha during his wandering days and discussed his philosophical ideas with him. Makkhali Gośala, the leader of the *Ājīvikas*, met Mahāvīra during his wandering years, and witnessed many miracles that Mahāvīra had performed. The tradition maintains that during his thirteenth year, after fasting for several weeks, Mahāvīra became the *jīnā*, the conqueror. He became a *tīrthaṇkara* (literally "one who makes a ford"), the omniscient one. Traditions reckons twenty-three prophets preceding Mahāvīra, who proclaimed that he was the last, the twenty-fourth, the first being Ṛṣabhadeva. Mahāvīra taught for thirty years as a *tīrthaṇkara*, and entered *nirvāṇa* at the age of seventy-two. He left behind a well-organized Jaina community, and thousands of monks, laymen, and laywomen.

The doctrinal content of the religion founded by Mahāvīra was already established by him, and—unlike Buddhism that traveled far and wide outside of India and underwent radical transformations over the centuries—Jainism remained, and remains, confined to India. Its doctrines have remained unchanged, with the exception of minor details. Contrasted with the Buddha's compassionate nature, Mahāvīra's doctrines and practices seem to have been marked by a severe austerity, and in the words of a modern scholar: a "peculiar stiffness"[1] characterizes these doctrines.

The philosophical outlook of Jainism is a metaphysical realism and pluralism as it holds that the objects exist independently of our knowledge and perception of them, and that these objects are many. Every living being has a soul as well as a body. The respect for life, i.e., non-injury to life, plays a very important role in its teachings. Additionally, the importance it places on the respect for the opinions of others finds expression in its theory of reality as multiple viewpoints (*anekāntavāda*), which gives rise to their logical doctrine that every judgment is conditional. Thus various judgments about the same reality may be true when each is subjected to its own conditions. I will begin with Jaina metaphysics.

I Jaina Metaphysics

At the outset it must be noted that Jaina metaphysics is a complete realism, which is best articulated in the position that whatever is manifested in the form of a cognition is the nature of the object of that knowledge. If in a cognition, the form "blue pitcher" is given, then there must be a blue pitcher that is being manifested. It is a complete realism, much like that of the Naiyāyikas, which I will discuss a little later. The Jainas take great pains to avoid absolutism and point out that everything is relational. Their decisive statement is: *a thing has infinite aspects.*

Every philosophical position has its truth and the Jainas sought to combine them all. These led to *anekāntavāda*, i.e. non-absolutism, which, in a way, synthesizes the various philosophical positions, not by putting them together as "p and q and r . . .," but as alternates (p or q or r . . .), each valid from a point of view known as a *naya*. This notion of a "point of view," to be sure, is not subjective. It is an objective point of view. Hence the perspectives are all objective and yield truths that are true, but only within that perspective, not absolutely. The Jainas argue that emphasis on one aspect to the exclusion of others is analogous to the story of seven blind men who upon seeing an elephant describe the elephant on the basis of the part (the trunk, the ears, the tail) of the elephant they had touched. Each judgment is partially true (*naya*), nonetheless each *naya* yields a true, but partial knowledge. These partial cognitions need to be synthesized into a total knowledge of the object.

Thus, the Jainas argue that given that the objects are complex in structure, they must be examined from various perspectives in order for us to comprehend their complete nature. The objects that we come to know have innumerable characteristics, positive as well as negative. For example, an object, say, a chair, has such positive qualities as shape, weight, color, etc., and negative characters, which distinguish it from other objects, say, a table, a stool, etc.

Additionally, when time is taken into account we see that an object may lose some of its characteristics, assume different characteristics, making us realize that an object really possesses innumerable characteristics. It is not possible for an individual to know an object in all its characters; only omniscient beings possess knowledge of an object in all its aspects.

The thesis of the infinite characters of an object leads the Jainas to make a distinction between that which possesses the characteristics and the characteristics themselves. The former is called the substance and the latter the attributes. Each substance has two kinds of attributes: essential and accidental. The essential characteristics (*guṇa*) of a substance are permanent; they belong to the substance as long as the substance exists. For example, consciousness is an essential attribute of the soul. Accidental characteristics, on the other hand, are transitory; they come and go. Desires, pleasure, pain, etc. are such accidental characteristics of the soul. It is through these accidental characteristics that a substance undergoes changes and modifications, which are called "modes" (*paryāyas*).[2] A substance is real; it consists of three factors: (1) permanence, (2) origination, and (3) decay of changing modes.

The Jainas classify substances as extended and non-extended. Extended substances are divided into *jīvas* (souls, conscious beings) and *ajīvas* (insentient or non-living objects). There are four *ajīvas*: (a) *pudgala* or matter (matter that has taken on the form of a body), (b) *ākāśa* or space, (c) *dharma*, the medium of motion, and (4) *adharma*, the medium of rest. *Kāla* or time is the only non-extended substance, because extended substances are collection of space-points, which time is not.

Let us quickly review the Jaina conception of substance.

Jīva *(Soul)*

The soul, though not perceivable by the outer senses, is perceived in such experiences of self-awareness as "I am happy," "I know," "I believe."[3] The body is not the soul. The dead body does not possess such properties as knowledge, desires, and feelings. The non-conscious body, the Jainas argue, cannot be the locus of these properties. The body is composed of physical elements. The sense organs are located in the body. The soul *uses* them as instruments to see colors, hear sounds, etc. But the soul in itself is identical neither with the body nor with the sense organs. It is the soul that remembers the past experiences, thus remembering is not the function of any one of the sense organs. Were it so, it would not have been possible for a person who has now become blind to remember his past experience of seeing something (or, if he is now deaf, of past hearing).

One of the unique features of the Jaina conception of the *jīva* is the belief that a *jīva* in its empirical state is capable of expansion and contraction according to the size of the empirical body.[4] The Jaina thinkers argue that just as a lamp illuminates the area, small or large, in which it is placed, similarly the soul expands and contracts contingent upon the size of the physical body. Most Indian thinkers on the other hand believe that the soul is not capable of expansion and contraction. This feature of the Jaina conception also explains their unique conception of knowledge. Knowledge is not a characteristic; it is an essence of the *jīva*. The *jīva*s therefore can know everything directly; sense organs, light, etc. are indirect aids giving rise to *jñāna* when the impediments are removed.

Past actions yield fruits now or will yield them in the future, because the actions, themselves, now gone, leave their impressions in the soul. Here the Jaina metaphysics comes to its peculiar position where it seems to contradict itself. The impressions left behind by actions are what they call "*karmas*." These *karmas* are material, but they are construed as clinging to the immaterial soul. *Karmas* in Jainism are construed on the analogy of atoms; they are tiny material entities, the impressions of past actions that cling to the souls. The souls are omniscient and every soul is capable of reaching omniscience only when the veil that conceals the nature of the soul is removed.[5]

There are infinite number of souls distinct from other bodies and the sense organs as is proven by the inner perception "I am happy," etc. Souls are classified into those that transmigrate and those that are liberated. The former are tied to their bodies owing to their *karma*. These transmigratory souls are either moving or unmoving, depending on the nature of their bodies. The immobile souls are one-sensed, the mobile ones are two-, three-, four-, five-sensed. Animals, plants, any particle of matter of earth, water, fire, and wind also possess souls.

Ajīvas *(Non-Souls)*

Pudgala or matter is capable of integration and disintegration. It possesses four qualities: taste, touch, smell, and color. Sound is not a quality but a mode of it. One may combine material substances to form larger wholes or break them into smaller and smaller units. The smallest part of matter is *aṇu* or an atom. Atoms may combine to form aggregates called "*skandha*." In the Jaina metaphysics these aggregates range from the smallest aggregate of two atoms to the largest aggregates which the entire physical world represents. The objects that we perceive in our everyday lives are compound objects, e.g., animal, senses, the mind, and so on.

Ākāśa or space is infinite and its function is to accommodate other substances. The Jainas distinguish between two kinds of space: *lokākāśa*, i.e., lived or mundane space, and *alokākāśa*, the space beyond this world. Space provides room for all extended substances. All extended substances exist in space. In other words, substances occupy the space, and the space is occupied. Thus, in contrast to the teaching of Descartes, substance is not the same as extension, but rather the locus of extension, along the lines of what John Locke talks about. Space is inferred, though not perceived.

Dharma and *adharma* are not taken in their usual senses as virtue and vice respectively, but rather as the conditions of movement and rest respectively;

they are eternal and passive extended substances. These two pervade the entire mundane space. Though these two substances are not perceived, they are postulated to explain the possibility of motion and rest that we perceive in our daily lives. It seemed to Jaina thinkers that since the world is constituted of atoms, these material elements would get scattered and distributed in the entire space, unless there is a principle to provide stability to material elements—*adharma* is such a principle. They further believe that an opposite principle was needed to explain movements—*dharma* is that principle. In the absence of these principles, there would be no worldly structure, no distinction between *loka* and *aloka*, no constancy; there would be utter chaos.

Time is infinite, though there are cycles of it. A thing changes, continues to exist, assumes new forms, discards the old ones, and all these presuppose time. Time, like space, is inferred, not perceived. Time is real. Time is constituted of the atomic moments of time. It does not extend in space, because it is indivisible and present everywhere in the world. Time does not possess extension in space.

II Jaina *Syádvāda* and Theory of Knowledge (*Pramāṇas*)

Syadvāda

The Jaina attitude to the nature of things, i.e., their *anekāntavāda*, yields a logic which is perhaps one of India's most important contributions to world philosophy. For the first time in the history of logic, the Jaina philosophers came to speak of a seven-truth-valued logic, known as "*syadvāda*," which has two components, "*syad*" and "*vāda*." "*Syad*" means "in some respect," or "from a particular standpoint," while "*vāda*" means "statement." The statement "this is a pitcher" is made, and is true, from a certain point of view. From another point of view, at the same time, this is not a pitcher. "*Syadvāda*" then says that a judgment is always made from a certain point of view from which it is true; however, from another point of view, the same judgment may be false. "*Syad*" should not be taken to mean "may be," "possibly," etc. It would be a mistake to regard "*syadvāda*" as a method of doubt, uncertainty, and skepticism. *Syadvāda* is certainty, not skepticism, but a doctrine of conditional certainty.

This leads the Jaina logicians to distinguish between seven perspectives from which the same statement or judgment can be evaluated.[6] Of the seven-fold judgments or predictions, there are only three primary modes: (1) existent, (2) non-existent, and (3) inexpressible. The seven are developed out of these three basic modes.

Given a judgment p, the Jainas hold that

1 there is a perspective from which p is true;
2 there is a perspective from which p is false;

3 there is a perspective from which p is both true and false; and
4 there is a perspective from which p is "inexpressible."

These four, the basic truth-values, were then combined into three more:

5 there is a perspective from which p is true and is also inexpressible;
6 there is a perspective from which p is both false and is inexpressible; and
7 there is a perspective from which p is true, also is false, and is also inexpressible.

Let me quickly explain these.

If p is "this is a pitcher," then from the perspective of a certain place, time, and quality (e.g., "brown"), p is true; the pitcher exists. But from the standpoint of another region of space, time, and quality (e.g., "red"), this statement is false, i.e., the pitcher does not exist. The two standpoints may then be combined and it may be asserted that as being in a certain region of space and time and as having a certain quality, this pitcher exists, but also from another perspective it does not, p is both true and false.

Being both true and false, and failing to combine the two values, p becomes inexpressible. The set of positive and negative properties of a thing cannot be exhaustively enumerated. Everything whatsoever has therefore an aspect of inexpressibility. From a purely logical perspective, "p" becomes undecidable.

Given these three possibilities, one generates the remaining four from them as the primary modes. The Jaina holds that such moral propositions as "truthfulness is a virtue," or "killing is a sin," can be regarded as having the seven truth-values.

Let us apply these forms to a common moral judgment, "you should speak the truth."

1 There is a perspective from which to speak the truth is a virtue (is);
2 There is a perspective from which to speak the truth is not a virtue (e.g., to speak the truth before a hunter who is searching for a deer, or to speak the truth to a wicked man who is after a woman) (is not);
3 There is a perspective from which to speak the truth is wholesome and is a virtue, but from another perspective to speak the truth is unwholesome and is not a virtue (is and is not);
4 There is a perspective from which without taking into account the situation or circumstance, we can never say whether truth-speaking is or is not a virtue (is inexpressible);
5 There is a perspective from which to speak the truth is a virtue, but without taking into account circumstances, we cannot say whether it is or is not a virtue (is and is inexpressible);
6 There is a perspective from which to speak the truth is not a virtue, but without taking into account circumstances, we cannot say whether it is or is not a virtue (is not and is inexpressible);[7]

7 There is a perspective from which to speak the truth is a virtue, but from another perspective to speak the truth is not a virtue; so, we cannot say whether it is or is not a virtue (is, is not, and is inexpressible).[8]

To sum up: *syadvāda* is a method of viewing a thing from different standpoints. The method is also called *anekāntavāda.* It is a method that synthesizes apparently incompatible attributes in a thing from different standpoints. As we will see shortly, different systems of Indian philosophy hold different views regarding the nature of reality. The Vedānta regards the *brahman* as absolutely permanent. Buddhism holds that reality is momentary and discrete, while permanence is illusory. The Sāṃkhya regards *prakṛti* as permanent-cum-impermanent, while the *puruṣa* as totally impermanent. For the Nyāya-Vaiśeṣika some of the real entities like atoms, time, soul, are permanent while others, e.g., a jar and a cloth, are impermanent.

The Jainas as distinguished from these maintain that everything is both permanent and impermanent. Every thing has origination, destruction, and persistence. A thing is permanent from the standpoint of substance, but is also impermanent from the standpoint of modes.

The Jaina Theory of Pramāṇas

Whereas a *naya*, as explained above, is the knowledge of a thing from a certain standpoint, a *pramāṇa* gives knowledge of a thing in its totality. In a *pramāṇa*, knowledge cognizes a thing with all its aspects. Such a knowledge combines all the different aspects of a thing. Jaina commentators state: "a manifold thing is the object of *pramāṇa*, while only an aspect of that very thing is the object of *naya*." Insofar as different strands of *nayas* spring forth from *pramāṇa*, *naya* is a part of *pramāṇa*. A *pramāṇa* lays bare the whole truth; a *naya* is a partial truth.

Initially the Jaina commentators make a distinction between two types of *nayas*: *dravyārthika naya* or substantial standpoint and *paryāyārthika naya* (or modal standpoints). The former focuses on a substance, the generic and permanent aspect. The *paryāyā naya* focuses on modes, changes, or transformation. Thus a pitcher as a substance, i.e., as a pitcher, is permanent. But as its form or quality, the pitcher is impermanent. Thus in *dravya-naya* grasps the generic aspect, while the *paryāya naya* grasps the specific aspect.

A *pramāṇa*, argues the Jaina, is self-illuminating, manifests its object, and is not subject to cancellation. A *pramāṇa* is free from three kinds of *bādha* or cancellations: doubt, error, and not knowing the specific features of the object. Right determination of the object is the main function of a *pramāṇa*.

The Jainas regard knowledge as evolution of the self, and deny any positive and direct determination by the object in the occurrence of knowledge. The knowledge in the long run must lie within self. The absence of object-determination in knowledge and the innate self-luminous character of knowledge give rise to the Jaina doctrine of omniscience. The self's original essence is pure luminosity. The self in the absolute state is a pure transcendental principle of self-luminosity.

The "object" according to the Jaina, is an independent real entity. It is not one, but many, and it is opposite to the self in nature. It is *jaḍa* or unconscious. It is constantly subject to *pariṇāma*, has different qualities (*guṇas*) and modifications (*paryāya*). The self also changes constantly. The self evolves into the form of knowledge of the non-self. The non-self evolves into the form of the knowable for the self. However, the object does not literally enter into the self. Thus the Jaina rejects not only the epistemological monism of Vijñānavada, but also the Advaita theory of identity.

The senses, according to Jainism, have a double character. They partake of the nature of the *dravya*, but their being is psychical. The Jaina accepts only five senses, not ten as the Sāṃkhya does. There are no sense organs of action, and the senses are not instruments of action. *Manas*, according to the Jainas, is the instrumental cause of the sense-functions, but in itself it is not a sense. However, the *manas* is an instrument, though the self is always the agent.

For the Jaina, valid knowledge is either direct or indirect. Direct knowledge or perception is either sense perception that occurs through sense organs, or such mental perceptions as perception of pleasure and pain within. Perceptual knowledge is defined as the knowledge that is detailed (*viśada*). In addition to empirical perceptions (external and internal), the Jainas speak of a more intimate perception, not dependent on the sense organs and the mind, a kind of immediate perception, which, again is of three kinds: *avadhi* is perception of things in remote space and time, and roughly corresponds to what modern psychology calls "clairvoyance"; *manaḥparyāya* is the direct cognition of the thoughts and ideas of other persons along the lines of Western telepathy; and *kevalajñāna*, knowledge *par excellence*, i.e., total comprehension of reality. It is omniscience, i.e., there is no distinction of time such as the past, the present, and the future.

There are certain interesting features of the Jaina theory of perception, which must be emphasized. Unlike the Nyāya and Mīmāṁsā, the Jainas do not define perception in terms of its causes (e.g., by the contact of the sense organs with their objects), but rather by the nature of the knowledge, namely, by its character of being a detailed and clear knowledge of its object. Thus in the Jaina tradition, *"pratyakṣa"* is not primarily a sense organ-generated knowledge, but also the self-knowledge that is obtained without any intervention from the sense organs. Again, the Jainas, unlike most other Indian schools, especially the Buddhists, do not admit any indeterminate or *nirvikalpaka* perception. What we perceive are objects in the world. The Jainas in this regard are realists. The Jainas respect the Buddhist thesis that perception in the strict sense must be free from all conceptual construction (*kalpanā*). Finally, it is worth noting that the Jaina conception of "*indriya*" or sense organs is very different from the other Hindu systems, which regard sense organs to be material objects of some sort or the other. The Jainas, on the other hand, regard them primarily as powers of consciousness of the self, although the external perceptible organs are treated only as their outer supports; in reality, they are powers of the self. "*Manas*," from a functional point of view, is also a power of the self, though it has body as its material support. The *manas* is extended all over the body and it is not atomic as the Naiyāyikas take it to be.

Among the *parokṣa pramāṇas*, the Jaina recognizes memory, recognition, *tarka*, *anumāna* or inference, and *āgama* or knowledge from authoritative scriptures. The Jainas are the only philosophers among Indian schools who recognized memory as a *pramāṇa*. In memory, an object which was already grasped by a previous *pramāṇa*, now referred to as "*tat*," is revived. Recognition is a complex mental act consisting of both elements of presentation and representation, both perception and memory, lacking in the sort of clarity which belongs to perception alone. As a *pramāṇa*, *tarka* is the means of knowing *vyāpti* or universal pervasion between the *sādhya* and the *hetu* to arrive at *anumiti*, the knowledge gained from an inferential process. Neither perception alone nor inference can yield the knowledge of *vyāpti*, argues the Jaina. *Tarka* is a unique source of such knowledge.

The Jainas, of all Indian philosophers, regard *āgama* or *śabda* as *parokṣa* knowledge. By *śabda* they do not mean either the Vedic texts or the words of the Vedic seers as the Hindus do, but the words of the perfected souls. The Jaina identifies *āgama* with *āptavacana*, i.e., words of the *āpta*. But he does distinguish between two kinds of *āpta*: the ordinary and the extraordinary. The extraordinary *āpta* is one who has attained omniscience. With regard to the meaning of a sentence or *vākyārtha*, the Jaina argues that words have meanings, both expressed and implied, by virtue of which they get connected to form a unified *vākyārtha* or sentential meaning.

While the Buddhists wavered a great deal on the issue of omniscience (some accepted while others did not) or even on the specific question whether the Buddha is omniscient, the Jainas had no doubt that the perfected souls, the *jinas* or the *tīrthaṅkaras*, attain omniscience. Once the covering *karmas* are removed by the long process of self-purification, any human can attain omniscience.

III The Jaina Ethics: Bondage and Liberation

The most important part of the Jaina ethics is the path to *mokṣa* (salvation). The Jainas argue that the contact between *jīva* and *ajīva* brings about birth and death. Bondage is the state in which the soul and matter interpenetrate. Freedom is their separation; it means attaining godhood. Matter particles are the obstacles that infect the soul. The soul can attain omniscience if the obstacles are removed.

It is important to keep in mind that *karma* in Jaina philosophy means both an action and the impression left by an act on the soul. *Karma* in the latter sense is *karmic* matter and is attached to the soul. Collectively the *karmas* are the sum total of tendencies generated in the past lives, and determine our present birth, i.e., the family in which we are born, our shape, color, longevity, etc., however, each is due to a specific kind of *karma*. The *karmic* matter is of eight kinds: knowledge-covering, vision-covering, feeling-producing, delusion-causing, longevity-determining, body-making, status-determining, and obstructive ones. These determine one's life until *karmas* are dissociated from one's soul. The *jīva*, on account of passions, desires, etc., attracts *karma*-matter, so there is an influx (*āśrava*) of the *karma*-matter in the soul. How much *karma*-matter one attracts depends upon the kinds of actions one has performed. Dissociation consists of two special kinds of entities, entities in a very peculiar sense, more appropriately process or steps: the stoppage of the *karma*-matter (*samvarā*) and the exhaustion (*nirjarā*) of already attracted *karmas*. (The soul is not devoid of extension; it is coextensive with the living body. The soul is the *jīva*; it is matter as well as consciousness).

The Jaina prescribes a path of self-purification, the path by following which the *karmic* matter that shrouds the self is gradually destroyed, and the self recovers its original omniscience. The path of self-*purification* is known as "*yoga*," which consists of the knowledge of the nature of the soul.

Right faith, right knowledge, and right conduct are the three jewels that together constitute the path to *mokṣa*.[9] Jaina commentators use the analogy of medicine as a cure to explain it. Just as the faith in the efficacy, knowledge of how to use it, and actually taking the medicine is mandatory for the cure to be effected; similarly, to get rid of suffering, the three principles of right faith, right knowledge, and right conduct are necessary.

Right faith is the basis and the starting point of the discipline. It is the attitude of respect towards truth. Such an attitude may be inborn or acquired. When one begins the study of the Jaina writings with partial faith, rationally examines what is taught by the *tīrthaṇkaras*, one's faith increases. The Jaina teachers believed that the more one studies the texts, the greater would be the faith. In other words, increase of the knowledge would increase the faith. Five signs of right faith are: tranquility, spiritual craving, disgust, compassion, and conviction.

Right knowledge is free from doubt, error, and uncertainty. It is the knowledge of the real nature of the ego. The Jaina writers outline different kinds of wrong views:

1 uncritical and obstinate acceptance of views. The wise person does not accept any view without critical examination;
2 indiscriminate acceptance of all views. Such as acceptance leads to a dull-witted acceptance of all views as true;
3 intentional clinging to a wrong view due to attachment—obstinate attachment to a wrong view in spite of knowing that it is wrong;
4 the attitude of uncertainty and doubt about the spiritual truths; and
5 sticking to the false beliefs and views owing to a lack of growth.

The Jaina prophets preach the essential equality of all living beings. Equality is natural to all living beings, while differences among them are adventitious, primarily owing to differences of auspicious and inconspicuous *karmas*. Besides, according to Jainism, any human can attain liberation. No particular status, or state, is a necessary condition for the attainment of liberation.

The soul in the body is God. God, according to Jainism, is not eternal, but has worked out his own freedom or liberation. The three categories (*tattvas*), God, spiritual teacher, and religion, in their true nature, are called *samyaktva*. Recognizing all living being as one's self is the root of right attitude. The opposite of *samyaktva* is *mithyātva* (wrong attitude). There are various types of wrong or false attitudes: about things, about the highest good, about the spiritual teacher, about God, and so on. One should cultivate the attitude of seeing all beings as equal to oneself. There are four such feelings: of friendliness, of gladness, of compassion, and of neutrality.

Right conduct is doing what is beneficial and avoiding what is harmful. The goal here is to get rid of the *karmas* that lead to bondage and liberation.

Right conduct has two levels: right conduct for the householder and that for the mendicants. The householder's rules are less stringent. These are: honesty in earning wealth, fearlessness and self-control, non-violence, not-lying, non-taking anything that is not given, refraining from illicit sexual relations, limiting one's possessions, limiting the scope of one's immoral activities, limiting the things one will use, not indulging in senseless harmful acts such as giving harmful advice, giving to others the means of destroying life, not indulging in harmful thoughts, not indulging in harmful behavior; the vow to remain equanimous for a certain period of time, the vow of fasting and living like a monk for a certain length of time, and the vow to share with guests.

For the mendicants, the rules of right conduct consist of observing five vows and gradual curbing of the activities of the body, speech, and mind. For the stoppage of the *karmas*, one takes the five great vows: *Ahiṃsā*, i.e., the vow of non-injury (non-violence), *satya* (the vow of truthfulness), *asteyam* (the vow of not taking what is not given), *brahmacaryam* (celibacy), and *aparigraha* (the vow of abstinence from all attachment). Overall, there is the lifelong vow of universal brotherhood.

Ahiṃsā or non-violence is the most important Jaina virtue, just as "compassion" is in Buddhism. It is one of the cardinal virtues; it signifies non-violence in thought, deed, and action. *Ahiṃsā* leads to pure love. Pure love or non-violence may be negative or positive. In the negative sense, pure love abstains from causing injury of any sort to any living being. In the positive sense, it is performing positive virtuous activities like serving or helping others and doing good to them.

To sum up: right faith, knowledge, and conduct are necessary for liberation. If one of the three is missing, there would be no *mokṣa*.

The perfected soul, according to Jainism, becomes a god. God, in Jainism, is not creator of the world. There are thus many perfected souls and so one could say that there are many gods (not in the sense of polytheism) but in the sense of a community of spirits. The perfected souls, as a matter of fact, are all alike, and so the Jainas speak of one god, although there are many perfected souls. God is to be worshipped, not to please him, but in order to pursue the ideal of complete freedom from *karmas*. One does not seek God's mercy and help; one pursues the ideal that is actualized in him.

Concluding Remarks

In reviewing the ancient Indian philosophies, we see that there existed many *nayas*. Of all the *nayas*, the most fundamental are two: the substance perspective (*dravya-naya*) and the process perspective (*paryāya-naya*). The Vedāntins adopt the former, the Buddhists the latter. The Jaina *naya* theory yields a guideline for synthesizing both of these. The Jainas sought to avoid the extremes and try to preserve the elements of truth in all these. Reality is both permanent and changing, both universal and particular, both positive and negative. There is really no opposition, the Jainas held, between these; each is valid from a certain perspective. The complete nature of reality consists both of identity and differences, of permanence and change, universal and particular. This synthetic approach of the Jainas is their most important contribution to Indian thought.[10]

The above discussion makes it obvious that the Jainas are not only realists and non-absolutists, they are also "relativists." A "perspective," on the Jaina thesis, *is not to be construed as a subjective way of looking at things, but an objectively partial view* which singles out one aspect out of the infinite, objective aspects of reality. Thus Jaina "relativism" is not subjectivism. Perhaps, it is more accurate to say that it is "relational-ism."

A comparison with A. N. Whitehead's metaphysical system worked out in his *Process and Reality* may throw some light on the nature of objective relationalism. In Whitehead's system, every actual entity is related to every other actual entity. Thus, a thing's having a certain color is always from a certain perspective. On Whitehead's account, an infinite number of perspectives constitute each and every entity. His system is much more complex than the Jaina system, but it is not an exaggeration to say that the Jaina *syadvāda* anticipates such an *objective relativism*. It is one of the great achievements of ancient Indian mind.

6

THE BAUDDHA *DARŚANA*

By the middle of the sixth century BCE, most probably about the time the major Upaniṣads had been composed, a new mode of thinking revolutionized the philosophico-religious scene of India, and, in course of time, almost all of Asia. This event—if any event could be said to have the decisive impact on the destiny of the people not only in Asia but the world over—was the birth of Gautama Buddha.

The Buddha was born in the foothills of the Himalayas around 560 BCE.[1] His early life is well known, but still inseparable from many legends that surround it. The name given to the Buddha at birth was Siddhārtha, and his family name was Gautama, so in his early years, the Buddha was known as Siddhārtha Gautama. The Buddha lived on the border of India in what is today known as Nepal. His mother's name was Māyā and father's name Śuddhodana, who was the chief of the *Śākya* clan; this explains why the Buddha is often referred to as "*Śākyamuni*," i.e., sage of the "*Śākyas*." Siddhārtha grew up in luxurious surroundings. When Siddhārtha turned sixteen, his father had him married to a beautiful princess named Yaṣodharā, and a year later Yaṣodharā gave birth to their son, Rahula.

The father, Śuddhodana, fearing a prophecy, shielded Siddhārtha from any kind of suffering and unpleasant experiences that might take him towards religious life; however, upon seeing an old man, a dead body, a sick person, and, finally, a recluse, Siddhārtha became restless. The sight of the recluse inspired him and one day, when his wife and son were asleep, he left home in search of truth.

We have already learned that there were two dominant trends of thought in those days: of the *brāhmaṇas*, the followers of the Vedic precepts and of the *śramaṇas*, the recluses. The *brāhmaṇas* followed the path of the Vedic rituals, recommended various sacrifices, and promised a life of enjoyment hereafter. The *śramaṇas* followed the path of austerity, inflicting pain on themselves by depriving themselves of all the pleasures of life, and offered a life of meditation as the road to the most sought after wisdom. The *brāhmaṇas* lived in society, the *śramaṇas* retired into the forest shunning all social responsibilities.

Siddhārtha initially followed the path of self-mortification. He met five ascetics who believed that practising austere self-mortification would lead the way to great vigor of the mind and to extraordinary insight and enlightenment. Hoping to attain insight, Siddhārtha began living on a smaller and smaller quantity of food, and by controlling his breathing, sought to fall into a state of trance in the hope of attaining illumination. Siddhārtha did not attain illumination; on the contrary, he fainted because of starvation. This experience convinced him that the path of self-mortification was of no use. He rejected the austere practices of self-mortification, and began his search for the truth *via* the path of meditation. He left the company of these five ascetics and took to wandering in search of the truth.

During his quest for the truth, the Siddhārtha, the future "Buddha," reportedly wandered far and wide in the Gangetic plains, meeting and talking to numerous ascetics, philosophers, and spiritual leaders. Chief among these, especially mentioned in the Buddhist records, were the skeptics, the *Ājivīkas*, and, above all Mahāvīra, the twenty-fourth *tīrthaṇkara* of Jainism. These ascetics shared a spirit of revolt against many key ideas of *brāhmaṇism*. Siddhārtha wandered to many places, followed various paths, and, after intense meditation under the *bodhi* tree, attained enlightenment (*nirvāṇa)*, and became the "Buddha." "Buddha" literally means "the awakened one." The title "Buddha," "the Enlightened One," was given to him after he attained *nirvāṇa*. His disciples mostly referred to the Buddha as *Tathāgata*, which means "he-who-has-thus-arrived there," and in his conversations with his disciples, the Buddha referred to himself as *Tathāgata*. After attaining *nirvāṇa*, the Buddha set out on a path to teach to the common folks (not particularly to the scholars), in a manner intelligible to them, in the language of the common people, the truth he had experienced.

When we do an in-depth study of the Buddha's teachings we begin to realize that his views were profoundly shaped by his conversations with the *śramaṇas*. Perhaps a major influence was Māhāvīra who was older to him by ten years. Māhāvīra denied the existence of God, gave a naturalistic account of the world, but believed in many souls, rebirth, *karma*, and the possibility of attaining perfection by one's own moral practices. The Buddha also rejected the teachings of the *brāhmaṇas*, their caste distinctions, and sacrificial rituals. However, it would be wrong to say that he rejected the entire Vedic tradition. He had sympathies with many of the Upaniṣadic beliefs and practices, for example, the conceptions of self-knowledge, the pursuit of the *yogic* practices, *mokṣa*, rebirth, and *karma*. He clearly rejected the belief in an eternal soul of each individual human being, as well as the thesis that the *brahman* is the only reality. It is also well known that the Buddha refused to answer questions about the existence of God, after-life, the status of the world etc., but strongly believed in the efficacy of ethical practices and the possibility of reaching perfection in this life.

I am not trying to suggest here that the Buddha's teachings were a mere hybrid of various ideas already around. Though influenced by many of the

Upaniṣadic ideas, he added his own touch and personal wisdom to them, and integrated them into a fabulous system. Nevertheless, it is always good to remember that no thinker, however original, is untouched by the cultural context that shapes his thinking, and the Buddha was no exception. Rejecting what he took to be unverifiable metaphysical dogmas, he held an empiricistic and pragmatic mode of thinking measured by whether it is verifiable in one's experience and whether it brings about good life and freedom from *dukkha* in the long run. He also rejected dry logical sophistry, but not the use of reason within the bounds of experience.

His teachings were neither metaphysical nor intellectual; they were primarily ethical and concerned with how to change one's life, not with the nature of reality. The Buddha's original teachings were understood and interpreted differently, and gradually evolved into a large and complicated system with many branches and doctrines.

After attaining *nirvāṇa*, the Buddha walked from his place of meditation called "*Bodhgayā*," a few miles along the river Vārāṇasī at the outskirt of this city called "Sārnāth," and delivered his First Sermon to a group of admiring and curious villagers who had assembled there. There was something unique about his speech as well as his audience. His audience did not consist of the members of the priestly class, of those who were adept in scriptures. It rather consisted of the common village folks, who neither spoke nor understood Sanskrit. The Buddha spoke in the Pāli language, and continued to preach in that language to make his teachings accessible to the common folks.

In his first sermon, the Buddha lays down two themes: the doctrine of the Middle Way and the Four Noble Truths. In the doctrine of the Middle Way, he rejects the two extreme paths of self-mortification and self-indulgence, and recommends to his audience a Middle Way between these two extremes. He says:

> There are two extremes, O recluses, which he who has gone forth ought not to follow. The habitual practice, on the one hand, of those things whose attraction depends upon the pleasures of sense, and especially of sensuality (a practice low and pagan, fit only for the worldly-minded, unworthy, of no abiding profit); and the habitual practice, on the other hand, of self-mortification (a practice painful, unworthy, and equally of no abiding profit).
>
> There is a Middle Way, O recluses, avoiding these two extremes, discovered by the Tathagata [*Tathāgata*]—a path which opens the eyes and bestows understanding, which leads to peace of mind, to the higher wisdom, to full enlightenment, to Nirvana[2] [*Nirvāṇa*].

He prefaced this sermon with some general remarks that proved to be very influential in the self-understanding of Buddhism, viz., the need to avoid the two extremes of self-mortification and of self-indulgence, of which the former is useless and the latter is demeaning. He informed his audience that he had found the "Middle Way" that leads to peace, insight, and enlightenment. The Buddha exhorted people to follow the Middle Path, asking them to steer clear of the two paths recommended by the *brāhmaṇas* and the *śramaṇas*. The *brahmaṇas* encouraged elaborate performance of various kinds of rituals and the *śramaṇas* practiced different kinds of self-mortification; the Buddha rejected both.

It is important to bear in mind that the doctrine of the Middle Way, so much reminiscent of Aristotle's Golden Mean, gradually becomes a major theme of Buddhist philosophy, so much so that an entire school of Mahāyāna Buddhism came to be known as "*madhyama*" or the Middle Path.

The second important theme of the first lecture focuses on the Four Noble Truths, which state the fact of suffering. These two, i.e., the doctrines of the Middle Way and the Four Noble Truths, form the foundation of Buddhist philosophy; they have been, and still continue to be interpreted, through the centuries.

"All is suffering (*dukkha*)" states the Buddha, which must be understood against the background of "all is impermanent (*anitya*)"[3] and "the aggregates of being are no-self (*anattā*)." I will begin with the truth of suffering.

I All is Suffering (*Dukkha*)

The truth of suffering as articulated as the Four Noble Truths is formulated in a manner and style that follow a pattern of Indian medical literature anticipated in *Caraka Saṃhitā*. The first Noble Truth identifies the disease, the second the cause, the third informs us that it is curable, and the fourth outlines the path, the procedure by which the disease is cured. The Four Noble Truths are:

1. there is *dukkha*;
2. there is origin of *dukkha*;
3. there is cessation of *dukkha*; and
4. there is a path leading to the cessation of *dukkha*, known as the Noble Eightfold Path.

There is Dukkha

In the First Noble Truth, the Buddha states the fact of *dukkha*. It concerns the basic fact of human existence, viz., that human existence is characterized by *dukkha*. The Buddha informed his disciples that the entire human existence is characterized by *dukkha*: Birth is painful, death is painful, disease is painful, and separation from the pleasant is painful. To drive home the omnipresence of *dukkha*, the Buddha told the story of a very distraught mother who came to the Buddha with her dead baby in her arms and asked him to restore him to life. The Buddha listened to her request and asked her to fetch a grain of mustard seed from a house where none had died. She searched for a long time in vain, and finally, returned to the Buddha and informed him of her failure.

> "My sister; thou hast found", the Master said,
> "Searching for what none finds—that bitter balm
> I had to give thee. He thou lovedst slept
> Dead on thy bosom yesterday; to-day
> Thou know'st the whole wide world weeps with thy woe;
> The grief which all hearts share grows less for one".[4]

One's understanding of the Buddha's teachings depends upon how clearly one comprehends the concept of "*dukkha*," and one of the roots of the development of Buddhism consists in precisely unfolding its meaning. The word "*dukkha*" has been variously translated as "pain," "sorrow," or "suffering." These translations, however, do not really capture the essence of what Buddha was trying to convey to his audience by this concept. The connotation of "*dukkha*" is much wider and comprehensive. First of all, it is good to remember that one's suffering (that is how we will translate *dukkha*) includes both pleasure and pain. Enjoyment and pleasures are also *dukkha*, inasmuch as the pleasures that one enjoys pass away; they do not last forever. The Buddha was aware that there are moments of pleasure, there are moments of satisfaction of one's desires, but he also realized that such moments are transitory; they are followed by experience of unhappiness and longing for what is no more. Even when one gets what one wants, either one cannot hold on to it or, alternately, one gets it and then wishes to have more than what he does have, and feels pain on account of the deprivation of what could have been. It is the very nature of desire to breed new desires. It stands not only for the well-known phenomena of illness, disease, old age, death, which the Buddha had witnessed early in his life, but also the deeper metaphysical truth that everything is impermanent. Thus, when rightly understood, the truth that existence is *dukkha* implies a rejection of all metaphysics of permanence and replaces it by the metaphysics of impermanence. It suggests that all metaphysical thinking, conceptual as it is, needs to be avoided. To sum up: *dukkha* is dissatisfaction, discontent, disharmony, incompleteness, imperfection, inefficiency, physical and mental suffering, conflict between our desires and our accomplishments, suffering produced on account of change, old age, disease, and death. It is the opposite of perfection, harmony, bliss, happiness, and well-being. In the final analysis,as we shall see shortly, impermanence, relativity of pleasure and pain, passivity (i.e., subjection to the causal chain), the lack of freedom and spontaneity, all point to the fact that existence is *dukkha*. Is there an end to it? If there is an end, how to reach it?

The Origin of Dukkha

The Second Noble Truth discusses the origin of *dukkha*, that there is a cause of *dukkha*. Like a true medicine man, the Buddha states that one cannot cure the disease unless one is able to identify its root cause. The Buddha says:

> Now this, O recluses, is the noble truth concerning the origin of suffering. Verily, it originates in that craving thirst which causes the renewal of becoming, is accompanied by sensual delight, and seeks satisfaction now here, . . . that is to say, the craving for the gratification of the passions, or the craving for a future life, or the craving for success in this present life (the lust of the flesh, the lust of life, or the pride of life).[5]

The immediate cause of *dukkha,* the Buddha argues, is *tṛṣṇā,* which is generally, though wrongly, translated as "desire." *Tṛṣṇā,* is rather, what is usually connoted by "thirst," the cravings of finite individuals, their selfish needs and desires. These desires in turn breed attachments resulting in frustrations and disappointments, i.e., *dukkha.* But the remote cause of *dukkha,* better yet the ultimate cause, is ignorance (*avidyā*) of the nature of things. The ignorance consists in mistaking what is impermanent to be permanent. There is nothing permanent, whether in the external world or within oneself. On account of ignorance, we ascribe to our own selves as well as to others a permanent soul, and permanent essences to the objects of the world. The belief in permanence leads to desires, which, in turn, leads to attachments causing rebirth, which is *dukkha.* Accordingly, we have here a large thesis ready for generations of Buddhist thinkers to reflect upon, viz., to determine what precisely constitutes existence and how precisely to construe the idea of "desire." One of the principal tenets of Buddhism, early and later, tries to give an answer to this question. It develops the very idea of causality, how everything arises depending on antecedent factors, and after coming into being, passes away. Thus, there is the inevitable chain of causation which technically came to be known as the doctrine of Dependent Origination. This doctrine, when applied to the specific case of human existence, takes the well-known form of a twelve-membered chain, which we shall discuss a little later.

At this juncture it is important to underscore an important point. There is no concept of "original sin" in Buddhism, and no one is foreordained to be damned. There is no forgiveness of sins, no atonement, because there is no one with the power to bestow forgiveness. Every cause gives rise to its inevitable effect; if we understand the cause-effect chain, then we can remove it, if we wish to do so. Otherwise, the cause-effect chain, i.e., the never-ending cycle of birth and death goes on.

The Cessation of Dukkha

The Third Noble Truth is an assurance that the disease, the basic problem of human existence, is curable. In other words, it is the assurance that *dukkha* can end. In the Buddha's words: "Now this, O recluses, is the noble truth concerning the destruction of suffering. Verily, it is the destruction, in which no craving remains over, of this very thirst; the laying aside of, the getting rid of, the being free from, the harboring no longer of, this thirst."[6] This cessation or extinguishing or extinction of all desires is *nirvāṇa,* the truth.

It is not easy to ascertain precisely what the Buddha meant by *nirvāṇa*. Scholars have raised such questions as: if to exist is to desire, then does the cessation of all desires means cessation of existence? Is *nirvāṇa* a negative state of ceasing to be? Or, is it also a positive experience of bliss? The Buddhist schools yet to be discussed differ among themselves on this most important question. I will discuss some of these in the concluding section of this chapter.

Etymological meanings of *nirvāṇa,* viz., the "cessation of" or the "ceasing to be" or "the blowing out" of a flame of a candle that is extinguished when there is no air (*nirvāṇa*), suggested to some scholars that in *nirvāṇa,* the existence which is characterized by *dukkha* is extinguished. Nothing could be further from the truth. Buddhist thinkers, even the Buddha himself, wrestled with the problem of describing *nirvāṇa* in more positive terms. One thing seems to be clear: it is not a negative state of merely ceasing to be. The Buddha's life testifies to this. The Buddha lived for forty-five years after attaining *nirvāṇa,* teaching and showing laypersons how to attain *nirvāṇa.* So, it is safe to say that in *nirvāṇa* what ceases to be is *dukkha,* not the person himself.

Nirvāṇa is freedom from *dukkha,* which encompasses within its fold grief, lamentation, pain, sorrow, sadness, despair, discontent, incompleteness, and so on. Given that *dukkhu* is due to desires, attachments, and cravings, freedom is freedom from these attachments. These three, namely, desire, attachment, and craving, however, are due to ignorance (*avidyā*), so the goal is to free oneself from ignorance.

Nirvāṇa, the highest accomplishment of life in Buddhism, has been used by various religious groups as a generic term to refer to enlightenment. If the Buddha were alive today, he would have said that the words "positive" and "negative" are relative; they are applicable in a realm that is characterized by conditionality, duality, and relativity. *Nirvāṇa* is freedom from relativity, conditionality, and all evils; it is not annihilation of a person, it is "Truth," the term that the Buddha uses unequivocally several times in the place of *nirvāṇa.* One who has attained *nirvāṇa* and has extinguished cravings is called "*arhat.*"

The question is often asked what happens to an *arhat* after death? This was one of the ten questions that the Buddha refused to discuss. Human language is designed to describe empirical objects. No word or sentence can capture meaningfully what happens to an *arhat.* But this much is certain: desires, passions, the feelings of "I" and "mine," etc., which are rooted in egoism, are completely destroyed upon becoming an *arhat.*

The Noble Eightfold Path

The Fourth Noble Truth lays down the path for the attainment of *nirvāṇa,* and this path is called the "Noble Eightfold Path."

The Noble Eightfold Path is usually divided into three groups: *śila, samādhi,* and *prajñā. Śila* consists of ethical practices (of right speech, right action, and right living); *samādhi* consists of different stages of meditation (right effort, right mindfulness, and right concentration); and *prajñā* of knowledge and wisdom (right views and right resolve).

The Buddha reiterates that these steps must be cultivated simultaneously, and not successively, because he believed that virtue and wisdom purify each other; the two are inseparable. One begins with the right views, and the remaining seven steps of the path are interdependent. Repeated contemplation, continuous effort by performing good deeds, and steadfast determination train the will and give rise to a personality in which one finds a fine assimilation of pure will and emotion, reason, and intuition, which is perfect insight, i.e., *nirvāṇa.*

The account of the Noble Eightfold Path, largely, though not entirely negative (i.e., what should be avoided), gives a preliminary impression, a moral catechism (list of virtues), but a proper understanding of it would consist in seeing how they steadfastly keep the practitioner along the Middle Way. The central question is: How precisely to orient one's life so that one is on the way to attaining *nirvāṇa*? For this purpose, the Buddha develops an eightfold path, and the major portion of the first sermon is devoted to describing it.

The Buddha repeatedly emphasized that one should pay close attention to how his actions affect those who are around them. Our actions should include the welfare of all, our own self and the selves of others. Five wrong actions are specifically mentioned in the Buddhist texts: killing and hurting others, stealing, false speech, immoral sex life, and consumption of alcoholic beverages. These are wrong because they cause harm to our own self and to others. Abstaining from these five wrong actions constitute the Five Buddhist Precepts:

> I undertake the rule of training to refrain from killing or hurting living things;
> I undertake the rule of training to refrain from appropriating what belongs to others;
> I undertake the rule of training to refrain from falsehood;
> I undertake the rule of training for self-control; and
> I undertake the rule of training to refrain from making myself a nuisance.

The Noble Eightfold Path follows a pattern which has been largely adopted by many writers, notably by Patañjali in his *Yoga Sūtras.* It is not only by following the strict path of ethical self-control, avoiding the extreme and following the Middle Path, but also by training the mind and thought, by exclusively focusing upon the truth, one eventually arrives at meditation and contemplation which brings about wisdom and freedom from suffering. As is the case with the first three noble truths, this truth—more important to the Buddhist resolute on attaining *nirvāṇa*—becomes also a matter of varying interpretations. Some of the questions that arose are: How to construe the idea of compassion in the context of the overall ethical sentiment of the Buddhist aspirant as well as of the one who has attained *nirvāṇa*? Eventually, this moral sentiment became the title for the entirety of the Buddhist practice and achievement. What is the nature of the wisdom, of the true perception of the nature of things which one arrives at after attaining *nirvāṇa*? We know, for example, that Nāgārjuna distinguished *nirvāṇa* from all *dṛṣṭis* (ways of looking) at things. Historically, it is also important to ask how does this account of ethical and spiritual practice differ from that which is adopted by the practitioners of the *yoga* and other spiritual disciplines? We will have occasion to discuss some of these questions when we discuss the Yoga school.

Concluding Reflections

The Buddha was an ethical teacher and reformer rather than a metaphysician. When asked if there is a life after death, or whether there is a beginning of the universe in time, he at times remained silent, and at other times emphasized that the answers to these questions were not necessary for a good life, and still at other times stated that whatever answer he might give is likely to be misunderstood. Let me summarize one of the conversations that he had with one of his disciples named Māluṇkyaputta, who demanded answers to the following questions, and threatened to leave the Buddhist order if Buddha did not answer these questions: These questions are:

> Is the universe eternal?
> Is the universe non-eternal?
> Is the universe finite?
> Is the universe infinite?
> Is soul the same as the body?
> Are the soul and the body different?
> Does the *Tathāgata* exist after death?
> Does the *Tathāgata* not exist after death?
> Does the *Tathāgata* both (at the same time) exist and not exist after death?
> Does the *Tathāgata* both (at the same time) not exist and not not-exist after death?

When Māluṇkyaputta went to the Buddha with these questions, the Buddha responded as follows:

> It is as if a man had been wounded by an arrow thickly smeared with poison, and his friends, companions, relatives, and kinsmen were to get a surgeon to heal him, and he were to say I will not have this arrow pulled out until I know by what man I was wounded, whether he is of the warrior caste, or a *brahmin*, or of the agricultural, or the lowest caste. Or, if he were to say, I will not have this arrow pulled out until I know of what name or family the man is . . . or whether he is tall, or

> short, or of middle height . . . or whether he is black, or dark, or yellowish . . . or whether he comes from such . . . . That man would die, Māluṇkyaputta. without knowing all this.
>
> It is not on the view that the world is eternal, Māluṇkyaputta, that a religious life depends: it is not on the view that the world is not eternal that a religious life depends. Whether the view is held that the world is eternal, or that the world is not eternal, there is still rebirth, there is old age, there is death, and grief, lamentation, suffering, sorrow and despair, the destruction of which even in this life I announce.[7]

The point that the Buddha was trying to make is as follows: Whatever opinions we might have of metaphysical issues do not matter. There is *dukkha*, birth, death, old age, etc., and there is the cessation of *dukkha*. We should focus on how to attain the cessation of *dukkha*, i.e., *nirvāṇa*.

The Buddha continued to preach and reply to questions and inquiries by his disciples for over forty years. These discussions brought to light his perspectives and views about many questions that were being discussed in those days. However, we have to remember that the words of the Buddha, no matter how simple, were always packed with meaning and one's understanding of their meaning depends on one's ability. Thus, it is not surprising that many of his statements aroused debates for generations to come.

Additionally, there are also problems of internal consistency, e.g., while rejecting the Upaniṣadic thesis about the eternity of the *ātman* or the Self, he placed strong emphasis on the principles of *karma* and rebirth. The question naturally arose whether these two positions are compatible. The Buddha characterized his teaching as *madhyama pratipad*, the Middle Way, because it avoids all extremes of being and non-being, self and non-self, self-indulgence and self-mortification, substance and process—in general, all dualistic affirmations.

All these problems gave rise to a variety of interpretations of the Buddha's teachings and sayings, and in spite of the Buddha's rejection of authority, and of *śabda* (word) as a legitimate means of knowing, his own words attained the status of one of the authoritative means of knowing the truth. During the one thousand years of the history of Buddhism in India, there took place the development of many philosophical schools, not to speak of the numerous schools of Buddhism that arose in Southeast Asia, Tibet, China, and Japan after Buddhism traveled to these countries. But, at the end, one advice by the Buddha on his deathbed to Ānanda, his closest disciple, remains symptomatic of the Buddhist spirit. Asked by Ānanda, "what shall we do after you are gone?" the Buddha replied "be a light unto thyself." (*ātmānaṃ pradīpo bhava.*") "Do not betake any external refuge; hold fast to the truth as a lamp."

The Buddha in some of his lectures distinguished his own position from those of both the empiricists and the rationalists (*tārkikas*), and characterized himself as an experimentalist. It is not an exaggeration to say that thousands of people found the spirit of Buddhism attractive in the sixth century BCE and that it has continued to attract millions of people even today. It stands against dogmatism and encourages an openness to experience by which truth claims can be verified. The *nirvāṇa* of the Buddha was a verified experience because he believed, thought, and acted the way he preached. It is clear that he thought that by following his path anybody could reach *nirvāṇa.*

II All Things are Impermanent (*Anitya*)

All is impermanent (*sarvam anityam*) was one of the Buddha's frequent utterances. All schools of Buddhism subscribe to this thesis of impermanence, though their interpretations vary. There are two aspects of it: negative and positive. The negative thesis states that there is nothing permanent; everything is in a perpetual flux. Due to the limitations of our sensory apparatus, we are not able to perceive changes that take place from moment to moment, but change is taking place all the time. Permanence, essence, unchanging substances, exist only in thought and not in reality. Regarding the positive thesis, there is no unanimity. One dominant version of the positive thesis asserts that everything is momentary. Modern scholars, e.g., Kalupahana, who represents the Ceylonese Buddhism, argue that the Buddha himself only taught the doctrine of impermanence, and that the "doctrine of moments" was "formulated from a *logical* analysis of the process of change" by the later Buddhists.[8]

The denial of permanence must be understood first in the context of the important idea of the eternal self or spirit in the Upaniṣads. There is nothing eternal, neither in the external world, nor in the inner life of consciousness. Given that everything is conditional and relative, everything passes through the process of birth, growth, decay, and death. The search for permanence leads us in a false direction, and all false doctrines arise from the misconception that there are permanent essences. The thesis central to all Buddhism concerns the all-pervasive nature of *dukkha* and how to alleviate it. The Buddha believed that craving for something or the other lasts forever, and the realization that everything is impermanent would lead to the pacification of cravings. Thus, the doctrine of impermanence not only has a theoretical importance but is also of considerable importance for the Buddhist practical and spiritual practices.

The idea of impermanence is certainly central to Buddhism; however, from the exposition of the Sanskrit critical literature on Buddhism, we learn that on the Buddhist view, everything is also momentary. Whether this positive thesis correctly represents the earliest Buddhist view, is difficult to ascertain. But there is no doubt that many of the Buddhist philosophies, found in the Tibetan and Chinese Buddhism, do in fact subscribe to the doctrine of momentariness.

The doctrine of momentariness states that things arise and then perish. Between the two, the arising and the perishing, there is only one moment of being, and in the disputational literature even this moment of being, which separates the arising from the perishing, came to be challenged. The thesis that things last only for a moment (leaving out the difficult question of what precisely is meant by a "moment") is made to rest upon an argument which runs as follows:

1 to exist is to be causally efficacious;
2 to be efficacious is to produce such effect as it is capable of;
3 then for an entity to exist is to produce such effect as it is capable of producing; and
4 since all its causal power is actualized, there is no more any causal efficacy and the thing by definition would cease to exist.

In this argument the first premise (to exist is to be causally efficacious) regarding the definition of existence is of central importance. Given this definition nothing can exist for more than a moment. The causal power that the thing has must be spent in the very first moment of its being. The Hindu writers who believed not only in the eternal soul but also that things may exist for a stretch of time, believed in the possibility that an entity's entire causal efficacy may be expended not at the very first moment of its being but over a stretch of time, implying thereby that while some power or efficacy is being actualized at the very first moment, some can remain potential. The Buddhists vehemently deny it. They argue there is no potential power; every power that we can meaningfully talk about is the power that is actualized. Therefore, given the two assumptions, viz.,: (1) to exist is to be causally efficacious, and: (2) to have causal power is to produce all the effects an entity is capable of producing at the very first moment of its being, it follows that an entity can exist only for a moment. Later Buddhist writers carried this thesis to its extreme consequence. Of the supposed three moments in the biography of an entity, arising → being → perishing, the second, the being, can be gotten rid of, leaving only arisings and perishings, which precisely is the doctrine of momentariness carried to the logical consequence.

The Buddhists, however, in their zeal of taking a thought to the logical consequence, did not stop even there. The Mahāyāna writers following Nāgārjuna argued that the moment of arising itself must arise and perish, and so also the moment of perishing, so that there would be an arising of arising, a perishing of arising, an arising of perishing, and perishing of perishing. Each of these again leads to similar internal splits and we find ourselves in a vicious infinite regress. All this leads to the consequence that the doctrine of impermanence, even in its version of momentariness, could not be taken to be a metaphysically true representation of reality, and like all representations, it is also *śūnya* or empty. Thus the doctrine of impermanence ends up in the thesis of emptiness.

In this brief account, I have tried to trace the development of the impermanence thesis from the early Therāvāda Buddhism to Mahāyāna *śūnyatā* thesis. It is always good to remember that the Buddhist philosophy has been a historically developing philosophy and it is always helpful to trace the path that its history has traversed. I will discuss some of these issues in the chapter on the schools of Buddhist philosophy.

III All Elements of Being are No-Self (*Anattā*)

As discussed earlier, the Upaniṣads postulate an identical *ātman* in all human beings, and hold that an "I," an individual self, is a combination of a body and a soul. The Buddha, in his sermons, gives a very different answer to the question: Who am I? The Buddha's *anattā* (no-soul), is the opposite of the Hindu doctrine of *attā,* that there is a permanent soul. The Buddha argues that there is no soul or *ātman*; a self is composed of five *skandhas*, viz., bodily form (matter or body), sensations (feelings, sensations, etc., sense object contact generating desire), perceptions (recognition, understanding, and naming), dispositions (impressions of *karmas*), and consciousness. These five aggregates together are known as "*nāma-rūpa.*" *Rūpa* signifies body, and *nāma* stands for such various processes as feelings, sensations, perceptions, ideas, and so on. These five *skandha*s that constitute the self are impermanent, so they cannot give rise to a permanent self.

The Buddha provides many similes to explain the arising of the self. One of his favorite examples was that of a chariot: As a chariot is nothing more than an arrangement of axle, wheels, pole and other constituent parts in a certain order, but when we take the constituents apart, there is no chariot, similarly, "I" is nothing but an arrangement of five *skandhas* in a certain order, but when we examine the *skandhas* one by one, we find that there is no permanent entity, there is no "I," there is only name (*nāma*) and form (*rūpa*).[9]

At this point, students may wonder, if there is no permanent self, who or what is reborn? The Buddha uses the metaphor of the flame of a lamp to explain rebirth. He argues that life is a flame, and rebirth is the transmitting of the flame from one aggregate to another. If we light one candle from another, the communicated flame is one and the same; the candle, however, is not the same. Upon death, the union of five *skandhas* dissolves, but the momentum, the *karmas* of this union give rise to another union of five *skandhas*. Accordingly, the Buddhist rebirth is the "endless transmission of such an impulse through an endless series of forms," and the Buddhist *nirvāṇa* is the coming to understand that self is a union of five impermanent *skandhas* that dissolve at death, and "that nothing is transmitted but an impulse, a *vis a tergo*, dependent on the heaping up of the past. It is a man's character, and not he, that goes on."[10] Any existent individual self is the *karmic* result of definite antecedents. Rebirth is only a manifestation of cause and effect. Impressions of *karmas* generate life after life, and the nature and character of successive lives is determined by the goodness and badness of the actions performed.

The rejection of an underlying permanent substance, e.g., soul, behind the ever-changing *skandhas* is not merely an intellectual analysis. The following points are worth noting:

First, on his analysis, the denial of a permanent self or soul does not destroy the notion of an empirical self or personality. Self or being means a union of *skandhas;* when the *skandhas* dissolve, the self disappears and we have death. In so denying, Buddhism de-emphasizes the ego-oriented framework of language, because if there are no "I," "you," and "my," then "I belong," "I own," etc., do not make much sense.

Secondly, although the Buddha denies the existence of a soul, he argues for the continuity of the *karmas*. A self, argues the Buddha, is a union of five *skandhas*; and as long as the *karmas* remain the same, we recognize the person to be the same for all practical purposes. But these *karmas* are not restricted to one union. They pass on to others and remain in them even after one's death. Thus, when one person dies, the *karmas* give rise to another union of five *skandhas*, and this process goes on until one attains *nirvāṇa*.

Thirdly, the denial amounts to rejecting all principles of identity in favor of the idea of difference. According to the *attā* theory, everything in the world—not only a human being, but also the mountain I see over there, this pen with which I write—has its own identity across time. A human being can be identified, reidentified, perceived, remembered, and referred to by such names as Devadatta, while perception and memory and recognition guarantee us that this is the same Devadatta I saw before. The Buddhist philosophers consider this position to be naive. Its naiveté is not only exhibited in believing that the names designate things but also in believing the validity of perception, memory, and recognition. Once the referential theory of meaning, which all Hindu writers accept, is rejected and the ability of perception to convey its own validity is questioned, then we begin to see the plausibility of the Buddhist theory. Names do not simply name a thing, but they help to bring together a large number of percepts under a common concept by virtue of their similarity and thus contribute to the construction of the world. The use of name "Devadatta" or the name "Ganges" creates the impression that there is identity between the person I saw in Pātaliputra then, and the person I see in Vārāṇasī today. The differences between these percepts are being glossed over aided by the use of the name. Likewise, the river Ganges in Patna and the Ganges near Vārāṇasī are not the same Ganges, and as Heraclitus argues that we never step in the same river twice, the Buddha argues that the inner is actually a process of change, but the process is arrested by the use of a name. Rapidity of succession creates an illusion of identity; identity is only the continuity of becoming. Ignorance creates the false impression of identity; however, only becoming exists.

It is important to remember in this context that things are really aggregates of parts, those parts again of other parts, and the last constituents are the momentary events that arise and perish. We do not perceive these momentary events, and given that we do not perceive the constituent parts, we cannot claim to be perceiving the whole. Indeed, the Buddhist denies the thesis that there are genuine wholes that arise out of the combination of parts. It is language that makes us believe that we perceive wholes even though we do not perceive its constituent parts. Thus, what we perceive is really a construct and in this construction language plays an important role. This chain of argument is designed to make us see that the alleged identical object is a construct out of differences that perpetually escape our grasping.

Fourthly, it follows from everything that has been said so far that there is no *sāmānya* of which particulars are instantiations as Plato and Naiyāyikas would have it; a universal rather is a construct from the particulars by virtue of their similarity aided by the use of language. Some Hindu metaphysical theorists, e.g., Mīmāṁsā, believed that the word "cow" means "cowness," alternately, on another account (Nyāya) the word "cow" means a particular cow as qualified by that universal cowness. The Buddhists reject this theory of meaning and replace it with what came to be known as the *apoḥa* theory (in its very general formation and overlooking its varieties), which holds that the word "cow" does not mean "cowness," but "not-non-cow," implying thereby that one of the functions of language is exclusionary, indicating what a thing is not (emphasizing difference), rather than what it is (emphasizing identity). In this context, there is no need to enter into the complicated and complex unending disputation between the Hindu and the Buddhist semantic theories; suffice it to note that the Buddhist *anātmā* theory, the anti-essentialism, the rejection of all referential theory of meaning, and prioritization of differences over identity, is such that all of them hang together. It is incredible to note the extent to which the Buddhist philosophers anticipated contemporary anti-essentialism and the prioritization of difference which one finds in the writings of philosophers emphasizing deconstruction, for example, Derrida.

Thus, the Buddha, on the one hand, rejects the Upaniṣadic essentialism that posits an enduring, substantial *ātman* in all human beings, and, on the other hand, the traditional Christian account that the individual soul is unique, and is incarnated only once. The self is an epi-phenomenon of the five impermanent *skandhas*, and, therefore, cannot give rise to a permanent self. The being of an individual, is, in fact, a becoming, an event, or a process. Any account of this process mandates that there must be an adequate cause to explain it. The Buddha explains *anattā* in terms of his doctrine of *karma*, i.e., the doctrine of cause and effect. Thus, the Buddha favors a process philosophy, although process with structure. The Buddha's doctrine of the twelve-membered chain of Dependent Origination illustrates this process philosophy, which I will discuss next.

IV Dependent Origination (*Pratītyasamutpāda*)

A common theme of all Buddhist philosophies is the doctrine of Dependent Origination. It is essentially the Buddhist doctrine of causality. Etymologically, "*samutpāda*" means, "arising in combination," or "co-arising." However, when prefixed with the term "*pratītya*" (which means "moving" or "leaning"), the term implies "dependence." Accordingly, "*pratītyasamutpāda*," has generally been translated as "dependent arising," "dependent origination," and so on. In the Buddhist texts, the formula of Dependent Arising has often been expressed in the following words: "When this is, that comes to be; on the arising of that, this arises. When this is not, that is not; on the cessation of that, this ceases."[11]

It means that, depending on the cause, the effect arises; when the cause ceases to exist, the effect also ceases to exist. *Dukkha* being a fact of existence must have a cause; if that cause is removed, the *dukkhu* will cease to exist. Thc doctrine of Dependent Arising, essentially a doctrine of causality, includes within its fold such important interrelated notions as, moral responsibility, rebirth, craving, death, consciousness, the nature of psychophysical personality, etc.

The Buddha details this doctrine in the *Discourse to Kātyāyana*. In the context of explaining the doctrine of the Middle Way, the Buddha advises *Kātyāyana* to avoid both extremes of existence and non-existence and exhorts him to follow the Middle Way. In the Buddha's words:

> On ignorance depends *karma*;
> On *karma* depends consciousness;
> On consciousness depend name and form;
> On name and form depend the six organs of sense;
> On the six organs of sense depends contact;
> On contact depends sensation;
> On sensation depends desire;
> On desire depends attachment;
> On attachment depends existence;
> On existence depends birth;
> On birth depend old age and death, sorrow, lamentation, misery, grief, and despair. Thus does this entire aggregation of misery arise.[12]

Given that everything arises depending on some conditions, if these conditions and causes are removed, the effect is also removed. In the Buddha's words:

> But on the complete fading out and cessation of ignorance ceases *karma*;
> On the cessation of *karma* ceases consciousness;
> On the cessation of consciousness cease name and form;
> On the cessation of name and form cease the six organs of sense;
> On the cessation of the six organs of sense ceases contact;
> On the cessation of contact ceases sensation;
> On the cessation of sensation ceases desire;
> On the cessation of desire ceases attachment;
> On the cessation of attachment ceases existence;
> On the cessation of existence ceases birth;
> On the cessation of birth cease old age and death, sorrow, lamentation, misery, grief, and despair.
> Thus does this entire aggregation of misery cease.[13]

In analyzing the above statements, we see that there are twelve links in the causal chain of dependent arising:

ignorance *(avidyā);*
karmas;
initial consciousness of the embryo;
psycho-physical organism;
sense organs;
sense object contact;
sense experience;
craving *(tṛṣṇā)*;
clinging;
becoming;
birth; and
death.

Because of ignorance an individual piles up impressions of *karmas,* which are responsible for bringing about a renewal of present embodiment. A vague consciousness provides the link between the past and the present embodiments, and the nature of this consciousness depends on the actions and desires of the previous embodiments. Gradually, the embryo assumes a psychophysical form with sense organs that come into contact with objects, resulting in all sorts of pleasant and unpleasant experiences. An individual craves for pleasant experiences, tries to avoid unpleasant ones, a desire to be born again is created, resulting in birth and death.

It is worth noting that each of the twelve factors is both conditioned and that which conditions. Thus the form one assumes is conditioned not only by what one experiences in this life but also by the way in which one responds to these experiences. Ignorance, *karmas* and the next five links, are the passive links insofar as one has no control over them, they result from past actions. But from the eighth link, i.e., *tṛṣṇā* (craving), moral will factors in, because, although the normal response to a pleasant experience is to prolong it and to try to cling to it, if one's moral will tells him otherwise, the person may proceed in the opposite direction. If a person realizes that pleasurable experiences are temporary and controls his cravings, desires, etc., he will begin to have a better understanding of his own personality and the world that surrounds him. On the other hand, if his actions are dominated by cravings and by clinging to pleasurable experiences, they will create in him a desire to be, in this as well as in the future lives, thereby giving rise to another collection of name and form. Thus, desire, clinging, and becoming are the active components of the twelve links of the wheel of Dependent Arising. In short, with the help of the doctrine of Dependent Arising, the Buddha provides an explanation of the nature of *saṃsāra* (the world where *dukkha* is manifested) as full of objects of attachments, as well as of the consciousness of "I."

The doctrine of Dependent Arising is the foundation of Buddha's teachings. It points to the relativity of all things. In the empirical world everything is relative, dependent, and accordingly, subject to decay and death. In order to understand the originality of this view we have to bear in mind several features of this doctrine:

First, the effect arises when all the causal conditions are there; it is constantly a new beginning and, in so asserting, the Buddhist position is close to *asatkāryavāda*.[14] Note that the Buddhist is not thinking of an event called "cause" and another called "effect." Causality is not a relation between two events but a relation between many preceding events, all of which lead to the arising of the succeeding event. The succeeding event arises or comes into being when all the causal conditions are present. Let me explain with the help of an example: What precisely produces a visual perception? For the Buddhist it includes a properly functioning visual sense organ, a visually perceptible object out there, auxiliary light, such conditions as the contact of the visual organ with the object, the previous perceptions, and their impressions. The twelve-membered chain of human life gives a picture of a similar chain of causation which binds the arising of one life, of embodied consciousness, to previous lives.

Secondly, the doctrine of Dependent Arising covers the three dimensions of time; it makes a person in the present life a result of the past and a cause of the future. The wheel of Dependent Arising operates without any *brahman*, a lawgiver, or God. There is no first cause, no absolute beginning; each cause is the effect of the preceding causes and gives rise to the succeeding ones. It postulates neither pre-determinism nor complete freedom of will. It explains an interdependence of conditions, some of which are within a person's control. In the final analysis, we are responsible for who we are and what we become. The cycle does not end with death; death is only the beginning of another life. It is a circular chain; the twelfth is joined to the first one. One may begin with the twelfth link, and ask:

> Why do we suffer old age and death?
> Because we are born. Why are we born?
> Because there is a will to be born. Why is there a will to be born?
> Because we cling to the objects of the world. Why do we cling to the objects of the world?
> Because of the craving to enjoy the objects of the world? Why do we crave?
> Because of sense-experience. Why sense-experience?
> Because of sense-object contact. Why sense-object contact?
> Because of sense organs. Why sense organs?
> Because of psychophysical organism. Why psychophysical organism?
> Because of initial consciousness of the embryo. Why initial consciousness of the embryo?
> Because of *karmas*. Why *karmas*?
> Because of ignorance.

Thus, ignorance is the root cause of *dukkha*. Impressions of *karmas* give rise to an unending series of physical and mental formations until ignorance is destroyed.

Everything depends on to what degree the cravings are brought under control. Until the impressions of *karmas* are completely rooted out, a fresh sprouting of the physical and mental formations is generated; the cycle comes to a stop when the impressions are destroyed by right knowledge.

While so much is common to all Buddhist philosophers, it is easy to see that this understanding of the chain of causation can only be provisional. For once one rejects the simple linear chain of cause and effect, i.e., one cause, one effect, one cannot remain satisfied with its expansion to four causes and one effect. In other words, one cannot stop short of saying that an effect arises dependent upon the entire universe, i.e., an effect prior to arising comes into being at any moment not only depending upon the conditions of my body, mind, and society, but also on the entire nature of the material world and the totality of the universe. This is what it should be on the Buddhist view, viz., I am not an identifiable entity standing apart from the universe, not an individual in the modern Western Cartesian sense of the ego, but a process upon which all nature and all other humans and living beings are impacting. This indeed has been the way Dependent Origination is understood in many schools of Mahāyāna, especially the Zen Buddhism. Thus, while the understanding and the formulation of Dependent Origination begins with the rejection of linear chains of causation, one cannot but expand it to the point where one begins to see that every change in the universe depends upon everything else. The only way to get out of this chain is by attaining *nirvāṇa*.

V *Nirvāṇa*

It may be obvious that the last understanding of Dependent Origination would completely transform the way one understands the concept of "*nirvāṇa*." Without doubt, the idea of *nirvāṇa* is the culmination of the Buddhist philosophy, just as attaining *nirvāṇa* is the goal pursued by the Buddhist aspirant. But what precisely is *nirvāṇa* and how to understand it? If we take the earliest reading of the Buddha, the word "*nirvāṇa*" conceals a metaphor, viz., that of blowing out a lamp as if by a gush of wind; it is complete overcoming of *dukkha*. However, many questions about *nirvāṇa* continue to be asked which have played an important role in the history of Buddhist philosophy. Some of these questions are:

1 Is *nirvāṇa* a negative state of cessation or a positive state of bliss? Or, is it something that can be described in neither terms?
2 Is *nirvāṇa* a state that one attains or arrives at the conclusion of a process? Is it brought about or is it eternally there?And if the last alternative is chosen, then one must ask can there be such an eternal *nirvāṇa* given that in Buddhism everything is impermanent?
3 Is the distinction between *saṁsāra* and *nirvāṇa* a distinction between two mutually exclusive realms so that the Buddha upon attaining *nirvāṇa* had left *saṁsāra*?

4 Is not the pursuit of *nirvāṇa* a selfish pursuit? To put it differently, is the expression "my *nirvāṇa*" a coherent notion? Or, can there be *nirvāṇa* of one person before everyone else attains *nirvāṇa*?

I think answering these questions, or at least trying to understand the *aporia* articulated in them would lead to a better and deeper understanding of the concept of "*nirvāṇa*." Given the space limitations, it is not possible to discuss these questions in detail. For our purposes the following should suffice.

In early Buddhism, at least in some of the schools, more specifically, the Sautrāntika, *nirvāṇa* was construed in purely negative terms as a complete cessation of suffering. But gradually this negative conception of *nirvāṇa* was replaced by a more positive understanding, according to which the cessation of *dukkha* brings about the complete transformation of existence, not its extinction. The Buddhist still hesitated to say that *nirvāṇa* is a state of bliss. Understandings and interpretations of *nirvāṇa* continued to change, culminating in Nāgārjuna's statement that *nirvāṇa* and *saṁsāra* are the same, that they are two sides of the same coin, a statement that has both puzzled and inspired Nāgārjuna scholars. What did he mean by it? *Nirvāṇa* is a mode of existence that one attains when one experiences the truth of *saṁsāra*. The picture that one has to transcend *saṁsāra* before reaching *nirvāṇa* is misleading and wrong. If suffering is due to craving, and craving is due to *avidyā* in which there is the illusion of permanence and eternity, then *nirvāṇa* is the realization or knowledge of the truth of things as impermanent and not transcending them into another world. The idea of permanence, as stated earlier, is due to the manner in which conceptual thinking embodied in language constructs the world, the path to *nirvāṇa* is the path of seeking complete deconceptualization, freeing oneself from the way our view of the world is bewitched by language and getting rid of all metaphysical representations of reality. As a consequence, nothing new happens, the world remains what it is, only it is now experienced in its truth, and that is *nirvāṇa*. Ignorance makes us ascribe identity and permanence not only to the self, but also to objects in this empirical world. This ignorance is dispelled by the right view that neither the self nor the things in the world are permanent; they are impermanent aggregates, better yet processes, bound together by the chain of causation. When we see the truth of things, we realize that there is no enduring self, no permanent things in the world. This realization results in a kind of desirelessness (because, *who* will desire *what*?), with no craving, there is no pleasure and pain, and so no suffering. This freedom is called "*nirvāṇa*." *Nirvāṇa* stops rebirth by breaking the causal chain of dependent arising. It is not the result of a process; it is not brought about by anything. Truth or *nirvāṇa* is.

The Buddhist thinking begins with the idea of individual *nirvāṇa*. In the Therāvāda Buddhism, an individual upon attaining *nirvāṇa* becomes an *arhat*. Mahāyāna replaces it by *bodhisattva*, who after attaining *nirvāṇa*, helps others to attain *nirvāṇa*. A *bodhisattva* recognizes that his own *nirvāṇa* is a lower *nirvāṇa* to be completed by *nirvāṇa* for all.

Scholars at times argue that *nirvāṇa* is the Buddhist counterpart of the Hindu *mokṣa*. It is true that the Buddha used a new word for a concept, which, in a certain sense, was already in the *Upaniṣads*, so in the *brāhmaṇic* culture. No body would disagree that *nirvāṇa* and *mokṣa* are the highest goals of life in Buddhism and *brāhmaṇic* traditions respectively. "*Nirvāṇa*," however, is not simply a new designation; the concept is markedly different from the Hindu *mokṣa*, especially when *nirvāṇa* is taken literally as "ceasing to be" or "extinction." The Hindu philosophers—with the exception of the Vaiṣeṣika[15] (one of the nine systems of Indian philosophy)—describe *mokṣa*, as a state of bliss. The Buddhist philosophers, over the centuries, have differed considerably in their understanding of *nirvāṇa*. No matter how one interprets *nirvāṇa*, it without any doubt is extinction, but not of the person himself, but of lust, hatred, passions. What are extinguished are selfish desires, cravings, and continued rebirth.

It is important to remember in this connection that neither the Buddhist *nirvāṇa* nor the Hindu *mokṣa* is "caused" (for whatever is caused, ceases to be); both are called "unconditioned," both are beyond time, and both are supersensible. For the Buddhists and the Hindus alike, ignorance leads to birth after birth. The goal is to free oneself from the clutches of *karma* and *saṁsāra*, and this freedom is the truth of things, only to be realized (not brought about) by the knowledge of the true nature of the self and the world. In this sense, everyone is "already" potentially free, though "realizing" this freedom requires effort, practice, meditation, and reflective knowledge. Though the Buddha rules out excessive self-mortification through extreme asceticism and endorses us to follow the Middle Way, some forms of renunciation, e.g., renunciation of family and social attachments, some forms of asceticism, etc., have been recommended. In short, all excesses of behavior are ruled out. The practice of some austerity and asceticism is part of training and discipline. The followers of the Buddha used to wear simple dress and wear robes of the cheapest cotton. Asceticism is detachment from the things that distract our desires.

Before concluding, I would like to note a point in this context: both the Hindu and the Buddhist traditions recognize that the weakness of the will causes human beings to act according to passions and desires. A famous Sanskrit prayer sums up this point beautifully: "*jānāmi dharmam na ca me pravṛtti, jānāmi adharmam na ca me nivṛtti*," which means "I know what is *dharma*, but cannot will to do it, I know what is *adharma* but cannot will to desist from it." Then the prayer continues: "*tvayā hṛṣikeśa hṛdisthitena, yathā niyukto'smi tathā karomi*," which means, "as you, O' Kṛṣṇa who resides in my heart, incite me, I will act accordingly." In other words, it reiterates that the moral will with its own efforts comes to a point when it surrenders its autonomy to divine guidance. This last point, of course, does not hold good of the teachings of the Buddha, because there is no "God" in Buddhism. Thus, the Buddhist has no choice but to rely on his own efforts in exercising moral will and freedom.

In the Western tradition, we find that both Aristotle and Augustine brought to the forefront the idea of the freedom of the will; however, in their philosophies freedom is the freedom of the will to choose, the Indian tradition focused upon the idea of freedom *from* (while differing among themselves as to what it is from which one seeks to be free, and the means by which such freedom is achieved). The Indian thinkers—both the Hindus and the Buddhists—understood true freedom as freedom *from* pain and suffering. Since suffering is due to desire and craving and the latter is due to ignorance, freedom in the strict sense must be freedom from ignorance (*avidyā*).

APPENDIX II

TRANSLATION OF SELECTED TEXTS FROM THE NON-VEDIC SYSTEMS

The Cārvāka Darśana

From the Play *Prabodahcandrodayam*[1]

Great Nescience: The doctrines of *Lokāyata* as a science are known to all everywhere, perception is the only (means of) true knowledge; earth, water, fire, and wind are the only realities; wealth and desire are the only two goals of human life. The elements are what form consciousness. There is not after-life, for death is one's salvation. Vācaspati composed this scripture in accordance with our intentions, offered it to Cārvāka. Cārvāka, through his disciples and their disciples, multiplied the work among his disciples and their disciples.

(Enter Cārvāka and his disciple)

Cārvāka: My dear child, you know that the science of punishment (or politics) alone is science (*vidyā*); *vārta* is included within it. The three Vedas, *Ṛg*, *Yajur*, and *Sāma*, are mere words of the cunning. In talking about the heaven, there is no special merit. See—

If the person offering a sacrifice reaches heaven after the destruction of the doer, actions, and instrumental entities, then there would be a large number of fruits in a tree that is burnt by a forest-fire. And—

If heaven is attained by the animal that is sacrificed in a sacrifice, then why does not the sacrificer slaughter his own father?

And—

Furthermore, if a *śrāddha* takes place in order to bring about the satisfaction of the dead ones, then pouring oil in a lamp which has gone off ought to increase its flame anew, which is absurd.

1 Kṛṣṇa Miśra's, *Prabodahcandrodayam* with Hindi commentary by Pandit Ramanath Tripathi Śāstri (Varaṇasi: Chaukhamba Amarabharati Prakashan, 1977), Act II, pp. 76–82.

Disciple: Oh, preceptor, if food and drink were the highest goal for persons, then why do they abandon worldly pleasures and take to very difficult penances . . ., take food only every sixth evening, and bear pain, etc.

Cārvāka: The ignorants prefer to abandon worldly pleasures in order to enjoy the pleasures promised in the *śāstras* composed by deceitful persons. Their bearing of all the sufferings is due to nothing but false hope promised by deceitful persons; they do not enjoy any of the happiness that is promised. Does one satisfy one's hunger by eating the sweets that one conjures up in one's mind?

The dopes that are duped by cults contrived by crooks are satisfied with cakes from no man's land! But how can fools' restrictions—alms, fasting, rites of contrition, and mortification under the sun—compare with the tight embrace of a woman with large eyes, whose breasts are pressed by intertwined arms?

The Disciple: Oh, teacher, the authors of the *śāstras* say that worldly pleasures should be abandoned since they involve suffering.

Cārvāka: *(laughing)* This game is indeed played with the feeble minded by men who are really beasts.

They say that you should throw away pleasures because they are mixed with pain. What person—who seeks his own good—throws away white and tender grains of rice just because they are covered with chaff?

Great Nescience: Yes, indeed, after a long time, I hear these well-reasoned words which give pleasure to my ears. Hey! Cārvāka, you are my dear friend!

Cārvāka: *(looking around)* It is His Majesty, the Nescience! *(Cārvāka goes closer to Great Nescience)* Victory unto His Majesty! This Cārvāka salutes you!

Cārvāka Refutation of Inference[2]

Refutation of the Naiyāyika View of Inference

Now inference will be examined. What, however, is inference? "Inference is preceded by that" (*Nyāya Sūtra*, I.1.5). How? This is how: one apprehends, in the kitchen, through the operation of the eyes, etc., the relation between fire and smoke. This gives rise to a *saṃskāra*, residual impressions (in the mind);

2 From Jayarāśi Bhāṭṭa, *Tattvopaplavasiṁha*, edited by Pandit Sukhlalji Sanghvi and Rasiklal Parikh (Baroda; Gaekward Oriental Institute, 1940), Chapter VII, pp. 64–67.

afterwards, at a later time one apprehends for the second time the mark (or smoke), after which the universal relation between them is remembered, after which there is a consideration (of the hill) as related to smoke. This causes the inference of fire (on the hill) from the mark (the smoke).

If one is absent, the other is also absent, for the one precedes the other. Without the cause, the effect is not seen to have occurred. Perception is said to be the cause; in its absence, how can there be any possibility of inference? If this were possible, then it would be an example of an event being produced when there is no cause. If perception is absent, so it is said, "it is impossible to apprehend an invariable relation."

There is reason why the invariable relation cannot be proved. Is it the apprehension of a relation between two universals, or will it be a relation between two particulars, or a relation between a universal and a particular? If it would be apprehension of a relation between two universals, that cannot be accepted because a universal is not possible (has not been demonstrated). That a universal is not possible has already been established. Nor can the relation (of *vyāpti*) be between a universal and a bare particular, for a universal is impossible (undemonstrated).

Nor is it (i.e., *vyāpti*) a relation between two bare particulars, for the particular fires and particular smokes are infinitely many. As we have already shown, the many particulars do not possess any common element. Even if that were possible, the infinity of particulars would still be there. If the numberlessness disappeared, then particulars would not exist. If there are no particulars, then, tell me, between whom would the relation of invariable succession be apprehended? . . .

It may be argued that the relation of invariable succession could be apprehended in the case of a few particulars that are present at that time, but not in the case of all particulars. Then, only those particulars may function as having the relation so that one of them establishes the other. But the relation cannot obtain in the case of all particulars if there is a relation between one pair of objects, it cannot be the basis of inference with regard to another pair. That would be an unreasonable extension. If there is a visual contact between Devadatta's eye and a jar, this would not produce knowledge of water, etc. A contact gives rise to a cognition of an object only with reference to a determinate time and place (and not at other times and places).

Refutation of an Inference whose *Hetu* is "Being an Effect"

Because of what follows, there cannot be knowledge of what is to be inferred, for it is impossible that smoke is an effect. It cannot be considered as an effect, because its cessation of existence is not apprehended. It cannot be said that it is to which is apprehended by perception, for (the question arises) does this perception arise by being directly perceived, or does it arise by being denied? If it is said that the cessation of smoke is directly perceived, then is smoke the object of that perception, or is it something else, or is it nothing? If the perception has smoke for its object, then this perception can establish only the existence of smoke and not its negation.

If the perception is of something else, then it cannot deny the existence of smoke, since something else is its object. If it has nothing for its object, then it would be like a person who is dumb, blind, and deaf. (i.e., it cannot affirm or deny anything).

The Jaina *Darśana*

The Doctrine of *Syadvāda*[3]

XXIII. When it is integrated, an entity is without modifications. When it is differentiated, this same entity is without substance. You brought to light the doctrine of seven modes which is expressed by means of two kinds of statements. This doctrine is intelligible to the most intelligent people.

(When one desires to speak of a single entity—self, pitcher, etc.,—having the form of substance only, without any reference to modification even if they are present, it is called "without modifications." It has the form of pure substance. In such expressions as "this soul," "this pitcher," only the form of substance is acknowledged, because of non-separateness of it and the modifications.

"Differentiated" means described with distinctions on account of its capacity for different forms. The same entity then is described as non-substance, without any underlying reference to the underlying substance. This is the sense. . . .

Thus although an entity consists of both substance and modifications, it has a substance-form when the substance standpoint is taken to be primary; it has a modification form when the emphasis on the modification standpoint is primary and the substance standpoint is subordinated; and it has the form of both when both standpoints are emphasized. . . .

What are these seven modes and what are these kinds of statements? When with regard to a single entity, e.g., the soul, an enquiry concerning modifications, existence, etc., without contradiction . . . a statement is made one by one with the word "somehow" in seven ways, it is called the "seven-mode doctrine." It can be expressed as follows:

(1) Somehow, everything exists. This is the first mode by affirmation.
(2) Somehow, everything does not exist. This is the second mode, by negation.

3 From Malliṣeṇa's *Syadmañjari with Anyayoga-vyavaccheda-dvātriṃśikā of Hemacandra*, edited by A. B. Dhruva (Bombay: S. K. Belvalkar, Bhandarkar Oriental Research Institute, 1933). Selections are taken from pages 138–159, which include Malliṣeṇa's text as well as Hemacandra's commentary.

(3) Somehow, from one point of view, everything exists, and from another point of view, it does not exist. This is the third mode, by way of affirmation and negation successively.
(4) Somehow, everything is indescribable. This is the fourth mode, by way of simultaneous affirmation and negation.
(5) Somehow, everything does exist, and is indescribable. This is the fifth mode, by way of affirmation and also simultaneous affirmation and negation.
(6) Somehow, everything does not exist, and somehow it is indescribable. This is the sixth mode by way of negation and simultaneous affirmation and negation.
(7) Somehow, everything does exit, does not exit, and is indescribable. This is the seventh mode, by way of affirmation, negation, and simultaneous affirmation and negation. . . .

We have said that the complex nature of an entity is intelligible to highly intelligent individuals. . . .

The absolutist who is highly unintelligent, points out the contradiction in affirming the contradictory modifications. . . .

XXIV. When non-existence is assigned to different aspects of an entity, it is not contradictory of existence in that entity. (Similarly) existence and indescribability are not contradictories. The unintelligent absolutists have not recognized this and are afraid of contradiction.

XXV. One and the same thing is eternal and non-eternal. Somehow it is of similar as well as dissimilar forms. Somehow it is both describable and indescribable, existent and non-existent.

XXVIII. With the words "it certainly exists, it exists, and somehow it exists," an entity is defined from false standpoints, by standpoints and by *pramāṇas.*

(In this verse, an object is defined in three ways: by false standpoints, by standpoints, and by the *pramāṇas.*)

The Bauddha *Darśana*

(i) The Teachings of the Buddha to Five Ascetics[4] (The Middle Way and the Four Noble Truths)

"There are two extremes, O recluses, which he who has gone forth ought not to follow. The habitual practice, on the one hand, of those things whose attraction depends upon the pleasures of sense, and especially of sensuality (a practice low and pagan, fit only for the worldly-minded, unworthy, of no abiding profit); and the habitual practice, on the other hand, of self-mortification (a practice painful, unworthy, and equally of no abiding profit).

4 From *The History and Literature of Buddhism,* by T. W. Rhys Davids (Varanasi: Bhartiya Publishing House, first appeared in 1896), pp. 68–90. The text edited and footnotes deleted.

There is a Middle Way, O recluses, avoiding these two extremes, discovered by the Tathagata—a path which opens the eyes and bestows understanding, which leads to peace of mind, to the higher wisdom to full enlightenment, to Nirvaṇa.

And which is that Middle Way? Verily, it is the Noble Eightfold Path. That is to say

Right Views (free from superstition or delusion)—
Right Aspirations (high, and worthy of the intelligent, worthy man)—
Right Speech (kindly, open, truthful)—
Right Conduct (peaceful, honest, pure)—
Right Effort (in self-training and in self-control)—
Right Mindfulness (the active, watchful mind)—
Right Rapture (in deep meditation on the realities of life).

Now this, O recluses, is the noble truth concerning suffering.

Birth is painful and so is old age; disease is painful and so is death. Union with the unpleasant is painful, painful is separation from the pleasant; and any craving that is unsatisfied, that too is painful. In brief, the five aggregates which spring from attachment (the conditions of individuality and its cause), they are painful.

Right Livelihood (bringing hurt or danger to no living thing)—

Now this, O recluses, is the noble truth concerning the origin of suffering. Verily, it originates in that craving thirst which causes the renewal of becomings, is accompanied by sensual delight, and seeks satisfaction now here, . . . that is to say, the craving for the gratification of the passions, or the craving for a future life, or the craving for success in this present life (the lust of the flesh, the lust of life, or the pride of life).

Now this, O recluses, is the noble truth concerning the destruction of suffering.

Verily, it is the destruction, in which no craving remains over, of this very thirst; the laying aside of, the getting rid of, the being free from, the harbouring no longer of, this thirst.

And this, O recluses, is the noble truth concerning the way which leads to the destruction of suffering.

Verily, it is this Noble Eightfold Path. . . ."

Then with regard to each of the Four Truths, the Teacher declared that it was not among the doctrines handed down; but that there arose within him the eye firstly to see it, then to know that he would understand it, and thirdly, to know that he had grasped it; there arose within him the knowledge (of its nature), the understanding (of its cause), the wisdom (to guide in the path of tranquility), and the light (to dispel darkness from it). And he said,

"So long, O recluses, as my knowledge and insight were not quite clear regarding each of these four noble truths in this triple order, in this twelve fold manner—so long I knew that I had not attained to the full insight of that wisdom which is unsurpassed in the heavens or on earth, among the whole race of recluses and Brahmins, gods or men. But now I have attained it. This knowledge and insight have arisen within me. Immovable is the emancipation of my heart. This is my last existence. There will be no rebirth for me."

Thus spoke the Blessed One. The five ascetics glad at heart, exalted the words of the Blessed One.

(ii) There is No Soul[5] (*Saṃyutta-Nikāya*, iii.66)

I The body, monks, is soulless. If the body, monks, were the soul, this body would not be subject to sickness, and it would be possible in the case of the body to say, "let my body be thus, let my body not be thus." Now, because the body is soulless, monks, therefore the body is subject to sickness, and it is not possible in the case of the body to say, "let my body be thus, let my body not be thus."

Feeling is soulless . . . perception is soulless . . . the aggregates are soulless. . . .

Consciousness is soulless. For if consciousness were the soul, this consciousness would not be subject. to sickness, and it would be possible in the case of consciousness to say, "let my consciousness be thus, let my consciousness not be thus."

Now, because consciousness is soulless, therefore consciousness is subject to sickness, and it is not possible in the case of consciousness to say, "let my consciousness be thus, let my consciousness not be thus."

What think you, monks, is the body permanent or impermanent?

> Impermanent, Lord.
> But is the impermanent painful or pleasant?
> Painful, Lord.

But is it fitting to consider what is impermanent, painful, and subject to change as, "this is mine, this am I, this is my soul"?

No indeed, Lord.

[And so of feeling, perception, the aggregates, and consciousness.] "Therefore in truth, monks, whatever body, past, future, or present, internal or external, gross or subtle, low or eminent, near or far, is to be looked on by him who duly and rightly understands, as, all this body is not mine, not this am I, not mine is the soul." [And so of feeling, etc.]

Thus perceiving, monks, the learned noble disciple feels loathing for the body, for feeling, for perception, for the aggregates, for consciousness. Feeling disgust he becomes free from passion, through freedom from passion he is emancipated, and in the emancipated one arises the knowledge of his emanci-

5 *Anattalakkhaṇa* Sutta, in E. J. Thomas, *The Life of Buddha* (Delhi: Motilal Banarsidass, 1997), pp. 88–89.

pation. He understands that destroyed is rebirth, the religious life has been led, done is what was to be done, there is naught [for him] beyond this world.

Thus said the Lord.

(iii) Translated from the *Visuddhi-Magga* (Chap. xviii)[6]

II Just as the word "chariot" is but a mode of expression for axle, wheels, chariot-body, pole, and other constituent members, placed in a certain relation to each other, but when we come to examine the members one by one, we discover that in the absolute sense there is no chariot; and just as the word "house" is but a mode of expression for wood and other constituents of a house, surrounding space in a certain relation, but in the absolute sense there is no house; and just as the word "fist" is but a mode of expression for the fingers, the thumb, etc., in a certain relation; and the word "lute" for the body of the lute, strings, etc.; "army" for elephants, horses, etc.; "city" for fortifications, houses, gates, etc.; "tree" for trunk, branches, foliage, etc., in a certain relation, but when we come to examine the parts one by one, we discover that in the absolute sense there is no tree; in exactly the same way the words "living entity" and "ego" are but a mode of expression for the presence of the five attachment groups, but when we come to examine the elements of being one by one, we discover that in the absolute sense there is no living entity there to form a basis for such figments as "I am," or "I"; in other words, that in the absolute sense there is only name and form. The insight of him who perceives this is called knowledge of the truth.

He, however, who abandons this knowledge of the truth and believes in a living entity must assume either that this living entity will perish or that it will not perish. If he assumes that it will not perish, he falls into the heresy of the persistence of existences; or if he assumes that it will perish, he falls into that of the annihilation of existences. And why do I say so? Because, just as sour cream has milk as its antecedent, so nothing here exists but what has its own antecedents. To say, "The living entity persists," is to fall short of the truth; to say, "It is annihilated," is to outrun the truth. Therefore has The Blessed One said—"There are two heresies, O priests, which possess both gods and men, by which some fall short of the truth, and some outrun the truth; but the intelligent know the truth.

"And how, O priests, do some fall short of the truth?

"O priests, gods and men delight in existence, take pleasure in existence, rejoice in existence, so that when the Doctrine for the cessation of existence is preached to them, their minds do not leap toward it, are not favorably disposed toward it, do not rest in it, do not adopt it.

"Thus, O priests, do some fall short of the truth.

"And how, O priests, do some outrun the truth?

"Some are distressed at, ashamed of, and loathe existence, and welcome the thought of non-existence, saying, 'See here! When they say that on the

6 From *Buddhism in Translations*, pp. 133–35.

dissolution of the body this Ego is annihilated, perishes, and does not exist after death, that is good, that is excellent, that is as it should be.'

"Thus, O priests, do some outrun the truth.

"And how, O priests, do the intelligent know the truth?

"We may have, O priests, a priest who knows things as they really are, and knowing things as they really are, he is on the road to aversion for things, to absence of passion for them, and to cessation from them.

"Thus, O priests, do the intelligent know the truth.

(iv) *Nirvāṇa*[7]

"Let us live happily then, free from hatred among the hating! Among men who hate let us dwell free from ill-will! "Let us live happily then, free from ailments among the ailing! Among men sick at heart let us dwell free from repining!

"Let us live happily then, free from care among the careworn! Among men devoured by eagerness let us be free from excitement!

"Let us live happily then, we who have no hindrances! We shall be like the bright gods who feed upon happiness!"

In a later prose description of the kind of feelings that lead a man to seek after Nirvana, we find the words—it is King Milinda who is speaking to Nagasena the Buddhist—

"Venerable Nagasena, your people say: 'Nirvana is not past, nor future, nor present, nor produced, nor not produced, nor produceable.' In that case, Nagasena , does the man who, having ordered his life aright, realise Nirvana, realise something already produced, or does he himself produce it first, and then realise it?"

"Neither the one, O King, nor the other. And, nevertheless, O King, that essence of Nirvana which he, so ordering his life aright, realises—that exists."

"Do not, venerable Nagasena, clear up this puzzle by making it dark! Make it open and plain as you elucidate it. With a will, strenuous in endeavour, pour out upon it all that has been taught you. It is a point on which this people is bewildered, plunged in perplexity, lost in doubt. Dissipate this guilty uncertainty; it pierces like a dart."

"That principle of Nirvana, O King, so peaceful, so blissful, so delicate, exists. And it is that which he who orders his life aright, grasping the idea of things according to the teachings of the Conquerors, realises by his wisdom—even as a pupil, by his knowledge, makes himself, according to the instruction of his teachers, master of an art.

"And if you ask: 'How is Nirvana to be known? it is by the freedom from distress and danger, by confidence, by peace, by calm, by bliss, by happiness, by delicacy, by purity by freshness.

7 From *The History and Literature of Buddhism*, pp. 113–115.

"And if again you should ask: 'How does he who orders his life aright realise that Nirvana?' I should reply: 'He, O King, who orders his life aright grasps the truth as to the development of all things, and when he is doing so he perceives therein birth, he perceives old age, he perceives disease, he perceives death. But he perceives not therein, whether in the beginning or the middle or the end, anything worthy of being laid hold of as lasting satisfaction. . . . And discontent arises in his mind when he thus finds a fever takes possession of his body, and without a refuge of protection, hopeless, he becomes weary of repeated lives . . . And in the mind of him who thus perceives the insecurity of transitory life, of starting afresh in innumerable births, the thought arises: 'All on fire is this endless becoming, burning and blazing! Full of pain is it, of despair! If only one could reach a state in which there were no becoming, *there* would there be calm, *that* would be sweet—the cessation of all these conditions, the getting rid of all these defects (of lusts, of evil, and of Karma), the end of cravings, the absence of passion, peace, Nirvana!'

"And therewith does his mind leap forward into that state in which there is no becoming, and then has he found peace, then does he exult and rejoice at the thought: 'A refuge have I gained at last!' Just, O King, as a man who, venturing into a strange land, has lost his way, on becoming aware of a path, free from jungle, that will lead him home, bounds forward along it, contented in mind, exulting and rejoicing at the thought: 'I have found the way at last!'—Just so in him who thus perceives the insecurity of transitory births there arises the thought: 'All on fire is this endless becoming, burning and blazing! Full of pain is it and despair! If only one could reach a state in which there was no becoming, *there* would there be calm, *that* would be sweet—the cessation of all these conditions, the getting rid of all these defects, the end of craving, the absence of passion, peace, Nirvana!' And therewith does his mind leap forward into that state in which there is no becoming, and then has he found peace, then does he exult and rejoice at the thought: 'A refuge have I found at last!' And he strives with might and main along that path, searches it out, accustoms himself thoroughly to it; to that end does he make firm his self-possession, to that end does he hold fast in effort, to that end does he remain steadfast in love toward all beings in all the worlds; and still to that does he direct his mind again and again, until, gone far beyond the transitory, he gains the Real, the highest fruit of *Arhatship*. And when he has gained that, O King, the man who has ordered his life aright has realized, seen face to face, Nirvāṇa."

Part IV

THE ANCIENT SYSTEMS

7

THE MĪMĀṀSĀ *DARŚANA*

Etymologically the term "*Mīmāṁsā*" means "solution of a problem by critical examination and reflection." The Vedas, the foundational texts of Indian philosophy, are divided into *Karma kāṇḍa* (the Portion of Actions in the ritualistic sense) and *Jñāna kāṇḍa* (the Portion of Knowledge). The Mīmāṁsā school has developed out of the ritualistic portion of the Vedas. As a school of Indian philosophy, Mīmāṁsā undertakes a systematic study of the *brāhmaṇas* (guidelines for the performance of sacrifices) and subordinates the other part of the Vedas (relating to hymns in praise of various deities and philosophic speculations and interpretations) to them. Vedānta, generally referred to as Uttara Mīmāṁsā, primarily analyzes the last (*uttara*) sections of the Vedas, that is, the Upaniṣads, which provide the philosophical interpretation of the texts. Accordingly, Mīmāṁsā school is known as "Pūrva (previous) Mīmāṁsā." It may be noted as a matter of interest from the philosophical perspective that there is a common assumption underlying the genre of Mīmāṁsā, both Pūrva and Uttara, that Vedic terms and concepts must be explicated in light of an understanding reflected in the language of the world.[1]

Jaimini's *sūtras*, known as *Mīmāṁsā Sūtras* (400 BCE), is the basic text of this school. Śabara (CE 200) wrote a principal commentary (*bhāṣya*) on it. Several scholars and commentators have written commentaries on Śabara's commentary. Among these two are most important: the one by Kumārila Bhaṭṭa and the other by Prabhākara. These two commentators are the founders of the two schools within the fold of Mīmāṁsā, and the schools are named after them, viz. Bhāṭṭa and Prābhākara respectively. Kumārila's commentary on Śabara's *bhāṣya* is entitled *Śloka-Vārtika* and Prabhākara's commentary is known as *Bṛhatī*. According to many accounts, Prabhākara was a student of Kumārila who disagreed with him on many important points. Kumārila's other well-known student was Maṇḍana Miśra, the author of several important works on Mīmāṁsā. Eventually Maṇḍana was initiated by Śaṃkara into Advaita Vedānta.

The central theme of the Mīmāṁsā is "*dharma*" (at the very outset Jaimini informs his readers: "now begins an enquiry into *dharma*").[2] What follows are attempts to define "*dharma*." *Dharma* is that which is indicated by the sentences of a certain form, i.e., "should-sentences," known as *codanā*. These sentences refer to the relevant Vedic discourse assuming the form "one should perform such and such actions." Consequently, the goal of Mīmāṁsā is to lead to a precise determination of the Vedic discourse, in order that practitioners may lead a life of "*dharma*." Thus it is not surprising that this school is also known as *Dharma Mīmāṁsā*.

Not having any theoretic use of the idea of God, the Mīmāṁsā explains the Vedic deities as posits implied by the performance of the rituals, and concerns itself with the motivation for such actions, e.g., the promised "other-worldly" consequences and their place in the ethical life of the community. It focuses upon the rules for interpreting the Vedas as a body of injunctions rather than as religious statements about God, soul, and the world. Much discussion is directed towards bringing out the precise meanings of words and sentences. Accordingly, Mīmāṁsā goes on to develop a rich philosophy not only of language but also of action.

In expounding such a system as Pūrva-Mīmāṁsā, it is imperative that we separate the ritualistic aspect of the system from the strictly philosophical ideas of this school. The key philosophical ideas include the Mīmāṁsā theory of the nature of knowledge, truth, and language. On all these counts, Mīmāṁsā commentators made important contributions and provided impetus for further discussions.[3] In my exposition in this chapter, I will primarily focus on the Mīmāṁsā epistemology. I will discuss key philosophical ideas and conceptions found in Mīmāṁsā and point out the differences between the Bhāṭṭa and Prābhākara schools where necessary. For the sake of understanding, I have divided the discussion under the following five headings: I. The Sources of Knowledge, II. The Nature of Knowledge: The Self-Validity of Knowledge, III. Error or the Falsity of Knowledge, IV. The Theory of the Meaning of Words and Sentences, and V. Self, *Dharma*, *Karma*, and *Mokṣa*.

I The Sources of Knowledge

The Mīmāṁsā, like most schools of Indian philosophy, makes a distinction between immediate and mediate knowledge.

Kumārila defines *pramā* as a valid cognition that presents a previously unknown object, is not contradicted by another knowledge, and is not generated by a defective condition, e.g., a defect in the sense organ in the case of a perceptual knowledge. The object of immediate knowledge must be existent, and when such an object is related to a sense (internal or external), there arises in the soul an immediate knowledge about it.

A *pramāṇa* is the efficient cause of a cognition. Kumārila recognizes six *pramāṇas*: *pratyakṣa*, *anumāna*, *upamāna*, *śabda*, *arthāpatti*, and *anupalabdhi*.[4] Prabhākara accepts the first five only and since he rejects *abhāva* as an independent knowable category, he does not need *anupalabdhi* to establish any such category. Both Kumārila and Prabhākara regard only perception to be immediate knowledge and admit two stages of perception.

Pratyakṣa

Perception is defined as a cognition that is produced by the contact of the sense organ with the mind, of the mind with the sensory organ, and the sensory organ with the object. When there is a contact of the sense organ with the object, initially, we have a bare awareness of it; we know that the object *is*, but we do not know *what* it is. In this cognition, neither the genus nor the differentia is presented to consciousness. This primary immediate knowledge is *nirvikalpaka* perception. At the next stage, i.e., the stage of *savikalpaka* perception, we come to know the object in light of our past experiences, understand it as belonging to a class, possessing certain qualities, and having a name. It is expressed in such judgments as "this is a chair," "this is a table," and so on.

Anumāna

Etymologically "*anumāna*" means the knowledge that "follows another knowledge." The Mīmāṁsā defines inference as the knowledge in which one term of the relationship—which is not perceived— is known through the knowledge of the other term that is invariably related to the first term. In other words, in inference, on the basis of what is perceived, we are led to knowledge of what is not perceived because the perceived and the inferred have a permanent, unfailing relationship. The Bhāṭṭas define invariable concomitance (*vyāpti*) as a "natural relation," and "natural" here means being free from limiting adjuncts. In the inferential knowledge that the "hill is fiery," we observe cases where smoke and fire are present together and also cases where they are not so present, and arrive at a general principle that governs all cases.

Unlike Naiyāikas who argue that an inferential argument has five members,[5] both Kumārila and Prabhākara hold that an inferential argument has three members. Both make a distinction between inference for oneself and inference for others. However, there is an important difference between Prabhākara and Kumārila: Prabhākara argues that the inference of fire on a hill does not present anything previously unknown, because the inference "the hill is fiery" is already included in the major premise that "all cases of smoke are cases of fire." Kumārila argues that the previous unknownness or novelty is an essential feature of inference, because although we know that smoke is invariably related to the fire, this hill as possessing the fire was not known earlier.[6]

Upamāna

Knowledge from comparison arises when, upon perceiving an object that is present before me, which is like an object that I have perceived in the past, I come to know that the remembered object is like the perceived one. This is knowledge by similarity. I see an animal *gavaya* that is similar to my cow and say "my cow is similar to this *gavaya*." Such a knowledge is not perception, because the object "my cow" is not being perceived; it is not an inference, because the knowledge is not derived from a *vyāpti* or universal concomitance; and the knowledge has not arisen from the testimony of another person.

Śabda

Among the sources of knowledge, Mīmāṁsakas discuss *śabda* in great detail because of their interest in the authority of the Vedas. This is the knowledge that arises from the testimony of a reliable person, and it may be of two kinds: personal (non-Vedic) and impersonal (Vedic). The first denotes either the heard or the written testimony of a person, the second the authority of the Vedas. The Vedic *śabda* produces a cognition of an object that does not have any contact with the sense organs; the cognition arises only on the basis of the *śabda* alone. Kumārila accepts both personal and impersonal *śabda*, but Prabhākara does not accept the authority of the non-Vedic *śabda.*

The emphasis of the Mīmāṁsakas, however, is on the testimony of the Vedas. Their primary goal is to determine the nature of *dharma*, and *dharma* as taught by the Vedic injunctive sentences. Other sentences of the Vedas are subsidiary to the injunctions. The injunctions are valid in themselves and do not derive their validity from any other source. The value and the sole use of the Vedas lie in giving directions for performing rituals. The remaining parts of the Vedas are useless.

The Vedas, like the words, are eternal.[7] They do not have either the personal or the divine origin.[8] It is asked: Are not the Vedas composed of the words that are non-eternal? The Mīmāṁsakas in response point out that the words are not really the perceived sounds, but are rather the letters that are uncaused and partless. For example, a letter, say, "s," is uttered by many individuals at different times, and in many different ways. The sound of the letters differ, however, we recognize the letter to be the same. Words as letters are eternal entities, and the relation between the words and their meaning is natural. I will discuss some of these issues shortly in the Section IV of this chapter.

Arthāpatti

Postulation (*arthāpatti*) is the necessary supposition of an unperceived fact which alone can explain a fact. A man fasts during the day but still gains weight and becomes fat. There is an apparent contradiction between his growing fatness and his fasting, barring some medical reasons. To reconcile the contradiction, we say that the man must be eating at night. Knowledge obtained from *arthāpatti* cannot be reduced to perception, inference, and comparison; it is not perception, we do not see the person eating at night; the knowledge is not derived on the basis of invariable relation between fatness and eating at night; and it is not obtained from the testimony of a person.

Anupalabdhi

Non-perception is the immediate cognition of the non-existence of an object. The question is: How do I know the non-existence, say, of an elephant in my room? It cannot be said to be perceived in the manner I perceive an object that I see before me. The Bhāṭṭas, like the Advaitins, argue that the non-existence of the elephant in the room is known from the absence of its cognition, that is, from its non-perception. This non-existence cannot be known by inference, because if we already had the knowledge of an invariable relation between non-perception and non-existence, i.e., if we had already known that the non-perception of an object implies its non-existence, then we would be begging the question and there would be no need to prove the non-existence by inference. We cannot explain the elephant's non-existence by comparison or testimony because the knowledge of similarity or words of a reliable person are not involved. Therefore, we must recognize non-perception (*anupalabdhi*) as an independent *pramāṇa*.

II The Nature of Knowledge: The Self-Validity of Knowledge

On the Mīmāṁsā theory, knowledge, by definition, is certainty about its object. Every knowledge is true of its object and so is *pramā*. Whenever adequate conditions for the generation of a particular knowledge exist, the knowledge arises without any doubt or disbelief in it. For example, in the day light when our eyes come in contact with an object, we have visual perception; on the basis of premises, we infer fire upon perceiving smoke; when one hears a meaningful sentence from one's friend, knowledge arises from testimony, and so on. In our daily lives we act on such knowledge without worrying about its truth and falsity and the fact that it leads to successful activity testifies that such knowledge is true. The invalidity of a cognition is arrived at by external means, especially by appealing to subsequent cognitions. When the conditions are defective—e.g., when the eyes are jaundiced, or there is lack of sufficient light—no such knowledge arises. Invalidity thus arises from subsequent experience or from some other data. At the moment a cognition arises, its validity is not, and cannot be, doubted. Thus to say that a knowledge is not true of its object is absurd. Knowledge does not need any special or additional excellence in the cause for it to be true. If the cause of a knowledge does not produce it, then no additional factor added to the cause can produce it. From this, it follows that once the cause of a knowledge produces the knowledge, this knowledge, by its very definition, will let the knower be cognizant of its object, and therefore it must be true. Given that the knowledge is already true, any further determination of the absence of any defect in the causal conditions cannot make the original knowledge true. Determination of the absence of defect only strengthens this certainty of truth. Besides, this determination of the absence of defect must itself be a knowledge which is also true of its object.

In this chain of argument, the emphasis is on the proper object of a knowledge. The object of a knowledge is only that which is manifested in that knowledge and not something else. What is not manifested in a knowledge cannot be the object of *that* knowledge. So the Mīmāṁsakas argue that the validity of knowledge (a) arises from the very conditions that generate it, not from any extrinsic conditions, and (b) is believed to be true as soon as it arises, so there is no need to verify it by any other *pramāṇa*. These two aspects taken together constitute the Mīmāṁsā theory of intrinsic validity, i.e., that cognitions are valid in themselves and do not need further proof to validate them.

Indian philosophers raised a questions regarding the truth or the validity of knowledge which the Western epistemologists did not. The questions is: Is the truth of a knowledge intrinsic or extrinsic to the cognition? They raised the same question about falsity. Those who answer this question in the affirmative, e.g., Mīmāṁsā and Vedānta, are known as the *svataḥ prāmāṇyavādins*, the upholders of the theory of intrinsicality of truth. Those who answer this question in the negative, e.g., the Naiyāyikas, are known as the *parataḥ prāmāṇyavādins*, the upholder of the theory of extrinsicality of truth. The questions discussed in this context are: Do the conditions which produce a knowledge also make it true? In addition, is it the case that when a knowledge is known to me, it is also at the same time known to be true? In this chapter, I am concerned with the Mīmāṁsā theory; accordingly, I will turn to it.

This doctrine of the intrinsic validity of all knowledge is one of the most important doctrine of the Mīmāṁsā school. In concrete terms it amounts to saying that all cognitions are produced and known to be valid, that there is no false knowledge. Both Prabhākara and Kumārila subscribe to the view that cognitions are intrinsically valid. However, there is an important difference between the two and the difference concerns the question: how is a cognition cognized?

Prabhākara holds that a cognition is perceived directly along with the object and the knowing self (articulated in the sentence "I know this pitcher"). Prabhākara accepts what is called *triputīvitti*, i.e., the three-fold presentation. Each cognition has three factors, the I (the subject or the knower), the known (the object), and the knowledge itself. In the cognition, "I know the jar"—the "I," the pitcher, and the awareness—all three are presented at once. Each is presented in its own way. The I is cognized as the I, but not as the object, the pitcher is presented as the object, and the cognition is known as a cognition, i.e., neither as the subject nor as the object. According to Prabhākara, when we know, we also know that we know. This knowledge, on his view, is self-revealing.

Bhāṭṭa Mīmāṁsā holds that knowledge by itself cannot be the object of itself. Kumārila and his followers, on the other hand, hold that a cognition is known by an inference from a new property called "knownness" that is produced in the object when it is known. Kumārila argues that knowledge is a process, an activity of the self. This process generates a property known as manifestedness in the object. A knowledge is not directly perceived, but is inferred from the manifestedness (*jñātatā*) that is produced in the object. Kumārila denies self-luminosity to knowledge; knowledge is rather inferred. The view that knowledge transforms the object from the existent object to the known object is challenged by the Nyāya-Vaiśeṣika who argue that knowledge cannot transform its object. This, however, is precisely what Kumārila holds, i.e., by being known, the mere object becomes the known object; it acquires a new property of knownness (*jñātatā*), from which the knowledge is inferred. There is no need to enter into this controversy; for our present purposes it is sufficient to note that the Mīmāṁsakas hold that whenever a knowledge is known ("I know"), it is known as being true of its own object; they believe in the *svataḥ prāmāṇya* of all cognitions.

Before proceeding further, let us pause for a moment to discuss what is meant by "*svataḥ*" in *svataḥ pramātva* of knowledge. "*Svataḥ*" means "by oneself." To say that the truth of a cognition is apprehended *svataḥ* is to say that a cognition apprehends its own truth. But "*sva*" may mean "by the cognition which apprehends the cognition itself." In that case "*svataḥ pramātva*" would mean that the truth of a cognition is apprehended by a cognition which apprehends that cognition. Thus to say that the *pramātva* is *svataḥ* may mean either of two things: it may either mean that the *pramātva* is apprehended by the knowledge to which it belongs or the *pramātva* is apprehended by the cognition which apprehends the knowledge whose *pramātva* it is. Therefore, one can say that the *pramātva* is *svataḥ* if it is either *sva-grāhya* (what is apprehended by the knowledge whose truth it is; *sva* is the original knowledge whose truth is under consideration) or *sva-grāhakagrāhya* (that in which truth is apprehended by a second knowledge which apprehends the first knowledge).

Against the second view, i.e., the truth is apprehended by a cognition of the cognition whose truth is under consideration, various objections may be raised. It may be asked: What is this cognition of the original cognition (*anuvyavasāya)*? Is it introspection of the first cognition? Does the Mīmāṁsā theory amount to saying that the *anuvyavasāya*, which apprehends the first cognition, also apprehends that cognition's *pramātva*? Since the introspection of the original *vyavasāya* is a cognition of that cognition, it may therefore apprehend that cognition's truth. This is the view of the Naiyāyikas and Murāri Miśra, who represents the third school of Mīmāṁsā. Kumārila, however, does not accept this as a viable alternative.

On Kumārila's view, knowledge is supersensible and is therefore always inferred; consequently, it cannot be an object of introspection. A cognition on his view is always known only by an inference which uses knownness as a reason. However, no matter whether the truth of a cognition is apprehended by a mental perception or *anuvyavasāya* or whether it is inferred on the ground of knownness of the object which serves as a mark, truth is not apprehended by the knowledge to which that truth belongs.

Against the Mīmāṁsakas, the following objection may be raised: Even when a cognition (*vyavasāya*) is apprehended in *anuvyavasāya* or in an inference with *jñātatā* as the mark, the *vyavasāya* is apprehended only *qua* knowledge, but not *qua* true knowledge. In response, Prabhākara point out that if we regard knowledge to be always *sva-saṃvedana*, i.e., that knowledge always apprehends itself, then we can also hold that knowledge, while knowing itself, also knows its truth. If knowledge is self-knowing or *sva-saṃvedana*, then it would also know its own truth.

Again, it may be asked: given that according to Prabhākara a cognition is self-knowing and that it knows its own truth, then if the knowledge were false, should not the error of knowledge also be similarly known thereby making falsity also *svataḥ?* When considering this objection against the Prabhākara view, we should bear in mind that Prabhākara does not regard error to be *svataḥ*.

Thus the question arises: If knowledge is self-evident, what accounts for the arising of the so-called error? How does the Mīmāṁsakas make sense of the alleged falsity of a knowledge?

III Error or the Falsity of Knowledge

If all cognitions by nature are valid, how do we explain erroneous cognitions? Prabhākara holds that given that every knowledge is true, nothing false ever appears in any erroneous cognition. In an erroneous cognition, one thing is taken to be the other. In the supposed false knowledge or erroneous cognition, i.e., "this is a piece of silver," one thing (e.g., a shell) is seen to be another (e.g., a piece of silver). The question arises: What is the object in this alleged false knowledge? It cannot be the shell, for the shell is not manifested in it. The cognition "this is a piece of silver" appears, though there is no silver in front of the perceiver. This false cognition is contradicted by a later cognition of the form "this is not a piece of silver, but a shell," which sublates the earlier knowledge and proves it to be false. The falsity of such a cognition is due to the presence of defects in its cause, in the present case, the distance, possibly defective visual organ, lapse of memory, and so on.

But what then is the status of the cognition "this is a piece of silver" when there is no silver there in front of the perceiver? Prabhākara argues that the cognition "this is a piece of silver," really consists of two cognitions, one perceptual, and the other, recollection. The component "this" expresses a perception, the component "silver" expresses a remembered thing. Each is a valid cognition; some thing is being perceived as "this," and a past cognition of a silver is being remembered. There is nothing false about these two cognitions. There is, however, a failure to distinguish between the two, not falsely taking the one to be the other. This non-distinction results in the perceiver's attempt to seize the silver. This view is known as *akhyātivāda* which means "no (false or invalid) knowledge"; one does not perceive the silver, one simply remembers it. The so-called false cognition is a mixture of two valid cognitions: the perception of "this" as characterized by features that are common to both the silver and the shell; there is no positive mistaking of one thing for another.

The Bhāṭṭas do not accept this theory. Kumārila points out that simple non-discrimination cannot explain error, because no one can deny that the false object appears. He recognizes a positive confusing of one thing with another, between a perception ("this") and a remembered ("silver"). When we perceive silver in a shell and make the judgment that "this is a piece of silver," both the subject and the predicate are real. The silver exists, say, in a department store, however, in this instance we bring the existing shell under the class of silver, and the error consists in relating these two really existent but separate things in the subject–predicate relation. Error is due to the wrong relationship, not because of the related objects which actually exist. These errors make us behave in a wrong way, which explains, why the Bhāṭṭas call their theory "*viparītakhyāti-vāda*" or the view that error is the opposite of right behavior.

To sum up: the Prābhākara school holds that every knowledge is *ipso facto* valid, and that there is no such thing as error. The Bhāṭṭas, on the other hand, concede that error may affect relationships though the objects perceived in themselves are free from error. Both, however, agree that error affects our activity rather than knowledge.

Against the Prabhākara theory, opponents argue that the failure to comprehend the distinction between the two is inadequate to account for erroneous cognitions. Error is not a simple absence of knowledge. It is not merely failure to comprehend the distinction between the two, because if that were the case, error would occur even in the dreamless sleep stage.

The main thrust of the objection is to ask whether actual experience testifies to the correctness of the Prābhākara theory. Is an erroneous cognition really the non-comprehension of difference? The opponents point out that actual experience testifies that in an erroneous cognition we initially have a cognition assuming the form "this is a piece of silver," which is sublated by "this is a shell, not a piece of silver." Furthermore, if error were simply negative (i.e., the non-comprehension of difference between the two), it would not bring about a positive practical reaction, such as withdrawing in fear, for example, in the snake–rope illusion, or proceeding to seize the silver in the case of the shell–silver illusion. Thus, it does not make sense to say that an erroneous cognition is the failure to distinguish between the "this" and the "silver."

The question is: What precisely is the nature of non-discrimination? The notion of non-discrimination or non-cognition of distinction between remembrance and perception is logically opaque. For what is the distinction other than the nature of distinct objects? The proposition that a table is distinct from a chair signifies that the negation of each obtains in the locus of the other. Distinction is a reciprocal negation (*anonyābhāva*). Therefore, along with the manifestation of the cognition and its objects, distinction also becomes manifest, the distinction being nothing more than the correlates themselves. It is incoherent to argue that although the distincts are perceived the distinction itself is not perceived. The Prabhākara argues that in an erroneous perceiving of the shell as "this is a piece of silver," perception and recollection respectively, of "this" and "silver" are not known to be different. This is inconsistent with his own admission that a distinction between one unit of knowledge and another is but of the nature of knowledge itself, and that knowledge is self-revealing. With respect to cognitions and their contents, differences are necessarily cognized along with the revelation of the nature of cognitions as well as the contents. In short, Prabhākara cannot explain the precise nature of non-discrimination. Additionally, we must remember that non-discrimination is not a necessary condition for the occurrence of an erroneous cognition.

This experience shows neither that illusion is simply negative non-distinguishing, nor that in an illusory cognition we have two experiences rather than the one. Positive identification, as well as non-knowledge of difference, can account for a positive activity. Never, indeed, does there arise activity on the basis of the mere non-comprehension of difference. In fact, as Vācaspati, the author of *Bhāmatī*, states, both verbal usage and activity are based upon the comprehension and not on the non-comprehension of difference. If it is insisted, however, that there could be activity by the mere non-comprehension of difference, then at the time of the cognition, say, of a pitcher, for example, if there is non-comprehension of the difference from the gem, then there would exist the possibility of activity with a desire to obtain the gem. The silver in the shell–silver example is perceptual. It is not a simple case of recollection. Without the identity of the silver with the "this" element before us, there would not be any activity toward it by merely recalling silver. Therefore, the Mīmāṁ sā view of error cannot be accepted.

IV Theory of the Meaning of Words and Sentences

The Mīmāṁsā holds that a word is a group of syllables arranged in a certain order that expresses a meaning. Each syllable is eternal, but its manifestation is a momentary event. Each such manifestation leaves an impression on the listener's mind. The last syllable (of a word) together with its impression, and all the earlier impressions, make the cognition of a word possible. The meaning of a word is not an individual, but rather a universal. The word "cow" means not an individual cow, but the universal, i.e., common features, of all individual cows. However, such sentences as "bring a cow" refer to an individual cow not by virtue of the meaning of the word "cow," but because of its being invariably associated with the universal feature cowness.

Another important theory of word meanings is that of the Nyāya, i.e., the word "cow" means an individual cow as qualified by the universal cowness. The Mīmāṁsā rejects this view. On the Mīmāṁsā theory, an individual and its universal features are not ontologically different entities; they are related by a sort of identity (*tādātmya*) by virtue of which, when the universal is meant, an individual is also comprehended and co-conveyed.

The relation between a word and its meaning is said to be "natural," and "eternal," i.e., not brought about by any human agency. It is "*apauruṣeya*" (authorless). The beginning of the relation is neither remembered nor comprehended. It is comprehended only through listening to the conversations of the elders. A word and its meaning arise together.

A word's primary denotative power is to convey the primary meaning. When the primary meaning is not suitable, one resorts to a secondary meaning or *lakṣaṇā*, which, however, must be related to the primary meaning. In a well-known example, the expression *"Gaṇgāyām ghoṣa"* ("the village on the river Ganges"), calls for the secondary meaning, namely, "the village on the bank of the Ganges river."

The Meaning of a Sentence

A sentence is a group of words satisfying two requirements: (i) the group must have a common purpose and a common meaning and (ii) the constituent words must be in need of each other, or arouse in the hearer the expectation of the other. We should note that the *Mīmāṁsā Sūtras*, in this context, discuss "*ekārthatva*," which means "having an identical *artha*." "*Artha*" may either mean "meaning" or "purpose"; thus, the unity of the purpose and the meaning go together. The primary purpose of a sentence, according to Mīmāṁsā, is an action (*kriyā*) and the other components fulfill the purpose of specifying the object, the agent, the means, and the end of the action. All component meanings center around an *action*.

Besides the unity of purpose and meaning, and expectancy (*ākāṅkṣā*), the Mīmāṁsā recognizes two other conditions for the constitution of a sentence. These two are: proximity (*sannidhi*) and appropriateness (*yogyatā*). The component words, and their comprehensions, must have spatial and temporal proximity. Words uttered or written at remotely distant places and times do not obviously constitute a sentence. "Appropriateness" requires that the component meanings must be compatible. A word sequence such as "this stone is virtuous" or "sprinkle the grass with fire," though they satisfy the first two requirements, fail the last test since the concepts of "sprinkling" and "fire" are not compatible, just as "virtue" is incompatible with "stone." Obviously, appropriateness here is semantical, not simply syntactical.

After determining the proper composition of a sentence, the Mīmāṁsā philosophies attend to the question: How does the cognition of a sentence arise? Is the word meaning apprehended first and then organized into the sentence meaning? Or, is the sentence meaning apprehended first and the word meanings apprehended separately later on? On this issue, the two main sub-schools of Mīmāṁsā differ, the Bhāṭṭas (i.e., the followers of Kumārila Bhaṭṭa) side with the Advaita Vedānta philosophers, and the Prābhākaras (the followers of Prabhākara) oppose them. The Bhāṭṭa theory is known as *abhihitānvayavāda* and that of the Prābhākaras is known as *anvitābhidhānavāda*.

The Bhāṭṭa (together with the Advaita Vedāntins) hold that the words convey individual meanings but when joined together, because of congruity, convey the meaning of a sentence. The sentential meaning is apprehended, *not from the component words, but from the word meanings* by a process of secondary meaning or *lakṣaṇā*. Being conveyed by the word meaning, a sentential meaning is not itself a *padārtha*, but rather an *apadārtha*, and so not a genuine entity. Hence, according to the Bhāṭṭa theory, a sentential meaning is apprehended by the following process:

1 each word conveys its own meaning by its primary *śakti*, known as *abhidhā* or designative power;
2 these meanings connect together by such factors as expectancy, proximity, and appropriateness; and

3 by a secondary signification or *lakṣaṇā*, these meanings generate a comprehension of sentential meaning as a related entity, this secondary meaning being produced not by the component words but, rather, by the word-meanings.

The second theory, i.e., the theory of the Prābhākaras, holds that the relation among the word meanings is the sense of a sentence, and such a relation is conveyed by the words themselves. Thus the sentential meaning is the meaning of the component words taken together. It is the words that designate, not unrelated objects or meanings, but objects as related to each other (*anvita*). A word is called *pramāṇa* because it designates a related structure, which constitutes the sentential meaning. The word meaning is related to other meanings *in general*, while a sentential meaning is the relatedness of other meanings in a specific manner. Otherwise, there is no difference between word meanings and sentential meanings.

Both schools accept that on hearing a word, there is knowledge of its meaning, i.e., *padārtha*. The difference between the two theories rests on the question, whether a word designates a pure unrelated object or an object as related to others in general. The Bhāṭṭa school subscribes to the former position, the Prābhākara school to the latter view.

Prabhākara holds that the *padārtha* that is meant by a word is related to the other *padārthas* meant by other words. Hence, the theory is called *anvitābhidhāna vāda*. The words mean the relatedness to other meant entities in general, the sentence means the specific relatedness to other meanings in particular. The followers of Kumārila, however, hold that the meaning of a word, unrelated to other such word-meanings, is what is intended by a word. Pure word-meanings, by virtue of *ākāṅkṣā, sannidhi*, and *yogyatā* get related to other such meanings. This is how a sentential meaning is constituted, which, however, is not a *padārtha*. The meaning of a sentence is not a *padārtha*. The Naiyāyikas believe that the word presents its meaning, i.e., causes the memory of the meaning of the word. Both Kumārila and the other Mīmāṁsakas reject this.

According to Prabhākara, words themselves have the inherent capacity to convey their individual meanings, that is, the construed sense of a sentence. Thus the words themselves make the sense of the sentence known. Upon hearing someone utter words in sequence, one immediately understands the meaning of the sentence that the words express. According to Prabhākara, the meaning of a word is like a *kadamba* flower; it consists of infinite little buds. The word meaning then refers to a sentential meaning. According to the Bhāṭṭa theory the word designates only its own pure meaning. The words have the inherent capacity to signify their senses alone, which in turn give rise to the sense of the sentence. In other words, the words cease to function after indicating their senses. Because the relation of the sense of the words is based on the words, Bhāṭṭas contend that the words have the capacity to connote the knowledge of their senses. In short, the word initially signifies its own meaning, then the words in a sentence are put together to construe the sentential sense.

The Meaning of the Injunctive Sentences

Injunctions or *vidhis* occupy a central position in the Mīmāṁsā ethics. In the sentence, "*svargakāmo yajeta*," i.e., the performance of sacrifice is enjoined for a person who desires *svarga* (heaven), an injunctive suffix conveys that the act leads to the desired object, that the act is within capacity of the person concerned, and finally, the act does not lead to any strong adverse consequence. This three-fold meaning constitutes *iṣtasādhanatā*, which prompts the undertaking of the act.

With regard to the sentences prescribing an action (*vidhivākyas*), e.g. "one who aspires to go to heaven should perform (the) sacrifice," the two sub schools of Mīmāṁsā differ regarding how best to construe their meanings.

The injunctive suffix (i.e., in Sanskrit grammar, the *vidhiliñ*) is the clause "you *should* offer sacrifice" means, on the Bhāṭṭa theory, that the action recommended is a means for the attainment of the desired result (*iṣtasādhanatājñāna*). This knowledge leads the agent to perform the action. But Prabhākara does not consider *iṣtasādhanatā* to be the import of the injunctive suffix. The suffix conveys *kārya*, the task to be done. The *kārya* is the import of the sentence. As a result of this controversy, we have to decide which of the two—the *kārya* and the *iṣtasādhanatā*—is the true import of an injunctive suffix. According to the Prābhākara school, the injunctive words themselves incite the person (who desires to go to heaven) to perform the action being recommended. The important step in this process is the realization that this course of action is a duty to be done.

The first view would seem to be closer to the consequentialist variety of the Western ethical theory, whereas the second view comes close to the deontological theory which privileges the sense of duty over the likely consequences.

V Self, *Karma*, and Liberation

Like the Nyāya-Vaiśeṣika, the Mīmāṁsā regards the self as distinct from the body, the senses, and the mind. They also regard intelligence, will, and effort as natural attributes of the self. The soul is an eternal, infinite substance having the capacity for consciousness, which is not an essential quality, but rather an adventitious quality of the soul, which arises when certain conditions are present. In the dreamless sleep stage the soul does not have consciousness, because such factors as the relation of the sense organ to the object are absent. For the Bhāṭṭas, the soul is both unconscious and conscious. It is unconscious as the substratum of consciousness, however, it is also the object of self-consciousness. For the Prābhākaras, the soul is non-intelligent, substratum of knowledge, pleasure and pain, etc. The self is the agent, the enjoyer, and omnipresent, but not sentient.

The two schools of Mīmāṁsā differ regarding the questions: How is the soul known? According to the Bhāṭṭa school, we know it as the object of the I; it is not known when the object is known. The Prābhākara school, on the other hand, argues that the self is known when an object is known; it is revealed in the very act of knowing as the subject of the knowledge under consideration. Both the Bhāṭṭas and the Prābhākaras subscribe to the doctrine of the multiplicity of souls; there are as many souls as there are individual beings. The soul survives death, so that it is able to reap the consequences of the actions performed.

The Mīmāṁsā emphasizes performance of *dharma* or moral duties to gain moral excellence. *Dharma* is that which is enjoined by the Vedas. They divide *karmas* into (i) obligatory (*nitya*), (ii) optional (*kāmya*), and (iii) prohibited. Obligatory *karmas* must be performed because their violation results in demerit, though their performance does not lead to any merit. Optional *karmas* are those that may or may not be performed; however, their non-performance does not lead to demerit. The performance of prohibited *karmas* leads to demerit. Obligatory *karmas* again are divided into those that are to be performed daily (daily prayer in the morning and in the evening), and those to be performed on special occasions (one should take a bath during eclipse). Optional *karmas* are done with a desire to get fruits; e.g., he who wishes to go to heaven should perform certain sacrifices. Finally, there are also expiatory actions in order to ward off the evil effects of the prohibited *karmas*. An aspirant in search of liberation must go beyond both merit and demerit. Obligatory actions must be performed following the guidance of the Vedas. Actions must be done without any desire for the results of the actions. For Kumārila actions are not an end in themselves; they must be done to realize the final goal by overcoming the past and the future accumulated *karmas*.

The Mīmāṁsakas theory of *śakti* has important implications for their theory of ritualistic actions. Mīmāṁsakas argue that the actions performed in this life, generate unperceived potency (*apūrva*), which remains and bears fruits in the future. Both Kumārila and Prabhākara accept *apūrva*, unperceived potency, as a necessary causal link between the ritualistic actions done and their fruits. Kumārila holds that it is produced in the soul of the sacrificer and it lasts till it begins to bear fruits in the future. Such injunctive statements as "*svargakāmo yajeta*" cannot be satisfactorily explained unless we accept *apūrva* as the connecting link between the ritualistic actions and the heaven. This concept provides an answer to the question how an action, e.g., a ritualistic sacrifice, performed here and now bears fruits later on, say, in the heaven. Prabhākara does not agree that *apūrva* is in the self, because the self on account of its omnipresence is inactive. *Apūrva* resides in the act or the effort that produces it. The act perishes after it is done, but the *apūrva* that resides in the act which the suffix "*liṅ*" or *kārya* in the Vedic injunction conveys—lasts till the production of the fruit. The effort or the exertion produces in the agent a *kārya* or the result, technically called "*niyoga*," which provides the incentive to the agent to act.

It is worth noting that both the Naiyāyikas and the Prābhākaras agree that a word has the power (*śakti*) to arouse experience of its meaning. Their difference is only this much: according to the Prābhākaras, this power belongs to the word, whereas according to the Naiyāyikas, the power belongs to God's desire. Only because of God's desire does a word has the power to mean what it means. The power does not reside in a word. The Prābhākaras recognize that a word itself has the power to mean what it means, when the word's power (*śakti*) is known, it generates the agreement with other meanings. For the Naiyāyikas, the word's *śakti* remains unknown, and yet generates the agreement with other meanings. On the Naiyāyika account, the memory of the *padārtha* is caused by a word, then it generates the knowledge of the meaning of a sentence, a thesis which the Mīmāṁsā does not accept. The deities occupy a secondary place in the Mīmāṁsā system. The primary aim of the Mīmāṁsakas is to persuade people to practice the Vedic injunctions, and not to teach them about God and the deities.

In the early Mīmāṁsā, the attainment of heaven as the state of bliss was the *summum bonum* of life; however, eventually the Mīmāṁsā commentators, like other Indian commentators, replace heaven with liberation (*apavarga*) from bondage. They came to believe that actions done with a desire to get fruits cause repeated births. The disinterested performance of actions, without any desire for the results, exhausts accumulated *karmas*. A person free from *karmas* is not reborn; liberation thus stops rebirths by destroying all the accumulated *karmas*. Past *karmas* should be exhausted without any residue. Obligatory and compulsory acts should be performed, and the non-performance of these acts would create demerit and result in suffering. Liberation is a state free from all kinds of painful experiences; it is a state in which soul returns to its intrinsic nature, freedom from pain and suffering. Kumārila and his followers subscribe to *jñāna karma samuccaya*, i.e., both knowledge and action lead to liberation. Prabhākara advocates actions as supreme and takes knowledge as the means to liberation.

The Mīmāṁsā take the Vedas to be self-revealed; they are not authored by God. The Nyāya and the Vedānta, on the other hand, hold that the Veda's are God's creations. The Mīmāṁsā argues that if the Vedas are taken to be authored by a human being, then the names of the authors would be known to us. The Vedas are handed down to us from the time immemorial in the form in which we find them today. Kumārila holds that the meaning of the words of the Vedic texts is understood in the same way as the words in the popular language. Let us take the famous Upaniṣadic *mahāvākya* "*tat tvam asi*."

The difference in their theory of meaning accounts for the differing interpretations of the terms "*tat*" and "*tvam*" in "*tat tvam asi*." In *anvitābhidhānavāda*, these words would convey the cognitions of their primary meanings—the cognition whose nature is memory. In *abhihitānvaya*, the terms "*tat*" and "*tvam*" convey the cognitions of their primary meanings, similar to memory. Accordingly, sentence-generatedness does not exist in "*tat tvam asi*": the knowledge simply arises from the individual word meanings. In other words, word meanings, not a sentence, cause a verbal cognition. Therefore, the cognition arising from "*tat tvam asi*" is not mediate in nature. The analogue offered for this mode of interpretation of the Upaniṣadic text provides one with the phenomenological clue for understanding the sense of immediacy attached to a cognition arising through language. The analogue "you are the tenth man" gives rise to a cognition that is perceptual in nature. I will discuss some of these issues in the chapter on Vedānta of this work.

Concluding Remarks

It is especially in their conceptions of knowledge, truth, and action that the Mīmāṁsakas left indelible mark on Indian philosophy. Subsequent schools of Indian philosophy further developed the ideas of Mīmāṁsā. *Mīmāṁsā Sūtras* and their commentators initiated a discussion of such issues as the sources of knowledge, relation between knowledge and truth, the intrinsicality or extrinsicality of knowledge, the relation between knowledge, truth and successful practice, and so on. The Indian philosophers of all persuasion struggled with these issues, interpreted and reinterpreted them, and in so doing further refined these ideas. Let me elaborate further.

1. The Mīmāṁsā theory of knowledge influenced other schools of Indian philosophies, and they further developed the initial insights of the Mīmāṁsakas. The Mīmāṁsakas were the first to develop the theory of *svataḥ prāmāṇya* and the Advaitins followed their lead.
2. The Mīmāṁsakas made the important distinction between the *nirvikalpaka* and *savikalpaka* perception, as the two stages in the development of knowledge. In general, Advaita Vedānta accepted the Bhāṭṭa view about knowledge, and thus preserved for later times the Mīmāṁsā view which otherwise would have been relegated to antiquity. This distinction between *nirvikalpaka* and *savikalpaka* perception remained with all Vedic systems, with the exception of the Buddhists who rejected it.
3. The Mīmāṁsakas started a way of understanding moral practices which still continues in the Hindu tradition and found its most famous expression in the *Bhagavad Gītā's* doctrine of *karma yoga*.
4. The Mīmāṁsakas tried to offer one of the first attempts to systematize Vedic interpretation, especially the *karma kāṇda* of the Vedas. It taught how best to interpret the Vedic injunctions regarding sacrificial acts, and raised many interesting philosophical questions about how to interpret them. Quite naturally, they did so without invoking the ideas of gods, deities, and God, which, for the Mīmāṁsakas, remained rather *posits* and not realities. Thus a Vedic sacrificial religion was admitted without invoking the idea of God as the creator of the universe. "God" was a theoretical posit, and nothing more.

Thus, it is not therefore surprising that the Vedāntins regarded Mīmāṁsakas as their close kin. Mīmāṁsā was called *Pūrva* Mīmāṁsā while the Vedānta remained as *Uttara* Mīmāṁsā. Their relationship remained a question to be deeply thought about. Connected with it were the general questions regarding the relation between knowledge and action and, of course, the relation between the earlier and the later parts of the Vedas. The Mīmāṁsā's overall contribution to Indian thought is immeasurable.

8

THE SĀṀKHYA *DARŚANA*

Of all the Indian systems of philosophy, Sāṁkhya is perhaps the most ancient and also most respected in antiquity. Historical antecedents of this school can be traced to the Upaniṣads, especially the *Svetāśvatara* and the *Maitrāyaṇīya*. The influential text of the *Bhagavad Gītā* is overwhelmingly Sāṁkhya. This school has been a major influence on *Ayurveda*, the Hindu medicine. The main developments of this school occurred in the period extending from the first century CE to the eleventh century CE.

Its supposed founder, Kapila, an atheist, is a mythical figure. Tradition maintains that he wrote a brief work entitled *Saṁkhya-sūtras* and another long work bearing the title *Saṁkhya-pravacana-sūtras*. Both of these works are not extant. A much later and the earliest available work, Īśvarakṛṣṇa's *Sāṁkhya-kārikā* (SK) is widely used as a source for this school. Many commentaries have been written on it. Among them, Gauḍapāda's *Saṁkhya-kārikā-bhāṣya*, Vijñānabhikṣu's *Sāṁkhya-pravacana-bhāṣya*, and Vācaspati's *Sāṁkhya-tattva-kaumudī* are most important. These works introduce many innovations; I will briefly review some of these.

The three pillars or the three fundamental concepts of this system are: *prakṛti* or Nature, *puruṣa* or self, and the theory of evolution. In this chapter I will primarily focus on these three.

I *Prakṛti* (Nature, Matter)

The Sāṁkhya school attempts to provide an intelligible account of our experiences in the world. Our everyday experiences consist of the experiencer and the experienced, the subject and the object. The subject and the object, *puruṣa* and *prakṛti*, are distinct; one cannot be reduced to the other. The Sāṁkhya metaphysics is thus based on the bi-polar nature of our daily experiences. We experience a plurality of objects. How do these objects come about? What is the ultimate cause of these objects? Cause is always finer and subtler than the effects. Thus, there must be a cause, some stuff that underlies the entire world of objects. Such a cause is *prakṛti*; it is the first uncaused cause of all objects, gross and subtle.

It is not possible for the senses to perceive *prakṛti* because it is extremely fine and too subtle to be perceived; therefore, it is imperceptible. Its existence can be determined by inference. Five arguments[1] adduced by the Sāṁkhya for its existence run as follows:

1 there must be an unlimited cause of all limited things;
2 there must be a universal or general source of pleasure, pain, and indifference;
3 the primary source of all activity must be a potential cause;
4 the manifested world of effects must have an unmanifested cause; and
5 there must be an unmanifest terminal of the cosmic dissolution.

Sāṁkhya conception of *prakṛti* is based on a theory which holds that changes in the world are not chance occurrences; they are, rather, caused. This theory of causality is known as "*satkāryavāda*" or the theory that the effect (*kārya*) is existent (*sat*) in the cause prior to its production. The question was asked: Is the effect something new or different from its cause? The Sāṁkhya school argues that the effect is nothing new, because what did not exist could not arise and origination is really a *transformation* of the cause. Obviously, "cause" here means the "material cause." Nothing new ever comes into being, only a new form is manifested; the matter remains the same. As yogurt is produced from milk, or oil from the oil-seeds, or jewelry from a lump of gold, a new form is imparted to the pre-existent stuff. No new stuff ever comes into being. This variety of *satkāryavāda*, i.e., the theory that the effect is a real transformation of the cause, is known as *pariṇāmavāda* (literally, "real-transformation-statement").[2]

In support of their theory that the effect is only a manifestation of the cause, Sāṁkhya provide five arguments,[3] which may be summed up as follows:

1 something existent cannot arise from the nonexistent;[4]
2 being invariably connected with it, the effect is only a manifestation of the material cause;
3 there is a determinate order obtaining between a cause and its effect so that everything cannot arise from everything;
4 only that cause can produce an effect of which it is capable, so that the effect must be potentially present in the cause; and
5 because the like is produced from the like.

Let me elaborate further on these five arguments.

The first argument, one of the great axioms of much of Indian thought, may be stated as follows: "What is, is, and what is not, is not." In other words, what is cannot become nothing and what is non-existent can never come into being. The *Gītā* in no uncertain terms declares: "Of the non-existent there is no coming to be; of the existent there is no ceasing to be."[5] Given this axiom, it was imperative that philosophers find a plausible explanation of change leaving aside the common sense view that things come to be and cease to be. Platonists gave one explanation while arguing that the forms, the universals, are eternal and the particulars exemplify the forms that are appearances. Sāṁkhya does not recognize universals as entities, thus the Platonists' solution was not an available option. The Sāṁkhya school argues that the effect pre-exists in the cause; a non-existent entity cannot be made existent by any operation unless it was already present in the cause.

The second argument points to a necessary and an invariable relation between cause and effect; a cause cannot produce an effect with which it has no relation. In other words, a cause cannot enter into a relation with what is not real. Thus, a material cause can only produce an effect with which it is causally related. Therefore, the effect must actually exist in the cause prior to its production.

The next three arguments are close to the Aristotelian notion of potentiality and actuality: certain causes produce certain effects. One can make yogurt only from milk; one can get mustard oil only from mustard seed, not from other grains. This determinate order is due to the fact that that alone which contains yogurt can be the cause of yogurt and that alone which contains oil can be the cause of oil, not just anything can be the cause of anything. The effect is another state of the cause. Causation is a process of making explicit what is already there implicitly. The cloth is contained in the thread, the oil in the mustard seeds.

The thrust of all these arguments is that the effect pre-exists in the material cause, if it were not the case that the effect preexisted in the cause, one could get any effect from any cause, which would deny the relation of causality altogether.

Before proceeding further, let me underscore two points about the above conception of causality: (1) between the two modes of causality, efficient and material, the latter is more fundamental because it is the latter that enters into the cause and produces the effect, and (2) the cause and the effect are the unmanifest/manifest, undeveloped/developed states of the same substance. Given this conception of causality, it is not surprising that Sāṁkhya philosophers argue that all worldly things are produced from an eternal, original stuff, known as *prakṛti*.

The process of evolution that explains the arising of things, I will discuss a little later. For the present it is worthwhile to emphasize that all worldly things include material objects, living beings, minds, and human bodies with their sensory structure, objects of thinking, feeling and willing. Pure consciousness alone is excluded from the list.

There have been since antiquity, two accounts of the original *prakṛti* from which objects of the world arise: one is atomism, the view that the original stuff really consists of infinitely small elements called "*paramāṇus*." The Vaiśeṣika school of Indian philosophy (which will be discussed later) develops this position. The other account held that the original stuff is a homogeneous mass with no internal differentiation, and that the things of the world arise by a process of progressive differentiation, the view that is represented by the Sāṁkhya school.

It is worth noting nonetheless that Sāṁkhya continues to have some traces of the first theory. The equilibrium of *prakṛti*, before the world comes into being, is an equilibrium of elements, but the elements in this system are not material atoms; rather they are the three *guṇas* ("quality," "constituent," "strand"), viz., *sattva*, *rajas*, and *tamas*, which are not qualities because they themselves posses qualities. These three constituents make up the *prakṛti*, which is partless and indivisible. They are called *guṇas* either because they are subservient to the goals of the *puruṣa*, or because they, like the three strands of a rope, bind the *puruṣa*.

Each of these three constituents is conceived atomistically, but none is an atom, each is rather described in terms of the qualities it especially promotes. The first, i.e., the *sattva*, engenders and promotes moral and intellectual qualities of goodness, virtues, and truth-seeking; the second, i.e., the *rajas*, promotes energy, activity, and movement; and the third, i.e., *tamas*, promotes and maintains laziness, inactivity, and sleep. These descriptions bring together a conception of atomistic elements and a qualitative notion of intellectual and ethical attributes (and propensities) and their opportunities in a curious manner. The word "*guṇa*," chosen for these elements of *prakṛti* by its equivocation, serves both purposes in an interesting way.

Irrespective of how one interprets this doctrine, it resists a purely physicalistic interpretation. It has been a standing influence on the Hindu way of looking at the world, even outside of a philosophical theory. All physical and mental phenomena, in fact, all thing in the world, represent these *guṇas* in different proportion. Indeed all human individuals are looked upon by their very nature as being of one of these three kinds. In some, *sattva* predominates; in others, *rajas*; and in still others, *tamas*. Not only the Hindu conception of personality types, but also food (and drink), is classified into three types contingent upon the proportion of the *guṇas*. One cannot determine precisely the proportion of each *guṇa* in the manifested world; nonetheless, the *guṇa* theory provides a powerful explanation of the physical, psychological, and moral aspects of the worldly manifestation. Critics like Śaṃkara[6] have accused this doctrine of confusing between the subjective and the natural, but this confusion misses the very point the Sāṃkhya makes, namely, the distinction between the subjective and the objective is a distinction within *prakṛti*, and *prakṛti* is *not* to be understood purely physicalistically.

One still faces the question how best to interpret this doctrine. One may elect to take it for what it says, i.e., ascribe some sort of qualities to the elements, and, as a consequence, understand *prakṛti* from the perspective of living beings, human bodies, and human intellectual and moral excellences found in varying degrees, so that even when conceived purely naturalistically, the elements of *prakṛti* contain the same *guṇas*, albeit only in low degrees. Or, one may seek a purely naturalistic representation of the three *guṇas*. Following a contemporary thinker, one may understand every element as having *three* properties, in different degrees of blending, of intelligible essence, energy, and mass.[7] Or, one may begin with *experience*—as it is prior to the subject–object distinction—and find in it all three tendencies towards the higher qualities of knowledge and goodness, movement, and rest.[8]

Whether in the original state of equilibrium or in the evolved state of disequilibrium in the world, the attributes or the *guṇas* are *for-another* in the sense that they, by a particular teleology internal to *prakṛti*, exist for the purpose of self, i.e., to serve his purpose. They are—even in the state of equilibrium *with-others*, i.e., when each *guṇa* is with other *guṇas* in a "mixing" in different proportions—struggling to increase itself and dominate over the other two. Each thus is in a state of motion; even the *tamas*, which promotes sleep, stupor and rest, struggles to overpower the other two. Thus, in a narrow sense, movement or energy, the *dynamis*, is generated and promoted by the *rajas*. In a broader sense, the sense in which *prakṛti* is always in motion, each of the three elements, internally as well as in relation to the other two, is constantly changing. Thus, within *prakṛti*, there are two kinds of changes or transformations: of the like to the like and of the like to the unlike. In the state of equilibrium, the former is ever-present, in the state of differentiation, only the latter.

But how does disequilibrium begin leading to the emergence of the world? To understand the system here, we must direct our attention to what was called, at the beginning of this exposition, the second pillar, the doctrine of *puruṣa* or self.

II *Puruṣa* (Self)

If materialism is the thesis that mind is reducible to natural processes, then Sāṁkhya, like all Indian systems, is materialistic. But *prakṛti* is not all of reality. There stands opposed and irreducible to it, consciousness, which limits the system's "naturalism" (which is a better characterization than "materialism"). *Puruṣa* is conscious. Not reducible to *prakṛti*, *puruṣa* stands apart. This brings me to the second axiom of Sāṁkhya: *the Principle of Irreducibility of Consciousness* to what is not conscious, thus, in the long run, to *prakṛti*. *Prakṛti* as well as its evolutes are possible *objects* of knowledge. Consciousness is the *subject* of knowing. All objects are manifested by consciousness, which alone is self-manifesting. Human mind, intellect, willing, and feelings, in fact all possible *objects* with varying degrees of transparency/subtleness are manifested by consciousness.

Among the properties of the *puruṣa*, the Sāṁkhya lists the following: *guṇa*-less, eternal, inactive, eternally free, not involved, i.e., a witness (*sākṣin*),[9] indifferent to pleasure and pain, beyond the three *guṇas*, the seer of all that is seen, and the subject for which all worldly things exist.

Sāṁkhya adduces five proofs[10] for the existence of *puruṣa*:

1 All composite things exist to serve the purpose of a being, and that being is *puruṣa*;

2 All objects of knowledge are composed of the three *guṇas*, which implies that there is a subject which is not an object of experience, that is *puruṣa*;
3 The experiences need to be co-ordinated; the consciousness that co-ordinates is *puruṣa*;
4 *Prakṛti* being non-intelligent cannot experience its evolutes; there must be an intelligent experiencer and that is *puruṣa*; and
5 There is the striving for release, which implies the existence of *puruṣa* that strives for and obtains release.

The points that SK is trying to make are as follows: Wherever there is an arrangement of parts, the arrangement is meant for someone else. *Prakṛti* is a composite of the three *guṇas*, so it must therefore be for the sake of, for the purpose of, something other than *prakṛti*. This other is *puruṣa*. *Puruṣa* in itself is not a composite of *guṇas*. The *guṇas* belong to *prakṛti*. Furthermore, *prakṛti* cannot manifest itself. *Puruṣa* is the principle of manifestation, self-manifesting as well as manifesting the other. It transcends time and space, a pure subject that can never become an object.

To sum up: the contrast between *puruṣa* and *prakṛti* is as follows: *Prakṛti* is the object, thus it is composite; *puruṣa* is the subject, the self. *Prakṛti* is enjoyed; *puruṣa* enjoys and suffers. *Prakṛti* is constituted of the three *guṇas*; *puruṣa* is beyond these *guṇas*; *puruṣa* is intelligent and strives after a freedom which it does not have; *prakṛti* is subject to the interplay of the three *guṇas*.

There are, however, on the Saṁkhya view, many *puruṣas*. Manyness of *puruṣas* is asserted on the following grounds:

1 because of the diversity of births, deaths, and faculties;
2 because of actions or functions at different times; and
3 because of differences in the proportions of the three *guṇas*.

Thus, the manyness of *puruṣas*—as opposed to the Vedāntic thesis that the Self in one—is established on the ground that birth and death, bondage and liberation, vary from person to person and occur at different times. Additionally, behavior of different persons also vary, and if there were only one self, these variations could not be accounted for. Each body is associated with a self.

Thus the Sāṁkhya advocates a dualism between *prakṛti* and (many) *purusas*, a dualism that is unlike the Cartesian dualism between matter and mind. In Sāṁkhya dualism *prakṛti* is ever there; *puruṣa* is always a witness of *prakṛti*. In Cartesian dualism on the other hand *res cogitans* (*puruṣa*) and *res extensa* are completely separate and it is only when *res cogitans* and *res extensa* meet that they come to know each other.

Pure, undifferentiated *prakṛti* evolves into the experienced world. Evolution, however, depends upon some relation between the two principles. But these two, *prakṛti* and *puruṣa*, are diametrically opposed to each other, so their being together is not intelligible. Additionally, their being together is not enough, because they are always together. Therefore, a relation closer than "being together" is needed in order for the *prakṛti* to evolve, for its equilibrium to stir, for its original homogeneity to start breaking up. But how can two things, so different, conjoin? Sāṁkhya literature calls it "*saṁyoga*," which means "conjunction." But conjunction holds good between two material substances, e.g., a book and my desk. How can there be a contact between a partless *puruṣa* and (original) *prakṛti* that has no internal differentiation?

The Sāṁkhya replies to this question using various metaphors. *Prakṛti* and *puruṣa* enter into a relationship "like the relationship between a lame man and a blind man" (in a well-known story). The *puruṣa* can see but cannot act (it knows, but has no agency); *prakṛti* can act but does not know (where to go and which path). When together, *puruṣa* knows the way towards the goal it aims at, *prakṛti* walks along the path shown. In the story, the lame man climbs on the shoulder of the blind man, and the two together follow the path to reach the goal.

But what is this goal? The SK states that the *puruṣa* has to accomplish two goals: "In order to see and in order to reach the state of alone-ness."[11] The *puruṣa* has the ability to see, but prior to the emergence of the world and its infinite concrete objects, *puruṣa* has nothing to see. The *puruṣa* needs to be a concrete subjectivity. Through this process of increasing concretization, the *puruṣa* aims at attaining the final liberation which is described in this system as "aloneness" or *kaivalya*. The goal is only of *puruṣa*; it alone can entertain a goal and determine the path appropriate for this goal, but *prakṛti*, being active, can be led along this path, and towards the goal. When the goal is reached, i.e., when *puruṣa* becomes free, their provisional co-operation ends, *puruṣa* is free i.e., alone, and *prakṛti* returns, or rather relapses, into its original state of pure undifferentiated homogeneity.

All along the way, nothing happens to the *puruṣa*. As *prakṛti* becomes differentiated, the world with its objects is created (note that Sāṁkhya works use the word "*sarga*,"[12] meaning creation although there is no creator), the *puruṣa* gets attached and tied to the world, there is a *mistaken appearance* of the *puruṣa* as being-in-the-world. Upon seeing this world, the *puruṣa* becomes free, so writes Gauḍapāda in his commentary on this *Kārikā*. But here "seeing" is to be understood as "experiencing." The same commentator adds an explanation, again a metaphor to elucidate the prior metaphor: just as from the union of a man and a woman a child is born, so from the union of *puruṣa* and *prakṛti* arises creation, and, I should add, through the world so created, liberation.

But is not the *puruṣa* eternally free, as we were earlier told? And if this is so, why should it now be striving for liberation? We will return to this question at the end of this chapter.

III Process of Evolution (or Creation)

In the title of this section, we have used both the terms "evolution" and "creation," which, in the Western popular discourse, are often set against each another. "Creation" is used when there is intelligence behind the world (i.e., an intelligent creator) and "evolution" when the process is mechanical or chance-regulated. To be fair, the word "evolution" captures only one aspect of what happens, and "creation" the other. There is, as stated earlier, no creation out of nothing, and "for the sake of an intelligent other" there is a teleology, and, in that sense, all creation is geared towards a goal. But there is no intelligent creator.[13] To the question, how a non-intelligent *prakṛti* could serve the purpose of intelligent beings, it is replied: "Just as non-intelligent milk acts for the nourishment of the calf, so does *prakṛti* to serve the ultimate purpose of the *puruṣa*."

The order in which the world emerges from undifferentiated *prakṛti* is as follows:

Mahat (The Great One) or *buddhi* → *ahaṁkāra* (ego-sense) → the five subtle elements (*tanmātras*) → 11 sense organs → five gross elements

Together with the original *prakṛti* and *puruṣa*, there are twenty-five principles (*tattvas*) or philosophical truths. Knowing these twenty-five *tattvas* (in their precise nature) is to gain wisdom that brings about liberation, at least that is what Sāṁkhya promises. These *tattvas* are not to be regarded as empirical facts, but each, a category, comprehends empirical facts. For a clear understanding of the Sāṁkhya theory of evolution, it is essential to understand not only the distinct function of these *tattvas*, but also to clearly grasp the order of appearance in the process of evolution.[14]

Let us briefly review these principles and their distinct functions. The first evolute is sometimes called "*buddhi*" or intelligence or intellect. In its psychological aspect, the *buddhi* is intellect, and its special functions are ascertainment and decision. *Buddhi*, as the discriminative faculty, makes it possible to discriminate between itself and the *puruṣa*, and makes liberation possible.[15] In its cosmic aspect, *buddhi* is intelligence, the origin of the manifest world. The idea echoes many statements of the Vedas and the Upaniṣads to the effect that first to appear from the *brahman* is the "Great One" (usually called the *Virāt*),[16] which is not to be construed as God. The point seems to be that the universal intelligence, the Great One, has to be differentiated into many centers of intelligence, each with its own ego (*ahaṁkāra*). The second evolute stands for the "I" the ego. Then we have many egos. It is on account of the feeling of the "I," and the "mine" that the self takes itself to be an agent and as having desires and as striving to achieve certain ends.

The constitution of the body follows next. It consists of *manas*, five sense organs, and five action organs, the five elements (known as the subtle elements) and then, of course, five gross elements. The mind synthesizes the sense data and transforms them into determinate perceptions. In short, evolution is a play of twenty-five principles including *puruṣa*, in which *prakṛti* is number one, and five gross elements the last.

The precise interpretation of this chain of creation is a matter of great interest for the Indian philosophers. Let me provide an explanation that I find appealing.

When the Sāṁkhya speaks of the "world," it understands by the word "the totality of human experience." Experience (*bhoga*) includes enjoyment, as well as its opposite, i.e., suffering. The Sāṁkhya in its theory of evolution gives an account of how pure consciousness, *puruṣa*, becomes the enjoyer-sufferer. The question arises: How does pure consciousness become an empirical ego, an enjoyer-sufferer as well as an empirical cognizer and agent?

First, a richly differentiated world of objects with varying proportion of the *guṇas* is required, which is possible only if there are gross elements or atoms. Gross elements are concretizations of pure sensory data, color, touch, sound, etc., the correlates of the five sense organs of knowledge and five sense organs of action. We thereby have all the *contents* needed for empirical ego's consciousness. These are unified in an "I"-sense. But the different "I"-senses are particularizations of the universal intelligence or *mahat.* This story retraces the chain from the evolved to their antecedent conditions. The Sāṁkhya account given above inverts this sequence as the order of creation and answers an old question, asked in the Upaniṣads: How does the one become many? The answer is by progressive differentiation and concretization.

It is worth noting that, as stated earlier, consciousness itself never arises from *prakṛti*. Both are original principles. As *prakṛti* becomes more and more differentiated, "consciousness" gets *reflected* in the constituted chain. The ego becomes "ego-consciousness," which is not an additional process, but occurs because of the "proximity" of the two. Thus, there is a certain phenomenality in this differentiation of consciousness as ego-consciousness, sensory-consciousness, body-consciousness, etc. Pure *puruṣa* appears to be an empirical person. He enjoys the world and experiences both pleasure and pain, which "entangle" him.

The bound self—now a-being-in-the-world, for whom the world is inextricably involved in enjoyment/suffering structure—is brought under the concept of "*dukkha*" or pain. He then wants to be free from this pain. "Pain" arises from the preponderance of *rajas*, the active energy, which is always left unsatisfied. Cessation of pain comes about through the knowledge of the true nature of the *puruṣa*, and requires an excess and predominance of *sattva* over *rajas* and *tamas.* A long and arduous process culminates in the self's clear and distinct knowledge of its own pure nature as distinguished from all "natural" or mundane elements with which he had so long identified himself. This Self is then "alone"; he is not in-the-world and also not with-others, which explains why liberation is described as *kaivalya.* All enjoyment and suffering ceases along with its content, i.e., the world. In Sāṁkhya terminology, the manifest world returns to its original home, namely, the undifferentiated *prakṛti.*

Undoubtedly there would be innumerable questions about this account. I will here mention and respond to some of them.

First to be noted is that the *puruṣa* as free is said to be lonely; he is by himself. There is no intersubjectivity, no being-with-other egos. Intersubjectivity is empirical. Pure subjectivity is "aloneness." Second, this tying of the experienced world to the *puruṣa* seems to make the world subjective-relative, as though each person, each ego, has his own world. With his liberation, his world would cease to be. What about the other subjects and egos? They would still be "bound" and so each "in his world?" This asymmetrical distribution of liberation and bondage is one of the premises from which the manyness of *puruṣas*—a cornerstone of the system—was in the first place inferred.

In response it may be noted that it is indeed true that Sāṁkhya writers did recognize *jagad-vaicitrya*, many different worlds, each a correlate of one *puruṣa*, but did not quite realize that they have to account for the possibility of one world being "constructed" out of these. Notice that the original unmanifested *prakṛti* is common to all selves, and remains, even after the liberation of one, where and how it was. It is the manifest *prakṛti* which dissolves. But how does *prakṛti* cease to undergo manifestation, if one self attains liberation?

The Sāṁkhya, in reply, uses another metaphor: Just as a dancer dances for the entertainment of the spectator(s) and, when the spectator is satisfied, etc., ceases to dance, the same is true here. *Prakṛti* "shows her manifest forms" until the seer no longer has the desire to see.[17]

To be noticed is the way Sāṁkhya uses metaphors: We have had three of them along the way, the metaphor of the lame man and the blind, the sexual "coupling" of a man and a woman producing a child, and finally, the spectator and the dancer.

Can metaphors be substitutes for philosophical argumentation? Can we say, in defense of the Sāṁkhya, that philosophical arguments may be either logical-analytical or poetic-metaphorical? The Sāṁkhya no doubt uses standard Indian logic's inferences to prove the existence of *prakṛti* and the manyness of *puruṣas*. But when it comes to speak of and make sense of the ultimate relationships (which are yet no relations), metaphors are needed *to illuminate* rather than to convince the skeptics. They show *the possibility* of such a relation, not a logical possibility, but an intelligible possibility. Besides, metaphors are so deeply embedded in the deep structure of language and thinking, and if Martin Heidegger is right in saying that original thinking is poetic, then through its metaphors, Sāṁkhya is expressing its thinking as intelligible, if not as actual. We have a rhetoric, which has not yet become logic, which is not to suggest that the Sāṁkhya did not have a theory of knowledge, which I will discuss next.

IV Sāṁkhya Epistemology

The Sāṁkhya did fall in line with the rest of the Indian systems and developed its own *theory of knowledge* with a logic or a theory of inferential knowledge subordinated to it. Knowledge of *objects* is obtained in the context of a relational structure found in the world; however, without some special relation to the *puruṣa*, the *puruṣa* would not be a knower and have the mode of awareness "I know." The faculty of *buddhi* makes this mode of awareness possible. It is transcendent and shining because of the preponderance of the *sattva guṇa* and creates the impression as if it were the *puruṣa*. Thus *puruṣa* is reflected in it, a reflection which is falsely taken to be an experience of the self assuming the form "I know." The commentator Vijñānabhikṣu, with his Vedāntic bias, takes this reflection to be the result of a superimposition of the *buddhi*-state on the *puruṣa*, a false ascription. The *puruṣa* now takes the *buddhi*-state, a mundane transformation, to be its own. This "taking it to be" is not a real content, but an appearing to be, which, according to some scholars, is "somewhat mythical."[18]

The close connection between the cognitive process and the *buddhi* as its instrument, because of its excess of the *sattva guṇa*, is a doctrine which is also found in Yoga and Vedānta. It is even found in Buddhism, which, uses the term "*citta*" for it. The influence of Sāṁkhya on these systems with regard to the cognitive process is indelible. In the *ānvīkṣikī* or logical-analytical systems, *buddhi* is deprived of this special role (because the word "*buddhi*" is used synonymously with "knowledge," and "experience," "*manas*" and the sense-organs are taken to be its instruments). Notice that I have not translated *buddhi* into English: If I were to do so its nearest approximation would be "intellect," but even that does not capture the entire connotation of *buddhi.*

There are three kinds of valid knowledge: perception, inference, and *śabda.*[19] The objects are determined, "measured," by the *pramāṇas* (which are like "measures"), in the same way as, in a measuring balance, things are measured. We will have other occasions to comment on the three cognate words, "*pramāṇa*," "*pramā*" and "*prameya*."[20] For the present, I will provide a quick explanation of the three *pramāṇas*, viz., perception, inference, and testimony, in Sāṁkhya.[21]

Perception is through the sense organs, each having its own specific object. Perception is the direct cognition of an object, when any sense comes in contact with it. The SK defines perceptions as "determination by judgment (*adhyavasāya*) of each object through its appropriate sense organs."[22] The definition suggests that perception does not merely receive a sensory datum, but also involves an interpretation, a judgment, founded upon such a datum. When an object, say, a chair, comes in contact with the eyes, it is synthesized by the mind. *Buddhi* then becomes modified in the shape of the chair. *Buddhi*, being an unconscious material principle cannot by itself know the chair; however, on account of the preponderance of the *sattva guṇa*, the consciousness of the *puruṣa* is reflected in it. With this reflection, the *buddhi's* unconscious modification becomes illumined as the perception of the object, in this case, a chair.

Inference or *anumāna* is the process by which what is not being perceived is determined. SK states: Inference, that follows the knowledge of a mark (the middle term) and that bears the mark (the major and the minor terms) is of three kinds.[23]

Inference is first divided into two kinds: inferences based on universal propositions (*vita*) and inferences not so based (*avīta*). The first one is again subdivided into *pūrvavat* and *sāmānyatodṛṣṭa.*

In the first case, i.e., *pūrvavat*, i.e., "like what has been before," one infers on the basis of past experience (hence this name), on the observed uniformity of concomitance between two things, e.g., one sees dark cloud and infers rain that is to follow. Let me give an example to explain the second, i.e., *sāmānyatodṛṣṭa*. The question is raised: how do we know that we have sense organs? It would not make sense to say that perception testifies to the existence of sense organs, because we perceive objects via sense organs. The Sāṁkhya argues that the existence of sense organs is proved by an inference assuming the following form:

All actions require some means or instrument.

The perception of color, etc., is an action.

Therefore there must be some means of perception. Here we infer the existence of sense organs on the basis of the acts of perception, not because we have observed the sense organs and the means to be invariably connected. The third inference *śeṣavat* proves something to be true by eliminating all other available alternatives; for example, when one infers that sound must be a quality because it cannot be either a substance, or an action, or a relation or anything else. The Sāṁkhya school subscribes to the five-membered inference of Nyāya, which I will discuss in the chapter on Nyāya.

The Sāṁkhya uses these inferences to prove the existence of the unmanifest *prakṛti* from manifest nature as well as the existence of *puruṣa*, and the manyness of *puruṣas*.

What is neither perceived nor inferred. (i.e., nor capable of determination by either) is known by the "words of a competent authority" by which is primarily meant the infallible words of the sages and the *śruti*. The extremely supersensible objects such as "after-life," "*karma*," and "*dharma*," are established by *śabda* alone, i.e., by words of the competent. The precise nature of *śabda pramāṇa* will be discussed later on.[24]

Things may not be perceived owing to various reasons: extreme distance (Caitra and Maitra, two persons are not perceived being at distant places now), extreme nearness (the eye may not see owing to extreme reasons), non-reception of sensations by sense organs (e.g., a blind person does not see since his visual sense organ does not receive visual sensations), subtleness (smoke and vapor are not seen owing to subtleness), lack of attention (attending to one thing exclusively, one does not see things nearby owing to inattention; attending to one thing exclusively, one does not pay attention to nearby things), being overpowered (stars in the sky are not seen during the days, being overwhelmed by sun-rays), aggregate of homogeneous things (one grain of rice is not discriminated after it is thrown into a heap of rice).[25]

Among these grounds, extreme subtlety is responsible for our not perceiving *prakṛti* and *puruṣa*. Atoms are not perceived because of extreme subtlety (fineness), and are inferred as causes from their effects. Similarly, original unmanifest *prakṛti* is inferred from such experienced entities as *buddhi* and ego-sense as their cause on the bases of similarity and difference. The effect must be like the cause in some respects but different in other respects (like the children are like their parents but unlike as well), i.e., on the basis of the fact that they are both *virūpa* and *sarūpa*.[26] Further inferences are used to prove that these effects must have been previously existent in the cause.

Concluding Remarks

The Sāṁkhya is a grand intellectual accomplishment by way of incorporating all aspects of human experience, in their variety as well as in their commonalities within one conceptual framework. It exhibits an overpowering tendency to take recourse to a monism, with materialism at the one end and monistic idealism on the other. The Sāṁkhya skillfully avoids these extremes, ending up with a dualism, not a provisional dualism, but a final, further irreducible dualism. Such a dualism, the *Gītā* incorporates into its monistic framework, albeit a provisional dualism to be ultimately overcome. In Sāṁkhya this dualism between Nature and Spirit continues even in the state of *mokṣa* when the world dissolves, experience ceases to be, *prakṛti* returns to its quiescent state, and *puruṣa* remains what it was originally.

In order to render their dualism intelligible, Sāṁkhya needed some kind of relationship—other than the simple difference between *prakṛti* and *puruṣa*. Accordingly, Sāṁkhya modifies this total otherness somewhat, and informs us that *prakṛti* is for the sake of *puruṣa*. This concession—namely, that *prakṛti*, despite its total difference from *puruṣa*, exists *for the sake of puruṣa*, for satisfying the goals *of puruṣa*, that *puruṣa* by "seeing" *prakṛti* comes to its own satisfaction and *prakṛti* returns to quiescent state—open up a Pandora's box. If *prakṛti* is totally other than the *puruṣa*, how can it yet be for the sake *of puruṣa*? Does not this "being for" militate against the autonomy of *prakṛti*? The idealists use this separation to make the case that the Sāṁkhya is only a stepping stone for Vedānta; thus, in the long run, *prakṛti* is only a "posit" *of puruṣa*, that the *puruṣa* sets up its own opposite, its own other, in order to achieve a goal. But, even for the Vedānta, what could be this goal? For both Sāṁkhya and Vedānta, it is *freedom*, no doubt; however, how could freedom serve as a goal if the *puruṣa* is eternally free? One answer, which the Sāṁkhya offers, is that in order to *strive after* freedom, *puruṣa* must get involved with *prakṛti*, that is to say, it must be "bound" and in chains. So we have a strange circularity: *puruṣa* gests imprisoned in order to become free, though it is eternally free (*nitya mūkta*). From this charge of circularity neither Sāṁkhya nor Idealism have any escape save by subscribing to the theory that *really* there is no creation, no imprisonment, no chain, no escape from it, excepting in the sense of removing an illusion. The realism of the Sāṁkhya, however, rebels against such a position. We must concede that Sāṁkhya realism is slightly softened by *prakṛti*'s being for *puruṣa*, though never abandoned.

How does all this hang together? Clearly by admitting a sort of "unconscious teleology," "a purposiveness but no purpose," a purposiveness built into *prakṛti* and manifested in its *ordered* development, the sequence being "naturally" geared towards that purpose. Notice that this is *the only system in Indian thought that has a teleology built into it*.

This teleology combined with the autonomy of *prakṛti* also saves the Sāṁkhya school from a gross naturalism or materialism; *prakṛti*, though unconscious (*jaḍa*), is not matter. It is *acit*, but consists not of atoms whirling about, but of the so-called "*guṇas*." Qualitatively, the *guṇas* are simple, their number "three" represents and is explained by the three groups of moral qualities which *puruṣa* may develop. According to one etymology, the "*guṇas*" are so-called because they *bind* the *puruṣa* or serve that purpose and also serve (in the case of "*sattva*") the purposes of both bondage and freedom. This is another consequence of the purposiveness without purpose. The constituents of *prakṛti* are intrinsically understood in relation to *puruṣa*.

Critics have taken the Sāṁkhya to task for their conception of the *guṇas*. Śaṃkara, for example, argues that the qualities represented can belong to a spirit, not to unconscious *prakṛti*, as Sāṁkhya ascribes them to it. The Sāṁkhya cryptic admission of "being for the other," of *prakṛti's* "being-for-the *puruṣa*" provides an explanation of the *guṇas* as moral qualities. The *guṇas*, as constituents of *prakṛti*, are *prone to* accentuate certain qualities in spirit; they stimulate appropriate dispositions. In other words, "*prakṛti*" is not to be understood naturalistically.

Finally, the state of liberation as "alone-ness," implies a total negation of inter-subjectivity which is not a very attractive goal no doubt, yet it is the original ontological state of the *puruṣa*. But how can it be so because *puruṣa* originally is not one but many? Manyness (of *puruṣas*) implies that they are mutually different, and this difference seems to be built into the domain of *puruṣa*. Is the *puruṣa's* oneness consistent with its manyness? Besides the sort of logic the Advaita Vedāntin employs to the effect that difference must be false, a mere appearance, infected with self-contradiction, mandates that the Sāṁkhya also explain how to distinguish the *puruṣa* from *prakṛti*. In Sāṁkhya any distinguishing feature of one person from another becomes a product of *prakṛti* and so an empirical feature deriving from the body-mind complex. When *puruṣa* is considered by itself in its purity, whence its differentiating feature? The Sāṁkhya arguments for manyness are double-edged. The determinate order of bondage and liberation, for example, the order, namely, that my bondage persists even when you are liberated, is tentatively persuasive. But recall that bondage and liberation are conditions of the empirical person not of the pure *puruṣa*. Yet the Sāṁkhya intuition that there is a manyness of the *puruṣa*s is undeniable, and the difficulty reappears from the other side as well: a monist has to explain how does even the phenomenon of manyness, of distinct spirits appear at all?

I concede the Sāṁkhya its fundamental intuitions. The system is a daring attempt to accommodate them skillfully no doubt but how successfully? I will let my students answer this question.

9

THE YOGA *DARŚANA*

Anybody mildly familiar with the Indian culture is well aware that the practice of *yoga* is an integral part of it. There had been a very ancient tradition of the practice of *yoga* in India, as is evidenced by the *Ṛg Veda* and some of the early Upaniṣads, the epic *Mahābhārata*, Cāṇakya's *Arthaśāstra*, and the early Buddhist writings. It is an important component of the spiritual practice of Indian ascetics of all brands and most schools of Indian philosophy recognize the importance of practicing *yoga* in some form or the other. *Yoga*, as a philosophical system, as a *darśana* along with other Indian *darśanas*, however, goes back to Patañjali's *Yoga Sūtras*. It is difficult to ascertain precisely when *Yoga* became a school of Indian philosophy, however, there is no doubt that Patañjali's *Yoga Sūtras* is the first systematic work on the *Yoga darśana*. Vyāsa's commentary on *Yoga Sūtras* entitled *Yogabhāṣya*, and Vijñānabhiksu's *Yoga Vārtika* and *Yogasāra Saṅgraha* are also very useful sources of *Yoga* school.

It has become common to couple Sāṁkhya and Yoga together. Sāṁkhya explicitly accepts *yoga* as the practical means to the realization of *mokṣa*, and Yoga subscribes to the theoretical framework of the Sāṁkhya school. Patañjali[1] is regarded as having been a brilliant compiler of the fundamental ideas of *yoga* and in that compilation exhibited his undeniable philosophical and systematic thinking. Today when works on *yoga* abound in all Western languages, it is worthwhile to look into the *Yoga Sūtras*, which is the classic text on the theme of the *yoga* and has stood the test of time. For all practical purposes, the *Yoga Sūtras* accepts the metaphysics of Sāṁkhya, has no theoretical need for God; it, however, adds the steps, parts, requirements of the discipline to enable the aspirant to progressively achieve the goal of *mokṣa*. The study of *yoga* is an important means to get to know a major component of Indian life and culture.

Etymologically the word "*yoga*" is derived from the root "*yuj*," meaning "to connect" or "to unite" two things, yoking the higher self with the lower self. Though the overall metaphysical and epistemological theses of the Indian *darśanas* vary considerably, the underlying idea—that the senses, passions, desires, etc. lead individual beings astray and the practice of *yoga* is the best way for self-purification by calming the senses—remains the same. As long as a person's mind and body are impure and restless, one cannot really comprehend spiritual matters. The *yoga* lays down a practical path for self-realization, i.e., the realization of the self as pure consciousness.

I Yoga Psychology

In the Sāṁkhya-Yoga school, the *jīva* or the individual self is of the nature of consciousness (*cit*), and is free from the limitations of the body, the senses, and the modifications of the mind. Knowledge, we must remember, is a product of *prakṛti* or nature, and is only falsely ascribed to the self or *puruṣa*. *Puruṣa*—the word *Yoga Sūtras* more often use for the self—by mistake regards itself to be the knower. All cognitive functions and the resulting cognitive products belong to *citta*, which is a product of *prakṛti*. The goal of the practice of *yoga* is to empty the thought process of phenomenality in order to gain knowledge of the true self, by distinguishing it from *prakṛti*.

Patañjali defines "*yoga*" as "*cittavṛttinirodha*,"[2] which means "the cessation of the modifications of the *citta*." So, before proceeding further, let us ascertain what is meant by "*citta*." In the Buddhist literature, "*citta*" is usually translated as "mind." On the Yoga view however, the *citta* is a comprehensive designation that includes among other things the *manas* or the mind, the "*ahaṁkara*" or "inner agency," and "*buddhi*" or "intellect," which assist the self to acquire the knowledge of the world. "*Manas*" in the narrow sense, receives and organizes sensations; "*ahaṁkāra*" is the source of self-awareness, self-identity, and self-conceit, and relates the sensory object to the ego; "*buddhi*," produces knowledge of the object, and makes judgments and discrimination possible. The *manas*, the *ahaṁkāra*, and the *buddhi*, have the three *guṇas*[3]—*sattva*, *rajas*, and *tamas*—in different proportions. The knowledge that brings about liberation puts an end to the incessant modifications of the mind (*cittavṛttis*).

In ordinary parlance, a *cittavṛtti* is a mental state or a modification of the mind which is in a constant process of change or flow. If *citta* is taken to be an ocean, then the *cittavṛttis* are its waves. In Western philosophical vocabulary, we can say that the *citta* is constantly outward-directed; its intentionality is in a process of change, which is the cause of suffering or *dukkha*. Patañjali defines *yoga* as a cessation of the changing intentionality of *citta*. When this is achieved, the self returns to its true nature as pure consciousness, and all suffering is eliminated.

Patañjali, after defining "*yoga*," goes on to distinguish between five kinds of mental modifications or *cittavṛttis* and five *kleśas* or defects. I will begin with the five *cittavṛttis*, which are: *pramāṇa* (right cognition), *viparyaya* (wrong cognition or error), *vikalpa* (imagination), *nidrā* (sleep), and *smṛti* (memory). Let me quickly explain each of these.[4]

The *pramāṇas* are ways of arriving at right knowledge. The Yoga school, like Sāṁkhya, accepts three *pramāṇas*: sense perception, inference, and verbal testimony.[5] In an external perception, there is a contact between the senses and the object, and the mind is transformed into the shape of the object. The *citta*—being extremely clear on account of the preponderance of the *sattva guṇa*

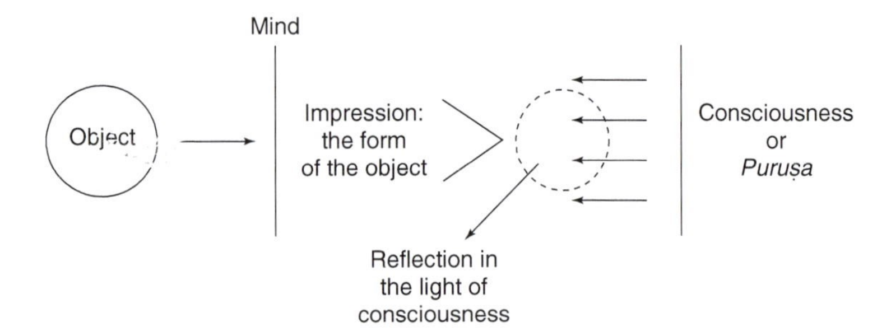

Figure 9.1

and being closest to the *puruṣa*—catches the reflection of the *puruṣa* and becomes conscious so to speak. Thus in every case of perceptual knowledge, I not only know the object but I also know that I know the object. For example, I know, upon perceiving a cow, that "this is a cow," and I also know that I know that this is a cow. In sense perceptions, we also apprehend the generic as well as the specific characters of an external object through the sense organs. Sense perception is a *vṛtti* which apprehends the specific and the generic nature of an external object through the channels of the five senses.

In inference, the object is not directly perceived, but its existence is mediately known through perception of another object with which it has the relation of universal co-presence. By inference one knows the generic nature of objects.

Verbal testimony is the way one comes to know an object (which one does not himself perceive or infer) on the basis of verbal reports of a trustworthy speaker who has known the object. The speaker must be free from defects, such as illusion, deceit, laziness, etc., and must also be compassionate. It is also the source of our knowledge of the super-sensuous entities. The most important kind of such knowledge is that which we derive from the "heard texts" *(śrutis)*.

Of these three means of right knowledge, perception is taken to be the most important by the Yoga system. The *Yoga Sūtras* does not appeal to any *śruti*, but rather to the direct experiences of the *yogin*, i.e., of the person who has achieved the goal of practicing *yoga*. This shows the empiricistic trend of the school. It is not surprising that some *yoga* commentaries recognize different kinds of perception, including *yogic* perception.

The second kind of *vṛtti* is "false knowledge" (*viparyaya*). It consists in taking something to be what it is not.[6] Taking a rope to be a snake is an example of false knowledge. It includes doubt as well as uncertain knowledge.

Three additional *vṛttis*, imagination or *vikalpa*, sleep or *nidrā*, and memory or *smṛti*, are unique to Yoga insofar as they are not generally recognized as *vṛttis* in other systems of Indian philosophy. Imagination or *vikalpa* is a verbal idea caused by words corresponding to which there is no object in reality. In the words of K. C. Bhattacharya, it is "the consciousness of a content that is not real, but is still verbally meant."[7] Thus, when one thinks of a "hare's horn" or of "a barren woman's son," there is a meant content, which though unreal, is presented to understanding. In Yoga philosophy, many such *vikalpas* or imaginative entities are recognized. For example, when one says "Rahu's head," it creates the impression that there is a distinction between Rahu and his head, whereas the fact of the matter is that Rahu is only a head. Similarly when it is said that "consciousness belongs to *puruṣa*," it implies that there are two separate entities consciousness and *puruṣa*, but in reality consciousness and *puruṣa* are identical.

In *nidrā*,[8] there is preponderance of the *tamas guṇa*, and the resulting cessation of waking and dream experiences. It stands for the absence of any cognition; however, it is a *vṛtti* because after waking up a person says "I slept soundly and did not know anything." Thus, "sleep" in this context refers to the deep sleep stage. The Yoga is unique in regarding sleep to be a *vṛtti* and comes close to Advaita Vedānta in this regard. Both agree that in sleep, even in deep sleep, there is consciousness that is recollected upon waking up.

The last kind of *vṛtti* is memory, which is defined as "holding on" or "not slipping away" or "retention" of the objects of the other four *vṛttis*.[9] K. C. Bhattacharya takes thinking (*cintā*) to be the second level of memory (i.e., memory of memory) and contemplation or *dhyāna* (which is a series of memories) to be the third level.[10] *Samādhi*, at which one arrives as a result of cessation of *vṛttis* is no longer a memory, but an intuition of the object. For Yoga, as we will see shortly, *samādhi* is of various grades.

The *puruṣa*, though eternally free, when reflected in the *citta* becomes a *jīva*, an ego, goes through pleasurable and painful experiences, takes himself to be an agent, enjoyer, etc., and subjects himself to various kinds of afflictions, which are either harmful or opposed to the practice of *yoga* or not so opposed.[11] The *vṛttis* that are opposed to the practice of *yoga* are really made so by five kinds of defects (*kleśas*): ignorance, ego, desire, aversion, and clinging to life.[12] If some *vṛttis* are free from these five defects, then these *vṛttis* must belong to the person who has achieved freedom in bodily existence and so has his *citta* functioning without the usual accompanying defects. Of all the five defects, ignorance or *avidyā* is the root cause of all.[13] Ignorance results in taking the self that is external, pure, blissful, to be the non-self, which is non-eternal, painful, unclean, and impure.[14] Non-self here includes body, mind, all material possessions, which an ignorant person takes to be one's self.

Egoism (*asmitā*) is consciousness of the seeming identity of the self and the *buddhi*, i.e., of the seer and the instrument of seeing. It is taking the *buddhi* or intelligence as the true self.[15] In reality, the self is unchanging while intelligence is always changing.

Rāga or attachment arises, holds Patañjali, from experience of happiness, i.e., from the memory of past experiences of happiness.[16] This memory gives rise to the desire to relive that experience. In the same way, aversion arises from experience of pain.[17]

Clinging to life is a fear of death that is common to all living beings, and is found not alone in the ignorant but, also in the wise individuals. This fear is due to the experience of death in a previous life and, for Yoga, it is a proof of the existence of a previous life. The desire has the form "let me be."

When these five detriments are "burnt," the *citta* is dissolved into its original *prakrti*. But the *vṛttis* of the *citta*, the cognitive modifications can be gotten rid of by meditation. As long as the detriments remain, there are cognitive modifications and there is suffering. Existence therefore is characterized by suffering, and the aim of *yoga* is to get rid of suffering. *Yoga Sūtra's* closeness to Buddhism is nowhere clearer than on this point.

II Yoga Ethics

The Five Levels of Citta

It should be obvious to my readers that the aim of *yoga* is to prevent the self from identifying itself with mental modifications by arresting or suppressing all modifications of the *citta*. The *citta* is constituted of three *guṇas*, i.e., *sattva, rajas,* and *tamas* in different proportions, which determine the different levels or conditions of *citta*. There are five levels of *citta* (*cittabhūmi*). These are: *kṣipta* or constantly moving, *mudha* being fixed on one object and without the freedom to move on to another, *vikṣipta* or distracted, *ekāgra* or one-pointed, and *niruddha* or restrained. In the *buddhi* at any stage, there is a flow into the form of self-identity, only this self-identity is not always explicitly manifest. When it is explicit, there is *samādhi.*

In the first two stages, there is primarily object consciousness, more specifically consciousness of the actual object. The mind is restricted to the presented object alone, though moving from one object to another without relating them. In the *kṣipta, rajas* and *tamas* predominate, and the *citta* is attracted by the sense objects. It moves from one object to another, without any rest. In the *muddha* only *tamas* predominates, and the *citta* is attracted to vices, sleep, inertia, etc. In the third, i.e. *vikṣipta* state, the *citta* is not under the influence of *tamas*; it has a touch of *rajas* in it. This stage has the capacity of manifesting all objects, virtues, etc. In this stage, *citta* is able to reach temporary concentration on some object, which is followed by the loss of concentration. In other words, the stoppage of mental modifications and *avidyā* etc., is not permanent. In the fourth, i.e., *ekāgra* or one-pointed stage, *sattva* predominates, and *rajas* and *tamas* are subdued. This stage is characterized by the beginning of prolonged concentration of the *citta*. In this stage mental modifications are suppressed, but only partially. This stage is preparatory to the next stage, which is called "*niruddha*," where all mental modifications including the mental concentration that characterizes the *ekāgra* stage cease to exist. In *niruddha*, the *citta* is calm and peaceful; it returns to its original state. The last two states are conducive to *mokṣa* insofar as both manifest the maximum of the *sattva guṇa*. In the *ekāgra* or one-pointed consciousness *buddhi* attains explicit consciousness of self-identity. The mind focuses on the object of meditation, the meditator and the object of meditation are fused together—though the consciousness of the object of meditation persists. In fact it is *samprajñāta samādhi* or the trance of meditation because in this state the mind establishes itself permanently in the object, has a clear and distinct consciousness of the object, and assumes the form of the object. The *niruddha* is *asamprajñāta samādhi,* the culmination of the process, the *yoga* in the strict sense. The *vṛttis* are arrested, though latent impressions persist.

It is not easy to attain the state of *niruddha*. The continually changing cognitive states can be restrained by practice (*abhyāsa*) and detachment (*vairāgya*).[18] Detachment is freedom from craving—again, a Buddhist-sounding idea—from sensory objects. One must cultivate detachment from two kinds of objects: they are either objects seen in the world, or object heard about in the scriptures (e.g., pleasure in the heaven). Patañjali rejects the heavenly worlds promised by the Vedic texts as rewards of the ritualistic performances. The *yogin* must have no attachment to the either one. Complete detachment is reached when the *yogin* knows the true nature of the *puruṣa* and does not desire anything material, i.e., anything constituted of the three *guṇas* (as all evolutes of *prakṛti* are, according to Sāṁkhya and Yoga). The final goal is not attained all at once. It is possible to attain prolonged contemplation, and relapse back into the pain and suffering on account of past tendencies and impressions. It requires a long and arduous training to attain the cessation of all modifications of the *citta* and destroy the effects of the *karmas*. It is important that one practices *yoga* with care and undivided attention, and the path that helps one attain the highest is called "*aṣṭāṅga yoga,*" which I will discuss next.

The Eight Limbs (Aṣṭāṇga Yoga)

Patañjali's *yoga* is said to be eight-limbed (*aṣṭāṅga*). The *aṅgas* or limbs are: (1) *yama* or control, (2) *niyama* or regulation, (3) *āsana* or bodily posture, (4) *prāṇāyāma* or regulation of breath, (5) *pratyāhara* or removal of the senses, (6) *dhāraṇā* or concentration, (7) *dhyāna* or meditation and (8) *samādhi* or absorption.

Yama and *niyama*, i.e., the first two of the eight *aṅgas*, are the needed preliminaries to any ethical and religious disciplines. The *Yoga Sūtras* prescribes five *yamas*, or ethical rules, negative in form. These are: *ahimsā* or non-violence, *satya* or truth-telling, *asteya* or non-stealing, *brahmacarya* or celibacy, and *aparigraha* or non-possession. Patañjali regards these five as "the great vows" that hold good universally at all places, times, and circumstances and for all classes of humans.[19] Of these five, *ahiṃsā*, coming as it does first on the list, is the most important. The remaining four *yamas* are geared towards it. Thus truth-telling is expected not to harm anyone; it is truth-telling not only in speech but also in thought. When one is established in non-violence, he has no enemy and is no one's enemy. In giving importance to non-violence, the *Yoga Sūtras* seems to have assimilated the moral doctrine of Jainism. Although the extreme version of non-violence found in Jainism is not found in the Yoga school, killing living beings and consequently meat-eating is absolutely prohibited for a *yogi* in the *Yoga Sūtras*.

Whereas the *yamas* are negative, the *niyamas* are positive and refer to places, times, and classes. They prescribe cultivation of good habits. The *niyamas* are also five in number: *sauca* or cleanliness (both natural and spiritual), purification of the body by washing it, and purification of the mind involved by cultivating such positive thoughts and emotions as friendliness, kindness etc.; *santoṣa* or contentment (being content with what one has without too much trouble), *tapas* or asceticism (enduring cold and heat), *svādhyāya* or the study of religious scriptures (study of religious books with uniform regularity), and *Īśvara-praṇidhāna* or contemplation of and surrender to God.

The difference between the two practices, *yama* and *niyama*, i.e., between morality and religious practice, may be stated in the words of K. C. Bhattacharya thus: "Morality is universal as the negative externality of spirituality, religious practice is its positive particularity and internality, while super-religious *yoga* is its transcendent individual reality."[20]

The next three steps constitute a process of spiritualizing the body. The disciples of ethical and religious practice must have already prepared the ground, now the body so trained must be subjected to a direct spiritualization. One begins with *āsana*, the right posture, which is rather a spiritual poise of the body, "steady and pleasant" to be achieved by relaxation and by absorption in the infinite.[21] *Āsana* spontaneously leads to the regulation of breath freely in accordance with the cosmic rhythm. There are many kinds of *āsanas* and these *āsanas* effectively keep the body free from all sorts of diseases, thereby keeping under check the factors that disturb the *citta* and make it restless. Prescriptions regarding the body are important because they secure the health of the body and make it fit for prolonged concentration.

Prāṇāyāma means breath regulation regarding the inhalation and exhalation. Here the Yoga prescribes suspension of breathing either after inhalation or before exhalation or retention of the breathing for as long as one is able to hold it. It must be practiced under the guidance of a person who has expertise in it. Such exercises strengthen the heart, help one control his mind insofar as it is conducive to the steadiness of the body and the mind. The longer the suspension of the breath, the longer would be the state of concentration.

The goal of *pratyāhara* is to cut off the mind from the external world. When the sense organs are effectively controlled by the mind, then it is not disturbed by sounds, sights, etc. This state, though not impossible, is very difficult to attain; it requires a resolute will and constant practice.

Now that the body is refined and spiritualized, the next three steps in the practice of *yoga*, which are constitutive of *yoga* proper, follow. Whereas the first five limbs are external in the sense that they are merely preparatory to the discipline of *yoga*, the last three are internal in the sense that they are constitutive of *yoga*. The last three—*dhāraṇā, dhyāna,* and *samādhi*— involve "bodiless willing," or rather spiritual willing. These three, when performed together, are known as "*saṃyama.*" "*Saṃyama*" leads to insight.[22]

The sixth and seventh, i.e., *dhāraṇā* and *dhyāna*, are preparatory to the eighth, i.e., *samādhi.* In *dhāraṇā*, one fixes the mind on a real position in space. An imagined object is placed in a position in space and is willingly visualized as being there. It is crucial to develop the ability to keep one's attention fixed on one specific object because it is the test of the fitness of the mind and signals that one is ready to enter the next higher stage, *dhyāna*, in which the object on which the mind focuses is continuously contemplated. It is the contemplation of the object without any disturbance. The sense of remembering becomes an uninterrupted stream of willing and imagining. This series merges into an *effortless samādhi*, subjectivity completely withdraws itself so that the *object alone shines*. In the words of the *Yoga Sūtras*, "*samādhi* occurs when the *dhyāna* shines as the object alone, and the mind is devoid of its own subjectivity."[23] The mind does not any more wander around, but becomes one-pointed or *ekāgra*.

Samādhi or concentration is the final step in the practice of *yoga*. In *samādhi*, all mental modifications cease and there is no association with the external world; they become one. The Yoga school here makes a distinction between two kinds of *samādhis*: *samprajñāta samādhi* and *asamprajñāta samādhi*. In *samprajñāta samādhi*, consciousness of the object is there; in *asamprajñāta samādhi*, it is transcended.

In *samprajñāta samādhi*, the consciousness of the *puruṣa* flows through the natural mind; it has an objective support to focus upon. But this *samādhi* itself has two sub-stages: *savitarka* and *savichāra*. In *savitarka* and *savichāra*, the *citta*'s focus is on a gross material object, e.g., the image of a deity, etc. In *savichāra* the gross object is replaced by its subtle equivalent, e.g., the *tanmātras*. "Subtle" means what is not perceptible by the senses. In other words, in *savitarka*, the object that is presented predominates; in *savichāra*, the act of presentation predominates. In *savitarka*, the body comes to the forefront and the mind is finitized; in *savichāra* the body drops out from consciousness and the act of apprehension becomes the focus, the pure self comes to be grasped, there being no object. This self-knowledge gives rise to two more forms of *samādhi* known as *sānanda samādhi* and *sāsmitā samādhi*: in the former, there is the absorption in the sheer bliss of self-knowledge, and in the latter, the mere "I am" awareness, the pure subject rather than the subjective act becomes the exclusive focus.

Another way of classifying the four *samādhis* would be to regard the *sānanda* and *sāsmitā samādhis* as *samādhis* in the subjective attitude, and the *savitarka* and *savichāra* as *samādhis* in the objective attitude. While *savitarka samādhi* is focused on gross material objects, *savichāra samādhi* focuses upon the subtle components of gross objects. One way of understanding the latter is to take the *samādhi* to be focused on the essences of color, sound, touch, etc., of which a gross material object is constituted, the meditation is on the *tammātras* of which gross objects are made, especially the gross objects here and now. At this point, the meditation may free itself from the object here and now and its subtle constituents, and move on to the subtle constituents of any object at any spatial and temporal position.

Irrespective of how one classifies the four stages of *samprajñāta samādhi,* the point that the Yoga is trying to make is as follows: *samprajñāta samādhi* is *ekāgra,* in it the focus is on the object of meditation, and the object of meditation and meditation are fused in it, though the consciousness of the object remains. *Asamprajñāta samādhi* is *niruddha*; there is no consciousness of the object. All mental modifications cease to exist, and the self realizes its own essence as pure consciousness. One attains *mokṣa,* the state of freedom from all suffering.

Before concluding this section, I will make some remarks about the body-mind relationship and the ordering of *samādhis* in Yoga.

The question is often asked: what is the relation between body and mind in *yoga*? *Yogic* practice, in a large measure, is bodily—both external and internal—physiological-breathing. This practice is supposed to have a wholesome influence on the mind. Likewise, mental practice of *abhyāsa, vairāgya,* and *dhyāna,* is supposed to bring the body under the control of the mind. There is mutual influence on each other. Considering the fact that both body and mind are the products of *prakṛti* and are due to the varying proportions of the three *guṇas* —one can say that both are *natural,* and that neither is spiritual. To be natural is *not* to be construed as being material. Sāṁkhya and Yoga, which share a common metaphysics, are to be sure, not materialistic. Both are naturalistic, but in both, nature is meant for the purpose of the spirit. Thus in both nature is ordered to serve the interests of the *puruṣa.*

It would therefore be wrong to ascribe to *yoga* a mind-body identity theory. In nature, as in body, there is a preponderance of the *rajas* and *tamas,* though *sattva* is not entirely lacking. In mind or *buddhi, sattva* predominates, thereby making it possible for the *buddhi* to know and to will not to will, thereby making *yogic* practice possible. Thus body is "spiritualized" through cleanliness, *āsana* or posture, *prāṇāyāma* or breath control, and *pratyāhāra* or merging of the sense organs in the mind. Likewise, through the purely mental operation of *dhyāna,* the body is freed from the *rajas* and the *tamas guṇas,* it becomes shining and lustrous. Both make the pure knowledge through *buddhi's* perfection possible. To sum up: the relation between body and mind is complex; they cooperate and mutually influence each other.

III *Īśvara* or God

The Sāṁkhya, as is well known, has no place for *Īśvara* in its metaphysics. The world has no creator; it evolves spontaneously from *prakṛti,* and from a teleological perspective geared to the purposes of the *puruṣa.* Yoga school, on the other hand, accepts the existence of God on both theoretical and practical grounds. Two arguments prove the existence of God: (1) The Vedas and the Upaniṣads declare that there is a God, a supreme self. So God exists because the foundational texts testify to its existence. (2) The law of continuity talks about the degrees, a lower limit and the upper limit of things that we see in the world. Similarly, there are degrees of power and knowledge. Thus, there must be a being who possesses perfect power and knowledge and that being is God.

The *Yoga Sūtras*, however, introduces *Īśvara* in the context of the discussion of the practice of *yoga*. There are, to my knowledge, at least four contexts in which "*Īśvara*" appears. In I.23, devotion to *Īśvara* is listed as an alternate route to *samādhi*. Commentators interpret this as meaning that devotion to *Īśvara* is the best and quickest way to attain *samādhi*. I.28 explains the nature of *Īśvara* as follows: "He is a special *puruṣa*, uncontaminated by the detriments to the practice of *yoga*, *karma*, the fruition of the *karma*, and by the *saṁskāras*, or dispositions left by the *karmas*." I.29 says that *Īśvara's* omniscience is unsurpassed. Much controversy surrounds the sense in which there are degrees of omniscience. I.26 states that *Īśvara* is the teacher of the earlier generations and also that he is not limited by time. The former statement means that he is the teacher of all teachers, the latter that time belonging as it does to *prakṛti* does not limit his being through devotion to him. The *yogi* comes to know his own self or *puruṣa*. Some of these themes are repeated in other chapters also.

The above makes it obvious that Patañjali accepts the existence of God, though his interest in God is only practical, from the theoretical-metaphysical perspective he abides by the Sāṁkhya doctrine. He does not regard *Īśvara* as the creator of the universe; God is only a special kind of *puruṣa*. God is the model of highest perfection and knowledge. He is a perfect being, all-pervading, omnipotent, omniscient, free from all defects. He does not bestow rewards or punishments, and has nothing to do with the bondage and liberation of individual souls. The goal of human life is not union with God but rather the separation of the *puruṣa* from *prakṛti*.

Concluding Remarks

It should be clear that the practice of *yoga* is an active process of willing. Spiritual activity, in this system, is understood as willing the goal to attain freedom. The will, however, is the "will not to will," i.e., the will to *nivṛtti*, not to *pravṛtti*.[24] In Sāṁkhya, the willing is a process of knowing, while in the Yoga system, it is a process of willing to free oneself from the natural will to pleasure or enjoyment. Here we see an interesting difference between Yoga and Vedānta and Vaiṣnava theism. Vedānta, especially of Advaita variety, aims at knowledge, Vaiṣnavism understands spiritual life as one of feeling, Yoga is a life of willing not to will.

One is struck by the *Yoga Sūtras* similarity with the Buddhist teachings. *Yoga Sūtras* emphasizes that the worldly existence, especially existence in body, is characterized by suffering, which is an important feature of Indian philosophies, especially of Buddhism. The *sūtra* II.15 categorically affirms that life is characterized by suffering. The *sūtra* in fact goes on to list various kinds of suffering, which include even pain arising from a moment of pleasure passing away.

The cause of suffering is given in II.17: the seer and that which is seen, i.e., the spirit and the material objects, are confused with one another. More specifically, *buddhi*, which is a product of nature, is taken to be the self. The knowable object is constituted of the three *guṇas* and exists for the sake of the self's spiritual purpose. The seer is the *puruṣa*, pure consciousness, the mere power of seeing. Suffering is overcome when this union of the self and *prakṛti* is dissolved, and the self is seen for what it is. *Yoga*, of course, is the means to accomplish this. Ignorance or *avidyā* is the cause of the union of the self and nature. This *avidyā* is destroyed by true knowledge of the distinction between the two.[25] But there is an important point of difference between the two: the fundamental error in Buddhism, is to mistake the momentary self as permanent, in the Yoga, however, it is to take the unchanging eternal self to be the changing natural processes. Patañjali's main criticism of Buddhism concerns the doctrine of momentariness (*kṣanikavāda*). Patañjali defends a realism regarding the things in the world; they are not mental constraints.[26] Like the Sarvāstivādins, he asserts that the past and the future also exist in reality,[27] the object and the mind are different,[28] and object is dependent neither on a single mind, nor on many minds.[29] What is self-luminous is not mind; mind is only an object. Only *puruṣa* is self-illuminating.

In view of the contemporary interest in the relation of *yoga* to Edmund Husserl's thinking, I will single out a few relevant points. First of all, both phenomenology and *yoga* seek to be descriptive sciences of experiences of different levels and types. Both avoid philosophy in the sense of system-building by speculative arguments. This alone creates the presumption that the two must be alike in many important respects, however, it must be noted that phenomenology restricts itself to perceptual experience and scientific experience, besides moral, aesthetic, and social experience; the Yoga, however, goes beyond these and ascends to supernormal experiences.

The central concern of phenomenology is the internal structure of all experience. Ordinarily, this structure is understood as consciousness' directedness to an object outside of it. But phenomenology brackets the object outside of consciousness, and is then left with the object as belonging to the internal structure, what it calls "meaning" or "*noema*" of the experience. The method of *epochē* thus makes it possible for phenomenology to study descriptively the internal structure of all experiences. Yoga's attitude towards intentionality is quite different. Its goal is to restrain the outward movement of mental modifications, their being of something out in the world. Intentionality is thereby progressively conquered, and the self as pure consciousness comes to the forefront. In this respect, Yoga and Vedānta schools differ from phenomenology. They begin with empirical consciousness, and through a series of moves aim at reaching pure non-intentional consciousness. These systems of Indian philosophy do not take intentionality to be a defining feature of consciousness, which has been defined rather in terms of its self-luminosity.

What Yoga proceeds to decipher by the method of reflective focusing, phenomenology proceeds to bring to light by the method of *epochē*.

Yoga of Patañjali does not deny the world; its goal is to restrain the movement of the mental states towards the world. Phenomenology does the same thing by a method of reflection and *epochē*. The *yogin* exclusively focuses upon an object, shutting off all other objects from its view. This is very close to the method of *epochē*, and is attained by a voluntary move. The phenomenologist, as is well known, proceeds through a series of *epochē*, the psychological, the phenomenological, and the transcendental being the primary. A *yogin* goes through different stages of *samādhi*: he initially focuses on the gross object, then on the subtle constituents of that object, its essential structures, leading to the focusing on the act of consciousness and on the pure subject to the complete exclusion of any object, and finally, on the pure non-objective self-luminosity of consciousness and consequent omniscience.

Another central theme of *Yoga* school of phenomenological significance is the gradual spiritualization of the body, beginning with the appropriately relaxed and effortless posture and breath-control, up until one reaches the complete indistinguishability of bodily and pure *buddhi's* subjectivity. The body, initially perceived as sinful and "dirty," becomes an effective means of willing not to will with "cleansing," "contentment" and ethical-religious practices.

Phenomenology continues to focus on meanings (*noemata*), ideal contents of experience; *yoga*, at some point in its progressive journey, totally overcomes all verbal reference and meaning, language drops out, making possible for the self-luminous consciousness to recede behind the object, so that the epistemic gap between the object in itself and the perceived content, i.e., the perspectival character of perception is overcome. The object stands luminously in its totality, reflected as it is in the consciousness. Phenomenology has no inkling of this grasp of the total object and the consequent omniscience. Descriptive phenomenology becomes, in Yoga, a *transformative* phenomenology.

The long, almost immemorial, practice of *yoga*, independently of and prior to the philosophical systems, has resulted in the concepts, possibilities and achievements of *yoga* practice being sedimented into the Indian life-world. It is not so much faith as recalling the possibilities actualized in the past that looms large before the Indian mind. Philosophy has tried to systematize the experiences whose memory is preserved in the *śruti*, the epics and poetry. The Yoga has become a part of the Indian life. Every philosophical system with the exception of Cārvāka, has accepted the possibility of *yoga* in some form or the other. However, there is room for a critical examination of actual achievements as well as the hope for the possibilities that always lie in such expectations.

10

THE VAIŚEṢIKA *DARŚANA*

The Vaiśeṣika is a very ancient system, most probably pre-Buddhist, whose earliest systematization was made by Kaṇāda in the *Vaiśeṣika Sūtras* which antedates most of the extant *sūtras*.[1] This is the first systematic work of this school. Not much is known about Kaṇāda. It is difficult to ascertain with certainty when exactly the compilation of *Vaiśeṣika sūtras* took place. The date of the *Vaiśeṣika sūtras* is said to range from somewhere between 200 BCE to the beginning of the CE, though it is very likely that some of the Vaiśeṣika doctrines were formulated much earlier. Other important works of this school are: Udayana's *Kiraṇāvalī* and *Lakṣaṇāvalī* and Vallabhāchāryā's *Nyāya Līlāvatī*. Praśastapāda's *Padārthadharmasaṅgraha* provides an excellent exposition of the Vaiśeṣika philosophy. The system embodies a naturalism which, since the beginnings of Indian thought, has opposed the mainstream non-naturalistic component of Indian thought. Again, the Vaiśeṣika, like the Sāṁkhya, does not amount to materialism,[2] although in many regards it comes close to Sāṁkhya. The school owes its name to recognizing the category of *viśeṣa* (particularity) as a necessary feature to account for the particulars of the world, e.g., atoms and souls, which are eternal. It accounts for and preserves this particularity despite recognizing many individuals. The objects that we experience in our everyday lives, on the other hand, are made up of parts, and so non-eternal.

As stated earlier, in the Indian thought one finds two naturalistic theories of the origin of the empirical world. On the one view, the world is a product of ordered evolution from an original undifferentiated Nature, the one becoming many, while, on the other, the world arises out of atoms combining together in various ways, which, in a limited sense, we may express by saying that the many become one. The Sāṁkhya represents the first, and the Vaiśeṣika the second view. Both of these schools, besides their naturalistic proclivities, propound a theory of the irreducibility of the self, recognize manyness of selves, and accept the doctrines of *karma*-rebirth, and *mokṣa*.

The Vaiśeṣika's primary concern is ontology; epistemology or theory of knowledge is subordinated to ontology. In ontology, it reduces all things in the world or beyond, to a minimum, i.e., further irreducible kinds. The world in all its variety and complexity is built up, within the theory, out of these irreducible entities. In this sense, it represents a grand intellectual adventure of ancient Indian mind. It is not surprising therefore that the ideas of the Vaiśeṣika remain the basis of the Hindu physical sciences,[3] just as the Sāṁkhya remains the basis of the Hindu medical science.

The Vaiśeṣika and the Nyāya are taken to be allied systems. Both subscribe to the view that the goal of human life is *mokṣa*, absolute cessation of pain and suffering. Both systems, however, differ on the number of the *pramāṇas* they accept; whereas the Nyāya accepts perception, inference, comparison, and verbal testimony, the Vaiśeṣika recognize only two, perception and inference. Again, whereas the Nyāya accepts sixteen *padārthas*, the Vaiśeṣika recognizes only seven. The Nyāya takes over the Vaiśeṣika ontology and defends it from opponent's attacks using canons of logical reasoning. I will discuss the *pramāṇas* and the conceptions of the self, bondage and liberation in the chapter on Nyāya, and primarily focus on the ontological categories known as *padārthas* in this chapter.

The *Padārthas*

Padārthas are usually translated as "categories." The term "*padārtha*" etymologically means "the meaning or referent" (*artha*) of words (*pada*). So by "*padārtha*," the Vaiśeṣika means "all reals" or "all objects that belong to the world." It is an object that can be thought of as well as named. If this etymology is scrupulously followed, then it would imply that any meaning of a word is a *padārtha*. That however is not the case. The word, "pitcher" signifies a pitcher, but "pitcher" is not a *padārtha*. Likewise, "red" means the color red, but the color red is not a *padārtha*; it is a quality. A *padārtha* then is a most general class under which referents of words fall, a class that is not included in any other class. It is a most general predicate of things. "Substance" is a predicate, a most general predicate, of pitchers, pens, and sticks, but not of "red," "blue," etc.

One generally compares the Vaiśeṣika *padārthas* to those of Aristotle and Kant. Whereas Aristotle's list is a haphazard group of very general predicates of things, the Kantian list, on the other hand, is systematic, being derived from the logical forms of judgment. It is traced to the forms of the faculty of "understanding," and so is subjective in origin. The origins of the Vaiśeṣika list we do not know. There is no principled deduction, though later commentators defend the list by critiquing suggested changes, additions, and subtractions in order to demonstrate that the list is almost complete.

All objects that the words denote may be divided into two kinds *bhāva* and *abhāva*, being and non-being respectively. Being includes all positive realities, e.g., physical objects, minds, souls, etc., and non-being includes non-existence. There are six kinds of positive realities and one negative *padārtha*. Thus, the Vaiśeṣika list (which from the literature appears to have slowly evolved) lists seven categories: *dravya* (substance), *guṇa* (quality), *karma* (action), *sāmānya* (universal), *viśeṣa* (particularity), *samavāya* (inherence) and *abhāva* (negation). In this chapter, I will primarily focus on these seven categories.

Dravya (Substance)

"*Dravya*" is usually rendered as "substance." But this translation does not really capture the meaning of "*dravya*" in the Vaiśeṣika system. The Aristotelian or Kantian "substance" has the sense of permanence in the midst of changes; the Vaiśeṣika *dravya* is not so understood. A *dravya*, according to the Vaiśeṣika, may change, or may last for some time and then cease to be, or may be eternal. By definition, it is the locus of qualities and actions (i.e., of the next two *padārthas*). A *guṇa* or quality, or an action, can only be in a *dravya*. A *dravya* is the locus (*āśraya*) not only of qualities, but also of actions. As a matter of fact, either proximately or mediately, all entities, belonging to all the different categories, reside in a *dravya*. A quality does not float around by itself. Any quality, say, "red" proximately resides, say, in a red flower. Such universal entities as "redness" reside in the color red, and the latter in a red object. Thus, in the Vaiśeṣika ontology, *dravya* occupies a preeminent place. The recognition of its primacy captures our naive realistic intuitions that *things* in the world have a prominent place in our picture of the world. It also captures—i.e., of the Sanskrit as well as the Indo-European languages—one important feature that nouns occupy a central place in a sentence.[†] In the Sanskrit sentence, "*ayaṃ ghataḥ*" ("this is a pitcher"), a substance is in the predicate place. Besides, a Sanskrit sentence does not always conform to the subject-predicate pattern. Again, and most importantly, Aristotelian, Kantian, and Lockean, notions of substance as a permanent substratum *underlying* changes is not found in the Vaiśeṣika. For these reasons, it seems more advisable to render "*dravya*" simply as "thing," the German "*Ding*."

To be noted is that many Indian systems, e.g., the Buddhists and the Sāṁkhya, do not accord primary ontological status to "*dravya*." They reject the things as a conglomeration of qualities, and then move on to regard each quality as a constantly changing process. For Vaiśeṣika such a position runs contrary to our everyday realistic intuitions. To perceive a quality is to perceive it as belonging to a thing. One never merely sees a color, but always sees a colored thing. The *dravya* therefore, according to the Vaiśeṣika, is not a Lockean unperceived substratum nor unperceivable "I know not what," but something that is perceived along with its qualities. Even the soul is perceived, on this theory, in such an introspective judgment as "I am happy" or "I am in pain." The "I" directly refers to my soul, and what is being perceived is not the pure soul, but the soul as qualified by the quality of happiness or pain. If a thing is not perceived, that is due to the fact that not all conditions of its perception are satisfied. Even the very small things, e.g., atoms, though not perceivable by us, are objects of special perception developed by a *yogi* known as *yogaja pratyakṣa*. The point I am making is that the Vaiśeṣika "*dravya*" is *not* an unperceivable thing only to be known by inference.

This definition of "*dravya*" that it is the locus of qualities has been subjected to many criticisms. I will mention only one: On the Vaiśeṣika thesis when a thing arises from the conjunction of its parts, because of the rule that the effect must be later than its cause, in the very first moment of its being, the thing is without any quality. The qualities which arise from the next moment onwards. If this thesis is admitted, then at that first moment the thing that has just come into being is without any quality and so is not the locus of any quality. But such Vaiśeṣika commentators as Vallabhāchārya and Udayana meet this objection by modifying the definition as follows: "*dravya* is never the non-locus of an absolute negation of quality." This definition follows the technique used extensively by the Navya-Nyāya logicians to replace a positive property by a double negation in the definiens.

Of all the categories, *dravya* is the most important, for there is a sense in which all the others—or, rather, instances of all of them—can *be* only in a "*dravya*." Anticipating our exposition of the other categories, we can say, such entities as a quality, an action, a universal, an inherence relation, particularity, and a negation (or absence) can have being only in a thing. Or, consider a thing like the pitcher I see in front of me. This pitcher is brown, so has the quality "brown," when it moves it becomes the locus of an action; it is the locus of the universal "pitcherness," also of the relation of inherence between that universal and itself as an instance of it, it also possesses its own particularity, and besides, is the locus of the negation, or absence, "the pitcher is *not* a glass" Thus, the entire set of Vaiśeṣika categories may be regarded as an elaborate ontological analysis of things we are familiar with, in this case a "pitcher."

The Vaiśeṣika, after defining *dravya* and explaining the nature of *dravya*, points out that all *dravyas* or things of the world can be classified into nine: Earth, water, fire, air, ether, time, space, soul and *manas* (mind). Each of the first five substances possess a unique quality, which makes the substance what it is. Smell is the unique quality of earth, taste of water, color of fire, touch of air, and sound of ether. To say that each of these substances possesses a unique quality does not amount to saying that it does not possess other qualities, but rather that the unique quality of a substance is what distinguishes it from other substances.

The first four are knowable by outer perception. The substances of earth, water, fire, and air are eternal and non-eternal. The atoms of these four substances are partless and eternal, because as partless they can neither be produced nor destroyed. All other objects made by the combination of atoms are non-eternal and subject to origination as well as destruction. All composite objects are constituted by a combination of atoms; at first the two atoms combine to form a dyad, a combination of three is called "triad," and so on. In this evolutionary process, there is no talk of the first creation of the world, because the process of creation and destruction of the world is beginningless. Every creation is preceded by destruction, and every destruction is followed by a creation. Atoms lack motion, therefore the will of God imparts motion to the atoms.

It is obvious that the Vaiśeṣika atomism is different from the Greek atomism on several key points; here I will make note of only two differences. Whereas the Vaiśeṣika atoms lack motion, the Greek atoms do not, and whereas the

Vaiśeṣika atoms differ both in quantity and quality, the Greek atoms can be distinguished only quantitatively.

The fifth substance that the Vaiśeṣikas accept is ether, which is indivisible, eternal, and non-perceptible. The first five substances are called the gross elements. The gross things, which must be different, and apart from each other, are then accounted for by space and time. Time is a common cause of all things. Space and time are imperceptible substances; they are one, eternal, and all pervasive; they are inferred. Space is inferred from our cognitions of "there," "here," etc., and time from our cognitions of the past, the present, and the future. The sixth *dravya*, namely, soul, is an eternal, all pervading substance. The soul is the substratum of consciousness. A distinction is made between two kinds of souls: the individual soul and the supreme soul. Whereas the individual souls, being different in different bodies, are many, the supreme soul is one and is the creator of the world. The existence of the supreme soul as the creator of the world is known by inference, but the individual souls, on the other hand, are perceived mentally, and such statements as "I am happy," "I am sad," testify to their existence. At the end comes "*manas*" without which nothing would be known. *Manas* is an inner sense and is atomic in size, and so cannot be perceived. Our experiences testify to the existence of the mind being atomic. The Vaiśeṣika argues that if the mind were not of an atomic size, then there could be simultaneous contact of its different parts with many senses leading to many different perceptions at the same time, which, however, is not the case. There is thus a rationale behind the order in which the *dravyas* are listed.

The Vaiśeṣika claims this list to be complete, and by way of disputations with other schools who add to or subtract from the list, undertakes to defend this list. The great medieval Naiyāyika Raghunāth Śiromaṇī, for example, reduced the three, ether, space and time to God's nature. He also does not regard *manas* to be a separate *dravya* —thereby reducing all *dravyas* to five. However, for our purposes there is no need to enter into such discussions.

It is worth noting that with this classification of *dravya* into nine, we are moving away from the ontological and coming a step, as it were, closer to the ontic discourse (using Heidegger's terminology). While this sub-classificatory scheme is *ambiguously perched between the ontological scheme of seven categories and the innumerable things of the world*, the task of philosophy is to connect the two. No Western philosopher, Aristotle and Kant including, provides such a sub-classification.

Guṇa (Quality)

Guṇa, generally rendered as "quality," is Vaiśeṣika's understanding of the word we have earlier discussed in the chapter on Sāṁkhya. The Vaiśeṣika, however, rejects the Sāṁkhya thesis of the three *guṇas* as the basic constituents of *prakṛti*. The Sāṁkhya virtually substantizes the "*guṇas*"; the Vaiśeṣikas take them to be qualities which are always found in some *dravya*. They do not exist by themselves. Besides they are not simply things; they are always qualified as being such and such. Yet the two, *dravyas* and *guṇas*, are ontologically different, though inseparable. The thesis that a thing and its qualities being inseparable must be non-different is rejected on the ground that (a) the color of the pitcher lies in the pitcher, while the pitcher has its being in its constituent parts each of which does not have that color, and (b) that their alleged non-difference would have the consequence so that we could say "this color *is* a pitcher," which is absurd. Add to these the third ground (c), already mentioned, that according to the Vaiśeṣika, when a thing arises out of combination of atoms, it is without a quality in the first moment of its arising.

Since, on the Vaiśeṣika theory, qualities are in a substance by definition, a quality, cannot itself possess another quality. Nor can a *guṇa* be a universal. What qualifies and so belongs to, say, this piece of paper (in "this paper is red") is red, but not red-ness. A quality or *guṇa*, very much like a substance it belongs to, is a particular. There is no universal *guṇa* (nor a universal substance). A *guṇa* is not always a substrate of an action. It cannot move from one place to another, a substance can and does. This is the reason why a knowledge, being a *guṇa* of the self, is not an action. It also does not have parts, although it is produced by causes. A substance alone has parts. A quality, then, we can say, is itself quality-less (*nirguṇa*), action-less (*niṣkriya*) and part-less (*niravayava*). But qualities belong to partless substances such as self. However, in the Vaiśeṣika system, substances and qualities are ontologically different entities. Unlike substances, qualities are always dependent; they are in substances. An action and a quality are two different aspects of a substance—the former its changing aspects and the latter its unchanging aspects.[5]

Kaṇāda lists twenty-four *guṇas*: These are: (1) color, (2) taste, (3) smell, (4) touch, (5) sound, (6) number, (7) size or magnitude, (8) distinctness, (9) non-distinctness, (10) conjunction, (11) disjunction, (12) remoteness, (13) nearness, (14) cognition, (15) pleasure, (16) pain, (17) desire, (18) hatred, (19) effort, (20) heaviness, (21) fluidity, (22) viscosity, (23) *dharma*, and (24) *adharma*. These twenty-four are classified into various groups (some belonging to one thing, some to many things; some to things which have a shape, some to things having no shape, some to both; some are specific qualities, some common qualities, and so on), which provides a rationale for the list of twenty-four.

In this list of qualities, some have become important for philosophers. These are such qualities of the self as knowledge, memory, pleasure, pain, desire and hatred, effort, as well as such supersensible qualities as *dharma*, *adharma* and dispositions called "*saṃskāra*." I will begin with these qualities of the self.

Pleasure and pain (*sukha* and *dukkha*) arise in the self as a result of knowledge; specifically, as a result of the contact between the self, sense organs, objects and mind (*manas*). Pleasure and pain are regarded as two different qualities of the self—the one not reducible to the absence of the other—both positive qualities as well as both different from knowledge. The object of pleasure is what is desired and favorable, the object of pain is not desired and regarded as unfavorable. We want pleasurable experiences to continue and wish that painful experiences end, that they cease to exist. Various kinds of pleasure and pain are distinguished: those that are caused by memory (of objects past), by imagination (of objects future) and, in the case of persons who have attained knowledge of the truth of the self, without any objects. Pain arises from objects or experience contrary to what the experiencer desires; otherwise stated, pain is that which a person does not desire and wishes to end after it arises.

Desire is caused by the thought of the enjoyment of objects, contrary conditions give rise to jealousy. Both may also arise from strong dispositions or habitualities, produced by objects that are dear, by objects that cause pain, and from appropriate *adṛṣṭa* or "unseen" potencies that have arisen in the self. A fourth kind of desire (and its opposite) arises from the intrinsic nature of the natural kinds to which an animal belongs: thus humans desire food, other animals desire grass or plants to eat, etc. Later authors classify desires into those whose objects are the intended results of actions, those whose objects are the means to reach the results, and those whose objects are actions themselves.

Dveṣa (hatred or jealousy) is described as what burns inside, causes constant remembrance of the object or the means for reaching it, and the thought of accomplishing it, causes the needed effort and produces in the self such qualities as *dharma* and *adharma.* Hatred is either simple anger or produces such deformations in the bodily expressions as vices, anger, impatience, and unforgiving feelings do.

The last of the qualities of the self discussed in the Vaiśeṣika is called *prayatna* or effort, often described as "enthusiasm" (*utsāha*) to do something which we all immediately experience within ourselves. The efforts caused by desire are called "*pravṛtti,*" those caused by hatred are called "*nivṛtti,*" both being different from the efforts (such as breathing, and other intra-bodily process) that are necessary for sustaining life.

Two unseen (*adṛṣṭa*) qualities are *dharma* and *adharma,* to be understood as moral virtue and its opposite, accruing to the soul. So important is the idea of "*dharma*" in the Vaiśeṣika that Kaṇāda in the very first *sūtra* explains "*dharma,*" and states that everything else, i.e., all other entities, are stated with the purpose of leading up to "*dharma.*" The second *sūtra* explains "*dharma*" as that which leads to flourishing (*abhyudaya*) in life and the highest goal in the next; the proof of "*dharma,*" we are told, is found in the Vedas. *Dharma* is brought about by performance of actions which are recommended; it is in itself a *guṇa* of the self. It is one of the specific qualities of the self, i.e., it cannot accrue to anything else. It is not a *guṇa* of the *buddhi* (like in Sāṁkhya), nor can it be there without being located in a self. It is brought about by the conjunction of the self with the inner sense, appropriate resolutions, and performances of actions recommended. *Adharma* is its opposite. Both *dharma* and *adharma* are called by a common name "*adṛṣṭa*" or "unseen," a word often used in the Vaiśeṣika works, but not in Gautama's *Nyāya Sūtras* or any other Nyāya work.

Saṃskāra or disposition (of past experience) is a special quality of the self, which is introduced as the cause of memory and recognition. It is this disposition that is either awakened or strengthened (or weakened) by appropriate conditions. Without positing such an unseen quality in the self, a past cognition (long since gone out of existence) could not be remembered. Habit strengthens dispositions, a special effort (e.g., to experience unseen entities) may cause especially powerful dispositions. The Vaiśeṣika recognizes three varieties of *saṃskāra*: (1) speed (*vega*) that keeps things in motion, (2) mental impressions (*bhāvanā*) that helps us to remember and recognize, and (3) elasticity (*sthitisthāpakatva*) that help a thing move to regain the equilibrium when it is disturbed, e.g., a string of rubber. It is worth noting that these dispositions do not belong to the self alone; they also belong to other things as well. It is not entirely clear why the Vaiśeṣika brings dispositions accruing to the self under the same genus as velocity of moving material things and elasticity of such things (as a string of rubber). A moving thing has the momentum in it to move. An elastic thing, when stretched, has the power, tendency, or built-in disposition to contract. Thus, one could argue that elasticity and momentum are not ordinary qualities, but rather dispositions to behave in certain ways.

Besides the specific qualities (of the self alone) just discussed (namely, cognition, desire, hatred, effort, *dharma* and *adharma* and dispositions), there are also qualities that belong to all things in common. These are: number, quantity, differences, conjunction, separation or disjunction, remoteness/non-remoteness, heaviness, fluidity, and viscosity.

An important Vaiśeṣika doctrine is that number is a quality of substances. All things whatsoever can be counted. It is often defined as the uncommon cause of "counting." Number really inheres in, or belongs to, more than one thing held together by a special act of mind, so to a collection or a set. Since number is a *guṇa* of substances, and since a *guṇa* cannot belong to other *guṇas*, number does not belong to qualities. Such modern logicians as Raghunātha Śiromaṇi reject this on the ground that one can also count three qualities, so number can belong to qualities as well. Also to be noted is that since number belongs to collections or sets, and since mathematicians of that time did not have the idea of a unit set, the Vaiśeṣikas regarded numbers to begin with "two"; "one" was not a number.

Parimāṇa, translated variously as "quantity," "size," "magnitude," etc., is either atomic or large, either short or long, and any of these either eternal or non-eternal. Non-eternal size is due to either number, or the size of component parts, or due to decay.

Pṛthaktva or separateness is the cause of determinations like "this is different from that." The judgment "a jar is not a glass" is about mutual difference of the two, but the judgment "this is other than that" is about their being *separate*. To many later thinkers, this is a distinction without difference.

An important *guṇa* is conjunction or contact (*saṃyoga*) when two things, which were not in contact, come into contact (as my two palms made to touch each other), a contact arises between them. Contact inheres in both. It is not regarded as a relation, but as a quality. Note that the system admits only one genuine relation i.e., inherence or *samavāya*, listed as an additional category. The opposite of contact is separation (*vibhāga*). Two conjoined things may be separated as when my two palms held in contact are made separate.

Otherness (and its opposite) denotes farness (and nearness), both in space and in time. So they can be translated as well into "remoteness" (and "nearness"). Temporally construed, they signify earlier and later.

Heaviness (*gurutva*) is defined as the special cause of falling down. It is found in two substances we are told, i.e., in earth and water, and belongs to the whole as well as to the parts. It is the cause of the fall of bodies. Fluidity or *dravatva* is self-explanatory; it is the cause of the flowing, for example, of water, milk, and so on. Viscocity exclusively belongs to water and is the cause of the different particles of matter sticking together to form the shape of a lump or a ball.

Karma (Action)

The next category is *karma* or action. Unlike the usages of "*karma*" in other systems, *karma* in this school is taken to signify movement of a thing from one place to another. It is different from voluntary actions done with subjective desire to do as well as effort, which is a variety of *guṇa*. *Karma* is simply displacement of positions in space, and it is with the help of *karma* that one thing reaches another place. It therefore does not belong to a quality, which does not move. While quality is a passive attribute, *karma* is dynamic. The Vaiśeṣika goes on to list five kinds of action that they admit: throwing upward, throwing downward, contraction, expansion, and movement. Among substances, all-pervasive ones cannot possess motion; thus, self, being all-pervasive, cannot move and so cannot act.

With "substance," "quality," and "action," we have circumscribed the basic core of the world according to the Vaiśeṣika. The world at its core consists of qualities and particular things in motion. But these three by themselves do not suffice to yield a complete ontology. We need (a) some features that things, qualities, and actions have in common and in which they differ, (b) some account of the incurable particularity of things; and (c) some basic relation that ties these entities together; and, finally, (d) some category that accounts for the pluralistic realism of the system. With this in mind, let us now turn to the next four categories that form the outer layer of the categorical structure of the world.

Sāmānya (Universal)

Universals, variously called "*sāmānya*" or "*jāti*," are entities which though one and eternal, inhere in many. They are real entities, not dependent upon the human mind. Thus the Vaiśeṣika advocates a realism with regard to universals which, in the Western world, was held by many realists beginning with Plato. But more akin to Aristotle, the Vaiśeṣika took universals to be natural kinds such as "cowness" and "redness." Particulars instantiating a universal come and go, but neither a particular's coming into being nor its going out of existence makes any difference to the being of the universal that belongs to them. Manifestation or lack of manifestation does not affect the being of an universal, because its being is eternal. Universals account for an infinite number of particulars appearing to be alike, though otherwise different. Universals belong to substances as well as to qualities and actions, as do cowness, redness and falling-ness respectively. If the instantiating particular is perceived, the instantiated universal is also perceived, as a matter of fact, perceived by the same sense organ as the particular. If sweet is apprehended by taste, then sweetness also is apprehended by taste. It is because of the universal that we designate different particulars by the same name, however, unlike many Western realists, the Vaiśeṣika does not believe that the universal "cowness" is the meaning of the word "cow." The Vaiśeṣika argues that if that were the case, then the sentence "bring a cow" would mean "bring cowness," which is absurd; it rather means a particular that is characterized by the appropriate universal, a cow characterized by cowness in this case.

Later Vaiśeṣika, led by the Naiyāyika Uddyotakara and Udayana introduced "*jātibādhakas*," i.e., "the features which rule out the being of a universal." Thus if there is only one particular of a kind, adding an appropriate suffix to its name, does not name a universal. Thus, space being one, space-ness (*ākāśatva*) is not a universal. Etherness, therefore, is merely a distinguishing characteristic (*upādhi*) and not a logical universal. Of the various defects discussed in this context in Udayana's *Kiraṇāvalī*, I will discuss only one that is known as *sāṅkarya*. Such a defect exists when two mutually exclusive characteristics are present in one and the same substratum. For example, the characteristic of being an element is common to the five elements—earth, water, fire, air, and ether; and the characteristic of being of a limited size is present in earth, water, fire, air, and mind. Thus both these characteristics have earth, water, fire, and air in common. Although the character of being an element applies only to ether and not to the mind, the characteristic of being of limited size applies to mind and not to ether. Therefore, if the "elementness" is taken to be a universal, it will apply to the four elements earth, water, fire, and air that are of limited size as well. Similarly, "limited sizeness" will apply to ether, which is not limited in size. That is why characteristics with partially overlapping denotations are not logical universals. Universals also cannot belong to a universal: "Cownessness" is not a universal. There are many such cases where an abstract noun does not designate a universal.

Before proceeding further, let me underscore an important distinction, i.e., the distinction between *jāti* and *upādhi*, which plays a very significant role in Vaiśeṣika ontology. It clearly brings out the Vaiśeṣika conception of universals as real, eternal, natural class essences existing in the objective world. A universal is a simple *padārtha*, and cannot be analyzed into other attributes, properties, components. That is why a general term, for example, "horse" would stand for a universal, but a term like "black horse" would not. "A black horse" represents a complex of properties and does not imply the existence of an additional ontologically distinct entity over and above blackness. In other words, the property of being a black horse is not over and above blackness and is not reducible to it.[6]

The Vaiśeṣika argues that without real universals, the world would consist of number-less transient particulars; it would not be the ordered distinct totality it is, and the use of language to describe the world would not be possible. Thus they totally reject the Buddhist position that only the particulars are real.

Believing that only particulars are real and that they too come and go, the Buddhists held that there is no universal, and that all classification is introduced by language. The idea of universal or sameness arises because of their being called by the same name. Only the name is general, which does not stand for any positive class essence. We call a certain class of animals as horse, not because they possess a common essence called "horseness," but because they are different from all other animals that are not horses. Accordingly, the Buddhists hold that there is no such thing as a universal, or a class concept; there are only particular objects of experience. Eventually, this account developed into the *apoha* theory that took the word "horseness" as not-being-a-non-horse. A particular horse therefore means a not-non-horse. There is no real universal; a universal is simply a name with a negative connotation. The Buddhist *apoha* theory is a sort of nominalism. Given that the Nyāya-Vaiśeṣika subscribes to realism, they argue that both particulars and universals are independently real.

The Vaiśeṣika distinguished between three orders of universals: the *parā* or highest, the *aparā* or lowest, and middle i.e., *parāparā*. *Sattā* or existence is the highest, and belongs to all substances, qualities and actions, "cowness" is of the lowest order belonging only to particular cows, while "substance-ness" of the middle rank belonging as it does to all substances.

Viśeṣa (Particularity)

Things not only are experienced as being alike, they are also perceived as being different, and even when they share the same qualities they are distinct, e.g., though all the cows have cowness, one cow is different from another cow. *Viśeṣa* is an entity, again a real entity, which accounts for this ultimate distinctness of individuals. The use of such indexicals as "this" or "that," does not explain individuality, but presupposes it. Therefore, we need a new category to explain individuality of entities.

The first attempt is to explain individuality by some quality (or *guṇa*) of an individual thing. But two things may have all the same qualities, e.g., twins, but they are still distinct. Could each one's distinctness be due to the stuff it is made of, its "matter" (a position which Aristotle held)? But then we are led to ask, what distinguishes the stuff of the one from the stuff of the other identical twin? We may ask, what distinguishes one atom from another? The Vaiśeṣika answer is: Each otherwise non-distinguishable partless particular possesses its own particularity, which is a real entity as much as the universals are. The particularity of wholes is accounted for by the particularities of its parts, but when we come to further partless entities the same explanation won't do; we have to stop somewhere in order to avoid an infinite regress and recognize a new real feature, its own particularity, only for individuals that do not possess parts. Each atom (also each soul) has its own particularity. So the Vaiśeṣika argues that particularity is the unique individuality of the eternal substances, e.g., space, time, ether, minds, souls, and atoms of earth, water, fire, and air.

It is worth noting that "particularity" is not a universal feature of distinct particulars. Ordinary objects of the world, for example, pitchers, tables, and chairs, are made up of parts, and so do not require particularity to explain them. Particularity is required to explain the differences among the partless eternal substances. The particularity of an atom or of a soul is not perceived, but inferred. Furthermore, to regard particularity as a universal would be self-contradictory, it would contradict the very sense of "particularity."

Samavāya (Inherence)

The one genuine relation which the Vaiśeṣika recognizes and admits as a distinct category is *samavāya*, often translated as "inherence." Etymologically "*samavāya*" means "the act of coming together closely," and is therefore used to denote a kind of "intimate union" between two things that are thereby rendered inseparable in such a way that they cannot be separated without themselves being destroyed. Annaṃbhaṭṭa defines *samavāya* as "a permanent connection existing between two things that are found inseparable."[7] By virtue of this relation, two such different things as substance and its qualities (e.g., a flower and its color red), a particular and the universal it instantiates (e.g., a cow and cowness), a substance and its action (a body and its motion), a whole and its parts (e.g., a cloth and the threads constituting it) become unified and represent an inseparable whole (*ayutasiddha*). It is an eternal relation. Excepting the case of a whole and its constituent parts, the relation holds good between entities belonging to two different categories. It also holds good between an ultimate, partless particular and its particularity. In the case of a blue flower, the flower is inseparable from its blue color; one could as well say that that blue particular is inseparable from the flower whose blue it is. In the case of a cow and its cowness, the cow will die but when the cow is dead and no more, cowness will be there only instantiated in other cows. There is a one-sided inseparability between the terms among whom this relation holds good.

Thus, this relation is one and the same, no matter what its relata are, it thus behaves like a universal. But on one view, the same relation, *one* ontological entity, obtains between all possible relata, so that it would be a mistake to regard each particular case of inherence to instantiate the universal "inherence-ness," for that would clearly lead to an infinite regress. It would be more economical to regard inherence always as the same identical relation, even when the relata vary.

One cannot ask how the relation of inherence is related to the terms. Positing another relation between a relatum and the relation would only lead to an infinite regress, so that it is more economical to recognize inherence to be a self relating relation and in that sense a genuine relation. Conjunction, by contrast, is not a self-relating relation. Annaṃbhaṭṭa defines *saṃyoga* as a contact between two things that were initially apart. Accordingly, no contact exists between entities that are all-pervasive and have never been apart from each other.[8] Additionally, it is a quality and so is related to the conjuncts by inherence. Inherence is a sort of *ontological glue*, which makes it possible for the entities to be unified, despite the categorical multiplicity. But it glues entities from different categories within limits; it does not weld all things in the world to one large thing, rather unifies the different entities that constitute *one* thing such as a white cow or a blue flower. We perceive the relation when the relata are perceived, as in the case of the color blue and a substance flower; we do not perceive the relation obtaining between an atom and its atomic size.

Abhāva (Negation)[9]

Because all knowledge points to an object that is necessarily real and independent, the knowledge of negation implies its existence apart from such knowledge. In other words, the absence of an object is different from the knowledge of its absence. The Naiyāyikas maintain that negation (*abhāva*) is always of a real negation from a real locus. There is no such thing as pure or bare negation. Both presence and absence are objective facts. Since the Vaiśeṣika is a pluralist and a realist, it admits many different reals, each different from the other. Of such finite things as this blue flower, it holds good that if it is *here* and *now*, it is *not*, at the same time, there and now; if it is blue, it is *not* also red.

The Vaiśeṣika therefore, for a complete theory or description of the world, needs only one more type of entity, besides those discussed so far, namely, "negation." In the judgments "A is not B," "A is not in B," and "A does not possess B-ness," we are affirming *real* negations, and these must articulate reality quite independently of any subjective point of view. Negation, according to the Vaiśeṣika, is an objectively real constituent of the world.

Now, already as the above examples show, "negation" is of many different kinds, and we can here lay down a broad typology of them in the following diagram under each heading I give, within brackets, the appropriate linguistic articulation for it.

Concrete examples:

1 There is no jar on the floor.
2 A pitcher is not a jar.
3 The pitcher is not yet made; it is not, but will be.

Negation

1. Absence ("A is not in B")

2. Difference or mutual non-existence ("A is not B")

3. Antecedent non-existence ("A will be")

4. Subsequent non-existence ("A is no more")

5. Absolute non-existence ("A is not here now")

Figure 10.1

4 The pitcher is destroyed; it was, but is no more.
5 There is no elephant in this room.

Let me elaborate these five negations further.

In the first there is the absence of something in something else. It is of three kinds: antecedent non-existence, consequent or subsequent non-existence, and absolute non-existence.

Antecedent or prior non-existence is the non-existence of a thing prior to its production, e.g., the non-existence of the house in the bricks, the non-existence of a pitcher in the clay, of jewelry in a nugget of gold, and so on. Annaṁbhaṭṭa defines *prāgabhāva* as that "which is without any beginning" (*anādi*) but "with an end" (*santa*). "Prior absence (*prāgabhāva*) is the absence of an effect before its emergence."[10] This non-existence has no beginning but has an end, because as soon as the house is built the non-existence of the house in the bricks, pitcher in the clay, jewelry in a nugget of gold, comes to an end.

Consequent non-existence is the non-existence of a thing on account of its destruction. A house after being built may be demolished. It is said to have a beginning but no end. The non-existence of the house begins when it is demolished or burned, however, this non-existence cannot be ended because one cannot bring the same house into existence.

Absolute non-existence is the non-existence of a connection between two things for all times, the past, the present, and the future. Annaṁbhaṭṭa explains absolute existence (*atyantābhāva*) as that absence "which abides through the three modes of time" (*traikālika*) and "the facthood of whose negatum" (*pratiyogitā*) is specified (*avachinna*) by a "relation" (*saṁsarga*); e.g. "There is no pot [pitcher] on the ground."[11] It neither has a beginning nor an end. In other words, it is both beginningless and endless. For example, horns are absent in a hare for all times, the past, the present, and the future.

Finally, mutual non-existence is the negation of identity, e.g., a table is not a chair. In other words, a table and a chair mutually exclude each other. Mutual non-existence, like absolute non-existence, is also beginningless and endless.

However, there is an important difference between the two. Whereas in absolute non-existence there are actual material objects, e.g., hare and horn and a negation of the relationship between the two, mutual non-existence is only a logical negation between two things that may not be actual. For example, "a red river is not a blue river" is true, though there is no red and no blue river.

Those schools of Indian philosophy that accept *abhāva* or non-existence differ regarding the question how it is apprehended. According to the Bhāṭṭas and the Advaitins, non-perception is the source of our knowledge of absence. In other words, the absence of knowledge causes the knowledge of absence. When all the conditions of perception are present but the object is not perceived, the absence of perception produces the perception of absence. In entering a room in the full day light, when there is an absence of the perception of an elephant, we perceive the absence of an elephant in the room. The Nyāya-Vaiśeṣika, on the other hand, argue that the absence of an elephant in the room means that the room is characterized by the adjective "absenceness," which is related to the room by the relation of *viśeṣaṇatā*, i.e., adjectivity, a kind of *svarūpa sambandha*, in which the nature of *abhāva* or absence is itself the "term" as well as the "relation." In other words, "absenceness" is the distinguishing characteristic as well as the relation of characterization. In short, the sense organ, i.e., eyes, perceive the room as well as the "absenceness" of the object in the room.

To sum up: negation or absence or non-existence as a category includes both negative entities as well as various types of negations. Acceptance of *abhāva* as a separate category recognizes the importance of this category for both epistemology and metaphysics.

We have now come to the end of our exposition of the Vaiśeṣika *padārthas*. It is close to Aristotelian and the Kantian lists, but more comprehensive and systematic. It provides the basis for a comprehensive description of the world, but not a list of categories used by modern science.

In its conception of the *padārthas*, the Vaiśeṣika provides an enumeration of reals without any attempt to synthesize them. It includes such categories as substance, quality, and action, but such formal categories as identity, difference, and *abhāva*, and such relational categories as conjunction, inherence, etc. One wonders how the Vaiśeṣika arrived at its list of *padārthas*. Why is causality not included in the list?

There is no reason why we should accept the list of Vaiśeṣika *padārthas* as absolute, it does provide a good starting point to begin a dialogue regarding the conceptions that underlie this list as well as reasons for its non-acceptance by those systems which do not accept it.

It is also worth noting that the Vaiśeṣika *padārthas* are not simply theoretical concepts; they reinforce the close connection between theory and practice in Indian thought. The very first *sūtra* lists the *padārthas*, includes *ātmā* in that list, and emphatically declares that knowledge of these *padārthas* helps to gain *mokṣa*. *Ātmā* is to be known in its purity as distinguished from other substances.

11

THE NYĀYA *DARŚANA*

The Nyāya school most likely had its origin in its attempt to formulate canons of argument for use in debates, which pervaded the Indian philosophical scene for a long time. The Nyāya derives its name from "*nyāya*," meaning the rules of logical thinking and the means of determining the right thing. Thus, originally indicated as a system of logic, laying down the rules of logical argumentation, Nyāya, also known as "*ānvīkṣikī*," blossomed into a systematic school and found its legitimate place among the six Vedic systems of philosophy. It found a close ally in the Vaiśeṣika school. The Naiyāyikas accept the ontology of the Vaiśeṣika school, and given that these two schools are closely allied in their realistic ontology, they are generally studied together forming a conjoint system called Nyāya-Vaiśeṣika.

The Nyāya was first systematized by Gautama, also known as "Akṣapāda," in the *Nyāya Sūtras* (250–450 CE), which belong to the post-Buddhistic period. In a brief exposition such as this, I will deal primarily with the Nyāya school as laid down by Gautama. Nyāya begins with the Gautama's *Sūtras* and Vātsyāyana's commentary (*Nyāya bhāṣya*, fifth century CE) on it, which were further explained and commented upon by Udyotakara in his *Nyāya vārttika* (seventh century CE). Vācaspati commented on *Nyāya vārttika* in his *Nyāya vārttika tīkā*. Other important works of this school are: Udayana's *Nyāya vārttika tātparyapariśuddhi* and *Kusumāñjalī*, Jayanta's *Nyāyamañjarī*. These works elaborate and develop the ideas contained in the *Nyāya Sūtras* and defend the doctrines against the attacks of hostile critics. Thus we can say that the ancient Nyāya (*prāchīna* Nyāya) developed out of the Gautama's *Sūtras*. The Navya-Nyāya (Neo-Nyāya) begins with Gaṅgeśa, the author of *Tattvacintāmaṇi*, the most remarkable among them being Raghunāth Śiromaṇi.

The most important difference between the old Nyāya and the Neo-Nyāya is as follows: The Neo-Nyāya discussed the same relational facts as the Nyāya did, however, in order to express their contents more adequately, they developed a new terminology and style. What the Naiyāyikas expressed in a simple language, the Neo-Nyāya expanded into much more sophisticated expressions using such technical jargons as *avacchedakatā* (the property of being the limitor), *viṣayatā* (the property of being the object), *prakāratā*, (the property of being a qualifier), and *saṃsargatā* (the property of being a relation). If the old Nyāya would say that the book is on the table, the neo Nyāya would express the same fact by stating that the book is being "qualified by the qualifier bookness," and state the relation of being on the table as the relation of conjunction, and also determine the table as qualified by "tableness." But note that this is only the beginning of the sophistication. Such authors as Gadādhara excelled in this sophisticated discourse. Thus, beginning with Gaṅgeśa in the eleventh century in Mithila, Neo-Nyāya had its high period in Navadeep, Bengal, where a galaxy of logicians flourished. Let me now turn my attention to the old Nyāya.

The Ancient or Old Nyāya

As stated earlier, the first systematizer of ancient Nyāya (henceforth referred to as Nyāya) was Gautama, also known as "Akṣapāda" who lived in Mithila. He not only systematized the already existing logical thought, but also used the occasion to respond to the Buddhist challenges. Vātsyāyana, the author of the principal commentary on the *Sūtras*, possibly belonged to the fourth century CE. Subsequent commentators did the same; they not only explicated the intentions of the *bhāṣya* but also defended the Nyāya against the opponent's criticisms. One may say that the Nyāya developed from the time of the Gautama up to the time of Śaṃkara (eighth century CE).

I will begin my discussion of the Nyāya with Gautama's *Sūtras* (henceforth NS). In the first *sūtra* sixteen entities are named, by knowing which one can attain the highest good. The sixteen entities are: (1) *pramāṇa* or the means of knowledge, (2) *prameya* or the objects of right knowledge, (3) *samśaya* or doubt, (4) *prayojana* or purpose, (5) *dṛṣṭānta* or example (required in inference), (6) *siddhānta* or conclusion, (7) *avayava* or components of an inference, (8) *tarka* or counterfactual argument, and eight pseudo-logical arguments (*nirṇaya, vāda, jalpa, vitaṇḍā, hetvābhāsas, chala, jāti, nigrahasthāna*). He concludes by noting that that a proper knowledge of these entities leads to the highest good.

The primary focus of my exposition in this chapter will be the Nyāya theory of *pramāṇas*, one of the sixteen topics mentioned in the first *sūtra*. It is not an exaggeration to say that the ancient Nyāya is an elaboration of these sixteen philosophical topics. For the sake of understanding, I have divided rest of the chapter in three sections: Section I discusses the *pramāṇas*, Section II the remaining fifteen Nyāya *padārthas*, and Section III explores the Nyāya conceptions of the self, bondage, and liberation.

I *Pramāṇas*

At the outset of his *bhāṣya*, Vātsyāyana notes as follows:

> when the object is known by the *pramāṇas*, one's practical response becomes successful, and the *pramāṇa* becomes objectively valid. In

> the absence of a *pramāṇa* there is no knowledge of the object, without knowledge of the object there is no ability of a *pravṛtti* to be successful. This knower, by experiencing the object by *pramāṇa*, wants either to acquire the object or shun it. His practical effort, as qualified by his desire to acquire or shun the object, is called *pravṛtti* . . . The intended object or *artha* is either pleasure or the cause of pleasure, pain or the cause of pain. The practical purpose of this *pramāṇa*, i.e., the goal which the *pramāṇa* has to reach is innumerable, because the differences among living beings are innumerable.[1]

A *pramāṇa* is an unerring concomitant of an object. As a *pramāṇa* articulates its object, so is the object in itself. By the success of a practical response is meant the response which leads to success. But a *pramāṇa* does not directly lead to successful practice. It leads to success via the true cognition of the object. After the practice is successful, the fact the *pramāṇa* has truly grasped the object is ascertained by inference. The point is that no cognition, without being true, can generate response which reaches the object.

Since the *pramāṇa* correctly apprehends its object, the knower, the object of knowledge, the knowledge itself, all three become invariable accompaniments of the object. Because without a *pramāṇa* there is no determination of the object. The knower is the one who has the practical response arising out of desire to possess the object or the hatred to shun it. *Pramāṇa* is that by which he knows the object, the object that is known is *prameya*. The knowledge of the object is *pramiti*. Since all these four invariably accompany the object, with these four, the nature of the truth (*tattva*) is exhausted. But what is this *tattva*? It is the being of what it is, the non-being of what is not.

This paragraph briefly, though pointedly, articulates the nature of the cognitive process, its relation to the being or non-being of things, the relation of knowledge to the object, the means of knowing, the object known, and the practical response which follows one's knowledge.

Vātsyāyana proceeds to maintain that when the being of an existent thing is apprehended, the non-being of what is not is also at the same time apprehended. Like a lamp, a cognition manifests what is there, but also at the same time manifests what is not there. The intention is to assert that an absence is also apprehended as much as the presence of a real entity. As a result, though Gautama does not mention it, absence is as much a *padārtha* as a positive entity is, whatever is determined by a *pramāṇa* is a *padārtha*, so is an absence.

Means of knowing or *pramāṇas* are four: perception, inference, comparison, and *śabda* or word.[2] When a *pramāṇa* is defined as the specific cause of a cognition, it actually can be brought under one or more of the *padārthas*. If a *pramāṇa* means the resulting knowledge itself, it comes under the category of quality, being a specific quality of the self. All the other remaining sixteen entities can be brought under the four. With this in mind, let us discuss the four *pramāṇas*, I will begin with perception.

*Perception (*Pratyakṣa*)*

The word "perception" applies both to a form of valid knowledge (*pramā*) as well as the method or *pramāṇa* of acquiring valid knowledge. Here we are concerned with perception as a *pramāṇa*.

For the Naiyāyikas, perception is cognition that is produced (*janya*) from the contact of a sense organ with an object; it is not itself linguistic, is not erroneous, and is well ascertained.[3] The self, the mind, sense organs, objects, and a particular kind of contact between them, are necessary conditions for perception. The contacts take place in a succession: the self comes in contact with the mind or *manas*, the *manas* with the sense organ concerned, and the sense organ with the object. This operation produces a cognition of the sort "this pitcher is blue." All knowledge is revelation of objects, and the contact of the senses with an object is not metaphorical, but literal.

The Nyāya definition of perception as a form of valid knowledge that originates and is caused by sense stimulation follows the etymological meaning of the term "*pratyakṣa*," which means "present before the eyes or any other sense organs," signifying direct or immediate knowledge. Gautama takes the term "object" to signify three kinds of objects: the physical objects (e.g., table, chair, pitcher),[4] specific objects (e.g., color, hard, soft),[5] and internal objects (e.g., pleasure and pain).[6] In short, perception is a cognition that is always of an object. Cognitions of substances like tables and chairs are called "external perceptions," of pleasure and pain "internal perceptions." Gautama further adds that perception is *avyapadeśa* (not impregnated by words) and *vyavasāyātmaka* (definite).

When we try to come to grips with the Nyāya definition of perception, we begin to see that the definition applies only to perceptions which are "*janya*," i.e., "produced"; these perceptions arise and pass away. It goes without saying that all human cognitions are generated. However, if there is an eternal being who perceives all things at all times, then the definition does not apply to this being's perception. The Naiyāyikas were aware of this difficulty, and such Nyāya philosophers as Gaṅgeśa define perception in a more general sense to include both. However, to understand the Nyāya theory of perception, it is essential that one has a clear conception of what the Naiyāyikas mean by "contact." On the Naiyāyika account, contact is a function of a sense organ through which it enters into specific relations with its appropriate object resulting in the perception of that object. This contact between the sense organs and their objects may be of various kinds.

The Naiyāyikas, after the commentator Uddyotakara, come to distinguish between six kinds of contacts[7] between a sense organ and an object. These are:

1. *Saṁyoga* (conjunction): a direct contact of the eyes with the object, say, a pitcher in the kitchen in full sight.

2 *Saṁyukta samavāya* (inherence in what is conjoined): an indirect contact of sense organ with its object through mediation of a third term that is related to both, e.g., when my eyes come in contact with the color of the pitcher through the pitcher in full sight.

3 *Saṁyukta samaveta samavāya* (inherence in what is inseparably related to what is conjoined): a still more indirect contact with the mediation of two terms that are related, e.g., in perceiving a pitcher in the kitchen, I also perceive "colorness" which inheres in the color of the pitcher, there is a contact of the eyes with the "colorness" with the mediation of the two terms "pitcher" and "color," i.e., conjunction with the pitcher and the second kind of contact with the color.

4 *Samavāya* (inherence): when I hear a sound, the sound inheres in the ear (according to the Vaiśeṣika ontology), so the sense organ of hearing is in contact with the sound in the relation of *samavāya.*

5 *Samaveta samavāya* (the relation of inherence in that which inheres in the sense): the contact between the sense and its object via a third term that is inseparably related to both, e.g., in the auditory perception of soundness, the ear is in contact with the "soundness" because it inheres in the sound, which, in turn inheres as a quality in the ear.

6 *Saṁyukta viśeṣaṇatā:* here the sense is in contact with the object insofar as the object is a qualification of the other term connected with the sense. This happens when I see the absence of a pitcher on the floor. The Naiyāyikas explain the perception of non-existence and the relation of inherence with the help of this contact. When I see the absence of an elephant on the floor of my room, the visual sense organ has a conjunction with the floor, but the absence is in the relation of *viśeṣaṇatā* with the floor.

These six kinds of contacts are called ordinary or *laukika.* The Naiyāyikas, in addition recognize three kinds of extraordinary or *alaukika* contacts. These are: *sāmānyalakṣanā pratyaksa, jñānalakṣaṇā pratyāsatti,* and *yogaja.* The first kind of extraordinary contact takes place when upon seeing the cowness in a cow, I also through that perceived cowness, perceive all other cows in whom the cowness inheres. In other words, the cowness serves as the mode of contact with all those individual cows in whom cowness is present. The second kind of extraordinary contact takes place when upon perceiving a piece of velvet, I also see its softness even though I am not touching it. The color of the velvet and its softness are so connected that when I see one of them in an ordinary contact, I also see the other in an extraordinary manner. Here the knowledge of the one, i.e., the texture of the piece of the cloth serves as the medium through which the softness is visually perceived. The third kind of extraordinary contact occurs when a *yogi* has the extraordinary power to perceive events yet to occur, or things at great distance or things like atoms, which are too minute to be ordinarily perceived. This kind of extraordinary contact is called *yogaja* and is possible only for persons adept in *yoga.*

Now, perception or rather a perceptual cognition takes place in two stages. At first with the contact of the sense organ with the object, there arises what is called "*nirvikalpaka*" cognition, and the cognition that arises after it is called "*savikalpaka*." Most systems of Indian philosophy recognize such a succession: first *nirvikalpaka* or non-conceptual perception, and then *savikalpaka* perception. But the systems differed as to the precise nature of the *nirvikalpaka* perception. On the Nyāya view, all the components of a *savikalpaka* perception are known in the *nirvikalpaka*, but only without being related to each other. In effect, *nirvikalpaka* is knowledge of a bunch of unrelated entities (e.g., "this" and "thisness," "jar" and "jarness," "blue" and "blueness"), but these entities are related into one complex structure in *savikalpaka*. The *nirvikalpaka* is a perceptual cognition, but there is no cognition of this cognition, so that I do not know immediately that I had a *nirvikalpaka* perception. Only its having occurred is known by inference after the occurrence of the *savikalpaka* perception. In other words, the perceptual cognition "this pitcher is blue," would not have occurred unless I had previously apprehended such elements as "this," "thisness," "pitcher," pitcherness," "blue," and "blueness" separately. Thus *nirvikalpaka* is the prior knowledge of the thing and its constituents as unrelated entities; it is known through inference from *savikalpaka*.

*Inference (*Anumāna*)*

With these remarks on perception, we may now pass on to the topic of inference or *anumāna,* which is the primary concern of Nyāya, and with which logic in the Western sense is primarily concerned. It is important to remember that in the Indian discourse the domain of logic is part of the theory of knowledge or the *pramāṇa* theory. The Indian theories discuss inference as *a pramāṇa,* i.e., as a mode of knowing, and not merely as a theory of valid thinking. This distinction, which cannot be overemphasized, will become clear as we proceed.

Whereas the inference as a means of knowing is called *anumāna*, the inferential cognition is called "*anumiti*." It is knowledge that arises after (*anu*) another knowledge. Accordingly, it is defined as that cognition which presupposes some other cognition. It is mediate and indirect and arises through the knowledge of the mark or *liṅga*. Consider the case of seeing smoke on a distant hill. Upon seeing the smoke on a hill, one infers that there is fire on the hill. In this case, the smoke serves as the mark of fire.

Inference has two aspects to it: under one aspect the theory gives a psychological account of how the process goes on; and in this aspect, it is called "*svārthānumāna*" or inference for oneself. Earlier in his life, a person, say, Shyam, had acquired the knowledge "wherever there is smoke, there is fire." Now upon seeing a column of fire rising up from a hill, Shyam remembers what he had learnt before, viz., that smoke is always accompanied by fire, and comes to the conclusion that the hill is fiery. With this memory, he now sees the smoke as that which is always accompanied by the presence of fire. This last perception (whose cognitive structure is more complex than the initial perception of smoke) would produce, in any rational mind, the inferential cognition "there is fire on the hill."

So far, the account given is entirely psychological, i.e., a description of the mental process which culminates in an inferential cognition. Clearly, the process is not a logical structure; it gives the story of a causal chain of how a cognition causes another whose final member is the inferential cognition. However, in the second aspect of the theory, for the purposes of convincing the other (*parārthānumāna*), one can transform the story into a logical structure, somewhat like a syllogism with the well-known five-membered structure, represented as follows:

1 there is fire on the hill (the proposition to be proved or *pratijñā*),
2 because there is smoke (states the reason or *hetu*),
3 wherever there is smoke, there is fire (*vyāpti*),
4 as in the case of the kitchen (example or *dṛṣṭānta*),
5 there is fire on the hill (conclusion or *nigamana*).

The first step is the assertion, the second gives the reason, the third illustrates the invariable concomitance (e.g., of smoke and fire), the fourth expresses "this too is like that," which in this context means that "this hill too is like a kitchen because it possesses smoke which is invariably concomitant with fire," and the fifth step is the conclusion where the initial assertion is asserted as established.

There are two important features of this Nyāya construction of an inference that must be noted. First, the conclusion is stated first, not as proved, but rather to be proved. Secondly, in (4) an example is given, an example that illustrates the *vyāpti*, or the universal concomitance between the *hetu* and the major term to be proved, or *sādhya*. The example rules out the possibility of using such a universal proposition as "all men are immortal," which are formally valid but materially unsound. Both the parties to the dispute must agree with regard to the instance. In other words, the inference must not only be formally consistent, but rather requires, to the contrary, that it must be materially true.

Those familiar with Aristotelian syllogism will easily recognize that the *sādhya* is the major term, the *pakṣa* the minor term, and the *hetu* is the middle. Accordingly, in the example under consideration ("this hill has fire, because there is smoke on the hill"), one could say that the "hill" is the minor term, "fire" is the major term, and "smoke," the middle, borrowing the technical vocabulary of Aristotelian syllogism. Modern scholars claim that (1) and (5) of the Nyāya inference are the same and so the first of them can be dispensed with, and that (4) is a mere repetition or application of the *hetu* and so it is superfluous. There remain, thus, only three propositions. Thus, many modern scholars tend to reduce the five-membered Nyāya *anumāna* to a three-membered syllogism. Such a reduction is misleading.

It is important to remember in this context that whereas Indian logic deals with entities, the Aristotelian logic deals with terms. In the Aristotelian logic, the validity of a syllogism depends on the extension of the minor term. The extension of the minor term "Socrates" (in the example, "All human beings are mortal, Socrates is a human being. Therefore, Socrates is mortal") is subsumed by the middle term "human being" and the extension of the middle term by that of the major term "mortal." In Aristotelian logic one finds three propositions; in Nyāya *anumāna* one finds that the five steps in an inference are descriptions of *jñānas*. A *jñāna* or knowledge, for Nyāya, is an event, an occurrence, and the five steps of the Nyāya inference are descriptions of *jñānas* which one undergoes in the process of inference. If the first four cognitions of the inferential process occur, the fifth one will follow.

Aristotelian syllogism concerns the formal principles of validity of arguments, the Nyāya inference seeks to have both formal validity and material truth. Material truth of an argument is assured by including the requirement of an example, acceptable to both the proponent and the opponent, within the logical structure of an inference. In addition, Western logic, especially in the modern form, completely separates logic from psychology, which one does not find in Indian logic.

Thus there are important differences between the Aristotelian syllogism and Nyāya *anumiti*. As long as one keeps these differences in mind, we can still call the Nyāya terms by their Aristotelian equivalents for easy reference. This is not to suggest that there is one-to-one correspondence between the Nyāya *sādhya, pakṣa,* and *hetu* and Aristotle's major, minor, and the middle term respectively.

Inference is generally taken to be of two kinds: *svārtha* and *parārtha*; I have already discussed these. Scholars raise various questions regarding the nature of inference and the methods of establishing *vyāpti,* and so on. In this introductory exposition it is not possible to deal with all of them. However, to give my readers a flavor of the kinds of questions raised and discussed, I will briefly review two classifications of inference: the first deals with the nature of inference and the second with the method of establishing *vyāpti.*

Gautama[8] makes a distinction between three kinds of inference—*pūrvavat, śeṣavat* and *sāmānyatodṛṣṭa,* i.e., that which infers from a cause (*liṅga*), that which infers from an effect to the cause, and that which brings together a number of singular judgments under a universal respectively. The first two are based on causation and the last one on simple coexistence. In the first case, i.e., *pūrvavat,* i.e., "like what has been before," one infers on the basis of past experience (hence this name): one sees dark clouds and infers rain that is to follow. In the second case, known as *śeṣavat* (i.e., like what follows), one infers the cause from the effect: one tastes a little water in the sea as salty, and infers that all sea water is so. In the third, i.e., *sāmānyatodṛṣṭa,* we infer the one from the other not on account of any causal relation but because they are uniformly related in our experience. One observes a person, Caitra by name, now to be at a place, and some time later sees the same person at a different place and infers that Caitra must have moved from one place to another. Seeing the sun in the eastern horizon in the morning and the sun in the western horizon in the evening, one infers the movement of the sun from the east to the west. On seeing some mango trees blossom, one infers *all* mango trees to be in blossom. The third inference is the same as an inductive generalization or bringing individuals perceived under a general concept that also applies to unperceived individuals.

Another way of classifying the inference is based on the nature and different methods of establishing *vyāpti.* These are: *kevalānvayi, kevalavyatireki,* and *anvay-avyatireki.*

In the first, the middle term is positively related to the major term, and the *vyāpti* is arrived at through the method of agreement in presence; there is no instance of their agreement in absence. For example:

> All knowable objects are nameable.
> The pitcher is knowable.
> Therefore, the pitcher is nameable.

This inference corresponds to the Mill's Method of Agreement. In this inference the universal premise "all knowable objects are nameable," is arrived at by an enumeration of the positive instances of agreement between "knowable" and "nameable."

In the second, the middle term is negatively related to the major term, and the *vyāpti* is arrived at through the method of agreement in absence, there being no instance of their agreement in presence. For example:

> What is not different-from-other-elements has no smell.
> The earth has smell.
> Therefore, the earth is different-from-other-elements.

Here smell is the differentia of "earth." In this inference, the smell is co-extensive with the earth, and there is no instance of the middle term "smell" with any term except the minor term, i.e., earth.

In the third, the middle term is both positively and negatively related to the major term. For example:

> All smoky things has fire.
> This hill has smoke.
> Therefore, this hill has fire.

And

> No non-fiery things have smoke.
> This hill has smoke.
> Therefore, this hill is not non-fiery, i.e., this hill has fire.

In this inference *vyāpti* is based on a universal relation between the presence as well as the absence of the middle and the major terms.

*Comparison (*Upamāna*)*

Let us now turn to the third *pramāṇa*, i.e., *upamāna*. Etymologically the word "*upamāna*" is derived from "*upa*" meaning "similarity" and "*māna*" meaning "cognition." Accordingly, *upamāna* means "knowledge by similarity." *Upamāna* as a *pramāṇa* has been defined as the "knowledge of the relationship that obtains between a word and its denotation." Resulting knowledge is called "*upamiti*." For example, a person who has never seen a *gavaya* and does not know what it looks like is told by his friend that a *gavaya* looks like a cow. Later on, he sees an animal much like, but not quite a cow. He then remembers what he was told by his friend, namely, that a *gavaya* is like a cow. The person then says: "this animal is a *gavaya*, because it is like a cow." This knowledge is arrived at by *upamāna*; the Naiyāyikas argue that this knowledge cannot be obtained either by perception or by inference. It is based on the knowledge of similarity.

Of the nine systems of Indian philosophy, the Buddhists reduce *upamāna* to perception and testimony, the Sāṁkhya and the Vaiśeṣika reduce it to inference, and the Jainas to recognition. The Mīmāṁsakas and Advaita Vedānta recognize it as a separate source of knowledge, though their accounts vary.

*Verbal Testimony (*Śabda*)*

Śabda is "verbal knowledge." This knowledge is derived from words and sentences. All verbal testimony, however, is not valid. When it is said that *śabda* as a *pramāṇa* is a source of valid knowledge, the reference is to the authoritative verbal testimony (*āptavākya*), the statements of a trustworthy person, who knows the truth, and speaks the truth to guide other persons. But it is not enough that the testimony is reliable; it is contingent upon understanding the meaning of the sentences uttered by an *āpta* person.

A sentence is a collection of words which has the power to convey its meaning. In order to acquire knowledge from a reliable testimony, one has to understand the meanings of the words. A word or *pada* is a collection of syllables or *varṇas*. Here a collection means "being the object of one cognition." Such a sentence, when uttered by a person who knows, is a *pramāṇa*. *Śabda* as a source of valid knowledge consists in understanding the meaning of words uttered by an *āpta* person. Thus we have (1) written or spoken testimony of a trustworthy person, (2) understanding of the meaning of the words uttered by such a person, and (3) the verbal knowledge of the objects under consideration.

A sentence, in order to make sense, must meet certain conditions. These are: "*ākāṅkṣā*" or expectation or mutual implication, "*yogyatā*," or fitness, "*sannidhi*" or "nearness," and "*tātparya*" or intention. A mere random group of words does not make a sentence, because they are not related by "*ākānkṣā*" or expectation

The words "cow, horse, man" do not form a sentence, because the words do not arouse expectations. The words must be related in such a manner that they need each other in order to make sense. The second condition outlines the fitness of the words to convey the meaning and not contradict each other. If someone says "sprinkle the grass with fire," we do not have a sentence, for the word "sprinkle" arouses an expectation which "fire" is not appropriate or fit to fulfill. Finally, even if the words are appropriate in this sense, they must be uttered in quick succession. Uttering words at long intervals would not constitute a sentence. Thus the words "bring --------a----------glass--------of---------water" does not make a sentence. In other words, the utterances must be close enough to constitute a sentence. Words—than they arouse expectations, are appropriate, and uttered in quick succession—constitute a sentence. For example, "there are five fruit trees on the bank of the river." Finally, the intention of the speaker is relevant, where various literal meanings are possible (as in "bring the *Saindhava*") the word "*Saindhava*" may mean a horse or salt. It is important to know what the speaker intends. If a man is eating dinner, he wants salt, not a horse.

Śabda as a *pramāṇa*, argue the Naiyāyikas, is of two kinds: *laukika* and *alaukika*. *Laukika* testimony is the word of a reliable human person and the *alaukika* is divine testimony, the words of the Vedas, which are uttered by God. Human testimony is fallible but the divine testimony is infallible.

In sum: *śabda* or word is an important *pramāṇa*. This is the way we come to know about things, simply by hearing sentences uttered by a competent speaker. We learn about physics or about history by listening to the lectures of a competent physicist or historian. We learn about contemporary events by reading reliable reports. This kind of knowing occupies a central place in Indian epistemologies—partly because it is by this means that we learn about what we ought to do, or how we ought to lead our lives, about *dharma* and *adharma*, from the discourses in the Vedas, for example. This kind of knowing is sometimes criticized as being dogmatic acceptance of authority, but this hasty critique fails to recognize its ubiquitous indispensability for our knowledge of the world. Just imagine what small fragment of the world we would be restricted to if we were to rely exclusively upon perception and inference.

At the end, it is important to reflect on the relative strength and weaknesses of the different *pramāṇas*. With regard to the sensible particulars, the Naiyāyikas regard perception to be stronger than inference. With regards to supersensible entities, inference is stronger than perception, and *śabda* is stronger than inference, *śabda* is the strongest with regard to what ought to be done. It is worth noting that the Naiyāyikas believe in *pramāṇasaṁplava* rather than in *pramāṇa-vyavasthā*. In other words, they believe that one and the same object can be known by perception, by inference, and by *śabda*. The Buddhists, in contrast, believe in *pramāṇa-vyavasthā*, i.e., in the thesis that to specific types of objects, there correspond specific *pramāṇas*. In general, the Vedic philosophers believed in *pramāṇasaṁplava*, i.e., the thesis that one and the same object is knowable by different *pramāṇas*, e.g., by perception, inference, and by *śabda*.

The Nature of Knowledge

We have examined the four sources or means of knowing that the Nyāya recognizes. Now we may turn our attention to the generic nature of "knowledge." Knowledge is called "*anubhūti*" or "*jñāna.*" According to the Nyāya, "consciousness" and "knowledge" are synonyms: not so, however, in other Indian systems of philosophy. The Nyāya also differs from the spiritual (*ādhyātmika*) philosophies in regarding consciousness as a quality (*guṇa*) produced in a self (*ātman*) only when the self is embodied, and there is appropriate contact of the sense-organs with the object. Without a functioning body, there is no consciousness. There is none, e.g., in the state of deep dreamless sleep. However, in spite of such dependence on bodily functioning, consciousness does not exhibit characteristics that are uniquely its own. Like a beam of light, it "shows up" or manifests whatever it falls on. It is also intrinsically of-an-object, there being no objectless consciousness. Knowledge is not an action, to know is not to act. Given that it arises in the self when certain conditions are fulfilled, it is not an essential quality of the self. However, only a self that is embodied can know. Contrary to the position of the spiritual philosophies—the Sāṃkhya-Yoga, the Bauddha, and the Vedānta—the Nyāya does not regard consciousness as self-manifesting. It only manifests whatever happens to be its object. Since it is not its own object, it cannot manifest itself. It is manifested, known, made aware of, only by another, subsequent, knowledge that makes it its object. Thus we have a knowledge K_1 whose object is O_1. K_1 manifests O_1. After K_1 has occurred, there may follow an introspective knowledge of K_1, let us call it K_2. K_1 is then manifested to the self.

> K_1 has the form "this is a jar."
> K_2 would have the form "I know that this is a jar."[9]

Knowledge is classified into two kinds: those that are "valid" (*pramā*) and those that are not (*apramā*). Valid knowledge or *pramā* is of four kinds, depending upon the causal process by which a knowledge is generated. Invalid knowledge is either error or doubt. Knowing a rope as a snake, or a white thing as yellow, are instances of error. Doubt, being uncertain knowledge, cannot be *pramā*. For instances of "doubt," we don't have to look far. Looking at a thing a little far away, in the dusk of evening, one wonders "is that a human or a tree?" Doubt arises from perceiving the quality common to both the alternatives ('human" and "tree") and not perceiving the specific properties that go with each.

A knowledge is valid or *pramā* when it is generated by an appropriate *pramāṇa*, and agrees with its object. A *pramāṇa* thus is both the proper cause of a valid cognition, but also its justification. This unique combination of a causal theory and a justification theory of knowledge is almost unique in the history of philosophy.

When the question is asked "how is true knowledge distinguished from false knowledge," the Naiyāyikas respond by saying that valid knowledge corresponds to its object and leads to successful activity. Invalid knowledge does not correspond to its object and leads to failure and disappointment. Suppose you need a pinch of salt with your evening dinner. You see a white powdered substance before, you take a pinch of it and put it in your soup, and upon tasting the soup you realize that it tastes right. On another occasion, however, when looking for salt you take a pinch of sugar, put it in your soup, and then realize that it is sugar and not salt. Thus, the Naiyāyikas argue that whereas the truth and falsity of knowledge depends on correspondence and non-correspondence to facts respectively, the test of its truth and falsity consists in inference from success and failure of our daily activities in relation to the object sought. True knowledge leads to successful activity, false knowledge to failure and disappointment.

The property of being a valid cognition is called *prāmāṇya* or *pramātva* (or validity). On the Nyāya theory, it is not intrinsic to a knowledge (contrary, again, to the spiritual philosophies).

Returning to the question as to whether truth (also falsity) of a cognition is *svataḥ* or intrinsic to the cognition or are extrinsic, i.e., *parataḥ*, the Naiyāyikas hold that truth and falsity both are extrinsic or *parataḥ*. In other words, when a knowledge arises from the causal condition which produce it, it is not *eo ipso* valid, nor it is, from the very beginning known to be valid (or invalid as the case may be). Validity needs a special causal condition for it to arise, this is, some special excellence in the generating conditions, just as invalidity is produced by some special defect in them. When a knowledge comes into being, it simply manifests its object, but not itself (as we have said), so it does not know its own validity or invalidity. It is only subsequently that the knower infers on the basis of success (or failure) of the practical action whether his knowledge was valid (or invalid).

Thus, according to the Nyāya, practical success (or failure) is the criterion of validity (or invalidity), while the nature of truth is taken to be correspondence between the structure of knowledge and the structure of its object.

II Nyāya *Padārthas*

As stated earlier, Gautama in his NS I.1.1 mentions sixteen *padārthas*.[10] Of the sixteen, the *pramāṇa* has already been discussed. I will in this section review the remaining fifteen *padārthas*.

Prameya literally means "a knowable or an object of true knowledge," i.e., reality. According to the Nyāya, there are twelve objects of such knowledge: (1) the self (*ātma*); (2) the body, the basis of organic activities, the senses, and the feelings of pleasure and pain; (3) the senses, e.g., of smell, taste, sight, touch and hearing; (4) their objects. i.e., the sensible qualities of smell, taste, color, touch and sound; (5) cognition (*buddhi*), which in the Nyāya school is used synonymously with knowledge (*jñāna*) and apprehension (*upalabdhi*); (6) mind (*manas*), the inner sense concerned with the perceptions of pleasure, pain, etc.; (7) activity (*pravṛtti*), includes both good or bad; (8) such mental defects (*dośa*) as attachment (*rāga*), hatred (*dveṣa*) and infatuation (*moha*) which make us do good or bad actions; (9) rebirth after death (*pretyabhāva*) result of our good or bad actions; (10) the experiences of pleasure and pain (*phala*); (11) suffering (*dukkha*); (12) liberation or freedom from suffering (*apavarga*), the cessation of all suffering forever.

Saṃśaya or doubt is a state of uncertainty.[11] In doubt, the mind wavers between mutually contradictory descriptions of the same thing, each of which is possible. A thing is known in general terms, but there is no apprehension of its specific nature. There is suggestion of different alternatives resulting in a doubt of the form, e.g., "is this a man or a tree?" Nyāya literature details the conditions and the many different ways in which doubts occur; all of them, however, involve different alternatives but no discernment of any specific mark to decide between them. Wherever there are conflicting opinions of philosophers such that the two contradictory possibilities are there, there is doubt.

It is worth noting that the resolution of doubt is a rational activity. Doubt precedes the exercise of *nyāya*, that is to say, of the different means of knowing in order to ascertain the nature of a thing and remove doubt. It is arguable that doubt and the effort to remove the doubt are rational activities, although, as has been argued, by Mohanty,[12] the Nyāya *saṃśaya* is perceptual doubt, while Cartesian doubt is an intellectual doubt. But there is no doubt that the resolution of doubt itself is a rational activity even if it involves *seeing* the thing more clearly and discriminatingly.

Prayojana[13] or purpose or an end-in-view is that object for which we act: either to desire it or to shun it. In other words, there is some goal, which, we think, we should reach or shun, and this determination or purpose leads to an application of *nyāya*. The primary purpose is the attainment of happiness and the removal of *dukkha*; however, everything that leads to the realization of the primary purpose can also function as a secondary or subsidiary purpose.

Dṛṣṭānta or example represents an undisputed fact that illustrates a general rule.[14] It is that entity with regard to which there is an agreement between both parties, i.e., between ordinary persons as well as critical thinkers. In other words, the ordinary person and the critical thinkers using logic must agree with regard to something and it is only such an agreed entity that can be used as an example. In other words, when one argues that the hill must be fiery because it is smoky, the kitchen may be cited as an example of that in which one sees smoke accompanied by fire. Example thus is a very important and necessary part of the Nyāya reasoning; it is a component of the Nyāya five-membered syllogism discussed earlier.

Siddhānta or conclusive view is the doctrine which belongs to a *śāstra* or a discipline or a science.[15] Conclusion is the definite ascertainment of an entity. Gautama divides it into four kinds[16]:

1 *sarvatantra siddhānta*, that which is not disputed by any of the sciences;

2 *pratitantra siddhānta*, that which is established by a particular discipline and by particular philosophers;
3 *adhikaraṇa siddhānta*, where in order to establish the property of a given thing we have first to establish another property of it. For example, the Naiyāyikas argue for the omniscience of creator by first establishing that an agent initially makes a binary combination of atoms possible;
4 *abhyupagama siddhānta* is provisional acceptance of a conclusion of the other. For example, when the opponent, in this case the Mīmāṃsaka, establishes that sound is a substance, the Naiyāyikas respond as follows: "We are not going to challenge this thesis; however, let us discuss the issue taking the thesis—either sound is eternal or non-eternal—for granted." The hope is that the idea of substantiality of sound will eventually be refuted if both alternatives (eternal or non-eternal) are set aside. Such a provisional acceptance of a conclusion of the other is called "*abhyupagama siddhānta*," which clearly has the structure of a hypothetical argument of the form "if S then either p or not-p," but if both alternatives, p and not-p, are shown not to apply, then the hypothesized premise must be wrong.

Avayava means "member" or "premises." A syllogism consists of five members or premises. These members have been discussed above.

Tarka in the *Nyāya Sūtras* is used as a kind of hypothetical argument, an indirect way of justifying a conclusion. It demonstrates that the presumed hypothesis to prove the conclusion leads to absurdity.[17] *Tarka* is an intellectual cognition produced by desire assuming the following form: "If smoke could exist in a locus which does not have fire, then smoke could not be caused by fire." The question is asked whether any absurdity would result if the given conclusion is accepted as true or rejected as false. This kind of argument is designed to remove any doubt in the *vyāpti*, e.g., "wherever there is smoke, there is fire," and, as a result, to strengthen the inference that proves the presence of fire upon perceiving smoke. Let me give an illustrative example of this sort of reasoning: in looking through the bay window of my house, I see smoke coming out of the house across the street and say that the house across the street is on fire. A friend sitting next to me argues that there is no fire, only smoke; in response, I advance a *tarka*: "if there could be smoke without there being fire, then one could produce smoke without fire, which is absurd." This proposition is deduced from the hypothesis because it follows from the hypothesis as a general rule: "whatever has a mark, has that which it is a mark of." To put it differently, the absence of fire is a mark of the absence of smoke. Accordingly, the modern Naiyāyikas define *tarka* as a process of deducing from a mark that of which it is a mark. It shows by a counter-factual argument that if things were of such and such nature, then absurd consequences would follow. For example, with regard to the eternity or non-eternity of the self, *tarka* removes the doubt by arguing, "if the self had an origin and an end, then *karma* and its consequences would not take place, which is not acceptable."

It is important to remember in this context that *tarka* does not give rise to true knowledge, i.e., it is not a *pramāṇa*, because one of its premises, the assumption of the contradictory of the conclusion is false. It confirms a *pramāṇa*; it is an aid to *pramāṇa*. This process of indirect proof in the Nyāya roughly corresponds to *reductio ad absurdum*, which one finds in Western logic.

Nirṇaya is the ascertainment of the truth attained by *pramāṇas* and *tarka*.[18] It is a doctrine that has been accepted and subscribed to by a school. It represents the removal of all preceding doubts, after an examination of views for or against a particular doctrine.

Vāda stands for analytic consideration in order to ascertain the truth.[19] It, like *nirṇaya*, also proceeds with the help of *pramāṇas* and *tarka* and uses arguments which are stated formally in the form of five-membered syllogism. The goal is not to refute any established theory but rather to arrive at the truth. In *vāda*, each of the parties involved in discussion—the proponent as well as the opponent—attempts to establish his own position and refute the position of the other.

Jalpa is wrangling in which both parties involved aim to defeat each other, but there is no attempt to ascertain the truth.[20] Given that the goal is to defeat others, it involves use of invalid arguments and reasons. (Lawyers usually use such arguments.)

Vitaṇḍā is a kind of debate in which the proponent does not aim to establish his own position, but simply aims to refute the position of the others.[21] Thus, whereas in *jalpa* each party's goal is to establish his/her respective position and to gain victory over the other, in *vitaṇḍā*, each party tries to win by simply refuting the position of the other. It roughly approximates what is called "sophistry" in Western logic.

Gautama defines "*hetvābhāsa*" as a "fallacious probans," because they do not possess all the characteristics of true probans," but they seem sufficiently similar to a probans.[22] Here *hetvābhāsa* does not mean a defective *hetu*, but rather a "seeming" or "pseudo" *hetu*, The Sanskrit term "*hetvābhāsa*," however, may be taken to mean not only the "semblance of a *hetu*" *(duṣta-hetu)*, but also a "faulty *hetu*" (*hetu-doṣa*). The older Naiyayikas do not make a distinction between these two meanings, Gaṅgeśa, however, does. For our purposes it is not necessary to go into a detailed investigation of this distinction. Suffice it to note that a *hetvābhāsa* prevents an inference from taking place.

In *chala* one of the parties to a dispute—after failing to give a good argument against his opponent—advances irrelevant or pseudo replies.[23] Here an attempt is made to contradict the argument of another person, by giving an unfair reply. The respondent contradicts a statement by taking it in a sense other than the one the speaker intended. In other words, when a person, say X, cannot respond to a fairly strong argument that Y provides, then X may contradict Y's statement by taking it in a sense that was not intended. For example, X may say "*nava-kambala*" meaning that the boy possesses a new blanket, and Y unfairly objects and points out that the boy has nine blankets, because the compound "*nava-kambala*" is ambiguous.

Jāti stands for all those futile arguments advanced by one party against the other, which instead of destroying the opponent's position really contradict the position of the one who advances those arguments.[24] It consists in advancing a futile argument based on similarity or dissimilarity between things. For example, in trying to meet the argument "sound, being an effect, is non-eternal, like a jar," the opponent may argue that the sound is eternal like sky because "sound shares with sky the property of being incorporeal." This is *jāti*. The Naiyāyikas enumerate twenty-four kinds of *jātis*.

Nigrahasthāna[25] is the last entity in Gautama's list. "*Nigraha*" means "defeat" and "*sthāna*" means "place" so that it leads to the final defeat of the proponent or the opponent. It includes many different kinds of arguments leading to the final defeat of one of the parties. Gautama in the second chapter of the fifth part of the *Nyāya Sūtra* lists twenty-two such arguments which lead to a final defeat.

This list of entities (it must be clear that these are entities in a highly abstract sense) shows what really occurs between the parties of a dispute, beginning with doubt and ending with ascertainment of truth, defeat of one of the parties and the victory of the other. Such an argumentative tradition, since ancient times, was a part of the rational discourses of the Indian philosophers, and the task of the Nyāya commentators was to give them precise definitions and formulations. It must also be evident that the concept of reason implicit in these discussions makes reason inseparable from proper, precise, and goal-oriented use of language and from intersubjective discourse.

III Self, Bondage, and Liberation

In the chapter on the Upaniṣads, we saw that they take *cit* or consciousness to be the same as *ātman*. For the Nyāya-Vaiśeṣika school, on the other hand, *ātman* includes both: the finite individual selves (and souls) as well as the infinite soul, i.e., God. I would like to draw the attention of my readers to the fact that in the list of *prameyas*, discussed in the previous section, *ātmā* appears first. Vātsyāyana states:

> The omniscient self is the seer, the enjoyer and the experiencer of all things, the body is the place of its enjoyment and suffering, and the sense organs are the instruments for enjoyment and suffering. Enjoyment and suffering are cognitions (of pleasure and pain). The inner sense or *manas* is that which can know all objects. Action (*pravṛtti*) causes of pleasure and pain; so do the *doṣas* (defects), namely, passion, envy, and attachment. The self had earlier bodies than this one, and will occupy other bodies after this one, until the achievement of "*mokṣa*." This beginningless succession of birth and death is called "(*pretyabhāva*)." Experiences of pleasure and pain, along with their instruments, i.e., body, sense organs, etc., are the "fruit" (*phala*). "Pain" is inextricably connected with "pleasure." In order to achieve *mokṣa* or *apavarga*, one should realize that all happiness is pain—which will result in detachment and in the long run freedom.[26]

It is worth noting that the above list not only includes the objects of true knowledge, but also body, sense organs, objects (of these senses), intellect (*buddhi*), mind (*manas*), action, (*pravṛtti*), defects (*doṣa)*, the succession of birth and death (*pretyabhāva*), fruits (*phala*), suffering (*dukkha*), and release (*mokṣa*).[27]

After this list of entities, the next *sūtra* proceeds to inform us how the "self" (or *ātman*) is known.[28] We are told that the self is too "subtle," and cannot be perceived by any of the senses. Such judgments as, "I am happy," "I am sad," do not provide any knowledge of the true nature of the self. Thus, the question arises: how is the self known? It is said that the self is inferred from pleasure, pain, desire, hatred, effort, and consciousness. These six are the specific qualities of the self, insofar as they belong *only* to the self. Of these six, three, namely, desire, effort, and consciousness, are common to both finite selves and the infinite self, i.e., God; hatred and pain belong only to the finite selves; and the sixth, namely, happiness, belongs to both the individuals and God, though God's happiness is eternal, while the happiness of finite individuals is non-eternal.

The Naiyāyikas take great pains to demonstrate that consciousness is a quality neither of the body, nor of the sense organs, nor of an action; it is rather a quality of the self, which exists independently and is different from the body, the senses, the mind and consciousness. The self, on their theory, is eternal; it cannot be produced and destroyed. Though consciousness is a quality of the self, it nevertheless is not an essential quality of the self, which explains why in deep sleep or coma one does not possess consciousness. Thus, the self may exist without consciousness. Self, however, is capable of having consciousness under suitable conditions; it arises in a self when the appropriate causal conditions are present, i.e., when the self comes in contact with the mind, the mind with the senses, and the senses with external objects. (These contacts are needed in the case of all kinds of cognition, including testimony and inference.) In other words, the self, though eternal, is by itself unconscious and thus is not different from material objects such as table and chair, excepting for the fact that the self alone is *capable* of having consciousness.

In the state of liberation, the soul is released from all pain and suffering. In this state the soul does not have any connection with the body. As long as the soul is associated with a body and the senses, it is not possible for it to attain liberation. If the body and the sense organs are there, there would be contact with the undesirable objects giving rise to feelings of pleasure and pain. Once the association between the body and the soul is severed, the soul would not have either pleasurable or painful experiences. Liberation is the cessation of pain, absolute freedom from pain. It is the *summum bonum*, the supreme good, in which the soul is free from fear, decay, change, death, and rebirth; it is bliss forever.

True knowledge of the distinction between the self and the not self is essential to attain liberation. To gain such a knowledge, one must hear (*śravaṇa)* the great sayings of the scriptures about the self, establish it by *manana* (reflective thinking), and meditate on the self (*nididhyāsana)* following *yogic* techniques and practices. When one realizes that the self is distinct from the body, one ceases to be attracted by material things, one is no longer under the influence of desires and passions that prompt an individual to undertake wrong actions and steer them in the wrong direction. One's past *karmas* are exhausted, the connection with the body ceases, and there is no pain, and that is *mokṣa*.

I have given a quick sketch of the Nyāya ontology as well as of Nyāya epistemology. It is, to sum up, a conceptualization of our ordinary concept of the world as consisting of many things. Perhaps this pluralism, we can safely say, is based on the way the Naiyāyikas use the category of difference.

APPENDIX III

TRANSLATIONS OF SELECTED TEXTS FROM THE ANCIENT SYSTEMS

I *The Mīmāṁsā* Darśana

The Mīmāṁsā Sūtras[1]

I.1.1 Then, therefore, an enquiry into *dharma*.

I.1.2 "*Dharma*" or duty is an object whose distinguishing feature (*lakṣaṇa*) is a command.

I.1.3 An examination of its cause (will now be made).

(The cause that will be examined is duty.)

I.1.4 Perception is the knowledge which arises from the senses coming in contact with the self. This is not the cause of duty, because it yields knowledge of an existing thing.

(*Pratyakṣa* is perception. It gives knowledge of an existing object. The object exists, i.e., can be perceived by the senses. It cannot yield any knowledge of *dharma* which is supersensuous. Other *pramāṇas* will be needed in the case of *dharma*. With regard to *dharma*, the Vedas are of supreme importance.)

I.1.5 The connection between word and its meaning is eternal. (The sentence which yields) its knowledge is (called) *updeśa* (precept). This sentence is never mistaken with regard to a supersensible object. It is a *pramāṇa* in Bādarāyaṇa's view, because it does not depend on any other (*pramāṇas*).

(The relation between word and its meaning is eternal. Word, or instruction is the means of knowing *dharma*. This knowledge is never wrong. It is infallible. It is under this aphorism that the other *pramāṇas*, e.g., inference, *arthāpatti* or presumption and *abhāva* or negation, besides perception, are discussed by commentators.)

I.1.6 (Eternality of words, objection:)

Some say that it is an action, because of seeing it there.

(Objection: word is not eternal, because it is an act and we see that it is produced.)

I.1.7 (Objection continues)

1 From Jaimini's *Mīmāṁsā Sūtras*.

By reason of no stability.

(The word, as soon as it is produced, vanishes.)

I.1.8 (Objection continues)

Because of the word "make."

It is said, "make a sound," which shows that sound is made and so is not eternal.

I.1.9 (Objection continues)

Because, it is heard simultaneously by all beings (who stand at a distance from the source.)

I.1.10 (Objection continues)

Because of the original and the modified forms.

I.1.11 (Conclusion of the objections)

When many persons pronounce it; it increases.

(What increases and decreases is not eternal.)

I.1.12 (The Mīmāṁsā position)

From here onwards, the objections raised against the eternity of sound will be replied.

I.1.13 (Answer to I.1.7)

That after coming into existence, sound disappears, is due to the object not coming in contact.

I.1.14 (Answer to I.1.8)

After the application.

(The word existed; it is made audible only by pronunciation.)

I.1.15 (Answer to I.1.9)

The simultaneousness is like the sun.

(Like the sun. There is one word and it is eternal.)

I.1.16 (Answer to I.1.10)

The changes of letters are no modifications.

I.1.17 (Answer to I.1.11)

Increase the noise concerns the tone (not the word).

I.1.18 (The conclusive Mīmāṁsā position, aphorisms 18–26)

On the contrary (the word) is eternal by reason of the manifestation being for the sake of others.

I.1.19 Because of simultaneity, the word produces the same effect everywhere.

I.1.20 Because there is no number.

(Even if pronounced several times, the word "cow" always produces the idea of one individual cow.

I.1.21 Because there is no correlative term.

(The *word* exists independently; it has no correlative; it is therefore eternal.)

I.1.22 The collection of words has no manifestation.

(The words collectively do not denote a class, but only an individual word does so.)

I.1.23 By seeing the force of the text.

(The Vedic text is taken to support the author's view.)

I.1.24 When manifested, it has no meaning, because the meaning does not depend upon it.

(The objector raises another objection.)

I.1.25 The pronunciation of the constituent words is with the object of an action, the sense is dependent upon them.

(The sentence, since it is composed of words which have meanings, must necessarily have a meaning. This is the reply to the objection raised).

I.1.26 In the world, you know an object when the object is in contact with the sense organ, so you have the knowledge of a sentence by reason of the arrangement of the words which are its constituents.

I.1.27 (Objection regarding the Vedas as authorless)

The opponent holds that the Vedas are modern because their names are derived from human names.

(The opponent argues that the Vedic names are of human origin.)

I.1.28 (Objection continues)

(The objector also) sees transitory things in them.

(Therefore the Vedas are human products.)

I.1.29 (Answer: Mīmāṁsā position, aphorisms 29–32)

It has already been said that the words are prior.

(Every word, human or divine, is eternal. The objection therefore has no ground.)

I.1.30 The names are because of their explaining them.

(The Vedas are called after great sages because they expounded them. But the Vedas themselves have no human origin.)

I.1.31 The Vedic words are used only in a general sense.

(So, names of persons are used in the Vedas, but they are common names, not proper names.)

I.1.32 On the other hand, the inducement is for the purpose of making persons do them, because such inducement is needed for the sacrifice.

(It is necessary that the person who is praised should perform the sacrifice.)

II The *Sāṁkhya Darśana*

Sāṁkhya-Kārikā[2]

(i) Five Arguments for Causation

9 The effect is existent, because the nonexistent cannot be brought into being, because there is a definite relation between the cause and the effect, because everything is not possible, because the efficient cause can cause only that which it is capable of producing, and because the effect is of the same nature as the cause.

2 From Īśvarakṛṣṇa's *Sāṁkhya-Kārikā* and *Gaudapāda's Bhāṣya* on selected *kārikās*.

(Arguments are given here to show that the effects of the primal nature are coexistent with their cause or source. They are therefore proofs of the existence of that primary cause or nature. Production is of that which is. This is the famous thesis of *satkāryavāda* or that the effect exists in the material cause prior to its production.)

(ii) The Three Guṇas *and the* Prakṛti

11 The manifest is "with the three attributes," "not able to distinguish," "objective," "common," "non-conscious," and "productive" in nature. The manifest Nature is likewise. The self is the opposite of this, and yet also similar.

(*Prakṛti cannot discriminate between* its three constituents. But the self, the *puruṣa* has discrimination. The products of nature are objects; the self is not an object. They, i.e., the products of nature, are *common,* but the self is specific. They are irrational; the self is rational. They are prolific; nothing is produced from the self.)

15 The unmanifest is the cause of the diverse finite things, because of homogeneous nature (of finitude), because of functioning through efficiency, because of division between cause and its product, because of the merger of the entire world.

16 It (the unmanifest) functions through the three constituents, by mixing up and modification, like water, because of the specific nature of the three constituents.

(iii) Puruṣa *(Self)*

17 The self exists, because all composite objects are for another's use, because there must be absence of the three constituents and of other properties, because there must be control, because there must be an experiencer, and because there must be tendency towards final release.

18 That there are many selves follows from the distributive nature of birth, death, and the instruments of cognition, from the engagement in actions not all at the same time, and also from different proportion of the three constituents.

(A multitude of selves is proved. From the contrary nature of the qualities, multitude is proved: or, from birth in general, one endowed with the quality of goodness is happy, another with the quality of foulness is wretched, and the third having that of darkness is apathetic.)

19 From this contrast, follows that this self is a "witness," free from suffering, neutral, seer, and inactive.

(The constituents as agents, act; a witness neither acts nor desists from action. The self is also a bystander like a wandering mendicant, so also the properties of being a spectator and passive. The self is a spectator, and not a performer of those acts.

But if self is a non-agent, how does it exercise volition. But there is a dilemma here: "I will practice virtues; I will not commit crime." Here the self must be an agent. The verse 20 explains this dilemma. It says that the self, the *puruṣa*, only appears to be the agent, by reason of the union with *prakṛti*.)

(iv) Evolution

21 In order to perceive nature by the self and for the isolation (freedom) of the self, there is a union of both self and nature, like that of the lame and the blind; from this association arises creation (or, evolution).

(As the birth of a child proceeds from the union of male and female, so the production of creation results from the connection of nature and self. The object of the union, or the final liberation of the self by its knowledge of nature is then explained.)

36 These special attributes, different from each other, as in a lamp, manifest the purpose of the self in its entirety, and present it to the intellect.

37 It is the intellect which accomplishes the self's experiences, it is the intellect which discriminates the subtle difference between nature and self.

(Here the function of discrimination between the self and the nature is assigned to intellect. As the intellect accomplishes this, consequently although it is as it were a chief principle, yet it is for another's use, not its own. Hence arises the purpose of liberation. Hence it is the intellect that discriminates the subtle difference between the nature and the self.)

52 Without dispositions, there would be no subtle elements; without subtle elements, there would be no dispositions. Therefore, there occurs two-fold evolution, the evolution of the elements and of the intellect.

53 The divine evolution is of eight kinds, the animal of five kinds, the human evolution has only one form. This in brief is the evolution of elements.

59 Just as a dancer stops dancing after having shown herself to the audience, so does nature desist after showing herself to the self.

III The *Yoga Darśana*

The Yoga Sūtras[3]

Chapter I Meditative Absorption (Samādhi)

I.2 Yoga is the restraint of the modifications of the mind.

I.5 There are five kinds of mental modifications; these are either detrimental or non-detrimental (to the practice of *yoga*).

I.6 (The *vrttis* are) right cognition, error, imagination, sleep, and memory.

3 From Patañjali's *Yoga Sūtras*

I.7 (The sources of) right cognitions are perception, inference and verbal testimony.

I.11 Memory is the retention of objects that are experienced (and not letting them slip away).

I.12 The mental modifications are restrained by practice and renunciation.

I.13 Practice is the effort to be steadfast in concentrating.

I.15 Renunciation is the controlled consciousness of the one who has no craving for sense-objects, whether such objects are actually perceived or heard (from the Vedas).

Chapter II Practice (Sādhanā)

II.1 The *yoga* of action consists of austerity, study, and submission to God.

II.2 It is for bringing meditative absorption and for the purpose of weakening the afflictions.

II.3 The impediments to *samādhi* are: ignorance, ego-sense, attachments, jealousy, and will to live.

II.5 Ignorance regards the self—which is eternal, pure, and of the nature of bliss—as non-eternal, impure, painful, and not-self.

II.6 The ego is to regard the nature of the seer and the power of the instrument of seeing as being the same thing.

II.7 Attachment is the consequence of happiness.

II.8 Aversion is the consequence of pain.

II.9 Clinging to life is an inherent tendency of even the wise.

II.11 Meditation eliminates the mental modification caused by afflictions (*kleśas*).

II.26 The means to liberation is undisturbed discernment that arises out of discrimination.

II.29 The eight limbs (of *yoga*) are: restraint, observance, posture, breath control, withdrawal of the senses, concentration, meditation, and absorption

II.30 The *yamas* are: nonviolence, truthfulness, non-stealing, celibacy, and non-possession.

II.32 The rules to be observed are: cleanliness, contentment, austerity, study of scriptures, and devotion to God.

II.46 Postures are to be steady and pleasant (comfortable).

II.47 Effort should be relaxed, and the mind absorbed in the infinite.

II.49 When the *āsana* is accomplished, *prāṇāyama* or control of breathing follows, which consists in the regulation of breathing in and breathing out.

II.54 When the senses do not come in contact with their respective objects, withdrawal from sensory objects takes place, corresponding, as it were, to the nature of the mind.

Chapter III Attainments (Vibhūtis)

III.1 In concentration, the mind is fixed in one place.

III.2 Meditation is the one-pointedness of the mind on one idea.

III.3 Meditative absorption occurs when the mind is without any conception of itself as reflecting and the object alone shines forth.

III.4 When these three (*dhāraṇā, dhyāna* and *samādhi*) are performed together, it is called "*saṃyama*."

III.5 As one becomes fixed in *saṃyama*, there arises insight.

III.6 *Saṃyama* is applied in the different planes of *samādhi*.

III.7 The three limbs of *saṃyama* are internal, when compared to the previous limbs.

III.9 In the state of *nirodha*, the outgoing *saṃskāras* disappear and the *saṃskāras* which restrain appear in the mind at the moment of restraint.

III.10 It is due to these *saṃskāras* that the mind flows undisturbed.

III.11 With the attainment of *samādhi*, the all-pointedness of the mind is destroyed and one-pointedness arises.

III.34 (Concentration) on the heart brings about knowledge of the mind.

III.54 The liberation is knowledge born out of discrimination; it knows everything as its object at all times simultaneously.

Chapter IV Complete Independence (Kaivalya)

IV.34 When the *guṇas* return to their original states, and when the power of consciousness is located in its own essential nature, liberation (complete isolation) takes place.

IV The *Vaiśeṣika Darśana*

The Vaiśeṣika Sūtras[4]

I.1.1 Now, therefore, we shall explain *dharma* (righteousness, duty).

(*Dharma* leads to knowledge by purifying the mind and producing thirst after knowledge.)

I.1.2 *Dharma* is that from which one achieves exaltation and the supreme good.

I.1.3 The authoritativeness of the Vedas is due to the words of God (or from being an exposition of *dharma*).

I.1.4 The supreme good arises from the knowledge produced by a particular *dharma* which teaches the categories, substance, attribute, action, universal, species, and inherence along with their common and differentiating features.

(This aphorism gives a list of the categories whose knowledge leads to the

4 From Kaṇāda's Vaiśeṣika *Sūtras* with the commentary by Śaṅkara Miśra

supreme good. Although six categories have been listed in this aphorism, the seventh, i.e., nonexistence or *abhāva*, is implied.)

I.1.5 The only substances are: earth, water, fire, air, ether, time, space, self, and mind.

(Substances are nine only, no more or no less.)

I.1.6 The qualities are: color, taste, smell, touch, number, measures, separateness and conjunction and disjunction, priority and posterity, understanding, pleasure, pain, desire, jealousy, and effort.

I.1.7 Throwing upwards, throwing downwards, contraction, expansion, and movement are actions.

I.1.8 Substance, quality, and action have the common attributes insofar as they are existent and non-eternal, have substance as their cause, are effect as well as cause, and are both genus and species.

I.1.9 What is common to substance and attribute is the property of being the cause of what belongs to their universals in common

I.1.10 Substances originate another substance, and qualities originate another attribute.

I.1.11 (But) an action that is producible by another action is not known.

(The question is: How is substance different from attribute and action?)

I.1.12 A substance is not destroyed by (its own) effect or by (its own) cause.

(Two substances that have the relation of effect and cause cannot have the relation of destroyer and destroyed. A substance is annihilated only by the annihilation of the supporting substratum and the dissolution of the parts that give rise to it.)

I.1.13 Qualities (are destroyed) in both ways.

(In both ways = by effect and by cause, e.g., the beginning sound in a series is destroyed by the effect, but the last sound by its cause, i.e., the last but one sound.)

I.1.14 Action is opposed by its effect.

(Action is destructible by subsequent conjunction produced by itself.)

I.1.15 *Dravya* possesses action and quality; it is an inherent cause—this is the defining mark of substance.

I.1.18 Substance is the one and the same cause of substance, qualities and action.

I.1.19 Likewise, attribute is the cause of substance, qualities and action.

I.1.20 Action is the common cause of conjunction, disjunction, and impetus.

I.1.21 Action cannot be the cause of substances.

I.1.22 (Action cannot be the cause of substances) on account of cessation.

(Substance is produced, when action ceases to be by conjunction. Therefore action is not a cause.)

I.1.23 A single substance may be the general effect of many substances.

I.1.24 An action cannot be the (joint) effect of many actions, because of the difference of their qualities.

I.1.25 Two-ness (duality) and other numbers, separateness, conjunction and disjunction (are caused by many substances).

I.1.26 An action, which is the joint effect of two or more substances, is not known as it cannot inhere in two or more substances.

(An action does not reside in an aggregate.)

I.1.27 A substance can be the (joint) effect of many conjunctions.

I.1.28 Color (can be the joint effect) of many colors.

I.1.29 Throwing upwards (as also throwing downwards, etc.) is the joint effect of gravity, volition, and conjunction.

(A single action may be the effect of many causes.)

I.1.30 Conjunction and disjunction are effects of actions.

I.1.31 Under the topic of causes in general, it is being said that action cannot be a cause of substances and actions.

V The *Nyāya Darśana*

The Nyāya Sūtras[5]

I.1.3 Perception, inference, comparison and *verbal testimony* are *pramāṇas.*

I.1.4 Perception is the knowledge which arises from the contact of the sense organs and (their) objects, knowledge which is not-linguistic, which is not erroneous (from the object) and which is of the nature of judgment.

(The cause of such knowledge is perception as a *pramāṇa.*)

I.1.5 After determining perception, inference is being determined. Inference "has that as its antecedent" or is a knowledge that is grounded in perception. It is of three kinds: "like what is before" (*pūrvavat*), "like what comes after" (*śeṣavat*) and "inference based on universal" (*sāmānyatodṛṣṭa*).

By "*pūrvavat*" is meant that where the effect is inferred from the cause, as for example, from the increase of cloud, one infers there is going to be rain.

Śeṣavat is that in which the cause is inferred from the effect. Upon seeing the river being full of water and the strength of the current, as contrasted with the water which was in the river in the past, one infers "there has been rain."

S*āmānyatodṛṣṭa* inference takes place e.g., when as contrasted with the thing seen earlier, the now seen object has fast moving current; with regard to the sun, which was seen at one place in the morning and is seen elsewhere now, one infers that even if it is imperceptible, the sun has motion (on the basis of inference).

Pūrvavat also signifies cases where upon seeing an entity, from among two entities which were earlier perceived together, which is the pervaded one, there is inference about the existence of the other entity which pervades the former, but is not being perceived now. This inference is also called "*pūrvavat.*"

Śeṣavat also means an inference of what remains. By denying this "remainder" and the entity which remains, there is no objection with regard to the

5 From Gautama's *Nyāya Sūtras.*

other entity. In such a case, the ascription of existence to the "remainder" entity is the cause of true knowledge which is inferential.

An example: if there is a doubt whether sound is a substance, quality, or action, then the one sound is not a substance since it is one, it is also not an action since it produces another sound, what remains is that sound must be a quality, this is the only remaining possibility.

Sāmānyatodṛṣṭa inference is the case where the relation between the mark and what is to be to-be-established, or the relation between that which is pervaded and the pervader, is not perceivable, and yet the mark leads to the inference of the to-be-established property, as when the self is inferred from desire, etc.

The object of perception is existent, but the object of inference is either existent or nonexistent. Why? Because inference apprehends "all three times," that is to say, an object which is related to the three temporal dimensions such as "shall be," "it becomes," and "it became." "Nonexistent" here means what is past and what is yet-to-be, future, entity.)[6]

I.1.6 *Upamāna* is the means by which one arises at a valid determination of an entity based on similarity with a well-known object.

I.1.7 *Śabda* is the verbal instruction of a person who knows what he is talking about.

I.1.8 That (*śabda*) is of two kinds: that whose object is perceived and that whose object is not perceived.

I.1.9 The objects of knowledge (*prameyas*) are: self, body, sense organs, sensory objects, intellect, mind, effort, fault, beginningless stream of birth and death, enjoyment of pleasure and pain, pain, and release.

I.1.10 Desire, jealousy, effort, pleasure, pain and knowledge are marks of the self.

I.1.11 Effort, sense organs and pleasure-pain are located in the body.

I.1.12 The five elements are apprehended by five sense organs: the organ of smell and taste, visual organ or the eyes, the skin which is the organ of touch, and the ear or organ of hearing.

I.1.13 The five elements are earth, water, fire, air, and ether.

I.1.14 The qualities of these elements are smell, taste, color, touch, and sound.

I.1.15 "*Buddhi*," "*upalabdhi*" and "*jñāna*" are synonymous, or mean the same thing.

I.1.16 The non-origination of several cognitions at the same time is a mark of existence of the mind.

I.1.17 Effort is the beginning of speech, knowledge, and of body (in that order).

I.1.18 The defects have urging for their mark.

I.1.19 Rebirth after death is called "*pratyabhāva*."

I.1.20 The "result" is that which results from effort and fault.

6 Vātsyāyana's *bhāṣya* (commentary) on *Nyāya Sūtra*, I.1.5.

I.1.21 Sorrow is attachment to the objects (defined earlier).

I.1.22 Freedom from all sorrow is release.

I.1.23 "Doubt" is (1) caused by the substantives which possess the common quality; (2) produced by the knowledge of the substantive which possess an uncommon quality; (3) due to the presence of contradicted opinions, (4) uncertainty attaching to perception, and uncertainty attaching to non-perception, is called "*vimarśa*" or wavering judgment.

I.1.24 Purpose is that object which, by being determined either as desirable or as fit to be shunned, gives rise to effort.

I.1.25 Example is that with regard to which both the ordinary, and those who are critical examiners, entertain similar beliefs.

I.1.26 Conclusion is the final determination that the entity has this property.

Part V

SYSTEMS WITH GLOBAL IMPACT

12

THE BUDDHIST SCHOOLS

After the death of the Buddha, the Buddhist monks began doubting and debating the Buddha's teachings and practices, and as a result of their inability to reach consensus, the basic ethical-philosophical teachings of the Buddha went through a long process of development. One may consider this process as consisting of three turns of the wheel of *dharma*, each turn spanning a period of five hundred years, determined by how the Buddha's teachings came to be interpreted. The Buddhist schools began proliferating, giving rise to as many as thirty schools in India, China, Tibet, and Japan. Whereas some took the Buddha's refusal to answer any metaphysical questions to mean a denial of the existence of reality and the means of knowing it, others took it to be a sign of empiricism. Some of the basic questions that arose are as follows: what is real? Is reality mental or non-mental? How do we know that external reality exists? Sarvāstivādins argued for the reality of all things; they took both the mental and the non-mental to be real. Regarding the question how we come to know the existence of the external world, the Sarvāstivādins were divided: the Vaibhāṣikas held that we perceive the external world directly and the Sautrāntikas held that we infer the external world; but we do not perceive the external objects. The Mādhyamikas argued that there is no reality, either mental or non-mental; all is void (*śūnya*). The Yogācāras held that only the mental is real and that the non-mental or the physical has no reality. Thus we have four main schools of Buddhism and in chronological order they are: the Vaibhāṣikas, the Sautrāntikas, the Mādhyamikas, and the Yogācāras. Correlating these four to a familiar but misleading distinction between two phases of the Buddhist religion, Hīnayāna and Mahāyāna, one could say that the Vaibhāṣikas and the Sautrāntikas belong to the Hīnayāna school, while the Mādhyamika, and the Yogācāra to the Mahāyāna school. This chronology, though helpful, is misleading because the Mahāyāna, i.e. both Mādhyamika, and the Yogācāra, had their beginnings very early in the history of Buddhism, even in the presumed Therāvāda writings, so that many scholars have come to doubt the validity of keeping the Hīnayāna and Mahāyāna completely separate. In any event, these four schools have much philosophical importance, and in such a short exposition as this, it is difficult to do justice to them. So without going into the details of the Buddhist hermeneutic, in this chapter I will discuss the basic doctrines of these four schools.

I The Vaibhāṣikas

The Abhidharma works form the foundation of this school of Buddhism. This school is called Vaibhāṣikas because they follow the commentary *Vibhāṣā* on Abhidharma*jñānaprasthāna*. The term "*abhidharma*" literally means "with regard to the doctrine," and initially referred to the commentarial literature. In time, however, Abhidharma teachers began systematizing their teachings and came to be known as the "superior" (*abhi*) "doctrine" (*dharma*), i.e., the study of the *dharmas*. This work also includes a comprehensive description of Buddhist doctrines, ranging from cosmology and theories of perception to issues surrounding moral problems, the virtues to be cultivated to attain *nirvāṇa*, *yogic* practices, and the meaning and significance of rebirth. Originating primarily in Kāśmīr, some of the principal teachers of the Vaibhāṣika school are: Dharmatrāta, Ghoṣaka, Vasumitra, and Buddhadeva.

The Vaibhāṣikas were realists, pluralists, and nominalists. The characteristic doctrines of this school are as follows:

1 Everything real is instantaneous, a thesis that is based on the Buddhist doctrine of conditioned arising or dependent arising;
2 Although everything is momentary, there are substantial entities (*dravyasat*), the basic constituents (*dharmas*) of reality;
3 Everything exists including the three dimensions of time, i.e., the past, the present, and the future; and
4 The existence of the external world is directly perceived, not inferred.

I will next elaborate on these theses.

One of the most important doctrines of the Vaibhāṣikas is *kṣanikavāda*, the thesis that everything real is instantaneous. Both mind and matter are momentary. Becoming is real; there is neither being nor non-being. The main premise of their argument is: "to exist is to be causally efficacious," i.e., to possess *arthakriyākāritva*. To be causally efficacious for them means to produce an effect. The production takes place at the very first moment of its being. With the production of the effect, all its causal power is spent out and the entity ceases to exist. The argument is examined threadbare by other schools, e.g., the Nyāya and the Vedānta, who believed and argued that a thing may have causal efficacy but may not produce all its effects in the very first moment of its being. The Vaibhāṣikas however, argued that if a being can withhold its power potentially without being actualized, then it might as well become eternal, an alternative they found unacceptable. Accordingly, they reject the possibility of unactualized power as an abstract concept. Everything real arises, produces its effects, passes away, and is replaced by its successor. Reality is a series of instantaneous events; there is no permanent substance, just as there is no universal property, *jāti* or *sāmānya*, instantiated in a class of particulars. There is only similarity between momentary events and mistaking similarity for identity we regard the particulars as possessing an identical feature in common. The illusion is sustained when we give the particulars the same name as jar, or tree, or God. The identity of name together with the resemblance among the particulars creates the illusion of real universals.

Not only the external world but also the alleged inner self consists of a series of changing particulars. The self according to the Vaibhāṣikas is not an identical substance; it consists of the intertwining of five different series: of material bodily changes, of thoughts, of feeling (*vedanā*), of volitions and forces (*saṃskāras*), and of changing events of consciousness (*vijñāna*). These five series, like five ropes, are intertwined in a complicated manner and create the illusion of an identical inner self. There is no lasting underlying substance; the series is held together by causality.

The Vaibhāṣikas accept the reality of the basic substantial constituents (*dravyasat*) called "*dharmas*." The term "*dharma*" has a variety of meanings in Indian tradition. In Buddhism the term usually refers to the teachings of the Buddha; however, in the Abhidharma context, a *dharma* denotes the basic, most primary, constituent present in experience. An element that cannot be further analyzed is a real existent (*dravyasat*) and has its own self-nature (*svabhāva*); it exists "in and of itself." An object, say, a chair, on the other hand, is an aggregate of *dharmas*, which are impermanent, momentary, and durationless.

Abhidharmakośa discusses seventy-five *dharmas* divided into conditioned ("*saṃskṛta*," literally, "co-operating") and unconditioned ("*asaṃskṛta*," literally, "non-co-operating"). The conditioned *dharmas* arise and perish, but the unconditioned, viz., *nirvāṇa*, empty space, and meditative emptiness of consciousness are eternal. Conditioned *dharmas* are classified into five groups: form (*rūpa*), mind (*citta*), mental faculties, forces not concomitant with the mind, and unconditioned *dharmas*. Of these *rūpa* includes eleven *dharmas*: five sense organs, five sense objects and unmanifested matter; mind includes, forty-six mental functions, and fourteen forces which are not concomitant with the mind. There are three unconditioned *dharmas, viz., nirvāṇa, apratisaṃkhyānirodha*, and *ākāśa* (two kinds of cessation and space). In short, *dharmas* refer to such elements as mind, matter, reality, ideas—in general to the basic factors or elements of experience.

It is not possible to go into an analysis of seventy-five *dharmas*. For our purposes it is sufficient to note that the conditioned *dharmas* constitute phenomenal existence. They are subject to the law of causality and in their flow they co-operate and perpetuate phenomenality. The unconditioned *dharmas*, on the other hand, are not subject to the causal law. *Dharmas* are also classified into impure and pure, bad and good in the moral sense. In this classification, the same *dharmas* are influenced by ignorance or wisdom (*prajñā*). Unconditioned dharmas are pure in the sense that they are free from defilements (*kleśas*), which cause body and mind to suffer. Greed, hatred, delusion, pride, wrong view, doubts, sloth, and distractions are the eight defilements, which defile any *dharma* to which they get attached. Conditioned elements, when defiled, taint each other, for example, lust may taint wisdom, as may an object of cognition which arouses passion. The Buddhist writers classified defilements into one hundred and eight, and proclivities into ninety-eight. The Buddha's saying "all are impermanent" is interpreted by the Vaibhāṣikas as referring only to conditioned *dharmas*.

There is a real transformation of the conditioned into unconditioned through insight. The *dharmas* conditioned by ignorance cause pain and sorrow, and the same *dharmas* when separated and suppressed by the ethical/spiritual discipline and knowledge, become *nirvāṇa* and *apratisaṃkhyānirodha* (cessation without a residue). Space (*ākāśa*), on the other hand, neither obstructs nor is obstructed; it is empty. In short, these *dharmas* combine in different ways and account for the phenomenal existence and the world-process.

As stated earlier, the Vaibhāṣikas were Sarvāstivādins because they believed in the existence of everything (*sarva asti*): the mental as well as the non-mental. Citing the Buddha's assertions that the past, the present, and the future exist, the Vaibhāṣikas argue that not alone the present but also the past and the future are real (*dravyasat*). They admit six categories of reality: the past, the future, the just arising, cessation with a residue (*pratisaṃkhyānirodha*), cessation without a residue (*apratisaṃkhyānirodha*), and space (*ākāśa*). For the existence of the past and the future, they advance the following argument:

There cannot be any knowledge if there is no "objective support" (*ālambana*). There does arise knowledge of the past and the future *ālambana*. Therefore, the past and the future must exist.

There is an important philosophical problem with the above position, inasmuch as the Vaibhāṣikas tried to combine two seemingly incompatible positions: on the one hand, they accept that nothing is eternal, that all reality is momentary, on the other hand, they make every moment eternal, inasmuch as each *dharma*, the past and the future as much as the present *is* or exists. When the Vaibhāṣikas were asked how they could hold that an object exists in three points of time and also hold that nothing endures, different Vaibhāṣikas gave different answers. Among these, four are worth noting.

1. Dharmatrāta advances the thesis of differences in forms (*bhāvas*): An entity, as it passes from the present to the past, remains the same, only its *bhāva* changes (in the same way as the form of gold changes from one jewelry to another). The substance or *dravya* remains the same.
2. Ghoṣaka held that what changes is *lakṣaṇa* (e.g., a person is attached to one woman, but gradually becomes non-attached).
3. Vasumitra held that the state or position or *avasthā* changes, not the substance (analogous to the value of "0" from the unit position to the hundred or the thousand depending on the place).

4 Buddhadeva held it is the *relations* that change depending on the context (just as the same woman in relation to one person is a daughter and in relation to another is a wife, etc.)

The first view looks like the Sāṃkhya position. The three temporal positions are related to three different relations to causal efficacy: when there is no efficacy, the entity is not yet; when it is causally active, the entity is present; when there is no causal activity, it is past.

The Vaibhāṣikas hold that the external objects are directly perceived by us. This is similar to the direct, common-sense realism of Western philosophy, according to which the color that I perceive is itself the color of the object in front of me. My mind directly knows the external world. We infer fire upon seeing smoke because in the past we have perceived smoke and fire together. One who has never perceived a fire would not be able to infer fire upon seeing smoke coming out of a building. If we never perceive external objects, as the Sautrāntikas believe, then we would not be able to infer them simply from their form (*ākāra*).

Concluding Remarks

1 The minute analytical listing of entities bears testimony to remarkable power of subtle observation, faithful articulation, and openness to new metaphysical thinking.
2 In this school, the ontological and valuational judgments are inseparably linked together. Every element of reality is either good or evil and the causal theory is as much about ontology as about values/disvalues. The two are not separated.
3 Given that there is a real transformation of the conditioned into unconditioned *dharmas*, conditioned and unconditioned have to be totally different. The unconditioned, the *nirvāṇa*, is a total extinction of the conditioned or the phenomenal. There are two levels of reality, *saṃsāra* and *nirvāṇa* (worldly and non-worldly) but nevertheless real. This dualism between the two levels of reality became a matter of great controversy among the Buddhist schools that followed. The Mādhyamikas argue against the Vaibhāṣika position and hold that *saṃsāra* and *nirvāṇa* are two sides of the same coin; the Sautrāntikas accept only the reality of the world and no separate reality of *nirvāṇa*, which on their view is a mere negation and not a positive entity; and the Yogācāras hold that *saṃsāra* is not real, only *nirvāṇa* is. Thus, it is not an exaggeration to say that the Vaibhāṣikas laid the foundation for the subsequent discussion of many philosophical issues among the Buddhists and the non-Buddhists alike.

II The Sautrāntikas

The Sautrāntikas accept the final authority of the *sūtra* literature which are the Buddha's own words. Of the three Pāli *Tripiṭakas*, the Sautrāntikas accept the *Vinaya* and the *Sutta piṭakas*, but do not accept the *abhidharma piṭaka* as the Buddha's words. Accordingly, the Sautrāntikas are said to be *sūtraprāmāṇika*, not *śāstraprāmāṇika*,

The founder of this school is taken to be Kumāralāta of Takṣaśila. The main literature of this school seems to have been lost. Our knowledge of the Sautrāntika doctrines is derived from what the followers of other schools have to say about them in the process of refuting them. Many of the Sautrāntika doctrines are known to us from the *Abhidharmakośa* of Vasubandhu, who prior to converting to Mahāyāna, was a Sautrāntika. The Abhidharma texts take Kumāralāta, Dharmatrāta, Buddhadeva, and Śrelāta to be the "Four Suns" of the Sautrāntika. Although they are said to belong to the Hīnayāna, Sautrāntikas are often considered as marking the beginnings of Mahāyāna. The Sautrāntikas were realists, pluralists, *kṣanikavādins*, and nominalists.

Some of the doctrines held in common by the Sautrāntikas are as follows:

1 The Sautrāntikas believe in momentariness and process-theory; every *dharma* is momentary. "Momentariness" means "perishing" in the moment after arising. It has no existence beyond arising. Perishing, being an absence, is not produced; it is *ahetuku*. Only being is causally produced, not non-being. Therefore, a *dharma*'s being is caused; it arises and then of itself perishes.
2 The Sautrāntikas rejected the existence of the conditioned or composite *dharmas*, because these elements are not real elements. The very existence of the *dharmas* consists in the process, stream or *pravāha*. There is no "origin," "existence," or "perishing." About the three unconditioned *dharmas* of the Vaibhāṣikas, the Sautrāntikas argue that "*ākāśa*" is nothing but the absence of anything tangible. *Nirvāṇa* is not a positive entity; it is mere absence. It is neither caused nor an effect. The same characterizes the "cessation without wisdom" or *apratisaṃkhyānirodha*; it too is a negative entity.
3 The Sautrantikas do not recognize the past and the future to possess reality. To accept them would be to regard them as present, which would be inconsistent.
4 When a *dharma* arises, along with it co-arise: arising-arising, existence-existence, decay-decay and non-eternity-non-eternity (the four *ana-lakṣanas*). These are conditioned entities. All conditioned entities have the marks of non-being becoming being, and being becoming non-being. A *dharma*'s being is its process; there is no substance called "arising."
5 Life again is not a separate entity; it is not a substance. It is a special ability (*sāmarthya*) which lasts for a definite period of time.
6 Word *(śabda)* is a mere utterance by a speaker whose function is to announce that the speaker has cognition of such and such thing.

The above theses of the Sautrāntikas make it obvious that they departed from the Vaibhāṣikas on several points; I will elaborate on the following three:

1 the reality of the past and the future;
2 the reality of the unconditioned or incomposite *dharmas* (*ākāśa, nirvāṇa*);
3 whether the external world is directly perceived or inferred.

Let me elaborate on these three:

The most important point of difference between the two concerns the reality of the past and the future. As we have seen, the Vaibhāṣikas hold that the past, the present, and the future, are all real. They hold that the present is undoubtedly real and it cannot be the effect of an unreal past and the cause of an unreal future. The Sautrāntikas argue that only the present is real. What is past has gone out of existence and is no longer real, and what is future has not yet come into existence and so is not yet real. The Vaibhāṣikas, on the other hand, argue that the past and the future are real; they are known, become objects of present knowledge, and exercise causal efficacy. The Sautrāntikas reject this argument, because reality, they argue, is *prajñapatisat*, not *vastu sat* as the Vaibhāṣikas believe. It is worth noting that although both the Vaibhāṣikas and the Sautrāntikas subscribe to "momentaries," their understandings of a moment is different. The Vaibhāṣikas understand by "moment" the last indivisible segment of time. For the Sautrāntikas, a *ksaṇa* is the time it takes for a *dharma* to arise; it perishes in the next *ksaṇa*. If it lasted for another moment, it would need another cause. The same cause, however, cannot produce a new effect, given that it has already produced its effect. Consequently, *kṣanikavāda* is transformed into a philosophy of process, because it does not make sense to say that every instant— even when it is gone and has not yet been—is eternally existing. Additionally, the Sautrāntikas argue that their conception is closer to the Buddha's doctrine of Dependent Arising. In the twelve-link chain of Dependent Arising, each link is both conditioned and that which conditions; one link does not cause the other link. Finally, they argue that to attribute duration to instants is to assign them a sort of permanency which goes against the doctrine of Dependent Arising. Thus, arising and passing are not two different processes, but rather a single continuous process.

The second difference concerns the reality of simple unconditional *dharmas*, viz., *ākāśa* or empty space and *nirvāṇa*. The Sautrāntikas reject that these two are unconditioned *dharmas*. They do not agree that the empty space is real. It is not a positive reality; there is absence of any tangible object. Likewise, *nirvāṇa*, which the Buddhist aspirant aims to attain, is a mere cessation comparable to the extinguishing of a lamp. Existence being *dukkha* according to the First Noble Truth, and *nirvāṇa* being the *nirodha satya* (the Third Noble Truth), i.e., the cessation of *duhkha* amounts to the cessation of existence, so that a person after attaining *nirvāṇa* ceases to exist. There is simply a blank nothingness. Its being is *prajñāptisat* and not *vastu sat*. It is to be noticed that many Western readers of Buddhism have wondered if *nirvāṇa* is not simply an extinction of *dukkha*. Only the Sautrāntikas held such a view, no other school did. Even Nāgārjuna in asserting that *nirvāṇa* is *śūnya*, was not affirming the Sautrāntika position. As we will see shortly, *śūnyatā*, for Nāgārjuna, is not of the nature of simple negation.

The third point of difference concerns the knowledge of the external world. The external objects, argue the Sautrāntikas, are not directly perceived; they are inferred, because being momentary, they disappear and cannot be perceived. The object of cognition, though it passes as soon as it appears, leaves behind a form, an image, and from these forms or representations of the objects in the mind we infer the existence of the objects, which are reproduced in the act of cognition. The Sautrāntika philosophy therefore came to be known as *Bāhyānumeyavāda*. The objects exist outside the mind. However, our perceptions depend not simply on the mind, but on four conditions: causes as a condition (*hetupratyayatā*), an equal and immediately antecedent condition (*samanantarpratyayatā*), an object as condition (*ālambanapratyayatā*), and a predominating influence as a condition (*adhipatipratyayatā*). The object must be there to impart the form to consciousness, the ability of the mind to receive the form, determination whether consciousness is visual, tactual, etc., and finally, auxiliary condition, e.g., light, etc. All these conditions combine and facilitate the perception of the object. When the form of the object is generated in the mind, the mind perceives not the object, but the copy of the object in one's own consciousness.

In many ways, the Sautrāntikas and the Vaibhāṣikas laid the foundations for the emergence of subsequent schools that developed within the fold of Buddhism. Many writers in English compare the Sautrāntika position to the Lockean representationalism as opposed to the direct naive realism of the Vaibhāṣikas. The existence of the external world is inferred on the basis of the constraint to which our internal representations are subject. We shall see that Vasubandhu rejects this argument and holds that consciousness apprehends only its own *ākāra* or form. The issue becomes whether this form of consciousness is derived from the supposed external object as the Sautrāntikas take it to be, or it is derived from the supposed *ālaya vijñāna*, the store-house of the needed prior experiences. Thus the Sautrāntika position on the one hand led to the *Vijñānavāda* view that consciousness alone is real and, on the other hand, to the Mādhyamika dialectic that there is no origination or cessation, no coming to be or going out, that everything is *śūnya*, which I will discuss next.

III The Mādhyamikas

The Mādhyamikas are those that follow the Middle Way of the Buddha. In his first sermon, the Buddha rules out the extremes of self-indulgence and self-mortification. In Sanskrit lexicons, one of the words for the Buddha is "*advayavādin*," i.e., "the one who asserts not-two." What are these two views? The Mādhyamikas take the "not-two" to mean that one should avoid all extremes of being and non-being, self and non-self, self-indulgence and self-mortification, substance and process—in general, all dualistic affirmations. The followers of this school take a middle position and subsequently came to be known as Mādhyamikas.

It is not an exaggeration to say that Nāgārjuna is the most important philosopher of the Mādhyamika school. It is generally believed that he was born in a *brahmin* family in Andhra Pradesh, in South India, in 150 CE. Many legends surround his name. According to some accounts, Nāgārjuna initially studied the Vedas and other important Hindu texts, but eventually converted to Buddhism. Numerous works have been attributed to Nāgārjuna. These works include public lectures and letters to numerous kings, in addition to metaphysical and epistemological treatises that form the foundation of the Mādhyamika school. But there is no doubt that his most important works are *Mūlamādhyamakakārikā* (abbreviated as MMK in this work) with his own commentary and *Vigrahavyāvartanī.*

The above account makes it obvious that Nāgārjuna lived five hundred years after the Buddha's death, during the transitional era of Buddhism when the Buddhist monks began debating Buddhist teachings and practices. One of the most important literatures belonging to this era is *Prajñāpāramitā*, which literally means "transcendent insight or wisdom," but usually translated as "Perfection of Wisdom." The principal theme of this work is the notion of *śūnyatā* (emptiness). Nāgārjuna analyzes this notion and develops its ramifications clearly and systematically. Although *Prajñāpāramitā* has been commented upon by both the Mādhyamika and Yogācāra schools of Mahāyāna Buddhism, in time it came to be used synonymously with the teachings of Nāgārjuna.

The Buddha had refused to answer any metaphysical questions. He characterized his teaching as *madhyama pratipad*, the Middle Way. Nāgārjuna was puzzled by the Buddha's silence and searched for the rationale behind it. He took the Buddha's silence to mean that reality could not be articulated by any of the commonly held metaphysical positions, e.g., the thesis of permanence and change, substance and causality, and so on. Because he rejected all such metaphysical positions, he thought he was taking a middle position and thus he called his philosophy "Madhyamaka."

In my discussion of the Mādhyamika school in this chapter, I am primarily going to draw from the *Mūlamādhyamakakārikā*, *Fundamental Verses on the Middle Way*. It contains 448 verses divided in to 27 chapters. The terse and dense nature of these verses continues to generate significant philosophical dialogue up to this day. The central theses of this work revolve around the notions of *śūnyatā* (emptiness) and *niḥsvabhāvatā* (lack of inherent essence or absence of essence of things).

Nāgārjuna rejects the doctrine of *dharmas* of the Vaibhāṣka Buddhists and argues that all *dharmas* are foundationless. No *dharma* has its own being or *svabhāva*. Things have no essence of their own, no immutable defining property; they are all dependent on one another. All these together form Nāgārjuna's famous thesis of *śūnyatā* (emptiness). It is important to keep in mind that Nāgārjuna is rejecting not only the philosophical thesis that things have their own essence, e.g., cowness belonging to all cows, but also the *brahman-ātman* of the Upaniṣads, the *puruṣa* and the *prakṛti* of Sāṁkhya, and the nine *dravyas* of the

Vaiśeṣika. Rejecting *svabhāva* (own being) amounts to rejecting the identity of a substance, the presence of a universal in many particulars, and any thesis which posits unchanging essences of things. Thus, Nāgārjuna rejects all metaphysical positions advocated by his predecessors, the Buddhists and the non-Buddhists alike. Taking the Buddha's doctrine of *pratītyasamutpāda*, i.e., Dependent Origination as his point of departure, Nāgārjuna uses a method known as *prasaṇga* or *reductio ad absurdum* to demonstrate that all perspectives about reality involve self-contradiction.

Prasaṇga *or* Reductio ad Absurdum

Prasaṇga is a method of analysis that exposes the inherent self-contradiction of any perspective to demonstrate its absurdity. The analysis consists in demonstrating that the proponent's theses lead to absurdity even when one uses the same rules and principles that the proponent himself has used. Let us examine how Nāgārjuna uses this method to accomplish his goals.

Nāgārjuna begins by noting that there are two possible predications about an object A: "A is" and "A is not." The conjunction and the negation of the conjunction give rise to yet two more possibilities: "A both is and is not" and "A neither is nor is not" (*catuṣkoti* or quadrilemma). This is also known as four-cornered negation. Nāgārjuna analyzes these four alternatives and, by drawing the implications of each alternative, demonstrates that it is impossible to erect any sound metaphysics on the basis of reason. Let me give an example. With respect to causation, these four possibilities translate into: (1) a thing arises out of itself, (2) a thing arises out of not-itself, (3) a thing arises out of both itself and not-itself, and (4) a thing arises neither out of itself nor out of not-itself. Nāgārjuna argues that on the first alternative (the Sāṁkhya view) cause and effect become identical; their identity points to their non-difference. Thus any talk about their being causally related is superfluous. On the second alternative (the Nyāya view) cause and effect become entirely different, and, accordingly, there can be no common ground between the two to make the relation of causality possible. Thus, the second alternative is equally meaningless. He further argues that since the first and the second possibilities are meaningless, the two remaining possibilities that arise out of the conjunction and the negation of the conjunction are equally meaningless.

The point that Nāgārjuna is trying to make is as follows: If the thing is already there, then it cannot not come into being. If it is not there, nothing can bring it into existence. To say that *it* originates, then *it*, i.e., the entity, must be there to originate, but if it is already there, then it cannot originate. Things arise neither at random nor from a unique cause nor from a variety of causes. An entity is neither identical with its causes nor different from them, nor both identical and different from them.

Nāgārjuna further argues that both the opposing views outlined above (i.e., (1). that the effect, prior to creation, is contained in the cause, and, accordingly, is not a new creation and (2). that the effect is an event, which is totally different from the cause and, accordingly, is a new creation) presuppose that the event which is called "cause" and the event that is called "effect" will have its own *svabhāva* or self-nature. If an event has a nature of its own then it will always have that nature; it will never change. When events have a nature of their own or are ascribed eternal essences, they are either totally identical or totally different. Qualification of the sort "some," or "partially" (i.e., to say that they are partially identical or partially different) is not permissible. In other words, such a self-nature by definition being eternal is free from conditions. Thus, it cannot be said to be caused in as much as being caused implies conditions; and therefore it cannot be brought into existence.

In short, we have two aspects of a causal relation that are not compatible with each other. One of these aspects is that causation involves Dependent Origination, the other points out that each cause and effect has eternal essence of its own which is not capable of origination. If we choose the latter, there is no Dependent Origination; if we choose the former, neither the cause nor the effect could have an eternal essence. If neither of the two has an eternal essence or self-nature, everything becomes conditional. Nāgārjuna argues that causes and effects when taken absolutely lead to absurdities; they are not self-existent entities that exist independently and unconditionally. Causal relations do not imply temporal sequence but rather mutual dependence. The conditioned entities have no essential nature of their own (*niḥsvabhāva*); they are *śūnya.*

Śūnyatā *(Emptiness) and the Levels of the Truth*

Nāgārjuna makes use of his theory of causal relation and applies it ruthlessly to demonstrate that not only the concepts and the doctrines of the rival schools (permanence, substantial self, etc.), but also the central Buddhist doctrines (momentariness, *karma*, *skandhas*, and even the very idea of *Tathāgata*), contain inherent self-contradictions. If there is no causality, then there is no change either, because change requires that one thing become another, which is impossible logically. The concept of time as consisting of the past, the present, and the future also goes with this. That which is present cannot become the past, that which is future cannot become the present, because in that case a thing would become what it is not, which, on Nāgārjuna's argument, is unintelligible

On Nāgārjuna's thesis, a being cannot change nor can it cease to be. The permanence of a thing requires that the thing remain the same in the midst of changes, but the idea of change being unintelligible, the definition of permanence is inapplicable to anything whatsoever. In effect, both permanence and change are metaphysical concepts that Nāgārjuna severely criticizes. It is worth noting that although his rejection of change and causal origination seems to bring him near Advaita position, the Advaitin still maintains that things have an eternal essence, *ātman-brahman*, while Nāgārjuna's radical thesis of essenceless –ness or emptiness remains far removed from such Advaita thesis.

Every concept, argues Nāgārjuna, acquires meaning only when contrasted with its complement and in that sense every concept implies its own negation. Other metaphysical categories that Nāgārjuna rejects are: substance and attribute, whole and parts, knowledge and object, universal and particular, the self and not self, the *pramāṇas* and the *prameyas*, bondage and liberation. One of the pervasive features of these metaphysical concepts is that they come in pairs, and of each of these pairs, it can be said that the members depend upon each other. If a substance is what underlies attributes, then the two concepts are dependent upon each other, and any definition of substance in terms of attributes has to be circular inasmuch as an attribute is what characterizes a substance. Likewise, if a whole consists of parts, then a part is a part only as belonging to a whole, and both concepts go together. Notice that in critiquing the concepts of whole and part, Nāgārjuna is critiquing the distinction between conditioned and unconditioned *dharmas* which was one of the central concerns of the early Buddhists. The same sort of mutual dependence affects the concept of *vijñāna* (cognition/knowledge) which both the Hindu and the Buddhist philosophers use. If an object is that which is manifested by a knowledge and a cognition or knowledge is that which manifests its object, then there cannot be one without the other but any definition is applicable to both of them together and not to each one separately. In so asserting, Nāgārjuna in effect is critiquing the Buddhist use of the word *vijñāna* and the fourfold conditions that give rise to it, especially the *ālambana patyayatā*.

Following the method outlined above, Nāgārjuna examines various metaphysical theories that existed in Indian thought during that time (e.g., Vaiśeṣika theory that a material object consists of simple atoms; the Sāṁkhya theory that material objects arise out of simple undifferentiated stuff called *prakṛti* or nature; the early Buddhist theory that reality is a process, or better yet, a series of instantaneous events) shows that in each of these cases the concepts employed (e.g., that of the part and whole, the simple and the composite, permanence and change, undifferentiated nature and differentiated entities) imply their opposites and to the extent they do, the thesis cannot be coherently formulated. Since a concept, say, a chair, is incoherent, the alleged thing called "chair" is also empty, argues Nāgārjuna, meaning thereby that it is devoid of self-nature. In such a scheme, it does not make sense to argue whether things exist or not. Ascribing existence to things is only a matter of pragmatic usefulness, not of ontological reality. Accordingly, Nāgārjuna concludes that since no entity can be characterized in itself to have an essence (i.e., being simple, being permanent, being instantaneous, being a whole, or being a part), such entities are *śūnya*.

The divergent theories of reality, on this view, are only conceptual constructions (*vikalpa*) in which each construction focuses upon a particular point of view. In view of this radical critique, the concept of *śūnyatā* itself may be said to undergo two levels of transformation: *śūnyatā* (1) as applied to the phenomenal world, and (2) as applied to the noumenal world. Thus, *śūnyatā* may be understood from the lower as well as from the higher point of view; from the lower point of view, it signifies lack of self-nature or absence of any substantial reality of its own; from the transcendent standpoint, it signifies the incoherence of all conceptual systems.

Nāgārjuna's thought thus implies a conception of levels of truth: conventional truth (*samvṛti*) and noumenal (*paramārtha sattā*) truths. In the phenomenal realm there is no absolute truth; truth is always relative to a conceptual system. The phenomenal world has only a pragmatic reality, which is also called conventional (*samvṛtti*). Conventional truth, however, is not the only kind of truth. There is also the *paramārtha-satya*, i.e., the higher or the absolute truth. The world, according to the Buddhist teachings, pertains only to the phenomena, the pragmatic, or the conventional level (these are used synonymously by the Buddhists); however, from the point of view of the absolute truth, the manifold world of names and forms is simply an appearance. Absolute reality transcends the perceptual-conceptual framework of language; it is unconditional and devoid of plurality. It is *nirvāṇa*. Such a truth is realized by intuitive wisdom (*prajñā*). It is non-dual and contentless. It is beyond language, logic, and sense perception.

It is important to remember that this *prajñā* begins at a lower level with the knowledge of the noumenal entities, e.g., *nirvāṇa*. At a higher level, even such entities as *nirvāṇa*, and *Tathāgata*, have to be dissolved into experiences. In other words, ontology is constantly being transcended by a series of negations, which may be represented as follows:

1 let p be a conventional truth;
2 –p is the higher truth (the negation being always higher than an affirmation);
3 the next higher truth may be represented as p and –p;
4 which again may be denied in –(p.–p)

In this way every affirmation can be negated leading to a higher level of affirmation, which again can be negated. All these lead Nāgārjuna to argue that *saṃsāra* or phenomenal conditioned reality, is not really different from *nirvāṇa*; they are the same.[1] In other words, *nirvāṇa* and *saṃsāra* are not two ontologically distinct levels, but one reality viewed from two different perspectives. The distinction between the two, like all else, is relative. The same reality is phenomenal when viewed conditionally; it is *nirvāṇa* when viewed unconditionally. Accordingly *nirvāṇa* is not something that is to be attained, but is, rather, the right comprehension of the *saṃsāra* in which the plurality of names and forms is manifested. Everything is *nirvāṇa*; it is *śūnya*. Thus, *śūnya* is an experience which cannot be linguistically and conceptually communicated, it is quiescent, it is devoid of conceptual construction, and it is non-dual.

Nāgārjuna further argues that no element of existence is manifest without conditions; therefore there is no non-empty element,[2] and whatever is conditionally emergent is empty. Thus there is a three-way relation between conditioned emergence, emptiness, and verbal convention. Nāgārjuna regards this relation as none other than the middle path: (1) conditioned emergence is emptiness; (2) emptiness and the conventional world are not two distinct ontological levels, but are rather two sides of the same coin. To say that a thing is conditionally emergent is to say that it is empty. Conversely, to say that it is empty is another way of saying that it emerges conditionally. What language articulates is the so-called conventional world, which is empty. Nāgārjuna did wrestle with the question: "in what sense do the words like '*śūnya*' and '*nirvāṇa*' verbally articulate what is incapable of being expressed"? He accepted the paradox involved to be unavoidable.

There have been endless questions and answers about the nature and validity of Nāgārjuna's thinking. How could he use logic when his thinking transcends it? Is it nihilism? To what purpose does he use logic when he has no position of his own to defend?

In reading Nāgārjuna, it is important to keep in mind that Nāgārjuna was neither a thorough-going skeptic nor a nihilist. T. R. V. Murti terms Mādhyamika dialectic "a spiritual *ju-jitsu*." He further adds that Mādhyamika "does not have a thesis of his own."[3] However, it seems that to interpret Nāgārjuna as the one whose arguments aim only at destruction is to miss the real significance of his philosophy. It is indeed true that Nāgārjuna demonstrates that one could expose self-contradictions in the opponent's arguments without making any claims about what in fact exists as long as one uses the rules accepted by the opponent. This, however, should not be taken to imply, contrary to Murti's contention, that Nāgārjuna did not have a thesis of his own. In his dialectical method, Nāgārjuna rejects the pretensions of reason to know reality. Nāgārjuna uses logic to destroy logical thinking and logically set up and defend positions. Just as one uses a nail to take out a nail from one's foot or one destroys the poison of a disease by using the poison in the medicine, so Nāgārjuna uses logic to destroy logic and to be free from its clutches. His mode of argumentation does not demonstrate the total inadequacy of reason, because he himself uses reason to demonstrate self-contradictions involved in the opponent's arguments. He shows that everything is conditional in the phenomenal world; that reality transcends both refutation and non-refutation, both affirmation and negation, and hence it cannot be captured by discursive reasoning.

What comes at the end and marks the highest point of wisdom is that *śūnyatā* itself is *śūnya*, emptiness itself is empty. This is to ward off any misconception that Mādhyamika thesis is nihilism or a conception of being as nothingness. Nāgārjuna's position, if he has a position, is very different from this. He warns us against reifying *śūnyatā* into an entity. Hence the culmination of wisdom is the knowledge that emptiness itself is empty. Reality can only be captured by rising to a higher level, which is the level of *prajñā*. Thus, in making these assertions Nāgārjuna indeed provides his readers with some theses of his own, in which case we cannot but ask, can he do so consistently?

IV The Yogacārās

The Yogācāra ("one whose practice is *yoga*") school is so-called because it recommends the practice of *yoga* to attain freedom (*nirvāṇa*) from the phenomenal world. The school is also known as Vijñānavāda, which derives from the school's explicitly stated position that *vijñāna* (consciousness) is the only reality.

Asaṇga, together with his brother Vasubandhu, are taken to be the co-founder of this school, though many important Yogācāra works, e.g., *Yogācārabhūmi* and *Saṃdhinirmocana Sūtra* predate them. Asaṇga's teacher was Maitreya who according to many was not a historical person but a *bodhisattva*. Asaṇga's important works are: *Aryadeśanāvikhyāpana* (an abridged *Yogācārabhūmi* that deals with the seventeen stages of *yoga* practice based on Maitreya's teachings), *Abhidharmasamuccaya* (a brief explanation from the Yogācāra viewpoint of the elements constituting phenomenal existence); and *Mahāyānasaṃgraha* (a comprehensive work on the Yogācāra doctrines and practices). According to Parmārtha's biography of Vasubandhu, Asaṇga initially belonged to the Hīnayāna Buddhism, but later converted to the Mahāyāna. Thus it is not surprising that Asaṇga's works are characterized by a detailed analysis of psychological phenomena that he inherited from the Abhidharma literature of the Hīnayāna schools.

Asaṇga's younger brother Vasubandhu is regarded as the most famous philosopher of this school. In my discussion of Yogācāra, I will primarily draw from his works.

Vasubandhu

Vasubandhu, the younger brother of Asaṇga, was born in Puruṣapura (today known as Peshawar) in the state of Gāndhāra in northwest India. Takasuku places Vasubandhu between 420–500 CE. Paramārtha wrote his biography sometime between 468–568 CE.

Although Vasubandhu began as a Sarvāstivādin, he converted to Mahāyāna Buddhism under the influence of his brother Asaṇga. Vasubandhu's two important works of this phase are: *Viṃśatikā* or the *Twenty Verses* with his own commentary, and *Triṃśikā* or the *Thirty Verses*. My discussion of Yogācāra school in this chapter is primarily based on these two works.

Gāndhāra in those days was heavily dominated by the Vaibhāṣika Buddhism, so it is not surprising that Vasubandhu's early writings were influenced by this school. In those days, Vasubandhu supported himself by delivering public lectures on Buddhism during the day and putting that day's lecture in a condensed verse form in the evening. In time, he composed over 600 verses. He collected these verses and entitled them *Abhidharmakośa*, which became one of the most important books of the Buddhist tradition. He also wrote a commentary on this work.

In *Abhidharmakośa*, the most important work of the early phase of his career, Vasubandhu describes the views of the different schools of the early Buddhist philosophy along with his own position. Vasubandhu arranges and systematizes all the *dharmas* recognized in the early Buddhist philosophy.

As a *Yogācāra*, Vasubandhu denies the existence of the external world. He begins by accepting the thesis that "all this," i.e., color, form, etc., are nothing but "*vijñaptis*." Everything that is being perceived is "perception only." He takes "*citta*" to be connected to "*caitta*," i.e., perception and what is being perceived, *citta* and *caitta* belong together. There is no external object that is outside and independent of *citta* and its correlate *caitta*. Some scholars argue that this thesis amounts to idealism insofar as it denies the existence of "external objects" (*vāhyārthabhanga*), Whether this thesis is an idealism in the sense prevalent in Western philosophy is debatable, and there is no need to enter into this controversy here. In any case, Vasubandhu is not asserting a purely theoretical thesis, but a thesis that would be conducive to the attainment of *nirvāṇa*. Precisely how, we will see soon.

Cognitions, argues Vasubandhu, arise without depending on the supposed object. In the *Twenty Verses* he defends *Yogācāra* from the objections raised by the realists who believe in the existence of an external world. In the *Thirty Verses* he develops his theses further. Various objections are raised and answered. Some of the objections raised against the "perception only" thesis, and Vasubandhu's answers in the *Twenty Verses* are discussed below.

One of the objections raised is as follows: If a perception does not arise from an object as its cause, then why are there spatio-temporal restrictions to a perception, i.e., my yellow-perception occurs only when I look *there* and *then*, not anywhere at any time? Why are they not restricted to one stream of consciousness (say, *mine*)? Why cannot the same perception occur in another stream as well (say, in *yours*)? In response Vasubandhu points out that external objects are perceived in dreams and hallucinations, although none are actually present. In dreams one experiences—sees, touches, etc.—objects, which do not exist. As regards "restriction of perceptions to space and time," he notes that the same restriction also characterizes dreams. Consciousness creates its own content; it does not need an external object. As regards "non-restriction regarding the different streams of consciousness" (the fact that different persons may have perceptions of the same object), such collective perceptions do occur (when admittedly there do not exist these objects) as in the case of all the dead perceiving rivers of fire along with their tormentors around. Such apparitions do not exist, yet all the dead sprits perceive them. As a consequence, we need not admit the existence of material objects to serve as causes of our perceptions. On the other hand, it is better to explain our present perceptions by past perceptions and actions.

We know that the Buddha spoke of sense-field etc. It is asked: why did the Buddha teach about "sense-fields," "sense-objects" such as "*rūpa*," etc., if there are no such sense-fields and how are we to understand his statements about them if there does not exist any perceived object? Vasubandhu argues that the Buddha's discourses about "sense-field" etc., are not to be taken literally but obliquely i.e., as having the intention of leading the hearers towards growing "selflessness." *Citta* is a series of continuous transformations brought about by appropriate causal conditions. The six types of consciousness—visual, touch, etc.—are being produced instantaneously by appropriate causal conditions. Appearances arise and perish without there being any material object outside of consciousness. In this series, there is no unity of a person or *pudgala*, neither the subject of consciousness nor object. All events are "without self."

In response to the question as to how to accommodate the theory of atoms as ultimate constituents of material objects, as held by the Vaibhāṣika and the Vaiśeṣika schools, Vasubandhu states that the atoms, if they have no parts and no sides or aspects, cannot simply combine to form a larger object. If there is no aggregate of atoms, then we would not be able to have any explanation of the objects of perception. If there is a difference of direction with regard to an atom, then the atom is neither one nor many. The same argument is used to critique the Vaibhāṣika doctrine that each sensory object—a color, e.g.—is a simple unity, an atom.

It is asked: is not perception the most basic *pramāṇa* by which the existence of objects is established? If the object of perception does not exist, how can it serve as a *pramāṇa*? Does not memory arise from the perceived object? Vasubandhu notes that direct perception arises as a momentary event, followed by a mental consciousness (by which time the perception has perished), followed by a memory. At no stage is there the experience of an external object. Memory is memory of the perception, not of the supposed object of perception. In this regard, perception is like a dream.

If there is no object of perception, then how does a person kill sheep, etc.? Vasubandhu argues that the body and its dying may be explained as special perceptions of willing caused by other-experiences and their traces by which there occurs a discontinuity in an appearance-series. Special perceptions in others may bring about discontinuity in a series by causing the other's life force to cease.

The point that Vasubandhu was trying to make is as follows: Perceptions do not justify the existence of external objects. He defines perception as an awareness that arises from the very object by which that awareness is specified. It is indeed true that the awareness of X, if veridical, is caused by X; but X, in this context, is not an external object but rather the percept or the object-form which "floats" in that very awareness, which Vasubandhu calls the *ālambana pratyaya*. The mind fabricates its own objects. Residual impressions generated by past experiences in turn generate ideas in the mind and these ideas are called "objects." How we see is, to a large extent, determined by previous experience and our experiences are intersubjective. To the question how an intersubjective world is possible in the absence of external objects, Vasubandhu refers to the illusory experience of hell shared by persons with a common *karmic* heritage. Vasubandhu concludes the *Twenty Verses* by noting that my knowledge of my *citta* and my knowledge of others *cittas*, are not like knowledge of objects and concedes that limitless depths of the series of perception-only cannot be comprehended by a person like him: Only the Buddha can comprehend the truth fully.

The above gives a brief synopsis of how Vasubandhu explains our everyday experiences, an intrasubjective world, the distinction between true and false knowledge. At times residual forces (*vāsanās*) cause internal modifications in a consciousness and as a result the object-content is manifested. States of consciousness alone are real and objects are wrongly superimposed on consciousness. Thus the external world is nothing more than the projection of consciousness.

At the outset of the *Thirty Verses*, Vasubandhu informs his readers that consciousness undergoes three stratifications. The first stratification is *ālaya-vijñāna* or store-consciousness, the repository of all *vāsanās* (traces of past experience). The "seeds" generated by good or bad action, are stored in the "*ālaya*-consciousness." It is the realm of potentiality. The second stratification is *manovijñāna* or thought-consciousness. It is the transformation of potentialities into actual thoughts. It is characterized by self-regard, attachment to the self, self-love, and the sense of I am. The third stratification is *pravṛttivijñāna* or active-consciousness, which manifests itself in the contents of various mental states and the alleged external objects. The third, the representational consciousness, includes visual, tactual, auditory, gustatory, and internal perception by the mind of *sukha*, *duhkha*, etc. Notice that Vijñānavādins are using *manas* in two different senses. In *manovijñāna* in the second level, it is used in the sense of self-attachment, and in the third level, it is used as an inner sense-organ, the sense in which it is usually used by Advaita, Nyāya, etc. Thus, in the reverse order, the three transformations are: sensory representation, self-awareness (as well as self-attachment, self-feeling), and the store-house consciousness where the experiences at the two levels deposit their traces as seeds which need to be actualized under appropriate conditions.

Besides these transformations of *vijñāna*, there is nothing else. Everything else is *vikalpa*, imagined. It has no reality. Hence, the thesis of *vijñapti*-only. *Citta* is one, undifferentiated being, but conceptually divided into the subject and the object. In reality, there is neither. The object of *vikalpa* is *asat*; *vikalpa* arises without a real object. These stratifications of consciousness create the mistaken belief that there are objects such as trees, tables, chairs, etc. that exist independently of consciousness. Vasubandhu outlines how each of these stratifications can be overcome and perfect wisdom attained. The state of perfect wisdom is pure, i.e., it has no object, no passions; it is a state of peace and joy.

It is worth noting that Vasubandhu distinguishes among three "natures" or "realms": (1) that which is imagined (*parikalpita*) but appears to be real. The imagined has only subjective being (*prajñaptisat*); (2) the empirical realm (*paratantra*) or the realm of causality (*pratītyasamutpāda*) which accounts for our mistaking impermanence for permanence. The dependent has both subjective and objective beings; (3) the absolute or perfect realm (*pariniṣpanna*) which is the ultimate truth of all events, the true nature of things (*dharmatā*). It is free from subject-object distinction It is "suchness" or "thatness," i.e., a nature which cannot be conceptually and linguistically articulated, which is not a universal shared by many particulars; it is uniquely each event's own nature. It is *nirvāṇa*. Repeated meditative practices remove past residual impressions, and when all defilements and conceptual constructions are purified, one is enlightened. The *tathatā* alone is pure *vastu-sat*.

All three are "*niḥsvabhāva*" (without own-nature). The first is *lakṣaṇa-niḥsvabhāvatā*, or empty by definition. The second is *utpatti-niḥsvabhāvatā*, or empty in the sense of Dependent Origination. The third alone is really empty, *paramārtaha-niḥsvabhāva*. Vasubandhu concludes by noting that when consciousness does not apprehend any "object," it is situated in consciousness-only.[4] This is trans-worldly consciousness. What happens is "resolution at its basis" (*āśraya-parāvṛtti*); it is called the *dharmakāya* of the Buddha.[5]

Concluding Remarks

The basic thesis of Vijñānavāda is that consciousness alone *is*. It is *sākāra*, i.e., has a form of its own, there being no formless consciousness. What passes as the object or *ālambana* of consciousness is really its form. Consciousness of yellow and consciousness of blue differ, not merely in the objects, which are yellow and blue respectively, but the consciousnesses in themselves are really different: one is the consciousness of blue, the other is the consciousness of yellow. To the ordinary mind, the *ālambana*, the object, seems to be out there in the world. For the Vijñānavādins, the so-called *ālambana*, that appears in a consciousness is nothing but the form of the consciousness and is given along with the self-manifestation (*svasaṃvedana*) of that consciousness. This is the basic thesis, but this thesis gives rise to both internal as well as external problems. Internal problems concern the relation of this thesis to the Buddha's own teaching and with the nature of the Buddha-consciousness, the consciousness of the enlightened one, irrespective of whether one is talking about the *arhat*, the *pratyeka buddha*, or the *bodhisattva*. The external problems concern the relation of this thesis to the ordinary point of view which is committed to the subject/object dualism.

Ordinarily, the objects that we perceive, the table, the tree, that mountain, have determinate places in space, and we take them to be caused by the supposed external object. But if there is no external object, why is it that our perceptions are of this place and not another place? Vasubandhu replies to such objections by citing the case of dreams in which we also perceive things at determinate places, "there" and not "here." If the objects of dream consciousness could have such determinants, so also could the seeming objects of our perceptions even if there is no real object outside. This is a difficult argument and requires a careful development taking into account the question whether the parallelism drawn between waking and dreaming holds good. It would be instructive to take into account in this context Descartes' so-called dream argument. Whereas Descartes asks how we can distinguish waking from dreaming, Vasubandhu says that waking experience and dream experience are so alike that representations in both have determinate positions without there being an external object. Dream representations arise without there being an external object, so also the ordinary waking perceptions could be law-governed without there being the causal influence of supposed external objects. In both cases, we have intentionalities, i.e., consciousness as being of something, which cannot be reduced to causality. One way of preserving the intentional relation without bringing in causality is to appeal to a coherence among different minds or to the intentionalities belonging to the same mind. I mention this idea of coherence because another example that Vasubandhu gives in his defense seems to appeal to such a coherence. How is it, he asks, that the evil spirits who suffer in the boiling caldron have those representations even though there is no such hell? In this case he seems to argue that it is because of their common representations, which they all share, so that there arises the appearance of something being really there.

But be that as it may, the Vijñānavādins hold that the representations are of something or the other, and this something or the other really belongs to the structure of those representations, so that only representations exist. The data of our experiences do not require us to posit anything other than our representations.

Vasubandhu also discusses our perceptions of other minds. In his thinking, other minds have a different metaphysical status from material objects. The material objects that appears, as we saw, are forms of consciousness, but other minds are independent realities. He therefore concedes that when I experience other minds, for example, that the other person is in pain, I am not experiencing what is simply intended by my intentionality, but I have an experience of what transcends it. Nevertheless my experience of other minds is intentional, and has a content that the other person is in pain, though I do not experience his pain directly. But when the Buddha knows the other minds, he directly experiences the experiences of the others, including their pain.

The contrast between the experience of a person which is intentional and the experience of a Buddha which is non-intentional causes Vasubandhu's exposition many problems. Perhaps the distinction between the representational consciousness of persons and the direct pure consciousness of the enlightened one, the Buddha, may provide further insights. *Nirvāṇa* brings about a complete reversal of consciousness. The *ālaya-vijñāna* is dissolved, so that the intentional consciousness—whose object-directedness was being determined by the *ālaya*—sheds its intentionality and becomes pure non-intentional knowledge; this is the knowledge of the Buddha. It is both *vijñapti* and not-*vijñapti*, both mind and not mind.

Whether Vijñānavāda can be called an idealism in the Western sense is difficult to decide because for that purpose we need to determine what is meant by idealism. There is no need to determine that here. What is essential is rather to understand *vijñāna* and the vocabulary that Vasubandhu uses in the context of Indian philosophical rhetoric. For a long time, the Vaibhāṣika discussions continued to determine the status of *vastu sat* and *prajñapti sat*. For Vaibhāṣikas everything is *vastu sat*, everything consists of real *dharmas*, even *nirvāṇa* is conceived as a *vastu*, a positive entity. The Sautrāntikas deny to *nirvāṇa* this status, only the present *dharma* is *vastu sat*; the others are absences. For the Mādhyamika everything is *śūnya* (empty), there is no *vastu sat*. For the Vijñānavāda, the positive entities that we take to be perceiving as things of the world are only *prajñaptisat*, only *jñāna* of the enlightened one, viz., *nirvāṇa* is *vastu sat*.

The truth of *vijñapti* or intentional consciousness is *śūnyatā*. But this nature of intentional consciousness as *śūnyatā* is realized only in the enlightenment. It is also called "*tathatā*" or "suchness,"[6] which is then seen to have been always the truth of everything including intentional consciousness. This is why the Buddha-consciousness, though non-representational and so non-mental, is also mental because it truly knows the truth of mental consciousness. This explains why the Buddha-consciousness is dealt within Vijñānavāda, as we find in Asaṇga, as being embodied, although one has to distinguish between three bodies of the Buddha, *dharma kāya, sambhoga kāya*, and *nirmāṇa kāya*.[7] The body, though a hindrance to the functioning of consciousness in the case of ordinary persons, still functions through its medium such that visual consciousness functions through the eyes, the tactual through the skin, and so on. The Buddha could not possibly have taught without having a body, so he freely assumes a body which, in his case, is not a negation or a limitation on his consciousness, but a freely used medium for showing his infinite compassion for others. Note that with the idea of the *tathatā* or suchness which is the essence of all beings, Asaṇga, and indeed all Yogācāras, come to a position which is very near the Vedāntic doctrine, i.e., that the *ātman* is the essence of all things.

13

THE VEDĀNTA *DARŚANA*

Of all the systems of Indian philosophy, Vedānta, at least in modern times, has been the most influential. This system differentiated into many sub-schools, each school having a well-argued philosophical position and a strong religious following. The term "Vedānta" (i.e., "Veda" + "*anta*") literally means "the end of the Vedas." "Veda," derived from the root "*vid*," means "knowledge"; "*anta*" has two meanings: the final place reached as a result of the effort, and the goal towards which all effort is to be directed, i.e. the Upaniṣads, which themselves are often referred to as "Vedānta." Accordingly, "Vedānta" refers to the doctrines set forth in the part of the Vedic corpus known as the Upaniṣads, one of the three bases of the Vedānta school.

The Upaniṣads, you might recall, are replete with ambiguities, inconsistencies, and contradictions; they do not contain a systematic and logical development of ideas. Several attempts to systematize the teachings of the Upaniṣads were made; one such attempt was made by Bādarāyaṇa in his *Vedāntasūtras* (aphorisms of Vedānta) or *Brahmasūtras* (aphorisms about *brahman*). These aphorisms constitute the second basis of the Vedānta schools. The third basis, the *Bhagavad-Gītā*, a chapter of the great epic *Mahābhārata*, probably was added much later to the list of the two bases.

The Vedānta school received its formal expression in the *Vedāntasūtras*. The term "*sūtra*" literally means "thread," and is related to the verb "to sew." It refers to a short aphoristic sentence, and, collectively, to a text consisting of such statements. It is difficult to date the *Vedāntasūtras*. However, given that these *sūtras* contain a refutation of all the schools of Indian philosophy, which date from 500 BCE to 200 BCE, they could not have been composed earlier than 200 BCE. *A sūtra* usually does not consist of more than two or three words and is characterized by brevity and terseness. The laconic contents of these *sūtra*s have given rise to various divergent interpretations within the Vedānta school. Their primary points of departure are interpretations of the nature of the *brahman*, relation between the *brahman* and the world, the self, and *mokṣa*.

One's interpretation of the Vedānta doctrines may be supported as much by independent reasoning as by citing and interpreting sentences from these three sources. One is regarded as a founder of a new sub-school if one has substantiated the interpretations of the doctrines by suitably commenting upon these foundational texts, in the technical jargon, by writing *bhāṣyas* (commentaries) on them.

The two better known schools of Vedānta are: Advaita Vedānta (non-dualism) of Śaṃkara and Rāmānuja's Viśiṣṭādvaita (qualified non-dualism). Besides these two, there are additional well-known sub-schools, e.g., those of Madhva, Bhāskara, Vallabha, Nimbārka, and so on. Each of these commentators earned the honorific title of "*Ācārya*" (though today, it is a much deflated title and has lost its past significance). These interpretations fall under two basic groups: non-dualistic and theistic interpretations. In this chapter I will discuss two schools of Vedānta: Śaṃkara's non-dualistic Vedānta and Rāmānuja's theism or qualified non-dualism.

I Advaita Vedānta

Advaita Vedānta, the non-dualistic school of Vedānta, has been and continues to be the most widely known system of Indian philosophy in the East and the West alike. Śaṃkara was the founder (primary explicator) of this school. Śaṃkara received most of his training under the guidance of his *guru* Govinda and attained the highest knowledge at a very early age. He traveled across India debating with opponents and reforming aberrant practices. He died at the early age of thirty-two. Śaṃkara was not only a philosopher; he was also a mystic, a saint, and a poet. An enormous amount of work has been attributed to him. His achievements are remarkable, and the short span of his life makes his contributions all the more remarkable.

Śaṃkara, according to a well-known legend, was asked to summarize his position in one verse. He summarized it in one-half of a verse, which runs as follows: "*brahma satyam, jagan mithya, jivo brahmaiva nāparaḥ*" (the *brahman* is the truth, the world is false, and the finite individual is none other than the *brahman*).[1] His major works reiterate this philosophy in different ways. In order to have a clear understanding of Śaṃkara's philosophy, it is essential that we understand the meaning and ramifications of these three assertions. I will begin with the first.

Brahma Satyam *(The* Brahman *is the Truth)*

Brahman, argues Śaṃkara, is the highest transcendental truth. It alone *is*. It is that state of being where all subject/object distinction is obliterated. It is pure consciousness that is timeless, unconditioned, undifferentiated, without beginning, and without end.

Śaṃkara's non-dualism denies all differences external as well as internal with regard to the real, the *brahman*. Other schools of Indian philosophy recognize some difference or other to be real: the Nyāya-Vaiśeṣikas recognize a real difference between consciousness and its object, not to speak of the plurality of conscious selves and of objects; the Buddhists of the Vijñānavāda school take consciousness or cognitions alone to be real, but recognize internal difference among the momentary cognitions arising and perishing; the Sāṃkhya recognizes an external difference among many selves and the one non-conscious *prakṛti*; and Rāmānuja's qualified non-dualism, as we will see a little later in this chapter, asserts an internal difference between *cit* and *acit* within the unity of one being, i.e., *brahman*. Śaṃkara's non-dualism denies all differences: external as well as internal. External differences may be heterogeneous, i.e., differences among things instantiating different classes (e.g., between a table and a chair); they could be homogeneous distinctions, i.e., differences among instances belonging to the same class (e.g., between a chair and another chair). Internal difference is the difference that exists between different parts of the same thing (e.g., between the one leg and the other leg of a chair).

Reality being one and differenceless neither admits of negation nor of antecedent negation nor of negation after destruction; therefore, it is beginningless, endless, eternal, and without any qualitative determination. Such being the nature of the *brahman*, the world consisting of different things as well as different types of things (conscious selves and non-conscious nature) is simply an appearance.

When it is said that the *brahman* is pure consciousness, it is not meant that consciousness is an essential quality of the *brahman*, for that would amount to introducing an internal distinction within the *brahman*, i.e., the distinction between a substance and its qualities. The *brahman* is not a substance, substance being an objective category. Likewise, when the Upaniṣads say that the *brahman* is *satyam* (truth), *jñānam* (knowledge), and *anantam* (infinite), it is not intended to imply that these are the qualities of the *brahman*, for that would amount to introducing an internal difference into *brahman's* nature. The Advaitins therefore construe such sentences of the Upaniṣads to mean three different ways in which, undifferentiated nature of the one, the *brahman*, is being articulated. These words serve to differentiate the *brahman* from their opposite qualities. To say that the *brahman* is truth, negates that the *brahman* is untruth, and so on. No positive determination of the *brahman* is possible. (This is very similar to Spinoza's assertion that every determination implies negation: *omnis determinatio est negatio*). As the Upaniṣads reiterate, the best way to describe the *brahman* is by saying that it is "not-this," "not-this." *Via negativa* orients the mind of the aspirants towards qualityless (*nirguṇa*) *brahman*. Nothing can be affirmed about it. Śaṃkara himself notes: "the reality is without an internal difference. . . .it is unthinkable; the thought can be brought to it via negation of what can be thought."[2] Nothing can be affirmed about the *nirguṇa brahman*. As *saguṇa*, the *brahman* is described as *satyam* (truth), *jñānam* (knowledge), and *anantam* (infinite) or *sat, cit, ānanda*" (existence, consciousness, and bliss), i.e., the *brahman* as interpreted and affirmed by the mind from a limited, empirical standpoint. It is that *brahman* about which something can be said.

The Upaniṣads contain both the negative and the positive descriptions of the *brahman*. Śaṃkara takes the negative statements to be higher than the affirmative ones, because negation becomes significant only after an affirmation has been made (which is then negated). It is a lower level of understanding to regard *brahman* as omnipresent, such that everything whatsoever is *brahman*. But it is only after one has made such a statement, that one can proceed to negate what has been affirmed and say "none of this is *brahman*." "This" refers to any possible object. The *brahman* transcends the world of objects (material things) and finite individuals. Manyness, plurality, differences, are all appearances. In reality, the two *brahmans* are one and the same. The teachings of Advaita affirm one simple truth: there is one reality, although it is known by different names. *Nirguṇa* and *saguṇa brahman* refer to one and the same reality; they have the same referent, although the senses vary, very much like the Fregean analysis of the "morning star" and "evening star." The *brahman* is one without any second; it does not admit of any change nor of any difference,

What then is the criterion of "reality" that the Advaitin applies to reach this ontological position? Śaṃkara uses "*bādha*," which in the context of his ontology has been construed as "cancellation" or "negation," or "contradiction." Cancellation is a mental process of correcting and rectifying errors of judgment. In this process one disvalues—more as a psychological necessity than from a purely logical point of view—a previously held object or content of consciousness on account of its being contradicted by a new experience. It is important to remember in this context that not all negations or contradictions are *bādha*. Suppose one believes that a certain hypothesis, say, a scientific concept, will work in a certain situation. A little later, one finds out that it will not. Cancellation of error has occurred. This, however, is not *bādha*, which not only requires rejection of an object, or a content of consciousness, but also that such rectification occurs in light of a new judgment to which belief is attached and which replaces the initial judgment.

Using this criterion of cancellation, Śaṃkara in his commentary on *Brahmasutras*,[3] discusses three orders of existence: Reality or Absolute existence (*paramārthika sattā*), empirical-practical (*vyavahārika sattā*), and illusory (*prātibhāsika sattā*).

Reality or Absolute existence is that which in principle cannot be cancelled by any experience, because no experience can deny or disvalue it. Reality is non-dual; it is the level of pure being. The act of cancellation presupposes a distinction between the experiencer and the experienced. It involves a plurality of objects because cancellation juxtaposes one object or content of consciousness against another incompatible object or content of consciousness and judges the first to be of lesser value. Thus, cancellation requires rejection, turning away from an object or content of consciousness in favor of something to which belief, more value, is attached. The *brahman* has no dichotomy within it; it is pure oneness and cannot be denied by any lower order of being. Therefore, no other object or content of consciousness can replace it. *Brahman* cancels everything while remaining uncancellable by any other experience whatsoever. "Consciousness is not," argue the Advaitins, is not a possible determination, for such a negation must itself be an act of consciousness, consciousness negating itself, which would be a self-contradiction. Given that consciousness does not admit the possibility of its being negated or cancelled, it is the only reality. Thus, the *brahman* or consciousness belongs to the highest level of being.

Appearance consists of those contents of experience that can be cancelled only by reality. This is the level of empirical existents. It includes our experiences of the world of names and forms, multiplicity of empirical objects, other finite individuals, in short, all subject-object distinctions that are governed by the law of causation. Most of us live at this level, die at this level, and are reborn to this level. At this level of experience, we take the world and God to be separately real, and attribute to God all the qualities that are generally associated with "God" in theism. God in this sense is *saguṇa brahman*, the creator, maintainer and destroyer of the world. He is an object of worship.

Illusory existent consists of those contents of experience that can be cancelled by reality or by the empirical existents. Illusions, hallucinations, dreams, etc., belong to this level. An illusory existent is different from an empirical existent insofar as it fails to fulfill the criteria of empirical truth. For example, a thirsty traveler passing through a desert runs to a particular spot to quench his thirst. However, upon reaching that spot he discovers that there is no water and realizes that his perception of water was really a mirage and that there is no water. The illusion of water comes to an end when the traveler, in light of new experience, discovers that it was a mirage. The illusory existent, i.e., the experience of mirage, is cancelled by another empirical experience. In short, all objects in principle can be negated. If x is an object, then the determination "x is not," is possible. It cannot therefore be ultimately real. The objects that belong to the empirical level can be cancelled; therefore, they are not real, better yet, false, which leads me to the second assertion mentioned above.

Jagan Mithyā *(The World is False)*

Let us now discuss what Śaṃkara meant by his assertion that the *jagat* is *mithyā*. "*Jagat*" is usually translated as the "world," the realm of birth and death; it is where suffering is manifested. The standard English translation of the word "*mithyā*" is "false." Thus, etymologically we can say that Śaṃkara is asserting the falsity of the world. However, one may wonder what does falsity mean? What is entailed in Śaṃkara's assertion? What is the relationship between the *brahman* and the false world? Why, or who, creates, this false world?

Adhyāsa

To understand what is entailed in Śaṃkara's assertion that the world is false, one must first understand two crucial Advaita concepts, i.e., "*adhyāsa*" (superimposition) and "*māyā*" (ignorance). These concepts lie at the basis of Advaita Vedānta metaphysics and epistemology and would go a long way in helping us to come to grips with the status of the world in Śaṃkara's philosophy. Superimposition refers to the simple, everyday experience in which one thing appears as another. It is an erroneous cognition, an illusory appearance; it is the cognition of "that" in what is "not-that."[4] In superimposition, one apprehends a thing to be other than what it is. Śaṃkara explains it thus: *adhyāsa* is one thing appearing as another, or rather "in one thing another appears," where the latter is "like something seen before" and the appearing is "like memory."

Most of us would agree that in everyday experiences we frequently perceive one thing as another or wrongly ascribe the properties of one thing to another. These are cases of erroneous perception, and the mechanism that underlies it is called "*adhyāsa*" or "superimposition," which not only explains an experience of perceptual illusion, but also, in Advaita Vedānta metaphysics, what occurs in the metaphysical situation of the *brahman* appearing to be the world, *ātman* appearing as a finite individual, the self appearing as body. In a superimposition, something functions as the locus, the underlying reality, while another entity is projected on it. The projected entity is false; the locus alone is real. When the error is corrected, the projected entity is cancelled, the locus stands out as real.

Let me explain superimposition further with the help of two examples: (1) one perceives a rope as a snake, and (2) perceives a crystal vase as red on account of the red flower placed near it. In the first case, one apprehends a thing to be other than what it is; in the second, one falsely attributes the qualities of one thing on another. These two types of perceptual error reveal the following characteristics of superimposition. Superimposition is: (1) the mixing of the real and the false, (2) seeing a thing in a substratum where it does not exist, (3) perceiving the attributes of one thing in another substratum, and (4) lack of discrimination or false knowledge.

The two examples given above concern things found in the world. But Advaita Vedānta affirms a more fundamental superimposition, i.e., superimposition of the world upon the *brahman*, which creates the sense that the world is real. The empirical world arises as a result of our superimposing the qualities on the undifferentiated reality, i.e., *brahman*. Just as in superimposition a rope is experienced as a snake, similarly, under the superimposition of names and forms, the *brahman*, the only reality, is experienced as the world. Thus, the Advaitins talk of superimposition with respect to particular experiences within the world of appearance as well as with respect to the appearance of the world in general. Some superimpositions, like a rope appearing as a snake, begin and end in time. Also, these experiences are private insofar as when I am misperceiving a rope as a snake, you are not. But there are superimpositions, e.g., the superimposition of the world on the *brahman*, which are beginningless; they are public insofar as all empirical individuals make the mistake of taking the world to be real, which it is not. Again, an illusory object, say, a snake, in the example given above, has no unperceived existence; its *esse is percipi*, i.e., its essence consists in being perceived. The empirically real objects, say, a rope or a snake or the world, on the other hand, have unperceived existence. Thus, when the world is said to be *mithyā* or false, it should not be construed as having the status of an illusory object. The world is empirically real prior to *brahman*-knowledge. With the dawn of the *brahman*-knowledge, the world betrays its falsity. The *brahman* is self-illuminating; it alone always *is*.

The Advaitins argue that our everyday experiences of superimposition assume various forms. Some superimpositions are that of identity (*tādātmya*)[5] as articulated in judgments like "I am this" (uttered pointing to my body), "I am a human." Here the superimposition is of the body on the self. Again, there are superimpositions of properties, substantives, and relations. There is the superimposition of the properties of the body on the self, e.g., "I am fat," "I am thin"; superimposition of the mental states such as desires, doubt, pleasure, pain, e.g., "I am happy," "I am virtuous"; and the properties of the sense organs on the self, e.g., "I am blind," "I am deaf." When a shell (on the beach) appears as silver, or a rope as a snake, a substantive is being superimposed upon another. But when I say "this is my body," it is a case of relational superimposition. At other times, a stone is worshipped as Viṣṇu, when one says "this is Viṣṇu." This is called "intentional superimposition." The point that the Advaitins are trying to make is as follows: Superimposition not only assumes the form of the "I" but also of the "mine." The former is the superimposition of the substance (*dharmī*), the latter of the attribute (*dharma*). The reciprocal superimposition of the self and the not-self, and of the properties of the one on the other, results in the bondage of the empirical self.

Given the centrality of superimposition in Śaṃkara's philosophy, it is not surprising that Śaṃkara begins his commentary on *Brahmasūtras* with a discussion of superimposition. The point that Śaṃkara makes is as follows: all appearances—the world appearance as well as the appearance of individuals—are due to superimposition (of one thing upon another). At this point, one may ask: why do we superimpose? Superimposition is due to ignorance (*māyā* or *avidyā*), a beginningless principle, argues Śaṃkara.

Māyā or Avidyā

Śaṃkara uses this concept to establish his central thesis that the *brahman* is the only reality, and that the multiplicity of names and forms (*nāma-rūpa*) is only an appearance. Etymologically the term "*māyā*" is derived from the root √*mā*, meaning, "measuring." With the concept of "*māyā*," Śaṃkara measures out the world, so to speak; or, the world is what is measurable. The term "*māyā*" can be traced as far back as the *Ṛg Veda*, where it has been used as the creative power of the deities. With this power, various deities for example, *Indra* and *Agni*, like a magician, assume many forms.[6] The Advaitins use the Vedic concept of "*māyā*" to explain the appearance of the world.

The term "*māyā*," is usually translated as "illusion." This translation, however, does not capture the full import of this concept. Rather than trying to give a one-word translation of this important concept, I will clarify it by setting forth its ontological, epistemological, and psychological meanings. Ontologically, *māyā* is the creative power of the *brahman* which creates the variety and multiplicity of the phenomenal world and makes us believe that the phenomenal world is real. Epistemologically, *māyā is* our ignorance *(avidyā)* regarding the difference between reality and appearance. *Māyā* disappears at the dawn of the *brahman* knowledge. Ignorance obscures pure consciousness and makes all empirical distinctions appear. Thus, epistemologically, the distinctions between the subject who knows, the object known, and the resulting knowledge are due to ignorance. From a psychological point of view, *māyā* is our tendency to regard the appearance as real, and *vice versa.* The empirical world is not real; however, our inclination is to believe that it is real. Another term used for ignorance is *avidyā,* which Śaṃkara in his writings uses more frequently than "*māyā.*" For him *avidyā* is the same as *adhyāsa*; it is a kind of psychic defilement, a "natural" propensity to err,[7] seed of the whole world,[8] and generates attachment from a psychological perspective.[9]

In his writings, Śaṃkara does not make a distinction between *māyā* and *avidyā;* he uses them interchangeably. For Śaṃkara *māyā* is *avidyā.* The followers of Śaṃkara, however, do make a distinction. Śaṃkara uses the word "*māyā*" in the sense of *śakti,* the power that creates the appearance of names and forms. But it is also used for the phenomenal world itself, for the world appearance, and in this sense, the creative, generative aspect is emphasized. Another way of explaining the distinction is to say that *māyā* explains the possibility of *Īśvara* or God, the creator, while *avidyā* accounts for the finite individual or *jīva.* According to this account, God, no less phenomenal, is the *brahman* as limited by *māyā,* while the *Īśvara,* also an appearance, is the *brahman* as limited by *avidyā.*

There are many ways of distinguishing the two, we, however, would settle for the simplest: *māyā* is cosmic, root ignorance of "world-experience," while *avidyā* is the individual ignorance. Upon attaining the *brahman*-knowledge, *avidyā* disappears, however, *māyā* still continues, because it creates the illusion of the world. The point to remember is as follows: Ignorance not only conceals the real nature of the *brahman,* it makes reality appear as something else. In other words, finite individual selves on account of ignorance not only do not see the *brahman* as the *brahman,* but also see it as something else, i.e., as the phenomenal world. For Advaitins, ignorance is not a mere absence of knowledge, it is rather a positive entity, although the negative prefix of the term "*avidyā*" ("a" = "not" + *vidyā* = "knowledge") creates the misleading impression that it is a negative entity, a mere absence of knowledge. The Advaitins advance the following argument for their thesis that ignorance is a positive entity: I have a direct awareness of my ignorance, which I articulate in such a sentence as "I am ignorant of X." How is such a direct awareness of my ignorance of something possible? If "ignorance of X" were the same as "the absence of the knowledge of X," then the latter absence could be perceived (within me) if and only if I know the counter positive of this absence, which is "knowledge of X." In other words, in order for me to perceive the absence of an elephant in my living room, I must have the knowledge of an elephant. But if I have that knowledge (of X), then I could not have the ignorance of X. So I could not have the knowledge of the sort " I am ignorant of X." This difficulty, argue the Advaitins, could be avoided only if ignorance were a positive entity, and ignorance of X were that this positive entity conceals X. The Advaitins argue that ignorance is not only a positive entity; it is also beginningless, because when one says, "I am ignorant," it does not make sense to ask when did you begin to be ignorant. Ignorance is beginningless, but does have an end.

Irrespective of whether ignorance is taken to be positive wrong knowledge, or lack of knowledge, or doubt, it is destroyed by right knowledge.[10] These three are similar insofar as they conceal the real nature of the *brahman* and are dispelled by the knowledge of the *brahman*. One reality appears in many different ways because of ignorance. For our purposes, it is sufficient to note that given his basic thesis of non-dualism, Śaṃkara uses the contrast between the *empirical* and the real to demonstrate the illusory character of the world, and to make the Upaniṣadic use of the "*saguṇa brahman*/God" intelligible. So, when the Advaita commentators emphasize that the false is indescribable what they mean is that it is neither real (*sat*) nor unreal (*asat*). False is that which is presented in experience but subsequently cancelled where it was presented. Given that it is experienced as being there, it cannot be unreal, because what is unreal (e.g., hare's horn, square circle, etc.) could never be presented. Unreal objects do not exist; they do not have any objective counterpart, so they can never become an object of experience. A false entity is given; it has an objective counterpart, so it is experienced, though it is cancelled subsequently, i.e., negated in the very same locus where it was experienced. Therefore, it is not *sat* or real either.

Advaita philosophers usually give the example of the experience of an illusory object—e.g., when one mistakes a rope for a snake in a dim light— to explain falsity. What does one see in such an illusory experience? One is neither perceiving a mental state, nor what does not exist, nor the rope that actually exists there; one is in fact seeing a snake out there in front of him, and this seeing—before the correction of the illusion—is hardly distinguishable from the veridical perception of a snake. However, when one's illusion is corrected, he does not see the snake any longer, and says "it was not a snake; it is a rope." In this illusory experience, one remembers the qualities of a snake, superimposes them on a rope, This peculiar kind of entity—a positive entity to be sure—is neither real nor unreal, it is indescribable as neither. It is *mithyā*. The superimposed is *mithya*, that on which it is superimposed is real. In other words, the rope one mistakes to be a snake, is a real rope— albeit only empirically real. Thus, when Śaṃkara argues that the empirical world is false, he is not saying that it is non-existent or unreal (non-being). The world is different from both the real (*brahman*) and unreal (non-being). It is not real because it is sublatable. It is not unreal because unlike unreal objects, the world appears to us; it is not non-being. The objects of the world, though not ultimately real, possess a different order of reality; they are empirically real. This explains why Śaṃkara describes the world as different from the real, the unreal, and the illusory existence (snake-rope illusions, mirage, and so on). It is the real that appears, and so every appearance has its foundation in reality. One does not experience a mirage in one's living room, but only under some empirical conditions.

Theory of Causality

Given that the world is false, the question arises, what precisely is the relationship between the *brahman* and the world? In what sense, if any, can the *brahman* be said to be the creator of the world? We know that there are two main theories of causality in Indian philosophy. The Nyāya-Vaiśeṣika subscribes to *asatkāryavāda*, which holds that the effect was non-existent in the cause prior to its production, so that the effect is a new entity, a new beginning. The Sāṃkhya defends the opposite point of view, namely, *satkāryavāda*, or the view that the effect is already there in the cause, that there is no new beginning, only a new formation, a transformation of the material cause, the original stuff, *prakṛti* or nature.

The Advaita Vedānta rejects the Nyāya-Vaiśeṣika view on the ground that what is non-being could never come into being, that *sat* cannot arise out of *asat*, that if it could, then anything would arise out of anything. The Advaita subscribes to the Sāṃkhya view insofar as they believe that that the effect preexists in the cause, that nothing new could ever come into being. Śaṃkara makes use of the Sāṃkhya theory of causation that the effect preexists in the cause prior to production to explain the relation. However, Śaṃkara replaced the Sāṃkhya theory of *pariṇāma* (a real transformation) by *vivartavāda*, the theory that there is only a seeming, an apparent transformation (*vivarta*) of the cause. In truth, there is no new production; nothing new arises, there is only a seeming production and destruction. Reality is unchanging; all change is apparent. Only in this sense the *brahman* is said to be the cause of this world. The *brahman*, in its creative aspect, is known as *Īśvara*, the lord, or the *saguṇa* brahman. The *brahman* as *Īśvara* is both the material and the efficient cause of the world.

Although the *brahman* creates the appearance of the world, it itself remains unaffected by the world-appearance. Śaṃkara uses the analogy of a magician and his tricks to explain this point. When a magician makes one thing appear as another, spectators are deceived by it; however, the magician himself is not deceived by it. Similarly, the *brahman* is that great magician who conjures up the world appearance and makes the multiplicity of names and forms appear. Finite individual beings are deceived by this appearance; they mistake appearance for reality. The *brahman* itself is not deceived by this appearance. Ignorance not only has the power of concealing reality but also of distorting reality. In other words, it is not only the case that we do not see the *brahman* as *brahman*, but we perceive it as something else.

If the question is asked: why create at all? Śaṃkara would respond by saying that it is "*līlā*," i.e., the divine play;[11] it proceeds from the nature of the *brahman*. There is no compelling necessity and it does not jeopardize the *brahman's* oneness. Thus, there is no "why" of creation. From the epistemological perspective, appearance comes first. *Avidyā* exists prior to both the individual self and God. This should not be taken to mean that *avidyā* is *temporally* prior to the individual self and God, because the relationship is beginningless; temporality is not an issue here. When viewed logically, on the other hand, we must have a conception of *avidyā* prior to one's arriving at conceptions of God and the individual self. From the ontological perspective, the *brahman* comes first. Once ignorance is destroyed by the knowledge of the real, the individual self is no longer subject to ignorance. Hence, the next question: what is the relationship between the individual self and the *brahman* and how does a finite individual dispel ignorance and see the *brahman* as *brahman*? This brings me to the last part of Śaṃkara's assertion.

Jīva brahmaiva Naparaḥ *(The Finite Individual and the* Brahman *are Non-different)*

The last part of Śaṃkara statement is that *jīva*-consciousness, i.e., the individual consciousness is non-different from the *brahman/ātman*. In his commentary on BS, Śaṃkara categorically asserts that the finite individual is seen to be different from the *ātman* on account of the limiting adjuncts (*upādhis*), but it is not different from the *ātman*, because it is the *ātman* who has entered in in all bodies as *jāvātmā*. Thus, we may call the *jāva* a mere reflection of the *ātman*."[12] Hence, the question: what is the nature of this *ātman* of which the *jīva* is a reflection?

Ātman

The Advaitins explain the nature of the *ātman* as follows:

1 *Ātman* is pure consciousness; it is self-luminous.[13] Following the Upaniṣads, Śaṃkara argues that it is on account of the light of the *ātman* that an individual self sits, goes out, walks, and so on. It is the light that illuminates everything;
2 Given that *ātman* is not an object,[14] none of the predicates that hold good of objects can be ascribed to it. Being radically different from objects in general, consciousness and (any) object cannot form an *intelligible* unity of the sort "consciousness-of-an-object";
3 *Ātman* or pure consciousness is not a phenomenon that is in space or in time;
4 Not being temporal, and not being an object of any sort, *ātman* by its very nature cannot be an object of any significant negation. For Advaita Vedānta, the expression "*ātman is not*" is meaningless, a possible

self-contradiction, while "*ātman is*" is a tautology, because the very negation of *ātman*, as in the statement "*ātman* is not," testifies to the existence of *ātman*. Whereas Descartes restricts the argument to doubt ("that I am doubting cannot be doubted"), the Advaitin argument is: "the act of negating consciousness is an act of consciousness, and so is incoherent"; and

5 A consequence of this last thesis is that self is eternal, having no beginning (that is to say, has no antecedent-negation), and has no end (having no subsequent negation). When in ordinary discourse, as well as in ordinary behavior, we ascribe consciousness, for example, to myself, or to you, to a body, such ascriptions are deeply misleading, because in such cases in spite of two things being totally different, the properties of one are ascribed to the other, or when one of the things is taken to be the other.[15] Likewise, when in ordinary life we distinguish between one state of consciousness and another by saying that one state of consciousness is of a table and the other of a chair, that is also misleading, for the distinction between a table and a chair, or between one object and another, does not contaminate the nature of consciousness.

To sum up: consciousness in Advaita is self-luminous, eternal, beginningless, undifferentiated, non-spatial, non-temporal, and non-intentional. One all-pervasive "spirit," the *ātman*, appears as if it were really divided in many centers of finite consciousness, but that appearance is due to many psycho-physical complexes. i.e., mind-body, ego-sense, and *buddhi* which create the misleading impression that each psycho-physical organism contains a distinct consciousness. In truth, however, as the Upaniṣads say "I am he" which is how the wise man expresses his experience of the non-difference from the *brahman* (the "I" refers to the finite *jīva* consciousness and "he" refers to the *brahman* consciousness).

Jīva

The goal of Advaita Vedānta, however, is to not simply understand the *ātman* but to know it, to realize it. So, the questions arose: How does *ātman* relate to the psycho-physical organism, or what we call "I"? How can one realize the true self, or the identity between the *ātman* and the *brahman*? The initial inquiry takes place in this context. Thus, the very question "who am I?" points to a kind of awareness of incompleteness and a desire to know more. Given that the *brahman* defies all characterizations and descriptions, it seemed entirely appropriate to the seers to begin with the self. Thus it is not surprising that the nature of the self became the focus of their investigation.

The *jīva,* argues the Advaitin, is a combination of two heterogeneous principles: *ātman*, pure consciousness and matter mind-body organism. So an individual self is neither pure spirit nor matter but a blend of the two. It is reality insofar as the *ātman* or the soul is its essence; it is appearance or false insofar as it is conditioned, finite, and relative. The first one is the essence, the *ātman*, which is shared by all human beings; it is common to me, to you, and to her. The matter, the mind-body organism, on the other hand, is a set of contingent features which provide the description, whether I am a male or a female, whether I am a philosopher or scientist, whether I am white or black, middle class or rich, and so on and so forth. The wrong identification (*adhyāsa*) between the self and the not-self is the basis of our empirical existence. Just as in a snake-rope illusion, the snake is superimposed upon the rope (the rope is the immediate datum of experience, the snake is an object of past experience, and illusion arises when the qualities of a snake, which was perceived in the past, are superimposed on "this," i.e., a given rope); similarly, the individual self on account of ignorance is superimposed on the pure self, the *ātman*, resulting in such qualities as egoism, etc., and the ego sees herself/himself as essentially separate from other individual selves as well as from the pure self. In other words, finitude and change that do not belong to the pure self are mistakenly superimposed upon it. In reality the *ātman*, the innermost self of a person, is pure formless, undifferentiated consciousness. It cannot be cancelled by any other experience whatsoever. Thus, the *ātman* and the *brahman* are not two different ontological entities, but two different names for the one and the same reality; the underlying self of the individual *is* the *brahman* (*tat tvam asi* or "that thou art").

The Advaita writers take recourse to two ways of describing the appearance of this difference. On the first account, the one *brahman* appears as many *jīva*s in the same way as one moon appears to be many when reflected in many different pools of water. The one consciousness is reflected in many ego-sense and *buddhi* complexes. On the second account, the situation is analogous to that between the one infinite space and the many finite spaces, the latter arising from the former because of the many dividers (such as the walls of a room). The two accounts are known as theory of reflection and the theory of limitation respectively. They use two different metaphors to understand the metaphysical situation of the one appearing as many. Though everything is the *brahman*, and there is no other reality than the *brahman*, it is known by different names. In the experience of the *brahman*, subject and object coalesce into each other. In this experience one realizes that the *brahman*, the unchanging reality that underlies the external world of names and forms, is also the reality that underlies the internal world of change and appearances. Śaṃkara repeatedly affirms that the *brahman* and *ātman* are one. Upon attaining the knowledge of reality (*mokṣa*), all subject-object distinctions are obliterated; the distinction between the self and non-self vanishes, ignorance disappears, and one experiences the *brahman* as pure being, consciousness, and bliss. The question that must be discussed before concluding this chapter may be formulated as follows: How does one attain this knowledge of non-difference?

The Brahman-*Knowledge or* Mokṣa

The goal of Advaita Vedānta is to teach the non-difference of the *ātman* and the *brahman*, the highest knowledge. Such knowledge of non-difference dispels ignorance and "brings about" *mokṣa* or freedom. *Mokṣa,* argues Śaṃkara, is realized through *jñāna-yoga,* the path of knowledge. Like most Vedic systems, but more so than others, the Advaita Vedānta depends upon the Vedas and the Upaniṣads to substantiate its position and shows that *jñāna-yoga* leads to self-realization. The Mīmāṁsā school, as we noted earlier, construes all Vedic texts to center around some course of action or other either to be performed or shunned. The Mīmāṁsā's primary concern therefore is with the *karma-kāṇda* (part concerned with actions) of the Vedas, and the Mīmāṁsā finds difficult to explain the Vedic sentences that merely state how things are without any reference to any course of action,. The Advaita Vedānta's primary concern is, however, with the *jñāna-kāṇda,* i.e., the part concerned with knowledge. Śaṃkara does not find it necessary that one should go through the Vedic ritualistic texts and practices in order to qualify to know the *brahman.*

Traditionally, in Hinduism, as we shall see in the chapter on the teachings of the *Bhagavad-Gītā,* three paths have been discussed: the paths of action, knowledge, and devotion. It is generally believed that all *yogas*, pursued properly, lead to the same end, namely, *mokṣa* (self-realization). Śaṃkara, however, argues that *mokṣa* is to be realized by pure knowledge of the identity of the *brahman* and *ātman. Karma* (action) and *bhakti* (devotion), at most can "bring about" the purification of the mind, but cannot "bring about" final liberating knowledge. Thus, devotion to God, leading an ethical life, or surrendering one's actions to God, while no doubt useful, cannot lead to the realization of the *brahman*, the ultimate goal of human endeavors. For Śaṃkara the study of the Vedāntic texts is necessary to destroy ignorance. However, prior to pursuing such a study, one should prepare one's mind in order to comprehend the deeper meaning of these texts. He discusses four qualifications that make one fit to study the Vedāntic texts by channeling the mind in the proper direction: (1) one must be able to distinguish between appearance and reality, the world and the *brahman*; (2) one must give up desires for pleasure and enjoyment, i.e., renounce all worldly desires; (3) one must develop qualities such as detachment, patience, and powers of concentration; and (4) one must have a strong desire to attain *mokṣa.*

After the mind is prepared, the aspirant goes to a *guru* (teacher) to study the Vedāntic texts. The Advaitins generally recommend a three-step process: *śravaṇa* ("hearing," that really consists in studying the Vedānta texts under a competent teacher), *manana* (reflective thinking, i.e., thinking in order to remove all doubts in the Advaita thesis, as well as advancing one's own arguments in support of that thesis) and *nididhyāsana* (contemplative meditation which strengthens the belief reached through the first two stages and culminates in the "intuitive" experience of one's identity with the *brahman*). With the constant meditation on the great saying of the Upaniṣads, "thou art the *brahman*," one realizes that he is the *brahman*. The final liberating knowledge (of the form "I am *brahman*") is an "intuitive" knowledge arising from verbal instruction (of the form "you are that"). One has the immediate experience of the *brahman;* the person realizes that he/she is non-different from the *brahman*. The Advaitins call it "an immediate knowledge arising from the verbal instruction"—analogous to a wise man's verbal instruction—"you are the tenth man."[16] The last cognition destroys the primal ignorance and the eternally self-illuminating self remains. This state is known as the state of *jīvanmukti*, freedom in this life. *Mokṣa* thus is not something that one looks forward to after death. It is a stage of perfection attained here; it is freedom while one is still alive. At death, such a person attains *videha-mukti*, the absolute freedom from the cycle of birth and rebirth, a state of equanimity, serenity, and bliss.

It is worth noting that *mokṣa* "brings about" freedom only in a very Pickwickean sense. In truth, nothing happens, nothing changes; no perfection is really brought about. Realization of *mokṣa* is not a new production; it is the realization of something that was always there. The self is *brahman*, and the perfection, *mokṣa,* is already an accomplished reality. There is nothing that has to be "brought about." Once the ignorance which had been covering the true nature of the self, is destroyed, the perfection that resides eternally in the self is brought to light, and the eternally free nature of the self manifest. In other words, *mokṣa* is coming to realize one's essence, which was forgotten during the embodied existence. It is the realization of one's potentialities as a human being; it is the highest realization.

A liberated person is an ideal of society, and his life worth emulating. After realizing *mokṣa,* a liberated person helps others to realize *mokṣa*. In other words, the *liberated* life is not a life of inactivity as some might assume. Scholars often argue that, in a philosophy in which the *brahman* is the only reality and the world an appearance, all distinctions between truth and falsehood become meaningless. Such an argument is based on a misunderstanding of the Advaita position; it stems from a confusion between the real and the empirical. Prior to realizing *mokṣa,* a person is responsible for his actions, reaps the consequences of his actions, and is subject to ethical judgments. In other words, from an empirical standpoint, distinctions between true and false are not only meaningful but also very important. It is only when *mokṣa* is realized that everything is seen to be a product of ignorance. Good actions take one toward the *brahman* realization, and bad ones away from this goal. The *brahman* is not an object of knowledge (it is not like Hegel's absolute coming to know itself); the *brahman* simply *is*. It is the highest knowledge.

Advaita Vedānta Logic and Epistemology

Let me begin with a few remarks about the use of the word "logic." "Logic," in the Western discourse, is generally taken to be formal logic; accordingly, any consideration of the issues relating to knowledge is taken to fall outside the scope of logic. But in Indian thinking, which will be clear as we proceed, there is no pure formal logic. It is assumed that the "*pramāṇas*" or rather the system of *pramāṇas* (means of true knowledge) constitute logic. Formal logic takes into consideration not only the formal validity of an argument but also the material truth. That being the case, "logic," as used here, becomes theory of knowledge, i.e., *pramāṇa śāstra*. In other words, logic considers the different ways we come to know reality. It discusses such questions as: How does knowledge arise? Is knowledge true of reality? Western formal logic abstracts from what is real, and considers only its form. Such an abstraction is not permitted in Indian logic. In order to isolate the bare form, Western logicians consider only the formal structure of an argument, and not the material truth of the premises and the conclusion. Accordingly, in Western logic, the following syllogism:

All men are immortal
All Greeks are men
Therefore, all Greeks are immortal

would be a logically valid argument. Indian logic does not allow such arguments into its discourse. The premise and the conclusion must both be formally valid and materially true. We already saw in the chapter on Nyāya that in order to disallow premises which are materially false, the Indian logicians stipulate that in stating a premise we must adduce an "example" to be admitted by both parties to a dispute. Thus, the proposition "all men are immortal" is not admissible because no instance of an immortal man can be found. We then begin to see how Indian logic becomes a logic of truth, and not a mere logic of formal validity. A true premise must be borne out by perception or by *śabda*. A false premise cannot function in an Indian inferential argument. It follows that logic in the narrow sense (perhaps, in the Western sense) of inference refers either to perception or to *śabda*, or indeed to the other ways of knowing a true state of affairs. Let me therefore begin with the means of true knowledge. My analysis in this chapter will primarily be based on *Vedānta Paribhāṣā*,[17] one of the most well-known Advaita epistemology texts, which offers its readers an analysis not only of the important issues surrounding Advaita epistemology, but also of basic ontological problems.

Means of Valid Knowledge

Like all other systems, the Advaita Vedānta also developed a theory of knowledge. A true knowledge is called *pramā*. A *pramā* (true knowledge), which *excludes* memory, is a cognition which is not contradicted by any other cognition and has for its content an entity that is not already known. A distinction is made between two types of *pramā*: the *pramā* that excludes memory, and the *pramā* that includes it. The former is regarded as the knowledge of an object that is neither contradicted nor previously known, and the latter as the knowledge of an object that is not contradicted by any other object of knowledge.

Non-contradiction is common to both definitions. In the erroneous perception "this is silver," the knowledge of silver continues to be true as long as the object of knowledge (i.e., the silver), is not contradicted by another object of knowledge (i.e., the shell). This implies that the knowledge of silver as silver must be taken to be true as long as it is not known that it is a shell.

The second characteristic of *pramā* is novelty or previous unknownness. This characteristic excludes memory from the ambit of knowledge. This characteristic raises the question regarding the status of a persistent cognition. When I look at a chair continuously, my experience of the first moment of course is knowledge, but what about my experience of the subsequent moments? Can it be called knowledge? Notwithstanding different answers, most schools hold that one's experience of subsequent moments is knowledge. The Advaitins, on the other hand, hold that such questions do not arise in their epistemology because for them a cognition is true as long as it is not contradicted by another cognition. The judgment "the table is" remains the same as long as it is not replaced by another judgment, making the questions regarding reproduction, subsequent moments, moot. Now, an opponent of the Advaita Vedānta may raise the following objection: for the Advaitin, an object, say, a pitcher (indeed, any material object) is just false. If that is so, how can knowledge of it be a valid knowledge? The Advaitin's reply to this question is as follows: until the *brahman* is realized, the knowledge of a pitcher remains true. The word "uncontradicted," when used to characterize the knowledge of a pitcher, means "uncontradicted prior to *brahman*-knowledge." In other words, the knowledge of a pitcher remains valid true to *brahman*-realization.

A *pramāṇa* is the specific cause of a *pramā*. Vedānta *Paribhāṣā*, discusses *pramāṇas* in its attempt to provide an answer to the basic epistemological question: How do we know? The Advaitins look to *pramāṇas* for removing doubts that may have arisen. They accept the four *pramāṇas* that the Naiyāyikas do, and add an additional two to the list. Thus the six *pramāṇas* that the Advaitins recognize are: perception, inference, comparison, verbal testimony postulation, and non-perception. Of these, perception is the most basic and of special importance; inference, comparison, and postulation are three non-perceptual *pramāṇas;* non-perception is the *pramāṇa* that apprehends non-existence, and verbal testimony, is a means of sensuous as well as supersensuous knowledge.

Pratyakṣa *(Perception)*

The term "*pratyakṣa*" is derived from the roots "*prati*" (to, before, near) and *akṣa* (sense organ) or *akṣi* (eye). So, etymologically the term signifies what is "present to or before the eyes or any other sense organ." It refers to sense-perception as a means of immediate or direct knowledge of an object. Broadly speaking, the Advaitins make a distinction between two kinds of perceptions: external and internal. Perception by any of the five sensory organs (sight, hearing, touch, taste, and smell) is classified as external, and perceptions of pleasure, pain, love, hate, and so on as internal.

The Advaitins argue that perception is immediate consciousness. However, for them, sense-perception is not the only means of immediate cognition: the immediacy of cognition does not depend on its being caused by sense organs. God, for example, has no senses, but those who believe in God believe that he has immediate knowledge of things.

Given that perception as a true cognition, i.e., *pramā*, is nothing but consciousness, the opponents might raise the following objection: if consciousness is one without a beginning, how can we say that the eye, ear, etc., or each sense organ can produce the knowledge, say, of a pitcher? How can a sense organ be the cause of pure consciousness? In reply, the Advaitin says that although consciousness is without a beginning, yet the mental mode (*vṛtti*)[18] which reveals it arises through the contact of the appropriate sense organ. To put it in another way, what is produced is consciousness qualified by a mental mode. The appropriate mental mode limits the resulting consciousness, so consciousness is figuratively spoken as knowledge.

The opponent may raise another objection: How can the mind or inner sense,[19] which has no parts, produce a mental mode which would be its modification? In reply, the Advaitins say that the mind does in fact have parts; it is a substance (*dravya*). Knowledge is an attribute of the mind. Other attributes of the mind are: desire, resolution, shame, intelligence, fear, etc. Just as a piece of iron, without having the property of burning, burns on account of false identification, similarly, the self, owing to false identification is said to have such properties as being happy or desiring, though these properties do not characterize the real nature of the self.

Given all this, it is imperative that the Advaitins provide an explanation not only of the perceptuality of knowledge but also of the perceptuality of the object (of perception)? The former, i.e., the perceptuality of knowledge is nothing but the non-difference of the consciousness reflected in the means of knowledge (*pramāṇas*) with consciousness as limited by the object (*viṣayāvachinna caitanya*). In other words, it is the non-difference between *pramāṇa caitanya* and *viṣayāvachinna caitanya*. They further note that an object is perceptual if and only if it is not different from the consciousness associated with the subject. An object is said to be perceptual, when it can be perceived, and is denied any existence apart from the subject-consciousness, which has for its limiting adjunct a mental mode in the form of object to be perceived. Let me elaborate on these further.

The theory of perception that the Advaitins develop is a kind of identity theory: in a perceptual cognition, the inner sense goes out through the visual sense organ (in the case of visual perception), and assumes the form of the object out there. This modification is called "*vṛtti*." The cognitive process of external visual perception contains the following five steps:

1 The inner sense comes in contact with the organ of vision, reaches out to the object and becomes one with it.
2 The mental mode removes the veil of nescience that had been hiding the object from the perceiver.
3 The consciousness underlying the object, being manifested as a result of the removal of the veil of ignorance, reveals the object.
4 The mind effects an identity between the consciousness conditioned by the object and the consciousness conditioned by the subject.
5 As a result, the cognizer perceives the object.

The Advaitins explain the process with the help of an analogy. In the words of *Vedānta Paribhāṣā*:

> Just as the water of a tank, having come out of an aperture, enters a number of fields through channels assuming like those [fields] a quadrangular or any other form, so also the inner sense, which is characterized by light, goes out [of the body] through the door [sense] of sight, and so on, and [after] reaching the location of the object, say a pitcher, it is modified in the form of the objects like a pitcher. This modification [of the inner sense] is called a mental mode (*vṛtti*). In the case of inferential cognition, and so on, however, there is no going out of the inner sense to the location of fire, because fire, and so on [other inferred objects], are not in contact with the sense of sight, and so on [other sense organs].[20]

The point that the VP is trying to make is as follows: just as the water of a tank, goes out through a hole, enters into a field and assumes the form of the field, rectangular or some other shape, similarly the mind, the inner sense, which is luminous, goes out through the eye, etc., and takes on the form of the object. In the perception of a pitcher for example, the mental mode and the pitcher occupy the same space. When one perceives a pitcher and says "this is a pitcher," the mental mode or *vṛtti* having the form of the pitcher, the consciousness limited by the pitcher and consciousness limited by that mental mode become non-different. This is how the pitcher is perceived.

Consciousness, in itself one, is said to be threefold depending upon the limiting condition. Object-consciousness is the consciousness as limited by the object (*viṣaya*), e.g., a pitcher. *Pramāṇa* consciousness is consciousness limited by the mental modification. The subject- consciousness (*pramātṛ*) is the consciousness as limited by the inner sense. In the case of perception an identity between these three is accomplished. Accordingly, pure consciousness, from an empirical point of view, becomes threefold: the object-consciousness, the means-of cognition consciousness, and the cognizer-consciousness. From the perspective of pure consciousness, these divisions are only apparent and not real; the plurality of objects is only apparently independent of the subject, but not truly independent.

It is worth noting that the Advaitins do not regard "being caused by sense organs" (as opposed to Nyāya) a defining property of perception. Perceptuality, as applied to a cognition, is made possible by a cognition on account of the identity of consciousness limited by *pramāṇas* and the consciousness limited by the object.

The Advaita theory of identity is a corollary of its metaphysics: only *brahman* or pure consciousness is real; it is all pervading, undifferentiated consciousness. Pure consciousness is also pure existence or being, and any assertions made about the latter are equally applicable to the former. Just as a clay-pitcher does not have any independent existence apart from the clay; similarly, the plurality of objects do not have any independent existence apart from pure consciousness, their source. In other words, these objects, though real empirically, are not real in themselves. The same can be said about the pure consciousness in a cognitive relation, which involves such elements as subject, object, and their relation. These elements are real insofar as they refer to pure consciousness, but are non-real in themselves. The Advaitins reiterate that as identical in essence with pure consciousness, these three terms of a cognitive relation refer to one and the same reality.

Perception is of two kinds: *savikalpaka* and *nirvikalpaka*. The former kind of perception apprehends relatedness of a substantive and its qualifying attribute. This occurs in the cognition "I know the pitcher." The second kind of perception, called indeterminate perception, is that knowledge which does not apprehend such relatedness, as in the case of identity statements, e.g., "this is that Devadatta" or "thou art that."

It is worth noting that the identity statement "thou art that" is not a tautology; it cannot be expressed as x = x. In logic, the sense in which the word "identity" is used by most contemporary philosophers, a tautology is a sentence that is true solely by virtue of its formal structure. Some people reserve the word tautology simply for logical truths or, possibly, for the subset of logical truths of propositional logic. Others use the word in a broader sense, such that not only logical truth, but analytic propositions, that is to say, propositions which are reducible to logical truths by the use of definition, would be considered tautologies. One must be very careful to understand the sense in which "thou art that" is an identity statement; it is not a tautology because what is meant by *ātman* for the individual is different from what is meant by the *brahman* for the individual. "Thou art that" is very similar to such statements as "this is that Devadatta." When I perceive Devadatta for the second time and report to my friend "this is that Devadatta" I saw yesterday, I do not mean to suggest that the two places and the times are identical. When I saw Devadatta yesterday he was in a school, and today I see him in the Columbia Mall. He was happy yesterday, and he is in pain today. The identity is the identity of "person" devoid of all accidental qualifications. The same is true of "thou art that" where the individual self as pure consciousness is said to be identical with the *brahman*, the pure consciousness.

To sum up: The immediacy of knowledge does not depend on its arising from the senses as is generally maintained, but rather on the object that is presented. The immediacy of the object presented to consciousness that apprehends it makes possible for knowledge to be perceptual. Although the phenomenal world rests on a distinction between the cognition and the content, no such distinction exists in the immediate consciousness of the *brahman*. Pure consciousness accordingly is the criterion of the perceptibility of objects. Since the cognizer-consciousness and the object-consciousness, e.g., a pitcher, share the same consciousness, in the perception of a pitcher, the pitcher becomes "immediate." Perception thus is of utmost importance, because the knowledge obtained is immediate, which is different from the non-perceptual knowledge obtained by inference, comparison, and postulation.

Anumāna *(Inference)*:

The next means of valid knowledge is inference (*anumāna*), which is the special cause of inferential cognition or *anumiti*. Here the Advaitins draw our attention to the fact that an inferential cognition or *anumiti* is caused by the knowledge of invariable concomitance purely as the knowledge of invariable concomitance. *Vedānta Paribhāṣā* defines *anumiti* or inferential cognition as the cognition that is produced by knowledge of *vyāpti* quā the knowledge of *vyāpti* (*vyāpti* being the invariable relation between what is inferred, the prodandum or *sādhya* and the reason), from which the inference is drawn, the mark, the *hetu*). The "quā . . ." is inserted to avoid the definition being too wide by applying to the unintended case of mental, secondary, reception of the knowledge of *vyāpti*. *Vyāpti* is defined as the relation of having the same locus belonging to the *sādhya* in all the loci of *hetu*.[21] I will illustrate this point with the help of an example typical of Indian philosophers, including Advaita:

> Whatever is smoky is fiery, e.g., a kitchen,
> The hill is smoky,
> Therefore, the hill is fiery.

Here the *vyāpti* is: "wherever there is smoke, there is fire." That is to say, wherever there is *hetu*, there is *sādhya*. The *sādhya* in other words is present in all those places where the *hetu* is present. *Vyāpti* then is "having the same locus" between a *sādhya* which is present in all the loci of the *hetu*. The *Vedānta Paribhāṣā* adds that *vyāpti* between fire and smoke exists when fire co-exists with all cases of smoke and is never known not to accompany smoke. This universal relation must have been cognized on a previous occasion and must be cognized, or better yet, re-cognized, in this particular instance (the hill) for inferential knowledge to occur. Cognition of a universal relation, though necessary, is not a sufficient condition of inferential knowledge. However, the cognition as well as the re-cognition of a universal relation together constitute the necessary and sufficient conditions.

According to Nyāya, we first see smoke on the hill, then remember that wherever there is smoke, there is fire as in our kitchen, consequently, there is smoke on the hill, which is a mark of fire, and so conclude that these must be fire on the hill.

We shall see where the Advaitin account differs from the Nyāya account. For the Naiyāyikas, the *parāmarśa* is cognition of the *hetu* for the third time, and this is the instrumental cause of inferential knowledge. The Advaita rejects this theory, and refuses to consider that *parāmarśa* in any sense is a cause of inferential knowledge. The knowledge of invariable concomitance is an instrument only with respect to the knowledge of fire, and not with respect to the knowledge of the hill. Hence the knowledge "this hill has fire" could not have been inferred with regard to the hill. With regard to the hill, the knowledge is rather a perception.

The Advaitins, like the Naiyāyikas, classify inference into inference for oneself (*svārtha*) and for another (*parārtha*). Whereas the Naiyāyikas recognize a valid inference for another to have five members, the Advaita Vedānta recognizes only three-membered inference for another. The three members that suffice are: the proposition to be established (known as *pratijñā*), the reason (*hetu*) and the example (i.e., *udāharaṇa*). In a concrete case, it is enough to argue: the hill has fire, because of smoke, as in the kitchen.

The Advaita logicians then proceed to prove one of their central theses, i.e., the empirical reality of the world, by an appropriate inference. The inference[22] would run as follows:

> Everything other than the *brahman* is false
> Because it is other than the *brahman*
> Whatever is other than the *brahman* is false, e.g., the shell-silver.

An appropriate definition of falsity would be: "something's being the counterpositive of the absolute nonexistence in whatever is supposed to be the substratum." Another way of proving the falsity of whatever consists of parts is this: "A cloth is a counterpositive of absolute nonexistence abiding in the threads, because it is a cloth, as is the case with any other cloth." The falsity of all things is the property of being the counterpositive of absence in all things appearing as its locus. The Advaitin obviously refuses to accept the Nyāya thesis that the whole resides in its parts in the relation of *samavāya.*

Upamāna *(Comparison)*

Knowledge obtained from comparison (*upamāna*) is derived from judgments of similarity, i.e., a remembered object is like a perceived one. Judgments founded on comparison are of the kind "Y is like X," where X is immediately perceived and Y is an object perceived on a previous occasion which becomes the content of consciousness in the form of memory. The Advaitins consider a typical instance of comparison given by Indian philosophers. A person has a *gau* (domestic cow), knows what it looks like, and has the capacity to apply its features to other cows. Upon running into a *gavaya* (a wild cow) in a forest he says: "the *gavaya* resembles my *gau*." The knowledge of similarity with a *gavaya* and my cow is the resulting knowledge called "*upamiti*." Its proximate cause is *upamāna*, the knowledge of the likeness of a cow which exists in a *gavaya*.

The Advaitins emphasizes that one has thus gained a new or better knowledge not about *gavaya*, but rather about the *gau*, since the person has a better understanding of the body of a *gau*. The similarity attaches to the cow; it is similarity with a *gavaya*. This similarity cannot be perceived, for when one knows this similarity, there is no sense contact with the *gau*. Nor is this cognition an inference, for the similarity of a cow with a *gavaya* cannot be the mark or *hetu* of the likeness of the *gavaya* in a cow. Knowledge of similarity in such situations deserves to be recognized as a new sort of knowledge.

Śabda *or Verbal Testimony*

For the Advaitins, verbal testimony "is a means of valid knowledge in which the relation among the meanings of the words that is the object of its intention is not contradicted by any other means of valid knowledge."[23] They further argue that a sentence is the unit of a verbal testimony. In other words, a sentence signifies more than the constituent words that compose it. To grasp the significance of a sentence, one must know not only the meanings of the constituent words, but also the relation among the meanings of the words that are conjoined syntactically. The apprehension of this relation is called the verbal cognition and if it is not contradicted, it is considered to be valid.

Four causes produce the knowledge by a sentence: expectancy (*ākānkṣā*), appropriateness or competency (*yogyāta*), contiguity (*āsatti*), and knowledge of intention (*tātparya*).

Expectancy is the capacity of the meanings of words to become objects of enquiry about each other. Hearing about action gives rise to the expectation about something connected with action, the agent or the instrument of action. For example, the sentence "get the umbrella," gives rise to a cognition. However, "umbrella" or "get" are uttered separately, would not give rise to this cognition. If the word "umbrella" is uttered, the question would arise what to do with the umbrella? If "get" is uttered, the question would arise, "get what"? In other words, both "umbrella" and "get" are required in order for that cognition to arise.

Competency or appropriateness is the non-contradiction of the intended relation desired to be set up in a combination of ideas. A sentence like "sprinkle fire on the grass to moisten it" lacks appropriateness, because fire can neither be sprinkled nor can it moisten anything.

By "contiguity" is meant that the meanings of words are to be presented without interval. Thus, the words must be uttered without a long temporal interval between them. "The door" requires to be preceded, without a long interval, by the verb "close" in order to close the door.

Words, argues the Advaitin, have primary as well as secondary meanings. Primary meaning is something that is directly meant by a word. A word in its primary meaning signifies a universal and not the particular in which it inheres. For example, the word "cow" stands for "cowness." A universal, in other words, is not an entity that stands over and above the individuals, rather it refers to the essential characteristics that are common to all members of that class. Thus, whereas the universals or class characteristics constitute the primary meanings of words, the individuals constitute their secondary meanings. In other words, although the word "cow" primarily means "cowness," it may signify individual cows by implication as those possessing universal cowness. To suppose that the word has the power to designate infinite number of individual cows would be to violate the principle of economy. Individual cows are meant by a secondary power of designation or implication (*lakṣaṇa)*.

A secondary meaning is something that is implied by a word. If the primary meanings of the words of a sentence do not adequately explain the import, then one looks for implied meanings. *Lakṣaṇa* or secondary designation is of two kinds: bare implication and a secondary designation that depends upon another *lakṣaṇa,* i.e., implication by the implied. Bare implication functions when the secondary meaning itself is related to the primary meaning. This occurs in "the village on the Ganges," which, secondarily, means "the village on the bank of the river." The second kind of implication is found when there is no direct relation to express the primary meaning. This occurs in the word "*dvirephā*," i.e., "having two *rephas*" whose primary meaning is "having two r's," but secondarily means a bee. A similar secondary designation occurs when it is said "a human like a lion," where not lion but lion's courage and strength are found in the man concerned.

Secondary meanings are also classified into three kinds: In the first case known as *jahallakṣaṇa*, the primary meaning is completely dropped in favor of a secondary meaning. This happens when after finding out that a person is about to dine with his enemy, you tell him "go and take poison." The intention here is not to ask the person to take poison but to make the point that dining with an enemy is like taking poison. In the second case, the primary meaning is there but the secondary meaning comes into play. In the sentence "white cloth," "white" includes "the property of whiteness" and by implication denotes the substance that white characterizes. Thus, there is cognition not only of the expressed sense, but also of the implied sense. This is called "*ajahatlakṣaṇa*." In the third case, one part of the original primary meaning is dropped, but another part is retained. When seeing a person "Devadatta," one says, "this is that Devadatta," "this" and "that" are taken to be the purport, and the meanings in terms of spatio-temporal locations are dropped. The identity between this and that Devadatta is only asserted leaving aside their differences. This case is called "*jahat-ajahat-lakṣaṇa*."

Very often, the principle of seeking a secondary meaning is employed to harmonize scriptural statements with one's own philosophical position. For example, in construing the meaning of the sentence "thou art that," the primary meanings of "thou" as "individual consciousness," and "that" as the "pure consciousness" are discarded. They are taken in their secondary meanings: the consciousness that underlies pure consciousness is the same consciousness that underlies the individual consciousness, thereby declaring that the text affirms the identity of non-dual pure consciousness.

Finally, *tātparya* or intention is the capacity to produce cognition of a particular thing. The question becomes important when there is doubt as to whether a particular sentence means this or something else. In such cases, i.e., when a word has more than one meaning, the context helps us to determine the intention of the speaker. For example, "*saindhavam-anaya*": Does it mean "bring a horse" or "bring some salt"? Generally, context helps us to decide. With regard to the Vedas, one needs reasoning aided by the principles of interpretation.

Arthāpatti *(Presumption)*

The Advaita Vedānta recognizes a unique mode of argument as a *pramāṇa* called "postulation." The argument is somewhat like what is called a "transcendental argument." Knowledge obtained from postulation (*arthāpatti*) involves assuming or postulating of some fact in order to make another fact intelligible. Supposing there is a fact p. If you say p is possible only if q, then you establish the validity of q. To take an example, let p be "Devadatta is growing fat even when he does not eat during the day." One must assume, barring physiological problems, that he eats at night, because there is no way of reconciling fasting and the gaining of weight. Therefore, Devadatta eats at night. In short, in *arthāpatti*, one assumes a fact without which a thing to be explained would not have been possible. The latter knowledge is the fact to be explained. Knowledge of the thing to be explained is the instrument, and the knowledge of the explanatory fact is the result.

There are two kinds of presumption. One is called *dṛṣṭārthāpatti*, the other *śrutārthāpatti*. In *dṛṣṭārthāpatti*, one supposes a fact in order to explain a perceived fact. For example, in a shell-silver illusion, when the judgment "this is not silver but a shell" negates the initial judgment "this is silver," we assume that the seeming silver must be illusory. The given fact p may also be a sentence from the "heard texts" (*śruti*), whose truth is taken for granted. Let p be "one who knows *ātman* overcomes all suffering." This can be true only if suffering being destroyed by knowledge has the status of falsity. Only the false is negated by another knowledge. The validity of this judgment is possible only if we assume that grief is false.

The latter, i.e., *śrutārthāpatti*, literally means the presumption of a fact in order to explain another fact known through testimony. It is of two kinds: *abhidhāna* (the supposition of a verbal expression) and *abhihita* (supposition of a thing meant). In *abhidhāna,* on hearing the part of a sentence, there is supposition of a verbal expression, for example, when the master of the house simply says "*dvāram,*" i.e., the door, the servant has to supply "close." The *abhihita* variety occurs when what is heard has no consistent meaning, so that the hearer supposes some other thing, e.g., upon hearing, "one who desires heaven should perform *jyotiṣṭoma* sacrifice," it is assumed that sacrifice must give rise to some unseen result.

Anupalabdhi *(Non-Apprehension)*

Another *pramāṇa* that the Advaita recognizes is non-perception, which is the specific way we come to perceive absences. It yields knowledge of an absence, where an object would be immediately perceived if it were there. Judgments based on *anupalabdhi* are of the sort "there is no X in the room," where X is an object which would have been perceived if it were there. To put it differently, if a pitcher were on my desk, I would have seen it in a well-lit room. The resulting knowledge of nonexistence is perceptual, nevertheless its instrumental cause viz. non-apprehension is a distinct means of knowing.

The knowledge derived from *anupalabdhi* has following features: Such a knowledge has for its object something non-existent, immediate, and such a knowledge cannot be produced by any other *pramāṇa.* Every instance of non-perception, however, does not prove its non-existence. A person does not see a chair in a dark room, which by no means proves that the chair is not there. Hence non- perception must be under appropriate conditions.

In connection with the six *pramāṇas* accepted by the Advaitins, it must be pointed out that they have limited applicability. The Advaitins by demonstrating the insufficiency and the relative nature of the six *pramāṇas,* pave the way for their transcendence in the *brahman,* the highest knowledge, the truth.

Thus there are two forms of knowledge: higher knowledge (*parāvidyā*) and lower knowledge (*aparāvidyā*). The first is the knowledge of the absolute; it is *sui generis.* It is attained all at once, immediately, intuitively. The second is the knowledge of the empirical world of names and forms, where *pramāṇas* are operative. All *pramāṇas* hold sway as "ultimate" until the *brahman* is realized, because when the *brahman* is realized nothing remains to be known. Each of the six *pramāṇas* has its own sphere of operation. They do not contradict each other. They are "true" only in the phenomenal world, but none of the *pramāṇas* are truly "true." The Advaitin doctrine of the intrinsic validity of knowledge supports and further explains what the Advaitins mean by this equivocation.

The Advaitins argue (1) that the function of knowledge is to manifest the object as it is; (2) that within dream, a cognition may lead to successful practice with regard to the dream object in a dream; and (3) knowledge is true in case it is not contradicted by subsequent experience. In the strict sense, only uncontradicted experience is ultimately true, however, the Advaita at the same time holds that no empirical knowledge satisfies both. Only the knowledge of pure *brahman* does. Any empirical cognition in principle is falsifiable, but as long as it is not actually falsified it *is taken to be true* by the cognizer. Thus, it is not the truth, but rather *falsity that happens to a cognition.*

The last sentence points to the Advaita theory of intrinsic validity, because the validity arises from the very conditions that produce it. The Advaita Vedānta theory of the intrinsic validity consists of the following theses: (1) every cognition, *as it were*, is *eo ipso*, taken by the cognizer to be true independently of any test, (2) there is indeed no criterion of truth, although (3) there is a criterion of falsity. A cognition is established to be false when it is contradicted by a subsequent experience. Any test of truth, if applied, leads to *infinite regress*, so better take truth to be "uncontradictedness." The truth is intrinsic to a knowledge; it originates as a cognition arises, and this is ascertained when a cognition is known.

The Mīmāṁsakas also subscribe to this theory, but their version is different. In the Prābhākara Mīmāṁsaka version, which we have already discussed, all cognitions being true, there is no error, no false cognition. What is called error or false cognition is really failure to distinguish between cognitions each of which is true. Thus, upon seeing from a distance a shell on the beach, one says "this is silver," which for practical purposes is false: in this instance there is a perception of the "this," a remembrance of "silver" and *a failure* to distinguish between the two; there is no false cognition. Although close to Mīmāmṣā, the Advaita Vedānta rejects the Mīmāmṣā theory that knowledge always is a means to action and true knowledge must lead to successful activity. It recognizes genuinely false cognitions in which one thing is taken to be what it is not. The object of the erroneous cognition, in the example under consideration, is not the shell, not an empirically real silver but a false "shell-silver," an object that is contradicted, and is indescribable either as *sat* or *asat*. Only the *brahman* experience is uncontradicted.

Thus the lack of uncontradictedness on the one hand while insuring the validity of the *pramāṇas* leads to the thesis that none of the knowledge gained by the *pramāṇas* is ultimately true. All knowledge gained through *pramāṇas* may be contradicted by an insight, an "intuitive" experience, that is qualitatively superior, the highest knowledge (*parā vidyā*), which dispels ignorance.

Readers might find the above claim i.e., that knowledge gained through *pramāṇas* may be contradicted by an intuitive insight, strange. Therefore, before concluding this section, let me make a few remarks about the concept of "intuition" vis-à-vis *pramāṇas* in Advaita Vedānta.

In order to ascertain the concept of "intuition" in Advaita Vedanta, one will have to contend, not with one but rather with four such concepts. Let me elaborate on these. To begin with, "intuition" would be an English word for the Sanskrit "*aparokṣa-jñāna.*" It stands for a knowledge, which is immediate, i.e., not mediated by any conceptual thinking and also a "knowledge by identity" in which the familiar distinction between subject and object is overcome.

1 We have already seen in discussing perception (*pratyakṣa*) that it is the knowledge, within the reach of everyone, i.e., within the bounds of ordinary experience, which gives some inkling of what an intuitive knowledge by identity must look like. The perceived thing stands there before me when I perceive it, I am in touch with it as it were, it is "given" (in Kant's language), and I do not go through a conceptual process of thinking to reach the objects. However, it is not unmediated, there is a mental process going on, and the perceptual cognition is the result of that process (*Leistung* or an "accomplishment" in Husserl's language). This process has been concretely described in *Vedānta Paribhāṣā*: the inner sense "goes out" as it were, assumes the form of the object, and an identification is achieved between the subject and the object. The result is a cognition founded upon an identification, but not identity brought about by a "going out" of the inner sense and assuming the form of the object. A process intervenes, a process of "mental modification." In the strict sense, the cognition is not immediate, though it seems to be immediate. Hence its intuitional character is a pretense. No concepts are involved; the language has no role to play, the non-conceptuality is not yet immediacy.

2 Perception's ability to result in a cognitive accomplishment is due to the fact that the mental modification or *vṛtti* itself is known immediately, without the intervention of another process. The object (let us say, a pitcher) is perceived through the *vṛtti*, but the *vṛtti* itself has to be known without the mediation of another such *vṛtti* if we are to avoid an infinite regress. This indeed is the case. The *vṛtti* is immediately present to the pure consciousness as it occurs. Here there is immediacy, no mediation (neither by another *vṛtti* nor by a conceptual thinking), no process is involved. But it is not a knowledge by identity, the pure consciousness and the *vṛtti* are not one nor can they be thought to be one. This is what the Advaita Vedānta calls "*sākṣī-pratyakṣa*," the witness-consciousness's immediate perception of all mental modification.[24] The witness-consciousness does nothing; it manifests the other, i.e., the *vṛtti* that is presented to it. But this other is not an external object; it is rather the form of the external object. Manifestation of the *vṛtti* is not an accomplishment, because by its very nature a *vṛtti* is present to the witness-consciousness. This cognition, if we call it "intuition," is immediate, but not the result of a process by which the otherness is overcome; the otherness remains.

3 The Advaita Vedānta entertains the possibility of working towards another experience which may be called "intuition." In this case, one begins with *śravaṇa*, i.e., "hearing" the texts of the Upaniṣads (being taught by a qualified instructor), then he reflects (*manana*) on the truths learnt, and finally contemplates (*nididhyāsana*) on them. This contemplation culminates in an intuitive realization of those truths which amount to intuitively knowing who he is, what is the nature of his self, and experiencing the identity of the *ātman* and the *brahman*. With this, the final remaining veil of ignorance is removed, and the self, eternally self-luminous, shines in its own light.

The question may be asked: Is this intuition, i.e., the knowledge of the identity of the self and the *brahman* a *vṛttijñāna*? As a matter of fact, the Advaita speaks of it as the final mental modification. Being mediated by a *vṛtti* (known as *akhaṇḍākāravṛtti*),[25] it is not immediate and so falls short of being an intuition in the strictest sense. But is the culminating stage in which the self shines by its own light my intuition? Again, it is not my knowledge, not knowledge by the subject who has reached this awareness. Who then may be said to be intuiting? And what does he intuit? The pure self is not an object of knowledge. It is eternally self-luminous, and is so now, only the veil of ignorance is gone. Again, strictly speaking, it is not an intuition by some knower. In other words, it is not as if a knower intuitively knows something other than itself.

4 Let us leave aside the process of progressing towards a goal for the time being, it is worth remembering that in itself, consciousness is ever self-luminous, *svayaṃprakāśa*. It apprehends itself by identity, without being an object of any cognition. We may at best call this aspect of consciousness an intuition of its own nature immediately and as identical with itself. Consciousness precisely is this intuition of itself. This alone, of all the four cases, is intuition in the strongest sense: intuition always by itself and of itself. If the Kantian consciousness is an "I think," the Advaita Vedānta consciousness is an "I intuit."

I hope the above discussion provides my readers some insights into the role of intuition vis-à-vis *pramāṇas* (i.e., the system of logic), which belongs to the domain of *avidyā*. The *pramāṇas* are not self-luminous; but they leave us at the door of the self-luminous consciousness so to speak. They are important insofar as they help us understand as well as transcend empiricality and lead to an immediate understanding of the self by destroying *avidyā*, but in the process of destroying *avidyā*, they destroy themselves. Only the self-luminous consciousness remains, which was always there.

To sum up, logic and intuitive experience are inseparably intertwined in Indian thought; they are two aspects of the same cognitive process. Thus *pramāṇas* is a system of logic, whose final basis is "consciousness" as the "witness" and the "judge" of all cognitive claims. The *pramāṇas* lead to an intuitive experience, where they have completely fulfilled their role and cease to be. Reason, in other words, is transcended by an intuitive experience, which is the goal of all rational thinking. Thus the standard Western dichotomy between reason and intuition collapses and both (reason and intuition) together form an integrated process of acquisition, validation, and justification of knowledge.

Concluding Reflections

Before concluding this section on Advaita, I would like to make some remarks about the relation between knowledge and ignorance in Advaita Vedānta.

The two, knowledge and ignorance (as the Upaniṣads repeatedly assert), are opposed to each other.[26] Śaṃkara, following the Upaniṣads, also reiterates that the two are as opposed to each other as light and darkness. Knowledge removes ignorance. Knowledge is what is intrinsically desirable; ignorance and its consequences are what we in fact desire. Although the opposition between knowledge and ignorance is a well-established doctrine of Vedānta philosophy (and of Buddhism as well, as certified by ordinary experience), the Upaniṣads sometime surprise us by bringing them together in a manner that seems to run counter to this opposition. The most important of such texts is to be found in the *Īśa*: "Those who worship *avidyā* enter into darkness and those who are engaged in *vidyā* enter into still greater darkness . . . Those who know both *vidyā* and *avidyā* together overcome death by *avidyā* and reach immortality by *vidyā*."[27] Clearly this text emphasizes the necessity of knowing both *vidyā* and *avidyā* for attaining immortality through knowledge. What, then, do these texts signify? These verses reinforce the dichotomy between work and knowledge and assert that those who pursue one to the exclusion of the other remain ignorant. Śaṃkara in his interpretation points out that "*avidyā*" in this context means action, i.e., the performance of the Vedic rituals, and "*vidyā*" signifies knowledge and thought of the deities. The performance of rites and meditation on the deities helps one attain immortality, which is not *mokṣa* or becoming identical with the *brahman*. Clearly these meanings are one-sided, so the question arises: Is there any other way of reconciling the text with the commonly acceptable meanings of words?

One way is to recall Plato's thesis in the *Republic* that when the prisoner in the cave first sees the light and the original realities, his eyes are blinded and dazzled. It is imperative that he sees both the original as well as the copies, so that he may begin to see the truth. In other words, knowledge of the one must be combined with the knowledge of the many. Performing the ritualistic actions with the vision shrouded by ignorance may lead one to pass from this world to the higher worlds, which is not *mokṣa*. Likewise, mere knowledge of the one to the utter exclusion of the experience of the world is not yet the highest knowledge. One must know both ignorance as ignorance and knowledge as knowledge. Is the *Īśā* saying something like Plato? I leave this question for the students to pursue.

It is possible to suggest that there are different levels of *avidyā* and that, to attain *vidyā*, one must go through the lower levels in order to reach the highest. In that case, one may want to maintain that *avidyā* is the pathway to *mokṣa* or *vidyā*, even if the path lies within the domain of *avidyā*. Thus, the initial opposition between *vidyā* and *avidyā* is softened, because all entry into knowledge must be through ignorance. But, at the same time, there is a "leap," a "jump" from the one domain to the other, a total transcendence, a discontinuity.

II Viśiṣṭādvaita

After Śaṁkara, the name that is most famous among Indian philosophers of the Vedānta school is that of Rāmānuja. Born two hundred years after Śaṁkara, Rāmānuja takes issue with Śaṁkara's conceptions of the *brahman*, the status of the world, *avidyā*, and argues that the *brahman* is real, the world rooted in the *brahman* is real, and in knowing we move from the partial to the complete. Using the principles of *dharmabhūta jñāna* or attributive consciousness, *apṛthak-siddhi* or inseparability, and *sāmānādhikarṇya* or the principle of coordination, Rāmānuja establishes his own version of non-dualism called "Viśiṣṭādvaita" or "qualified non-dualism."

Rāmānuja remains one of the most influential interpreters of a theistic variety of Vedānta. As a young man, he stayed in the company of such poet saints as Yamunā, Mahāpurāṇās, Goṣṭhipūrṇa who exercised a profound influence on him. These poet saints of South India were known as "*Ālvārs*." The term "*ālvar*" etymologically means "one who has attained a mystic intuitive knowledge of God." These poet saints upheld a theistic interpretation of the Upaniṣads, the interpretation that shaped Rāmānuja's philosophical outlook. Rāmānuja worshipped the god Viṣṇu and had many Viṣṇu temples and *maṭhas* built during his lifetime. The catholic spirit of his religion made it possible for him to acquire a large number of devoted scholars, who carried on his religion and philosophy for centuries to come. Rāmānuja died in 1137.

Rāmānuja's philosophy is a creative and constructive effort to systematize the teachings of the *Upaniṣads*, the *Gītā*, and the *Brahmasūtras*. One of Rāmānuja's primary contributions lies in reconciling the extremes of monism and theism, while providing a formidable opposition to Śaṃkara's Advaita Vedānta. If for Śaṃkara reality or the *brahman* is pure consciousness, pure existence, and pure bliss on which individual consciousness ("I" and "mine"), the world, etc., are superimposed owing to ignorance, Rāmānuja takes *brahman* to be the God of religion, an all-inclusive being. Rāmānuja, like Śaṃkara, believes that *brahman* is the only reality, and in so believing subscribes to a kind of non-dualism; however, whereas Śaṃkara's non-dualism takes the world and the God to be appearances, Rāmānuja's non-dualism takes them to be real, and in so believing satisfies the religious yearning for a self-conscious supreme person, who is nevertheless the totality of all beings, conscious and non-conscious.

Rāmānuja begins by asking the basic Upaniṣadic question: "what is that by knowing which everything else is known? The answer is: the "*brahman*." The *brahman* is knowable; he is realizable. Let us see what Rāmānuja has to say about this important concept.

Brahman

At the outset of his philosophy, Rāmānuja informs us that all knowledge necessarily involves discrimination and differentiation; it is impossible to know an object in its undifferentiated form. Knowledge is the affirmation of reality and every negation presupposes affirmation. The knowable is known as characterized in some form or the other by some specific attributes.

Rāmānuja refuses to divorce the manifold from the one; his unity contains within itself the diversity. Since knowledge always involves distinctions, both pure identity and pure difference are not real. He concurs with Śaṃkara that the *brahman* is real. Being the all-inclusive totality of beings, the *brahman* is the whole of which there are two kinds of parts: consciousness or *cit*, and matter or *acit*. The *brahman*, then, is *cit-acit-granthī*, "a knot of consciousness and matter." Finite centers of consciousness as well as the material nature, both belong to *brahman*, are in it, and as belonging to the *brahman*, they are ultimately real. The *brahman* is an organic unity, a unity which is characterized by difference. Rāmānuja recognizes as real three factors: the *brahman* or God, soul, and matter. Though equally real, the last two are absolutely dependent on the first.

In this metaphysical theory, the category of substance (*dravya*) predominates. One substance, which is a part of another, functions as the latter's qualifying attribute. The human individual consists of two substances, body and soul. The two, being parts of a whole, are inseparably connected with each other. Perhaps the most original aspect of Rāmānuja's philosophy is the rejection of the principle that to be real means to be independent. Although soul and matter in themselves are substances, in relation to *brahman* they become his attributes. They are *brahman*'s body, and he is their soul. Rāmānuja's notion of *apṛthak-siddhi* or inseparability explains this relation.[28] This relation of inseparability that obtains between a substance and its qualities may also be found between two substances. Just as qualities are real and cannot exist apart from the substances in which they subsist, similarly matter and soul are parts of the *brahman* and cannot exist without the *brahman*. The soul of a human being, although different from his body, controls and guides his body; similarly, the *brahman* although different from the matter and souls, directs and sustains them. To put it differently, the *brahman* is like a person and the various selves and material objects constitute his body. Thus Rāmānuja's *brahman* is not an unqualified identity; it is identity-in-difference, an organic unity, or better yet, an organic union in which one part predominates and controls the other part. The part and the whole then become a prototype of the large ontological relation. Body and soul are related with this sort of inseparability as much in the case of human individuals as in the case of the *brahman*. Just as knowledge is substance-attribute, similarly the self (*cit*) is itself a substance as well as a quality of the Being or the *brahman*. The negative way of indicating the relation emphasizes the identity of Being and its attributes on the one hand, and at the same time retains the conception of relation in the integrity of Being by rejecting absolute oneness (identity) which one finds in the Advaita Vedānta of Śaṃkara. Thus, as the logical subject, the *cit* is a mode (*prakāra*) of the *brahman*, but as an ethical subject, it is a monad which has its own intrinsic nature.

Thus, whereas for Śaṃkara, the *brahman* as pure intelligence is devoid of any distinctions, pure identity without any difference (*nirguṇa*), Rāmānuja's *brahman* is identity-in-difference. When the Upaniṣads describe the *brahman* as devoid of qualities, they mean that the *brahman* does not have any negative qualities, not that it does not have any qualities whatsoever. It possesses a number of characteristics (*saguṇa*). Existence, consciousness, bliss, knowledge, truth are some of his attributes. These attributes are responsible for his determinate nature. The *brahman*, for Rāmānuja, is not different from the personal God of theism. But as the one reality, it includes, rather than excluding all differences between conscious individuals and the material world. The fundamental principle of thinking then becomes identity-in-difference rather than pure identity. Everything is real, but only as included in the one reality, but when considered as independent of, and falling outside *brahman*, as autonomous, all difference is an appearance. This totality is the supreme person, the *puruṣottama*, who is all-knowing, all-powerful, blissful, and infinite.

The Brahman *and the World*

Rāmānuja argues that the *brahman* is real and the world rooted in the *brahman* is also real. He takes the Upaniṣadic account of creation literally: the omnipotent God creates the world out of himself. During dissolution, God remains as the cause with subtle matter and unembodied souls forming his body. This is the causal state of *brahman*. The entire universe remains in a latent and undifferentiated state. God's will impels this undifferentiated subtle matter to be transformed into gross and unembodied souls into embodied ones according to their *karmas*. This is the effect state of the *brahman*.

Creation, for Rāmānuja, actually takes place, and the world is as real as the *brahman* itself. Accordingly, Rāmānuja holds that such Upaniṣadic texts as "there is no multiplicity here" ("*neha nānā asti kiñcana*"), do not really deny the multiplicity of objects, of names and forms, but rather assert that these objects do not have any existence apart from the *brahman*. It is indeed true, concedes Rāmānuja, that some Upaniṣadic texts articulate the *brahman* as wielder of a magical power (*māyā*), however, *māyā*, argues Rāmānuja, is a unique power of God by which God creates the wonderful world of objects. He vehemently criticizes Śaṃkara's theory that the world is false; it is a creation of *māyā*. The created world of the *brahman*, for Rāmānuja, is as wonderful as the *brahman* itself.

There is, according to Rāmānuja, no special kind of object which is neither *sat* nor *asat* (as Śaṃkara argues). All things are real or *sat*. Even when I mistake a rope for a snake, what I see is real (not the Naiyāyika's elsewhere-existent, but here and now before me). Error is due to the fact that in this case because of darkness etc., I do not perceive everything that is there. The longish shape, size, color, etc., that I see are all there, but the fibrous texture, etc., I do not see. When an error is corrected, I do not have a total negation of what I saw, but additional knowledge supplements what was perceived there. Error is *partial truth*. Rāmānuja uses the doctrine of quintuplication to substantiate his theory, which holds that from a metaphysical perspective everything is present everywhere. Some particles of silver, it is conceivable, are present in the shell. When the shell is mistaken for silver, one may say, silver is there in a miniscule form. Not all illusions, however, can be explained in this manner. A person's perception of a white conch as yellow requires a different explanation. How do we account for the yellowness of the conch in such cases? Rāmānuja maintains that a person with a jaundiced eye, perceiving a white conch as yellow, actually transmits to the conch the yellowness of the bile through the rays of the eyes, and as a result the new color is imposed on the conch and its natural whiteness is obscured. Hence there is no subjective element in error. Error is only partial knowledge.

A corollary of this thesis is that knowledge implies both subject and object.[29] It is the subject that knows the object with the help of its essential attribute (*dharmabhūta jñāna*). All knowledge is characterized by attributes, and there is no knowledge devoid of attributes.[30] Hence, Rāmānuja's theory is known as *satkhyātivāda*, which literally means "*sat* (existence) alone is cognized." Applied to the relation between the *brahman* and the world, we can say, the world is real, but only a part of the totality that is *brahman*. Error consists in mistaking the part to be an autonomous whole. Thus, correction of error is not total negation (as Śaṃkara argues), but additional knowledge, one knows more about that yonder objects than he did originally.

Rāmānuja rejects Śaṃkara's theory of causality according to which only the cause is real, while all effects are false appearances. Rāmānuja's own theory comes rather close to the Sāṁkhya *satkāryavāda* that there is a real causation, the effect being a real transformation of the cause. Finite individual souls and material nature are real transformations, so that even in the causal state, the *brahman* contains matter and souls within it. Rāmānuja distinguishes between the body of the *brahman* and his soul, on the analogy of finite individuals. The body of the *brahman* consists of matter and finite souls, and his soul is his infinite, all-knowing consciousness.

The *brahman* thus is both the material and the efficient cause of the world, and continues to be "the inner controller" of what he creates. There is no contradiction in saying that the same thing is both the material and efficient cause. The potter's wheel, e.g., is the efficient cause of a pitcher, and material cause of its own form and qualities. As both *cit* and *acit*, the *brahman* is the material cause, while as idea and will he is the efficient cause. It must be noted that this view of God is radically different from Śaṃkara's, according to whom the material cause of the world is *avidyā*, while the *brahman* is the ground of the appearance of the world (and finite individuals) Finally, we must note that for Rāmānuja, time is real, and is directly perceived as a quality of all perceived entities. Time is eternal in the sense that it is never destroyed.

If someone were to ask, "how does the one contain the many?" Rāmānuja in response would put forth the grammatical principle of *sāmānādhikarṇya* or the principle of coordination. With the help of this principle, Ramanuja rejects both the concepts of *bheda* (difference) and *abheda* (non-difference) and institutes the concept of *viśeṣa* (predication). Following this principle, Rāmānuja argues that in all cases of predication what is predicated is not a bare identity but a substance that is characterized by different attributes.

In order to explain this, let me turn to Rāmānuja's interpretation of the classic Upaniṣadic text, "So 'yam Devadatta," i.e., "this is that Devadatta," which, for Rāmānuja, is not an identity judgment as it is for Śaṃkara. Rāmānuja argues that the words in a sentence with different meanings can denote one and the same thing. For example, Devadatta of the past and the Devadatta of the present cannot be entirely identical, because the person seen at the present and the person seen in the past are different, have different meanings, yet both refer to the same person. Similarly, unity and diversity, the one and the many can, co-exist and can be reconciled in a synthetic unity. Thus, with the help of this rule, Rāmānuja, on the one hand rejects the principle of abstract bare identity, and, on the other, institutes a principle of differentiation at the very center of identity. There is no need to deny the many; the many characterize the one.

The Self, Bondage, and Liberation

Each individual self (*jīva*) is a substantial reality, but a substance can, on Rāmānuja's theory, serve as a quality of the whole of which it is a part. Then a stick, or *daṇḍa,* is a substance, a thing, but also qualifies the person who carries it, who is called *daṇḍin.* To the question, then, whether the individual selves have their own substantive being or are merely adjectival, Rāmānuja's answer is: both. A finite substance depends, in the long run, on the infinite whole, i.e., *brahman.* The *brahman* is qualified by both *cit* and *a-cit*; it is *citacitviśiṣta.*

Human beings, according to Rāmānuja, have a real body as well as a soul. Given that the body is made of matter, it is finite. The soul, on the other hand exists eternally, though it is also a part of God. It is subtle, which allows it to penetrate even into unconscious substances. Consciousness is not an essence, but an eternal quality of the soul. There is no state—waking, dreaming, and dreamless sleep—in which the sense of "I" is missing. Waking up from deep sleep, one says "I slept well," "I did not know anything," which implies that one did not know any object. The soul remains conscious of itself as "I am" in all states. In the *Bhagavad Gītā*, Rāmānuja argues, that even God refers to himself as an "I." He is a person, the supreme person.

Both the individual souls and God then are embodied. A brief review of Rāmānuja's concept of "body," or "*śarīra*" would provide further insights and help my readers understand this complicated sense of embodiment. Whereas the Naiyāyikas define "body" as the locus or the support (*āśraya*) of effort, sense, and enjoyment, Rāmānuja defines "body" in terms of "subservience to the spirit." The body depends on the will of the spirit for its movement. There never was, or will be, a time in which this relation between body and soul did not exist. It is a necessary relation of "inseparability." Even before creation, God's body existed, but only in its original state, i.e., *prakṛti*, the stuff that undergoes change. Apart from his body, God is unchanging. Thus, God's being has both a spiritual as well as a material part, though matter originally, i.e., prior to the world creation, as belonging to God's body, is pure ("pure" in the sense of being only of *sattva* quality).

In *saṃsāra* (the embodied existence), the soul wrongly identifies itself with the body on account of *karmas* (past deeds) and ignorance. Though the soul is infinitely small, it illumines every part of the body in which it is housed. Accordingly, Rāmānuja distinguishes between two meanings of the "I": in one sense, the "I" means the *ahaṁkāra* or egoism, which is to be overcome and conquered, while, in another sense, the "I" means "the knower." The knower self refers to himself as the "I." The soul is an I. There are innumerable individual souls; they are qualitatively alike but differ in number. In this respect, Rāmānuja's conception of the individual soul corresponds to that of Leibniz, who advocates qualitative monism and quantitative pluralism of monads.

Mokṣa, according to Rāmānuja, cannot be brought about by mere knowledge. Work, knowledge, and devotion to God are needed to get freedom from ignorance, *karma*, and embodied existence. "Work," for Rāmānuja, means different rites and rituals prescribed in the Vedas according to one's caste and situation in life. These duties must be performed without any desire for the rewards. Disinterested performance of one's duties is the key here. Such a performance destroys the accumulative effects of actions. The study of the Mīmāṁsā texts (texts that explain how the rites and ceremonies should be performed) is necessary to ensure the right performance of duties. Accordingly, Rāmānuja makes the study of Mīmāṁsā a necessary prerequisite to the study of Vedānta.

The study of the Mīmāṁsā texts and the correct performance of one's duties lead one to realize that sacrificial rites and ritual do not lead to freedom from one's embodied existence, hence the necessity of the knowledge of Vedānta, which aids in developing one's intellectual convictions about the nature of God, the external world, and one's own self. Such a knowledge reveals to the seeker of wisdom that God is the creator, sustainer, and destroyer of the world, and that the soul is a part of God and is controlled by him. Study and reflection further reveal to the aspirant that neither the correct performance of one's duties nor an intellectual knowledge of the real nature of God can lead to freedom from embodiment. Such a freedom can only be attained by the free, loving grace of God. Accordingly, one should dedicate oneself to the service of God. Rāmānuja, in short, unlike Śaṃkara, maintains that the path of devotion leads one to freedom. Knowledge, combined with *bhakti*, can destroy ignorance, but *mokṣa*, in the long run, is brought about not by the individuals' own efforts, but by God's grace (*dayā*). One needs to give up a false sense of independence, i.e. pride, and seek his mercy by completely surrendering himself to God, which is called "*prapatti*."

Thus what brings about *mokṣa* is not the aspirant's self-surrender, but God's own infinite compassion for the devotee. The followers of Rāmānuja differ as to the extent of activity and passivity involved in the process. Some emphasize more initiative on the part of the aspirant, others more passivity. Some prefer to use the analogy of a monkey's little one who actively clings to the mother's body: others prefer the analogy of the kitten's complete passivity such that the mother cat just picks him up at the neck. In any case, the steps in the process are: (1) knowledge of God's infinitely perfect nature, (2) constant meditation (*dhyāna*) on him, (3) resulting in uninterrupted thought of God culminating in immediately experiencing him, (4) one's completely surrendering oneself to him, (5) leading to God's infinite mercy that destroys one's *karma*, ignorance, and bondage.

To sum up: the path of devotion, for Rāmānuja, involves constant meditation, prayer, and devotion to God. Meditation on God as the object of love accompanied by the performance of daily rites and rituals, removes one's ignorance and destroys past *karmas*. The soul is liberated; it is not reborn. It shines in its pristine purity.

Unlike Śaṃkara, the soul according to Rāmānuja does not become identical with God; it becomes similar to God. *Mokṣa* is a state in which the individual self becomes pure and perfected and enjoys eternally God's fellowship. The last vestige of egoism is removed. But all this, i.e., the highest goal, cannot be achieved simply by one's own effort, or even by knowledge alone.

Rāmānuja rejects the notion of complete identity between the *brahman* or God and finite selves. Individual selves are finite and cannot be identical to God in every respect. God not only pervades but controls the entire universe. As the existence of a part is inseparable from the whole, and that of a quality is inseparable from the substance in which it inheres, similarly the existence of a finite self is inseparable from God. Accordingly, his interpretation of the Upaniṣadic statement "that thou art" is very different from that of Śaṃkara. For Śaṃkara, the relation between "that" and "thou" is one of complete identity. Rāmānuja, on the other hand, maintains that in the Upaniṣadic statement under consideration, "that" refers to God, the omniscient, omnipotent, all-loving, creator of the world, and "thou" refers to God existing in the form of I-consciousness, the finite human consciousness. The identity in this context should be construed to mean an identity between God with certain qualifications and the individual soul with certain other qualifications. To put it differently, God and finite selves are one and the same substance, although they possess different qualities. Hence, the name of the system, Viśiṣṭādvaita ("qualified identity" or "identity with certain qualifications.") Thus, whereas in the non-dualistic Vedānta of Śaṃkara liberation implies the total effacement of the self, in the qualified non-dualistic Vedānta of Rāmānuja, the liberated self lives in eternal communion with God.

Before concluding this chapter, let me briefly sum up the important differences between Śaṃkara and Rāmānuja.

Śaṃkara and Rāmānuja

Interpretation of the Upaniṣadic Texts

We already know that there are two kinds of texts in the Upaniṣads; the so-called positive and the negative texts. To recapitulate: we find texts that describe the *brahman* as being the origin and the sustainer of all beings, into which they all return. The Upaniṣads also assert "none of this is the *brahman*." These texts throughout the centuries have posed problems for commentators as to how to reconcile these seemingly inconsistent statements? According to Śaṃkara, affirmative sentences are only provisional, only to be denied afterwards, and the negative sentences state the higher truth, articulated as *brahman* is none of these. The world and the finite individuals are not real, the *brahman* alone is real. According to Rāmānuja what is negated is the presumed autonomous reality of finite things, but all of them have their reality as parts of one all-comprehensive totality, i.e., *brahman*.

The Brahman *as Indeterminate and Determinate*

Śaṃkara regards the *brahman* as pure existence, an indeterminate being without any external or internal differentiation as well as without any qualities. According to Rāmānuja such an entity can never be apprehended by any of the *pramāṇas*. What is not a possible object of a *pramāṇa* must be a non-entity. Pure existence is not known. Every *pramāṇa* knows an object as being such and such. The *brahman* is *saguṇa*; it is not a distinctionless reality.

Consciousness as Self-manifesting vs. Intentional

On Śaṃkara's theory, pure consciousness is self-manifesting, and it is not a possible object of a *pramāṇa*. Rāmānuja considers this to be totally mistaken. Consciousness is always *of an object*, and it is self-manifesting only when it is directed towards an object. When I am apprehending a thing in perception *now*, then only, i.e., *at that very moment*, my perceptual consciousness manifests itself *to me*. Later on, i.e., at other moments, that consciousness does not manifest itself to me, nor does it ever manifest itself to other selves. So on Rāmānuja's theory, consciousness manifests itself to its own subject at the moment it also manifests an object. Śaṃkara's pure consciousness which has neither subject nor object, and yet always self-manifesting is a figment of imagination. In modern western philosophical language, Rāmānuja ties intentionality and reflexivity to consciousness closely together. Without intentionality, consciousness cannot be reflexive.

Brahman *as* Sat, Cit, *and* Ānanda

Śaṃkara regards *brahman* to be pure bliss. Its nature is bliss or *ānanda*, just as it is also pure knowledge. Rāmānuja considers that statement to be meaningless.

"Bliss" and "knowledge" are qualities of the *brahman*. It is absurd to take them to be identical with the *brahman*. If that were the case, such texts such as the "*brahman* is *sat, cit,* and *ānanda*" would be tautologies, and the words "*sat,*" "*cit,*" and "*ānanda*" synonymous. A string of synonymous words does not make a sentence. Each of the constituent terms must stand for a quality belonging to the *brahman*. *Brahman* is a qualified whole which contains within its being the world and finite selves.

Status of Avidyā *or Ignorance*

For Śaṃkara, the silver or snake that appears in illusory perception is neither real (*sat*) nor unreal (*asat*), but indescribable either as *sat* or *asat*. This new category of entity is presented in experience but is subsequently totally negated in the same locus in which it was presented. Such an object is called "*mithyā*" or false. Ignorance is beginningless; it is a positive entity having two functions: concealment of the real and the projection of the *mithyā* upon it. The world and the finite things are *mithyā* in this sense.

Rāmānuja launches a severe critique of Śaṃkara's theory of error (and of the associated theory of ignorance). Of the various objections that Rāmānuja raises against Śaṃkara's account, I will here mention only four. Rāmānuja asks: What is the locus or *āśraya* of ignorance? To put it differently, where does ignorance reside? It cannot reside in the finite individual, because the individual self is a product of ignorance. The *brahman* cannot be its locus either, because the *brahman* is of the nature of knowledge, which destroys ignorance. Ignorance and knowledge being contradictories cannot have the same locus. Thus, it is impossible to determine the locus of ignorance.

Secondly, ignorance, argues Śaṃkara, veils the self-luminous *brahman*. Rāmānuja asks: what is meant by the "concealment of luminosity"? It may mean either the obstruction in the origination of luminosity or the destruction of the luminosity. Rāmānuja argues that the luminosity is not produced, so the question of its obstruction does not arise. Thus, the concealment of luminosity can only mean the destruction of the *brahman's* luminosity, which would amount to the destruction of its essential nature.

Thirdly, Rāmānuja points out that on the Advaita thesis the self-luminous consciousness becomes conscious of the world of objects on account of some defect. What is the exact nature of *avidyā* as an imperfection or defect in *cit*? Is this defect real or not real? Śaṃkara argues that it is not real, but it cannot be taken to be not real either because it explains our errors; it not only explains such illusions as rope-snake, but also the appearance of the world. If it is said that the *brahman* itself may be regarded as having the defect, then there would be no need of postulating *avidyā*, because then the *brahman* itself would be regarded as the cause of the world, but, in that case there could not be any release for the finite individual, because the *brahman* being eternal, its defect also would be eternal.

Fourthly, Rāmānuja points out that it is impossible to define ignorance. Śaṃkara argues that ignorance is indescribable, because it is nether *sat*, nor *asat*, nor both *sat* and *asat* at the same time. Rāmānuja argues that "*sat*" and "*asat*" are contradictories; there is no third possibility. Thus to say that the false object is neither *sat* nor *asat* is to violate a basic principle of logic. Rāmānuja concludes that ignorance cannot be defined.

The above discussion will give my readers an idea of the kinds of objections Rāmānuja raised against Śaṃkara's theory of ignorance. The followers of Śaṃkara have systematically refuted these objections to substantiate their own theory of ignorance. Irrespective of which account one finds plausible, there is no doubt that Rāmānuja's critique of Śaṃkara has left its indelible mark on the Advaita philosophy. Rāmānuja steers clear of both monism and dualism, and provides his followers with a spiritual experience of the *brahman* or God that harmonizes the demands of reason and immediate experience, philosophy and religion. Traditionally, a person must belong to one of the three higher castes to pursue the path of *mokṣa*. Rāmānuja recognizes that irrespective of caste and rank, one may follow the spiritual path to attain union with God. This accommodating spirit made it possible for Viśiṣtādvaita to acquire a large number of followers and make it popular in India through the ages. It uplifted the lower castes, and therein lies one of its most important contributions.

APPENDIX IV

TRANSLATIONS OF SELECTED TEXTS FROM THE BUDDHIST SCHOOLS AND THE VEDĀNTA *DARŚANA*

The Yogacārā School

Vasubandhu[1]

1 Our thoughts arouse the false ideas of the ego and the elements of existence; as a result, there arise various transformations of consciousness which are mainly of three kinds.

2 There are consciousness of ripening, consciousness of the discrimination of the objective world, in the first place, the *ālaya* (store-house) consciousness, which leads all seeds into fruition.

3 (As a state of pure consciousness) it is not conscious of its clingings and impressions, in both of its functions, objective and subjective, it is always connected with touch, volition, feeling, thought, and cognition. But it is ever indifferent to its associations.

4 Not affected by the darkness of ignorance or by the memory or by touch, etc., it is always flowing like a fast moving stream, but is abandoned only in the state of *arhat*.

5 (This was the first transformation). The second transformation is called the mind-consciousness which both depends on the store-house consciousness and also conditions it. Its nature is intellectual thinking.

6 It is accompanied by four afflicted desires, which are: ignorance of the self, wrong view of the self (self as permanent), self-pride and self-love, and also by touch (feelings, desires), etc.

7 It is free from memory (of the distinction between good and affliction), but not from the dark ignorance. Wherever it arises, so do contact and the others. But it also does not exist in the state of *arhat*, or in the state of cessation, or in a super mundane path.

8 The third is the apprehension of sense-objects of six kinds. Its nature and characteristic consist of the discrimination of objects, either beneficial or not or neither.

1 Vasubandhu's *Thirty Verses*.

9 Mind functions consist of general mind functions; particular mind functions, good and afflicted functions; minor afflicted and indeterminate mind functions—all these impress mind in three ways (joy, suffering, and indifference).

10 Touch, etc. (volition, feeling, thought and cognition) are the general mind-functions. Particular mind-functions are desire, resolve, remembrance, concentration, and wisdom. Each depends on many conditions.

11 The beneficial mind-functions are: faith, inner-shame, fear of blame, lack of greed, vigor, tranquility, carefulness, and nonviolence.

12 The afflictions which are secondary are: anger, malice, hypocrisy, envy, selfishness, and deceitfulness; The primary afflictions being aversions, confusion, pride, and doubts.

13 More secondary afflictions are: mischievous exuberance, desire to harm, lack of shame, lack of fear for blame, mental confusion, excited-ness, lack of faith, laziness, carelessness, and lack of mindfulness.

14 Still more afflictions are: to be distracted, lack of recognition, regret, torpor, distraction and non-discernment. Intermediate mind functions are repentance, drowsiness, reflection, and investigation. The former two pairs compose a different class from the latter.

15 Based on the mind-consciousness, the five consciousnesses (of the senses) are manifested along with the objective world, sometimes together and sometimes not, like the waves in water.

16 The sense-consciousness always arises and manifests itself except when born in the realm of absence of thought, in the state of unconsciousness, and in the two forms of attainments, in sleep and unconsciousness.

17 Transformations of consciousness are many; what is imagined does not exist; therefore, everything is perception-only.

18 As the result of various seeds, transformations take place in accordance with a reciprocal influence so that such and such types of discrimination may take place.

19 The residual impressions of various actions give rise to residual impressions of both the six organs and their objects. When the ripening in a previous life is exhausted, another ripening in a different life is produced.

20 Various things are falsely discriminated because of false discriminations. What is grasped by such false discrimination has no self-nature at all.

21 The own-being, which results from interdependence, is produced by the conditions of discrimination. The Absolute is different from the interdependent; the former is eternally free from what is grasped by false discrimination.

22 The Absolute and the dependent are neither the same nor different; the one can be seen only in the other as in the case of the impermanent and the permanent.

23 The three different kinds of absence of own-being have been taught in the three different kinds of own-being. The Enlightened one has taught that all *dharmas* have no entity.

24 The first is the non-entity of phenomenon, the second is the non-entity of self-existence, and the last is the non-entity of ultimate existence. Of what are falsely posited, the ego and *dharma* have to be eliminated.

25 The ultimate truth of all *dharmas* is nothing other than such-ness. This is the truth of all events all the time. It is perception-only.

26 Until consciousness is awakened, its mode of being is not mind-only. The six sense organs, objects, and the seeds of evil desires cannot be controlled and eliminated.

27 The same is true even of the consciousness "all this is perception only." This also involves apprehension, and is not situated in "consciousness-only."

28 Consciousness is situated in "consciousness-only" when it does not apprehend any object. When there is nothing that is apprehended, there is no apprehension of it.

29 The supra-mundane wisdom of *bodhisattvahood* is there without any grasping, and beyond thought. There occurs revulsion at the basis, and the end of both kinds of susceptibility to harm (conditional knowledge).

30 This is the realm of passionlessness, beyond description, good and eternal. Here one is in the state of emancipation, peace and joy.

The Mādhyamika School

Nāgārjuna

Pratyaya Parīkṣā *(Examination of Conditions)*[2]

1 Entities can never exist by originating out of themselves, from others, from both or from no cause nowhere and at no time.

2 There are only four conditions: cause, objectively extending, contiguous, and dominant. There is no fifth. Of the positive entities, there is no self-nature. From the nonexistence of self-nature, other-nature also cannot exist.

3 Action does not belong to what has relational conditions. Nor does it not belong to what does have these conditions. The conditions do not have the force of activity nor does such force not belong to the conditions.

4 As originated and uniquely related, entities can have relational conditions. How can non-relational conditions be asserted of entities which have not come into being?

5 Relational conditions do not belong either to being or to nonbeing. What use is it, if it belongs to being? Whose use is it if it belongs to nonbeing?

6 When an element does not evolve from being, non-being nor from both, how can there be a producing cause? Thus such a cause is not permissible.

7 When a *dharma* does not have a supporting condition, in such a *dharma* how can there by a supporting condition?

2 From Nāgārjuna's *Mūlāmadhyamakakārikā*, Chapter I.

8 When a *dharma* has not arisen, how can there be extinction? In an extinguished state, of what use is a condition?

9 Entities without self-nature have no real being. The dictum "this being existent, that becomes" is not possible.

10 Effort does not exist separated from all conditions, nor does it exist together with these. In that case, how can it arise out of these conditions?

11 If non-entity can arise from these conditions, why cannot the effect arise from non- conditions?

12 The arisen entity has the conditions, but the conditions have no self-possessing nature.

13 An effect therefore is neither made with conditions nor without non-conditions. The effect has no existing status, where then are the conditions and non-conditions?

Nirvāṇa Parīkṣā[3]

EXAMINATION OF *NIRVĀṆA*

1 If all is *śūnya*, and there is neither arising nor destruction, then what needs to be destroyed or abandoned for *nirvāṇa* to be possible?

2 If all is *aśūnya* and there is neither production nor destruction, then what has to be extinguished or abandoned for *nirvāṇa* to be possible?

3 What is called *nirvāṇa* is—unrelinquished, not reached, not annihilated, not eternal, never ceased, non-created.

4 *Nirvāṇa*, first of all, is not a kind of being, for if it were, it would then have decay and death. There is no positive entity, which is not subject to decay and death.

5 If *nirvāṇa* were a positive entity, then it would be produced by causes. Nowhere there is an entity which is not produced by causes.

6 If *nirvāṇa* were to be a positive entity, how can that lack a substratum? There is no positive entity without a substratum.

7 If *nirvāṇa* is not a positive entity will it be then a non-entity? Wherever there is no entity, there can be no corresponding non-entity.

8 If *nirvāṇa* is a non-entity can it then be independent? For, an independent entity is not to be found anywhere.

9 Coordinated or caused are separate entities this world is called phenomenal. The same is called *nirvāṇa* when abstracted from causality.

10 The *Buddha* has taught that any entity, positive or negative, should both be rejected. *Nirvāṇa* therefore is to be understood neither as a positive entity nor as a negative entity.

11 If however *nirvāṇa* were both (positive) entity and *abhāva*, final release would also be both reality and non-reality at the same time. This, however, is not possible.

3 Ibid., Chapter XXV.

12 If *nirvāṇa* were both positive entity and (its) absence, then *nirvāṇa* could not be uncaused, because both positive entity and non-entity are dependent on causation.

13 How can both positive entity and negative non-entity be together in *nirvāṇa*? *Nirvāṇa* is un-caused while both being an entity and not-being-an-entity are productions.

14 How can both being-an-entity and being-a-non-entity be represented in *nirvāṇa*? Like light and darkness, they cannot be simultaneously present.

15 *Nirvāṇa* being neither an entity nor a non-entity, we could understand if we knew what each one means.

16 If *nirvāṇa* is neither an entity nor a non-entity, by what means is it made known as both entity and non-entity?

17 It cannot be asserted that the Buddha exists after *nirodha*. Nor can it be asserted that he does not exist, both exists and not exist, and neither after *nirodha*.

18 It cannot be asserted that the Buddha exists in this life. Neither it is asserted that he does not exist, or both, or neither. We will never understand it.

19 Between *nirvāṇa* and *saṃsāra* there is not the least difference. Between *saṃsāra* and *nirvāṇa* there is no difference at all.

20 The limits of *nirvāṇa* is also the limit of *saṃsāra*. Between the two, there is not the slightest difference.

21 The views regarding what exists beyond *nirodha*, the end of the world, permanence, are based on *nirvāṇa*, posterior and prior extremes of existence.

22 Since everything is *śūnya*, what is finite and what is infinite? What do both together mean? What does negation of both mean?

23 What is identity and what is difference? What is eternity, what is non-eternity? What do eternity and non-eternity together mean? What does the negation of birth mean?

24 All acquisitions and thought are in the quiescence of plurality. The Buddha—never, nowhere—taught conciliation of all objects.

Dvādaśāṇga Parīkṣā[4]

EXAMINATION OF TWELVE LINKS

1 Deluded by ignorance, they create their own residual impressions (*samṣkāras)* in order to cause rebirth, and then, by their deeds, go through the various forms of life.

2 Consciousness, owing to the *samṣkāras*, sets up the various forms of life. When consciousness is thus established, name and form become apparent.

3 When name and form are established, the six *āyatanas* (seats of perception) arise. With the six *āyatanas*, touch evolves.

4 Ibid., Chapter XXVI.

4 As in the case of the eye and its material form, consciousness arises in a similar relational nature of name and form.

5 From form, consciousness, and eye issues forth touch. From touch arises feeling.

6 Conditioned by feeling, craving arises. It "thirsts" after the object of feeling. In the process of craving, the fourfold clingings (grasping for desires, views, rules and rights, and conceptions about the self) arise.

7 With clinging, the perceiver gives rise to becoming. When there is no clinging, he will be free, and there will be no becoming.

8 Becoming consists in five *skandhas*. From becoming arises birth. From birth arises old age, death, suffering, misery, and . . .

9 . . . grief, despair, and lamentation. In this way, the simple suffering attached to the *skandhas* arises.

10 The ignorant creates the mental *saṃskāras* which are at the root of *saṃsāra*. Thus the ignorant is the doer, but the wise, seeing the truth, does not create anything.

11 When ignorance disappears, *saṃskāras* also disappear. The cessation of ignorance is dependent on wisdom.

12 When a link of the causal chain ceases to be, the subsequent link will not arise. As a consequence, suffering that belongs to the *skandhas* is extinguished.

The Vedānta *Darśana*

I Advaita Vedānta

(i) "Adhyasabhāṣya"[5]

What is this *adhyāsa* (superimposition)? This is being said—(superimposition is) an appearance like memory of what was seen before in something else. Some call it the superimposition of the properties of one thing on a quite different thing. Some others consider it to be an erroneous superimposition due to non-apprehension of the distinction (between two things). Others hold that when one thing (x) is superimposed upon another (y), x will have properties opposed to those of y. From every point of view, however, that (in superimposition) one thing appears as having the properties of another is not contradicted. Thus, ordinarily there is the experience: a shell appears as silver, one moon appears as two. Everywhere, there is no contradiction of one thing's appearing as having properties of another. These people ordinarily experience: a shell appears as (if it is) a silver, one moon appears as if it has a second.

Objection: However, again (we may ask), is there superimposition of an object and its properties on the self which is not an object? Everybody

5 From "Adhyāsabhāṣya" of Śaṃkara's *Brahmasūtrabhāṣya* (BSBh).

superimposes something on an object which is in front of him, and you state that the self is opposed to the non-self and therefore is free from the sense of "you."

The reply is: it (i.e., the self) is not entirely a non-object, since it is the content of the sense of "I," and because the self as opposed to the non-self is well known in the world as the direct (self-luminous) self.

(ii) The Brahman and the World

MUBH, I.1.7

The Imperishable is taken to be the source of all beings, in fact, of the entire creation. For example:

It is a well-known fact in this world, that a spider spins forth threads from itself alone without needing any other cause; the threads are really non-different from its body, and it withdraws the very same threads into itself and makes them one with its own body. We know herbs ranging from corn to trees grow out from earth. These herbs grow as inseparable from the earth. Likewise, we know that hair grows on the head as well as on the other parts of the body, differing (from the body) in nature. As with these illustrations, similarly, from the Imperishable that does not need any auxiliary, the entire universe—similar as well as dissimilar—originates.

These illustrations are given to help the student understand the point without difficulty.

BSBH, II.1.6 (THE REAL WITHOUT ANY INTERNAL DIFFERENCE) DIFFERENCE IN NATURE

The word "but" excludes the opponent's position. The view that the *brahman* could not be the material cause of this universe because the two are different in nature, cannot be wholly true. For it is a matter of common experience that from a man, a conscious being, insentient hair, nail, etc., originate, and that scorpion and other animals come into being from cowdung which is also insentient.

The Advaitin answer is as follows: "There is nevertheless this much of a difference that some insentient things form the basis for some sentient ones, while others do not." . . .

"Here the Upaniṣad reveals the presence of the supreme cause in the whole of creation when it says: 'It became the sentient and the insentient.' On the ground of this text, it can be argued, on the one hand the sentient cannot become insentient owing to dissimilarity, so also it can be argued, on the other, that the insentient (*pradhāna*) cannot become the sentient creatures. However, the dissimilarity (between the *brahman* and creation) has been explained away, therefore a conscious cause has to be accepted, as stated in the Upaniṣads."

BUBH II 4.14 (DUALITY IS ONLY AN APPEARANCE)

The question is: Why is it said that the self does not have consciousness any more after attaining oneness (with the *brahman*)? Listen . . .

The *brahman*, the really one without a second, appears to be something different from the self; however, owing to the limiting adjuncts of the body and organs conjured up by ignorance, there is duality, as it were, in the individual self

Objection: if duality is being used as an object for comparison, is it not taken to be real?

Reply: "no," because *śruti* asserts: "All modifications are simply names due to speech . . . Where duality arises, there one smells the other, one sees the other, one hears the other, one greets the other, one thinks of the other, one knows the other; this is the state of ignorance . . .

But when ignorance has been eradicated by the knowledge of the *brahman*, there is nothing but the self . . . there who smells what, who smells and through what instrument? . . . Ignorance conjures up the non-self, in reality, there is only the one self . . .

To the aspirant—who has realized the *brahman* by discriminating between the real and the apparent—there only the absolute subject, one without a second, remains; O, Maitreyi! through which instrument should one know that knower?" (In other words, when everything is the self, what does that self know except its own self? The object of the perception and the perceiving have become non-different.)

BSBH, II.1.9 (*MĀYĀ* DOES NOT AFFECT THE *BRAHMAN*)

(There is an objection that if the effect returns to the cause at the time of dissolution, then it will contaminate the cause.)

The answer is that there is nothing incongruous here . . . because there are illustrations which support our point. They show that even though the effects merge in their causes, they do not contaminate the latter with their own peculiarities . . . Nor do products such as necklaces made out of gold transfer their individual peculiarities to gold when they merge into it . . . Though cause and effect are non-different, the effect has the nature of the cause, but not vice versa . . .

As the magician himself is not affected at any time by the magic conjured up by himself, it being illusory, so also the supreme self is not affected by this world which is an appearance. . . . As *Gauḍapāda Kārikā* (I.16) states: "the moment the individual self is awakened from the influence of the beginningless *māyā*, that very moment, he realizes the non-dual which is beyond birth, dreamless, and sleepless."

We also find here the answer to the objection regarding the rebirth of free souls, because their false knowledge is eradicated by the knowledge of the real. Another objection—that even at dissolution the universe with all its diversities will continue in the supreme *brahman*—is also dismissed by not accepting such a position (i.e., a dualistic poition). Hence this position of the Upaniṣads is quite logical.

BSBH, II.1.33 (THE WORLD AS MERE SPORT OF THE *BRAHMAN*)

Just as a king whose desires have been fulfilled engages in activities like sport; again, just as the activities of breathing in and breathing out continues naturally, likewise god may have creative activity as "sport" without presupposing any need or motive , even if we take refuge in logic or by *smrti.*

(iii) Knowledge and Ignorance

KAṬHA UPANIṢAD, I.2.4

Of these two, that which is superior becomes good, but that which men prefer causes destruction. This has been said, but why? These two are separated by great distance, opposed to each other, mutually exclusive, have divergent paths, produce different results being the causes of bondage and freedom. What are they? That is being said. They are *avidyā,* or whose object is desired, and *vidyā* or one whose object is preferable. The learned prefer the latter and I regard you Nachiketa as belonging to this group. You are not attracted by many objects of desire—you are fit to realize enlightenment.

BSBH, I.2.21

In the Upaniṣads, we read: "There is then the higher knowledge by which that immutable is realized." (MU, I.1.5) We also read "By the higher knowledge, the wise realize everywhere that which cannot be perceived and grasped, which is without source, features, eyes, and ears, which has no hands, no feet, which is eternal, multiformed, all-pervasive, subtle, and not diminishing, the source of all." (MU I.1.6). In connection with this, the doubt arises: is it *pradhāna,* or the embodied soul, or God that is spoken of as the material cause of all things and as endowed with qualities such as "not being perceived," etc.?

The opponent replies to this question thus: "it is the insentient *pradhāna* which is the material cause of everything . . . ."

[The rest of the aphorism refutes this opponent's view and holds that the *brahman* alone could be the source of all things.]

The entity that is the source of all things and is possessed of such qualities as not being perceived, and so on, must be the highest god only. And none else . . . Neither *pradhāna* which is insentient, nor the embodied soul which is limited in its vision by limiting adjuncts, can possibly be omniscient in general and all-knowing in details.

(iv) Ātman

I.3.22 (ĀTMAN AS SELF-LUMINOUS)

(When the MU speaks of "light," this light must be none other than the *brahman.*)

". . . Now the doubt arises with regard to these texts (MU, II.2.10; Kaṭha, II.2.15) as to whether this entity, which when shines, all things shine, is some naturally lustrous substance or the conscious self."

(There is the opponent's view that this is the light of some shining substance. Śaṃkara rejects this and goes on to say . . .)

"Under such circumstances we say: It must be the conscious, self-shining self . . . for it is not a matter of experience that the sun and other things shine in accordance with some other shining substance . . . A lamp does not shine in imitation of another lamp."

"The *brahman* manifests all things; the *brahman* is not manifested by them (these things), as the Upaniṣadic texts state: "It is the light of the self which makes one sit (goes out, works, and comes back)" (BU, IV.3.6), "It is not perceptible, because it is never perceived" (BU, III.9.26), and so on."

II Viśiṣṭādvaita

Rāmānuja's Critique of Śaṃkara's Avidyā[6]

Rāmānuja raises seven objections against Śaṃkara's conception of *avidyā*:

1 IMPOSSIBILITY OF A LOCUS FOR *AVIDYĀ*

(Rāmānuja's says:) What is the locus of *avidyā*? You have to say, being located in whom does ignorance produce error? It cannot be said to be located in the finite individual, because the finite individual is a product of ignorance. Nor can it be said that ignorance rests in the *brahman,* because the *brahman,* being of the nature of self-luminous knowledge, is opposed to ignorance.

2 IMPOSSIBILITY OF CONCEALING THE BRAHMAN BY *AVIDYĀ*

(According to Śaṃkara *avidyā* conceals the nature of the *brahman*; however, concealment of luminosity, argues Rāmānuja, means the destruction of the nature of the *brahman.*) Concealment of luminosity may men either the obstacle in the appearance of the manifestation of the *brahman,* or the destruction of the self-revealing nature of the *brahman.* It cannot mean the obstacle in the appearance of the manifestation of the *brahman,* because the manifestation of the *brahman* is not accidental, it follows from its nature. Therefore, concealment means the the destruction of the *brahman*'s self-luminous nature.

6 From Rāmānuja's *Śrī Bhāṣya* with the commentary *śrutaprakāśīkā,* edited and published by T. Srinivasa Sarma (Bombay: Nirnayasagar Press, 1916), pp. 166–216. In this section I have given a summary of Rāmānuja's arguments against *avidyā* as an "illusory" power of the *brahman.* Advaitins reply to these objections one by one, and these replies again are refuted by Advaitins.

3 IMPOSSIBILITY OF DETERMINING THE EXACT NATURE OF *AVIDYĀ* AS AN IMPERFECTION

(It has been argued that on account of some defect (*doṣa*) the self-luminous *brahman* becomes an object of knowledge.) The question is: Is the defect residing in consciousness real or unreal? It is not real, because its reality is not admitted (by the Advaitins). It is not unreal, because then there would be infinite regress. If we take the defect to be the essence of the *brahman*, then the *brahman* being eternal, the defect would be eternal, and there would be no *mokṣa*.

4 IMPOSSIBILITY OF DEFINING *AVIDYĀ*

What is intended by "being indescribable?" If what is meant is "different from being (*sat*) and non-being (*asat*)," than such an entity would have no *pramāṇa*, and it would become *aṅrvacaṅya* (indescribable) indeed. What is meant is this? Everything that is an entity is establishable by cognition, and all cognitions are of the nature of either *sat* or *asat*; thus, if you say that its object is neither *sat* nor *asat*, then everything would be the object of every awareness.

5 IMPOSSIBILITY OF FINDING A PROOF FOR THE EXISTENCE OF *AVIDYĀ*[7]

The question is: By what *pramāṇa* is *avidyā* cognized? Avidya cannot be perceived because it is neither real not-real. It cannot be inferred, because inference needs a valid mark or the middle term; *avidyā* lacks this mark. Nor can it be cognized on the authority of the Vedic texts, because Vedas take *avidyā* to be the wonderful power of creation that really belongs to god.

6 IMPOSSIBILITY OF FINDING A PROOF FOR THE REMOVAL OF *AVIDYĀ*

What has been said (by the Advaita Vedāntins)—that ignorance is dispelled by the knowledge of the *brahman*, free from any qualification—is false. Such sentences of the Upaniṣads as "I know this great self, which is of the color of the sun, from behind darkness," etc., come into conflict with the Advaita point of view.

7 IMPOSSIBILITY OF THE REMOVAL OF *AVIDYĀ*

What has been said (by the Advaitins), namely, that the knowledge of the identity of the *brahman* and the self brings about the total cessation of ignorance—that is illogical. Since bondage is real, it cannot be eliminated by knowledge . . . what is more, the knowledge which, according to you, dispels ignorance, is false, it needs another knowledge to negate it, and so on.

7 Rāmānuja's arguments regarding the impossibility of finding a proof for the existence of *avidyā* are too complicated to detail here. For purposes of this work, I have briefly summarized Rāmānuja's arguments in this regard.

Part VI

THE TEACHINGS OF THE *BHAGAVAD GĪTĀ*

14
THE BHAGAVAD *GĪTĀ*

The *Bhagavad Gītā* has acquired a place of incomparable honor in the religious and philosophical literature of India. It is not an exaggeration to say that the *Bhagavad Gītā* is the most well-known and one of the most discussed Hindu texts. The fact that Śaṃkara and Rāmānuja, two important classical commentators of the Vedānta school, regarded the *Gītā* as one of the three primary sources of the Vedānta tradition, provides an eloquent testimony to its importance. Scholars are not unanimous regarding the dates of the *Gītā*; tradition, however, maintains that it was authored somewhere between the third and the first centuries BCE and is taken to be a part of the epic *Mahābhārata*. It is safe to say that it is post-Buddhistic because in it the references to the Buddha's views abound. The *Gītā* expresses the quintessence of the Vedas and the Upaniṣads, and has been translated and commented upon by classical and modern scholars in the East and the West alike. Wilhelm von Humbolt characterizes the *Gītā* as the most beautiful and truly philosophical poem; Mahatma Gandhi calls it the guide and solace of his life; and the poet T. S. Eliot considered the *Gītā as* one of the two most important philosophical poems in world literature, the other being Dante's *Divine Comedy*. Thus, it is not surprising that the *Gītā* has been translated into all the major languages of the world, and there are close to 100 translations of it in English.

To interpret the teachings of the *Gītā* is not an easy task. Many technical terms found in the *Gītā* give interpreters considerable latitude in interpreting its teachings. Different facets of the *Gītā* lend themselves to different interpretations. Translators, in translating and interpreting the *Gītā*, emphasize whichever interpretation suits their metaphysical stance, and make the *Gītā* a gospel of war, of action, of duty, of devotion, or of knowledge to suit their personal agenda. Additionally, the *Gītā* refers to many beliefs of its time, yet does not subscribe to any of these completely. In this chapter, I am going to examine the *Gītā* in its own terms. I will discuss the three paths founds in the *Gītā*: the paths of action, knowledge, and devotion. The primary focus of my attention will be the path of action.

There are eighteen chapters in the *Gītā*. In these chapters, Kṛṣṇa gives metaphysical, religious, and epistemological arguments to Arjuna to persuade him to fight. In response to questions by Arjuna, Kṛṣṇa gradually develops a philosophy of life, consisting of guiding principles for human conduct. In verse seventy three of chapter eighteen, Arjuna informs Kṛṣṇa that his doubts are dispelled, his delusion is destroyed, and that he is prepared to do what is chosen for him by Kṛṣṇa. He will do God's bidding. As a result, Arjuna fights and wins.

To understand the teachings of the *Gītā* adequately, one must have some sense of the setting and the background in which the *Gītā* was composed. Therefore, before I go into the insights that the *Gītā* has to offer, I will give you a flavor of the context and the setting in which this great work was composed.

For the sake of understanding, I have divided this chapter into four sections: Section I discusses the historical context and the setting of the *Gītā*; Section II provides a detailed analysis of the path of action; Section III discusses the paths of knowledge and devotion, and Section IV concludes with remarks about the relationship that exists among the three paths discussed in the *Gītā*.

I The Historical Context and the Setting of the *Gītā*

In format, the *Gītā* consists of a dialogue, which, however, for all practical purposes, is a monologue. The principal speaker is Kṛṣṇa, who, according to the *Gītā*, is an incarnation of the Lord Viṣṇu in human form. Hence, the title "The Song (*Gītā*) of the Lord (*Bhagavad*)." The other speaker in the *Gītā* is Arjuna, one of the five Pandavas, the hero of the epic *Mahābhārata* and the *Gītā*. The enemies of the Pandavas are one hundred Kauravas, the villains. The Kauravas were first cousins of the Pandavas. The Kauravas cheated the Pandavas out of their legitimate kingdom in a gambling match and had them banished to the forest for thirteen years. It was understood that after thirteen years the Pandavas were to return, and then the Kauravas were to return the kingdom to them. During the period of the Pandavas' exile, the Kauravas consolidated their position, made allies with the neighboring kings, and, when the Pandavas returned after completing the term of their exile, and asked for their kingdom, the Kauravas refused to return the kingdom. The Pandavas made every effort to resolve the issue amicably, but failed; thus, the war became inevitable.

The first chapter of the *Gītā* describes the two armies on the eve of the war. Arjuna is sitting on his chariot and Kṛṣṇa is acting as his charioteer. Arjuna sees his teachers, friends, uncles, etc., standing on the opposite side; he is horror stricken by the thought of killing his friends and relatives. Arjuna's dilemma is as follows: he belongs to the *kṣatriya varṇa* (warrior class) which mandates that he fight in an impending war which is righteous; however, his familial duties (*dharmas*) and obligations mandate that he protect his family members. Arjuna is overwhelmed with the thought of killing his kinsmen; he is confused and is not sure of what is his duty in this situation. He lays down his arms in frustration and tells Kṛṣṇa that winning the battle at the cost of killing his own friends, relatives and teachers would bring him no credit. He would in effect be guilty of killing his own relatives, an act that would destroy his family, and he would incur great demerit. He turns to his charioteer, his counselor, Kṛṣṇa (Arjuna was not aware of Kṛṣṇa's real identity at the time), and informs him that he has decided not to fight.

In Arjuna's words[1]:

> I do not wish to kill them, even if I am slain, Kṛṣṇa . . . (1.35)

> The sins of men who destroy the family create disorder in society that undermines the eternal laws of caste and family duty. (1.43)

> The flaw of pity afflicts my entire being and conflicting sacred duties have bewildered my reason; I ask you to tell me decisively—which is better? I am your student, teach me for I have come to you [for instruction]. (2.7)

It is worth recalling here that the meaning of the word "*dharma*" is notoriously varied, and that *dharma* stands for all those virtues and duties which determine a person's relationship to himself/herself, to other persons and to society, to the gods, and to the universe as a whole. Our sources of knowledge of *dharma* are the scriptures and the tradition. The world of *dharma*, therefore, is enormously complex, differentiated, and structured. Taking into view the ancient Hindu belief, which the *Gītā* also articulates, all human beings are divided into four classes depending on a person's aptitudes and abilities. These are the *brahmins*, i.e. priests and scholars, the *kṣatriyas* or the class of warriors, the *vaśyas*, the businessmen, farmers and tradesmen, and the *śūdras* or the class that serves the other three. Each class has a set of duties attached to it. *Dharma* is divided into the virtues and the duties of the members of each class, and also to those virtues and duties that are obligatory for every human being. Thus, it is the duty of a warrior to fight for a noble cause as against the forces of evil. The context of *Bhagavad Gītā* precisely is constituted by the relationship between the two parts of the world of *dharma*: viz., the *dharma* belonging to the specific classes and the *dharma* that is common to all humans. The teachings are, on the face of it, intended to resolve a perceived contradiction between the two.

In response to the question why Arjuna should fight, Kṛṣṇa initially helps Arjuna resolve his dilemma from two standpoints: the absolute and relative. From the ultimate or absolute standpoint, Arjuna is reminded that self is immortal, while the body of any human being is going to be destroyed sooner or later; hence to mourn over those bodies killed in battle is futile. The soul, on the other hand, is immortal; it transcends birth and death. In Kṛṣṇa's words:

> He who believes that this self slays and he,
> who believes that this self is slain,
> both fail to understand;
> the self neither slays nor is slain. (II.19)

The self is neither born, nor does it die,
nor having been can it ever cease to be.
It is unborn, eternal, permanent and primeval.
It is not slain when the body is slain. (II.20)

The Spirit that is in all beings
is immortal in them all;
for the death of what cannot die,
cease to sorrow. (II.30)

Just as a person abandons old clothes, Kṛṣṇa continues, and takes up new ones, so do the selves abandon old bodies and take up new ones. No weapon can pierce this self, fire cannot burn it, water cannot drench it, air cannot dry it. This self is eternal, unmoving, present in everything, unmanifested, unthinkable; so Arjuna should not mourn death. Or, alternately, Kṛṣṇa tells Arjuna, reminding us of the Buddhist view, if you consider this self as being ever-born and ever-dying, still you should not mourn its passing away. For the one who is born, death is a certainty, and the dead will surely be reborn. Arjuna should not mourn for what cannot be otherwise. Thus continuing his understanding of the nature of the soul, Arjuna is eventually asked not to grieve for the possible death of his opponents.

From the relative standpoint, Kṛṣṇa reminds Arjuna that since he (Arjuna) belongs to the warrior class, it is his duty to fight. In Kṛṣṇa's words:

If you fail to wage this war
of sacred duty,
you will abandon your own duty
and fame only to gain evil. (II.22)
. . .
. . .[C]onsidering your own (*sva* = one's own being or nature) duty as a soldier, you must not falter,
there exists no greater good for a warrior
than a war of duty. (II.31)
. . .
But if you do not fight
this righteous war,
then you will abandon your duty and
you will incur sin. (II.33)
. . .
The great warriors will think
that you fled from the war on account of fear
and those who hold you in high esteem
will despise you. (II.35)

Your enemies will slander you,
scorn your skills.
What could be more painful than this? (II.36)

"Duty" (*dharma*) here is taken in its inclusive sense, in the context of its philosophical and religious foundations. In this story, moral and spiritual values are at stake; all amicable means of settlement have failed. It is thus the *dharma* of a soldier to fight in a righteous war in order to establish truth and righteousness, and to restore the moral balance of his society. So doing his *dharma*, fighting in the war, is the only right thing for Arjuna to do.

In short, initially, Kṛṣṇa gives arguments to persuade Arjuna *why* he ought to fight. Kṛṣṇa makes the following points in the verses quoted above:

1 the real self or soul is neither born nor does it die;
2 in killing his kinsmen and friends in a righteous war, Arjuna is not going to incur any sin;
3 if Arjuna did not fight he would gain *karmas*;
4 Arjuna belongs to the warrior class and it is his duty to fight; and, finally,
5 if Arjuna did not fight, he would be considered a coward and would be disgraced by his friends and enemies.

Although Kṛṣṇa begins by pointing out *why* Arjuna ought to fight, very soon in the second canto, Kṛṣṇa changes his tune and explains *how* Arjuna ought to fight, i.e., with what spirit Arjuna ought to fight, and with this Arjuna's thoughts move to *karma yoga*, which I will discuss next.

II *Karma Yoga* (Path of Action)

Kṛṣṇa tells Arjuna to do his duty with a spirit of detachment, without any desire to receive any benefits. Let us, once again, listen to Kṛṣṇa's words:

On action alone be your interest never on its fruit. Let not the fruits of actions be your motive *nor your attachment to inaction* (II.47)

Perform action that is necessary; it (action) *is more powerful than inaction*. . . . (III.6)

Always perform without attachment, any action that must be done.
Because in performing action with detachment, one achieves supreme good. (III.19)

Abandoning all attachments to the fruits of action, ever content, independent,
he does not do anything whatsoever even when he is engaged in action. (IV.20)
. . .

> Disciplined in discipline, he purifies, self-subdued masters his senses, unites himself with the self of all, *he is not contaminated though he works.* (V.7)

> Treating alike (*sama*) pleasure and pain, gain and loss, success and defeat, get ready for the battle, you shall not incur any sin. (II.38)

The verses translated above express the crux of the path of action outlined in the *Gītā*. In terms of action, Kṛṣṇa asks Arjuna to perform actions without any desire for the fruits of the action for himself. In other words, actions must be done from a sense of *dharma* without any desire to gain benefits. Desires and passions can lead a person astray, lead a person to perform selfish actions, while performance of *dharma* without any attachment to their *consequences* purifies the self and leads to *mokṣa*.

Let us discuss what the *Gītā* means by "consequences" (*phala*). Kṛṣṇa repeatedly asks Arjuna to remain non-attached (to consequences), and asks him to perform his *dharma*, that performance of duty without desires, leads to *mokṣa*. There are ample examples of this in history. Kings like Janaka and Aśvapati achieved *mokṣa* by performing action without any desire for consequences. Additionally, one may be inspired by the idea that one's own performance of duties would set an example for others to emulate. In giving this advice to Arjuna, Kṛṣṇa gives Arjuna his own example and points out that he engages in action for the good of humankind (*lokasaṃgraha*), that if he did not engage in desireless actions, human beings may follow him and become renunciants, which would create confusion among humankind. Additionally, he asks Arjuna to do his duty with the spirit of rendering it as an offer to the "highest lord," and without any desire for the consequences for himself, without a sense of "I," "mine," "hate," jealousy," pleasure, and "pain," etc. Kṛṣṇa goes even a step further, and points out that it is more important for one to do the duties of one's own *varṇa*, no matter how imperfectly done, than to do the superior performance of the duty of another *varṇa*:

> It is better to perform one's own duty though void of merit, than the superior performance of the duties of another caste; better to die while doing one's own duty, perilous is the duty of other human beings. (III.35)

He reiterates this point when he says:

> It is better to do one's own duty, though devoid of merit, than to do another's, however well performed. By doing the duty prescribed by one's own nature a person does not accumulate any *karma*s. (XVIII.47)

Let me sum up the main points of Kṛṣṇa's discourse:

1 One should do one's duty for its own sake without being attached to its consequences.
2 You may do your duty in the spirit of *lokasaṃgraha*.
3 Perform your own *dharma*, and not that of another person

Let me briefly comment on these three. First, the *Gītā*'s thesis of doing duty for duty's sake has had many followers, the most notable among them is Gandhi. This thesis, however, has given rise to numerous problems.

An important question arises: How to understand the principle of doing your duty for duty's sake? It has been held by some scholars (e.g., Hegel) that it is not possible to eliminate the desire for consequences and still go on performing action. Consider the case of a physician or a surgeon who treats a patient. Should he not desire that his treatment cure the patient? Is the *Gītā* asserting that the surgeon should do his duty of treating his patient without any consideration of the likely results that might follow from his treatment of the patient? Or is the *Gītā* asserting that the surgeon's efforts should be directed towards curing the patient? Would the second alternative amount to saying that the surgeon is interested in the consequences? Is it not rather the case that a doctor or a physician indifferent to what his treatment yields give rise to the judgment that the doctor does not care?

I would suggest two replies both intended by the *Gītā*. The first is a straightforward reply which makes a distinction between consequences for the patient irrespective of whether he is cured or not and consequences for the doctor himself. By "fruits" the *Gītā* and the Indian psychology of action generally means the latter, as is borne out by verse II.38 given above.

In other words, the *Gītā* recommends that the physician should not be motivated by the likely consequences for herself (viz., whether she suffers financial loss, makes profit, or whether she receives praise or blame for her success or failure as the case may be). This is true inner freedom, non-attachment, but she should not be indifferent to whether her treatment cures the patient or hurts her. To be a responsible agent the latter concern is important, while the concern about her own fortune is not.

The second answer is a little more difficult, not exactly stated in the *Gītā* but may nevertheless be taken to be not only compatible with the teachings of the *Gītā* but needed for it to hold good. This reply would require asking what constitutes the identity of an action. The identity of an action depends upon how far the action he performs extends. In the example under consideration, the identity of an action extends up to curing the patient, but not to money, fame, and fortune. In other words, curing the patient is a constituent of what a surgeon is supposed to do, and these constituents are not the "consequences" that the *Gītā* has in mind. Kṛṣṇa recommends that the surgeon should be indifferent to the external consequences for himself, e.g., money, pleasure and pain, success, and defeat, etc. One should not be attached to these feelings because their pull over the human mind is very strong.

The second issue is, does working for *lokasaṃgraha* contradict the themes that the agent should do his duty for the sake of duty and not for any consequence *for himself*? I will argue in the same way as above that what Kṛṣṇa recommends is that a *karma yogin* does not aim at his own success or failure. One way this can be achieved is by aiming at the good of humankind (of the community included), but not for his own benefit. The larger the goal one entertains, the lesser would be the concern for the agent's own fortune and fame.

An analysis of an action may be undertaken to make the point: agent → motivation → action → consequence—for oneself or for another. Kṛṣṇa says that the agent should not be motivated by the thought of benefit for himself, rather the thought of consequences for others (the patient, the community, humankind, etc.) should be the motive.

Finally, how are we to construe the point about *svadharma*? A traditional construal holds that a person's *svadharma* is determined by his *varṇa*. If he is a *kṣatriya*, his *svadharma* is to fight for a righteous cause. But such a construal takes away from the *Gītā* the universality of its message, and makes it relative to the Hindu *varṇa*-bound duty. I would prefer to say that *svadharma* signifies that each person has his "station in society and the duties attached to it." In that case, *svadharma* would mean the individual's *own dharma*, something along the line of Bradley's idea of "my station and its duties."

To all these, I will add another point which distinguishes the *Gītā's* conception of duty from that of Kant. It appears as though *Gītā's karma yoga* is very Kantian in spirit. But unlike Kant, the *Gītā* does not give any criteria of a person's duty. Kant's three formulations of Categorical Imperatives help us to determine whether a purported course of action is a duty or not. The *Gītā* does not provide any such criteria for deciding what is my duty. It is assumed that every person knows his duty. The *Gītā* focuses on *how* one should do one's duty. I should perform my duty in the true spirit, with the right attitude, and never because it helps me or serves my own interest. Unlike Kant, the *Gītā* gives no formal criteria of duty. The source of duty in the *Gītā* is tradition, whereas in Kant it is reason. With this in mind, let us move to the path of knowledge.

III *Jñāna Marga* (The Path of Knowledge) and *Bhakti Marga* (The Path of Devotion)

"*Jñāna*" means "knowledge," "understanding," and "intuition," and when used in conjunction with the word "*yoga*," signifies the path that helps intellectuals attain self-realization (*mokṣa*); it prescribes a rigorous intellectual discipline. Advaita Vedānta school recommends the aspirants to follow this path to realize the *brahman*.

The path of knowledge is of primary concern in the following verses: II.54–72; IV.33–42; V.13–29; VII.I–30. At the beginning of the *Gītā*, to persuade Arjuna to fight, as we have already seen, Kṛṣṇa makes a distinction between what is mortal and what is immortal or eternal. Such a person is a truly wise person.[2] A wise person not only understands this distinction in theory, but also implements it in practice. A wise person is courageous; his courage comes from within. It is the courage of wisdom, courage to do the right thing, courage to endure. Such a person is not affected by the rise and fall of material things; he is not affected by cold and warmth, success and failure, pleasure and pain. Of such persons, all the *karma*s are burnt by the fire of knowledge.

Thus, from the standpoint of knowledge, Kṛṣṇa reminds Arjuna that the soul is immortal, it never dies. The body, on the other hand, is going to be destroyed upon death.[3] By pointing out the inevitability of the destruction of the physical body and the impossibility of the destruction of the immortal soul, Kṛṣṇa asks Arjuna to remain firm in the discharge of his duty. Such a knower rises above the vicissitudes of everyday concerns of life and is not affected by pleasure and pain. Kṛṣṇa says:

> The wise man, O' Arjuna, remains equal in pain and pleasure, and, who is not troubled by these; he indeed is fit to attain immortality (self-realization). (II.15)

Another sense of knowledge in the *Gītā* is knowledge of Kṛṣṇa as the lord of the universe. In Advaita Vedānta, the absolute reality, the *brahman*, is said to be the first principle; in the *Gītā*, on the other hand, Kṛṣṇa is said to be the origin of everything[4] and a person is asked to know Kṛṣṇa's majesty, and to be attached to Kṛṣṇa. Kṛṣṇa says:

> At all times think of me while fighting, with your mind and intellect focused on me you will come to me without any doubt. (VIII.7)

To sum up: Knowledge is used in at least two different senses in the *Gītā*: (1) the knowledge of distinction between the lower or mortal self and the higher or the immortal self, and (2) the knowledge of Kṛṣṇa as the higher self, the lord of the universe. In other words, in the *Gītā*, Kṛṣṇa is identified with the higher self. Meditation helps one to realize the distinction between the mortal self and the immortal self.

The path of devotion is another path found in the *Gītā*. "*Bhakti*," means "devotion," "love," and signifies an intense relationship with which one approaches the divine. It is loving worship of a specific chosen deity; in the *Gītā*, it refers to Kṛṣṇa. Kṛṣṇa tells Arjuna that a *jīva* is saved by keeping in mind the highest lord, *parameśvara*, "that human beings who are focused on my cosmic form, whose hearts are devoted to me and spend days and nights in this state, in my opinion, are the best *yogis*. Such persons offer all their actions to me, think of me as worth worshipping as the highest, their minds are entirely preoccupied with me, and these *bhaktas* are saved by me from the ocean of *saṃsāra*." So, Kṛṣṇa asks Arjuna to focus his mind and intellect on him, and that if he is able to do it, there is no doubt that after death, Arjuna would obtain an existence in Kṛṣṇa. In Kṛṣṇa's words:

A man who dies meditating on me;
At the time of death enters my being;
When he is freed from the body;
There is no doubt of this. (VIII.5)
. . .
Revere with unswerving thoughts;
Knowing me as the origin of all beings (IX.13)

Gītā emphatically declares that those who do not worship Kṛṣṇa cannot attain *mokṣa*, and asks for single-minded devotion to Kṛṣṇa.

Kṛṣṇa, however, does not stop at this; he goes a step further and states that the worship of other Hindu deities is wrong, and that individuals worship other deities because they do not have the true knowledge. By worshipping other gods, one does not receive any benefits, though one might wrongly believe that he is receiving benefits. In reality, any benefit a worshipper receives comes from Kṛṣṇa. Worship of other gods takes one deeper and deeper in the world of ignorance which is characterized by rebirth. Again, those who follow the Vedas do not attain *mokṣa*. At places, the *Gītā* even asserts that other deities and gods are ignorant of the knowledge of Kṛṣṇa, which, in the final analysis, leads to liberation.[5] Kṛṣṇa recommends "*abhyāsa-yoga*," i.e., repeated practice of fixing the mind on Kṛṣṇa, however, if Arjuna is not able to do that then he should dedicate all his actions to Kṛṣṇa. Only by working for Kṛṣṇa, Arjuna will gradually purify his mind and attain *mokṣa*.

The *Gītā* also articulates the nature of a true devotee or *bhakta*. A true devotee has no jealousy for any living being; he is friendly towards all, and is free from the sense of "I" and "mine," free from attachments to pleasure and pain, and his mind is always focused on Kṛṣṇa. Such a person is Kṛṣṇa's dearest devotee. Kṛṣṇa provides in a series of verses his criteria of a true *bhakta*.

IV Relationship among the Paths

The question is often asked: What is the central teaching of the *Gītā*? Which one of the three paths is primary? Is it *karma yoga* (path of action), or *jñāna yoga* (path of knowledge), and *bhakti yoga* (path of devotion)? Given that the concluding chapter of the *Gītā* explains devotion as the highest achievement, and emphasizes that one attains *mokṣa* through devotion, many scholars claim that the *bhakti yoga* is the most important path of the three paths discussed in the *Gītā*. On my interpretation, the *Gītā* does not favor one path over the other, rather that the central teaching is a synthesis of the three paths discussed in the *Gītā*.

In order to understand the relationship that exists among these three paths, one must keep in mind that the two paths, those of action and of knowledge (*jñāna*), had already been advanced as two paths to spiritual freedom in Hinduism. The Vedic religion focused on the path of action (action understood in the narrow sense of ritualistic actions) as undertaking all obligations in the world, while the path of knowledge, inspired by the Upaniṣads, focused on the renunciation of worldly roles and duties. One of Kṛṣṇa's achievements in the *Gītā* lies in breaking down the opposition between these two paths. At the same time, another path, perhaps more recent in origin, called "Kṛṣṇa Vasudeva cult," had already made its appearance. Kṛṣṇa adds this path, i.e., the path of devotion, to the other two paths. Thus, one finds three paths in the *Gītā*: *karma yoga* (path of action), *jñāna yoga* (path of knowledge), and *bhakti yoga* (path of devotion). These three paths are not mutually exclusive alternatives; rather, they complement each other. Let me elaborate on this point.

For example, Kṛṣṇa tells Arjuna that knowledge consists in attaining the attitudes appropriate to further actions without any attachment to results; it consists in removing one's attention from the lower self and focusing on the higher self. This knowledge allows a person to perform actions without any desire for the fruits of the actions, which shows that the paths of knowledge and action go together. Kṛṣṇa says: "One who is able to turn his mind inwards and finds contentment in the self is the person who loses interest in actions and is able to perform actions without any desire for the results of the actions."[6] In other words, action and knowledge are not opposed to each other; rather, the former is not possible without the latter. In order to act without any desire for the results of the actions, one must have the right attitude. This attitude comes by way of an understanding that only the empirical self performs actions, and that the real self is not an actor per se. Kṛṣṇa says:

> He—who, treats alike pleasure and pain, is given to contemplation with firm resolve without any sense of ownership and attachments, is dedicated to me—is dear to me. (XII.18–19)

Only a true *jñānī* (knower) can turn his attention inwards, find contentment in the self, and has the ability to perform actions without any desire for the fruits of actions. He treats alike enemy and friend, honor and dishonor, cold and heat, pleasure and pain, and is free from attachment. He is neutral to praise and blame, restrained in speech, and content in whatever happens.

Again, when Kṛṣṇa at the end of the fourth chapter exhorts Arjuna to do his duty, and Arjuna cannot muster the courage to do so, Kṛṣṇa suggests that Arjuna should use meditation to gain victory over his desires and passions, i.e., his lower self. Thus, non-attached actions are to be accompanied by meditation in order to gain knowledge of the distinction between the empirical self and the supreme self. Devotion to Kṛṣṇa helps an aspirant realize that the lower self performs actions, by the lower nature of Kṛṣṇa. Here, devotion must be accompanied by both knowledge and action. Kṛṣṇa says:

> Surrendering all actions to me,
> Fixing your mind on your higher self

> Having no desires and selfishness;
> Fight, surrendering this fever. (III.30)

Thus, devotion is an important aspect of action[7] and is related to knowledge.[8] Knowledge and action along with devotion are also called worship.[9]

In short, the practice of *karma yoga* does involve, in the long run, knowledge and *bhakti*, just as practice of *jñāna yoga* also involves practice of selfless action and whole-hearted devotion. Likewise, a true and dedicated devotee needs no less to perform selfless action and eventually to know the *brahman*. Thus while one can distinguish between the three paths, the matter is actually more complicated. We can therefore formulate the situation thus.

How one should begin one's spiritual life depends upon the kind of person one is. One may begin with action, pursue the ideal of selfless action, but in course of that pursuit be drawn into knowledge of the one and an attitude of devotion towards the one being. Likewise, if a person is of contemplative sort, he would find it in accord with his nature to begin with *jñāna yoga*, and while he will find it in accord with his nature to begin with *jñāna yoga*, and while pursuing knowledge will be involved in *karma* in the true spirit as well as in devotion to his own god. But he may begin with *bhakti* and be led to traverse the other two paths as well. Thus the three paths all come together irrespective of where one chooses to begin, consistently with his own nature.

In summary, the *Gītā* does not speak of three mutually exclusive paths to spiritual freedom, but rather synthesizes all three in one path. One may begin with any of these paths; however, the path that leads to the attainment of *mokṣa* includes non-attached actions, knowledge of the distinction between the lower and the higher self, and single-minded devotion to the supreme self. It is wrong to interpret the *Gītā* merely in terms of caste duty; it is universal in its scope and has a message for the role of humankind insofar as it tells us to do our duty without any desire to get the benefits from it, by renouncing selfish desires. Although the path with which one starts his journey depends upon his psychological make-up (in Arjuna's case, it is *karma yoga*), the aspirant has to go through the other two before reaching the goal. Śrī Aurobindo, a contemporary Vedāntin, calls the integration of these seemingly different paths "Integral Yoga."

The three paths are unified on the basis of the conception of highest reality as the highest *brahman* or the highest puruṣa (*puruṣottama*) which the *Gītā* develops. In this conception, Sāṃkhya and Vedānta are unified. The Sāṃkhya, as is well known, admits two principles: *puruṣa* and *prakṛti*. The *puruṣas* are many, i.e., these are many individual selves. *Prakṛti* is one Nature, a complex of three *guṇas*, *sattva*, *rajas*, and *tamas*. The Vedānta recognizes the highest Being to be *brahman* or pure consciousness, and synthesizes these two ancient philosophies. The unity of the *Gītā* may be represented by the following figure:

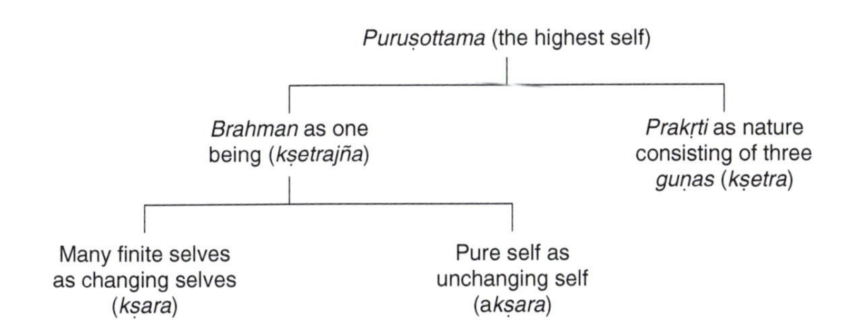

Figure 14.1

Traditional Vedanta and Sāṃkhya, in this scheme, are synthesized under integral Vedānta. Thus it is not surprising that all through the ages, the *Gītā* has been accorded one of the highest places in the religious and philosophical literatures of the Hindus.

It is unfortunate that the topic of caste duty obscures the universality of the *Gītā*'s message. The context of the Hindu life of those days introduced the theme of caste, but nothing in the *Gītā's* teaching requires that it be dependent on that context. The message is universal. Arjuna's situation represents a universal situation, a "moral dilemma" and the consequent breakdown of conventional moral ideas, requiring a transition to religion and spirituality.

Part VII

MODERN INDIAN THOUGHT

15

MODERN INDIAN THOUGHT

The classical philosophical systems had reached their high point by the time the British rule in India began. The Sanskrit pundits continued to instruct students in the classical systems, and no new major innovation seemed to be in the offing. These Sanskrit scholars applied themselves to the school of Navya-Nyāya (new logic); outstanding scholars devoted themselves to teaching and writing about this school. However, no major works were published, although it does seem that a whole lot of "private papers," known as "*kroḍapatra*" continued to accumulate.[1] Students used them to defend their own positions and criticize their opponents. Lineage of such students traced back their ancestry to great pandits. How far new philosophical innovations were made, is hard to say.

In the nineteenth century, with the spread of English education, scholars well versed in Western philosophy and the English language appeared on the Indian philosophical scene. Some of these scholars learned Sanskrit and read original Sanskrit texts of the classical past, but still wrote in English, comparing Indian philosophies to Western philosophers. As a result, a discipline called "comparative philosophy" came into existence.

The political, social, and economic effects of the British rule on India were far more profound. Tension between the forces of tradition—through which the Indian culture had grown—and the forces of modernity had increased. The Hindu intelligentsia found themselves in an ambiguous situation; there was an awareness of the sense of responsibility to its own culture as well as a sense of distance from it. They studied, absorbed, and understood the Western social and political concepts, and seized this opportunity to demonstrate that Indian philosophy is as great as any other philosophies.

As a result, there arose a wide spectrum of social reformers, philosophers, political leaders, religious innovators, and cultural critics, such as Vivekananda, Raja Rammohan Roy, Aurobindo, Tilak, K. C. Bhattacharyya, Tagore, Seal, Halder, Gandhi. Some of these figures were not professional philosophers, but educated, literate, action-oriented public figures. Nevertheless, their ideas are of great significance even for academic philosophy. The fact that Tagore, a poet and a non-academic figure, was elected as the President of the first Indian

Philosophical Congress in 1925 testifies to the importance and impact of such figures in India.

In this essay, it is not possible to discuss all these figures and their contributions. I will only discuss two figures: K. C. Bhattacharyya and Śrī Aurobindo, the latter of whom was not a professional philosopher. Both Bhattacharyya and Śrī Aurobindo belonged to the pre-independence era. These two individuals influenced the modern minds at many different levels and in many different ways. They brought to the forefront the fact that modern Hindu intelligentsia, while professing loyalty to its own tradition, transformed the Hindu tradition, perhaps partly under the influence of Western thinking and partly to meet social and political challenges of the day. These individuals re-read, re-understood, and re-interpreted the Vedānta school, which influenced not only the philosophical, but also the religious, political, and social thinking of Hindu minds. Thus it is safe to say that Vedanta, especially Advaita Vedānta, has played an important role in the self-understanding of modern Hindu intelligentsia.

K. C. Bhattacharyya

It is not an exaggeration to say that K. C. Bhattacharyya is one of the leading contemporary Indian philosophers. Although all of K. C. Bhattacharyya's published works are contained in two volumes of *Studies in Philosophy*,[2] one can say that the pages of these two volumes are filled with original thoughts on many topics spanning the entire range of Indian and Western philosophy. Bhattacharyya had carefully studied ancient Indian philosophical schools, e.g., Advaita Vedānta, Sāṃkhya-Yoga, and Jainism. He was also very well versed in classical German philosophies, especially of Kant and Hegel. In his philosophy, one finds an assimilation of both Eastern and Western philosophies. The goal of his philosophy was neither to espouse a particular philosophical perspective nor to provide a defense of any particular *darśana* of Indian philosophy. One marvels at his understanding of philosophers Indian and Western alike, as well as at the originality of his thought.

Kalidas Bhattacharyya,[3] the youngest son of K. C. Bhattacharyya, divides his father's philosophy into three phases: the first stage extends from 1914 to 1918, during which he published three papers: "Some Aspects of Negation," "The Place of the Indefinite in Logic," and "The Definition of Relation as a Category of Existence."[4] The second stage extends from 1925 to 1934,[5] during which he published five papers and his monograph entitled *The Subject as Freedom*. The five papers are "Śaṃkara's Doctrine of Māyā," "Knowledge and Truth," "Correction of Error as a Logical Process," "Fact and the Thought of the Fact," and "The False and the Subjective." The third stage, the shortest of the three, lasted a little more than a year (1939), during which he published three papers: "The Concept of Philosophy", "The Absolute and its Alternative Forms," and "The Concept of Value."[6]

In this brief essay on Bhattacharyya's philosophy, it is not possible to do justice to all the issues that his philosophy raises. I am going to focus on the concept of "absolute" in Bhattacharyya's philosophy. Limiting this essay to the concept of the absolute makes sense for many reasons, and I will name only a few. Bhattacharyya discusses this concept in two of his articles, viz., "The Concept of Philosophy" and "The Absolute and its Alternative Forms." These articles appeared in the third and the final phase, the richest and most profound phase of his writings, and reflect the culmination of his philosophical thinking. Secondly, Bhattacharyya's concept of the three absolutes is strikingly original and is a unique contribution to the philosophical world the world over. Thirdly, the search for the absolute has been the primary concern of Indian philosophy from the Upaniṣads (600–300 BCE) to the neo-Vedānta of the twentieth century via the classical Vedānta of Śaṃkara and Rāmānuja. By focusing on this concept, we would get a better understanding of how the concept of "Absolute" developed in the entire spectrum of Indian philosophy. Finally, discussion of this concept would not only show how Bhattacharyya's philosophy fits into Indian philosophy historically, but would also show the development of his philosophy through three phases insofar as Bhattacharyya discusses absolute as "indefinite" (first phase), "freedom" (second phase), and "alternation" (third phase).

The Absolute as Indefinite

Those of us who are familiar with Bhattacharyya's philosophy know very well that he was very much influenced by Jaina logic. Bhattacharyya's conception of the absolute as indefinite follows his interpretation of the Jaina theory of *anekāntavāda.* In his article, "The Jaina Theory of *Anekānta*," Bhattacharyya shows that neither the category of "identity" nor of "difference" is basic to philosophy and that the alternation of the two is more satisfactory. At the outset, Bhattacharyya notes: "The Jaina theory of *anekānta* or the manifoldness of truth is a form of realism which not only asserts a plurality of truths but also takes each truth to be an indetermination of alternative truths."[7] He further adds that the purpose of his paper is "to discuss the conception of a plurality of determinate truths to which ordinary realism appears to be committed and to show the necessity of an indeterministic extension such as is presented by Jaina logic . . ."[8]

Bhattacharyya analyzes the definite and the indefinite and, from the contrast between the two, deduces the seven modes of truth. To say that from one perspective a determinate existent X *is* and from another perspective *is not,* does not imply that X is X and is not Y. It rather means that an existent X, as an existent universal, is distinct from itself as a particular. Accordingly, every mode of truth is a determinate truth as well as an indetermination of other possibilities or alternative modes of truth. These modes of truth, argues Bhattacharyya, are not merely many truths but "*alternative* truths."[9] From one perspective, X is existent; from another perspective, X is non-existent; however, when X is viewed as existent and non-existent simultaneously, it becomes indescribable (*avaktavya*); there exists an "undifferenced togetherness" between the two, which Bhattacharyya calls "indefinite." Each mode of truth, as an alternative to others, is objective.

Bhattacharyya applies the above conception of the definite and indefinite to the concept of "*brahman*." The Upaniṣads, as we know, identify a single, comprehensive, fundamental principle by knowing which everything else in this world becomes known. This fundamental principle, *brahman* or absolute, defies all characterizations. BU categorically asserts that there is no other or better description of the *brahman* than *neti, neti* ("not this," "not this"). In the classical non-dualist Vedānta of Śaṃkara, the *brahman*, or the Absolute, is that state where all subject/object distinction is obliterated. The *brahman* simply *is*. Bhattacharyya takes for his point of departure this consciousness that transcends both the subjective and the objective. Since this principle cannot be defined in terms of the objective and its correlate, the subjective, he calls it the "indefinite." Given that the absolute is not limited (not definite), it can only be indefinite. In other words, both the subjective and the objective belong to the realm of the definite, and that which transcends both is the indefinite.

Every definite content of experience, holds Bhattacharyya, implies an indefinite out of which it is carved. The indefinite points to a primary distinction between the definite and the indefinite, the known and the unknown: "the indefinite *is not* and *is* indefinite at once."[10] To put it differently, "the indefinite and the definite *are* and *are not* one." The line between the definite and the indefinite is itself indefinable; the definite, being a mode of the indefinite, embodies the indefinite.

Bhattacharyya does not discuss the question whether absolute exists; he rather attempts to understand it. Paradoxically, it is understood as that which cannot be understood; it is indefinite (not comprehensible) and definite (somehow comprehensible) at once. Bhattacharyya was well aware that this logical absolute as indefinite cannot be an object of one's experiences, that in order for it to be the basis of objects, it must be understood as the subject of our experiences. Thus it is not surprising that he does not rest satisfied with the logical absolute, and eventually takes a psychological approach in which the absolute as indefinite is construed as the absolute as subject or freedom.

The Absolute as Subject or Freedom

The most comprehensive statement of the absolute as freedom is analyzed in the work *The Subject as Freedom*, which was written long before Bhattacharyya wrote the articles "The Concept of Philosophy" and "Alternative Forms of the Absolute." In this work, Bhattacharyya begins with an analysis of the distinction between the object and the subject. "Object" is what is meant by the "subject;" the "subject" is other than the object. When one knows an object, one becomes aware of the meaning of the term "object." Thus, the word "this" may be taken to symbolize the object. When one uses the word "this" to signify a specific object, others also use "this" to denote the same particular object. Thus, the pronoun "this" has a general meaning and both the speaker and the hearer use it to refer to an object. The subject, on the other hand, is not meant; it has no universally accepted meaning. When Paul uses "I," he uses it to refer to Paul, but when Timothy uses "I," he uses it to refer to Timothy, not Paul. The word "I," argues Bhattacharyya, symbolizes the subject, so he prefers the word "I" to both "you" and "he."

The distinction between these two symbols "this" and "I" throws light on the important distinction between the subjective and the objective. The point that Bhattacharyya is trying to make is as follows: the subject is not a meant entity. The word "this" symbolizes an object and has a generality about it. However, the same does not characterize the word "I" which is neither singular nor general; it is rather both singular and general. "I" takes on generality insofar as each speaker uses it, although in the singular, because each speaker uses it for himself or herself only. Thus, though the subject sometimes may be spoken of as an object, it is not meant as an object. In other words, when the subject is understood through the word "I," it is not known as the meaning of the word. It is possible to objectify the subject, but the objectification cannot be a determinant of the subject. When one refers to the subject as the object, the subject does not become the object. Moreover, the reality of what is meant can always be doubted. In Bhattacharyya's words: ". . . the object is not known with the same assurance as the subject that cannot be said to be meant. There may be such a thing as an illusory object."[11]

After articulating subjectivity as an awareness of the subject's distinction from the object, Bhattacharyya distinguishes between three stages of subjectivity. In the first stage, the self identifies itself with the body; in the second, the self identifies with the images and thoughts; and in the third, initially there is a feeling of freedom from all actual and possible thoughts, which is followed by an awareness of the subject as "I" in introspection, eventually leading one beyond introspection to complete subjectivity or freedom.

The different stages of subjectivity are reached progressively: the denial of the preceding gives rise to the succeeding stage until there is nothing left to deny. At each stage there is an inner "demand" to go beyond that stage. It is important to note that the introspection of the subject as the "I" is the realization of the free nature of the subject, where one has an awareness of the subject's freedom. However, this awareness must be denied to make way for complete freedom. Bhattacharyya here is making an important distinction between the "subject as free" and "subject as freedom"; the former being the introspective stage of subjectivity and the latter the ultimate stage, the ideal, the subject's ultimate goal.

At this juncture, one might ask why assume this subjective attitude? Assuming that it does lead to freedom, can one not make a similar case for the objective attitude? He discusses some of these issues in his articles "The Concept of the Absolute and Its Alternative Forms" and "The Concept of Philosophy."

The Absolute as Alternation

At the outset of his paper on the absolute as alternation, Bhattacharyya informs his readers that philosophy begins in reflective consciousness, i.e., an awareness of the relationship between reflective consciousness and its content.[12] Reflective consciousness and its content imply each other, and he takes this relation of "implicational dualism" as the starting point to discuss his concept of "alternative absolutes."

Using Kantian distinction between the "forms of consciousness," Bhattacharyya argues that consciousness functions diversely, better yet alternately, as knowing, willing, and feeling. The implicational dualism, i.e., the relation between consciousness and content is different in each case. In knowing, the content is not constituted by consciousness; in willing, it is constituted by consciousness; and in feeling, the content constitutes a sort of unity with consciousness. In each attitude the dualism of the content and consciousness can be overcome; consequently, each has its own formulation of the absolute. There are three absolutes corresponding to three forms of consciousness: knowing, willing, and feeling, in K. C. Bhattacharyya's words, "truth, reality (or freedom) and value."[13] In knowing, the content is freed from consciousness and the absolute is truth. In willing, consciousness is freed from content and the absolute is freedom. In feeling, there is a consciousness of unity and the absolute is value. The Absolute, when freed from this trifold implicational dualism, by its very nature has to be understood in a triple way. Let us examine it further.

The Absolute as Truth

In knowing, the object of knowledge stands independent of the act of knowing. The content is "unconstituted by consciousness." "It may, accordingly, be (loosely) called a known no-content. It is explicitly known as what known content is not."[14] The act of knowing, rather, discovers the object. Thus, in Bhattacharyya's view, the realistic position is closer to the phenomena than idealism. The known content need not be known, which explains why Bhattacharyya even asserts that to know an object is to know a timeless truth. "The object may be temporal but that it is in time is not itself a temporal fact."[15] Thus, according to K. C. Bhattacharyya, the realist's definition of knowledge is valid, but what is claimed to be known may not really be known in the realist's sense of the term.

Space limitation does not permit me to make an in-depth examination of how the process of knowing leads to the absolute as truth, because that would necessitate a detailed study of the issues discussed in his article "The Concept of Philosophy." For our purposes, the following will suffice. In this article,

Bhattacharyya argues that the task of philosophy is the justification of beliefs by a "higher kind of knowledge" which can be arrived at by analyzing speech and thinking. Speech and thinking admit of grades. As a result, we get the grades of thought and the grades of thinking corresponding to each other and pointing to grades of theoretic consciousness.[16] The belief that "The absolute is" is implied in the theoretic consciousness of "I am not." The denial of "I" is possible because of our belief in the absolute.

By "thought," Bhattacharyya means all forms of theoretic consciousness involving the understanding of a speakable. Philosophy presents beliefs that are speakable and are an expression of the theoretic consciousness, which as an understanding of the speakable, consist of the four grades of thought: empirical thought, contemplative thought or pure objective thought, spiritual thought, and transcendental thought. In empirical thought, the content refers to an object perceived or imagined to be perceived. Such reference constitutes a part of the meaning of its content. Pure objective thought involves reference to an object but not necessarily to a perceived object. Subjective or spiritual thought does not involve any reference to an object. It is therefore purely subjective. Transcendental thought is the consciousness of a content that is neither subjective nor objective. It refers neither to things, nor to universals, nor to individuals, but rather to absolute truth.

Science deals with the content of empirical thought which Bhattacharyya calls "*fact*." The other three thoughts have contents which are either self-evident, objective contents, or truth, or reality. In science, the content, according to Bhattacharyya, is literally speakable. In the pure objective attitude of philosophy, the contents "demand" to be known, but are not actually known. Here we get metaphysics or philosophy of an object. The third level of thinking is philosophy of the subject, and in the fourth and the final kind, we have philosophy of truth.

This distinction among the various grades of theoretic consciousness is of serious import since Bhattacharyya's philosophy is concerned not with the first but with the last three grades of theoretic consciousness. The last three stages are not, in fact, entirely different from each other and, according to Bhattacharyya, one stage necessarily leads to the next. The absolute is reached through a series of denials. Each earlier stage is negated, and each negation leads to the formation of the beliefs contained within the next higher stage.

Whereas the spiritual reality is symbolized as "I" and expressed literally as self, truth is symbolized as "not I" and is therefore not reality, not to be enjoyed, and not literally expressible. For Bhattacharyya, truth is "being spoken as what I is not."[17] Consequently, it is not identical with the self as Advaita Vedānta maintains, but is definable as what the self is not. The last stage is beyond negation since the theoretic denial of the self in the form "I am not" leaves one remainder. What remains to make such self-denial possible is the Absolute. As an undeniable being, the absolute is truth. The absolute does not have anything outside from which to be distinguished. Truth is the absolute but the absolute is not the only truth. It can be distinguished from alternative forms of itself. As undeniable being it may be truth, or as the limit of all transcending negating processes it may be freedom, or as their indeterminate togetherness, it may be value.

Absolute as Reality (or Freedom)

The second is the absolute of willing. In this absolute, the content is constituted by willing. Willing is active; it is constructive. In the absence of willing this absolute is nothing; it is understood as a negation of being. Willing, as a matter of fact, is willing of itself which in reality is its denial. When a will is satisfied, it is superseded, and in that sense denied.

The process of willing, which leads to the absolute as freedom, is analyzed in the work *The Subject as Freedom*, which I have already discussed. In this work, no clear distinction has been made between knowing and willing, resulting in the impression that the absolute as freedom is also the absolute as truth. In "The Concept of Philosophy," as has been explained earlier, the pursuit moves from empirical fact to self-subsistent object, from objectivity to subjectivity, and from subjectivity to the truth. Thus, the individual self is transcended in favor of truth, and the absolute object is more fundamental than facts or universals. In the work, *The Subject as Freedom,* the individual self is transcended in favor of the subject, the "I," which in turn is transcended in favor of freedom itself.

The Absolute as Value

The third is the absolute of feeling and the matter is quite different in the case of feeling. The beautiful object appears as beautiful in feeling, and "shines as a self subsistent something," distinct from its knowable parts. In other words, there is a unity free from the duality of content and consciousness. It is a content "that is indefinitely other than consciousness" or consciousness "that is indefinitely other than content." The term "indefinitely," for Bhattacharyya signifies that the absolute of feeling is indifferent to both being and non-being, and accordingly, the absolute is transcendent. Value is the unity of the felt content and its feeling. It is different from its knowable relations and its relation to its parts. This is how Bhattacharyya suggested we should understand the being of value.

Felt content, though not definite in itself, is understood "*as though* it were a unity."[18] Reflection demands such a unity. The realist position that the value is objective and the idealist position that the value is subjective are not preferable and their alternation is stopped when the unity becomes definite. "The unity of felt content and feeling may be understood as content that is indefinitely other than consciousness or as consciousness that is indefinitely other than the content."[19] Value as such is unity which is the indetermination of content and consciousness and not identity. This relation defines the absolute of feeling.

Concluding Reflections

Bhattacharyya's thesis of the triple absolutes is indeed unique, interesting, and thought provoking. The absolute of knowing may be understood as truth, the absolute of willing as freedom, and the absolute of feeling as value. The triple absolute is the prototype of three subjective functions, which are mixed in our everyday experiences. However, each experience can be purified of the accretions of the other functions and can become pure or absolute. Absolute knowing is apprehension purged of all non-cognitive elements; it is an apprehension of the object-in-itself. Absolute willing is willing purged of all objective elements. Absolute feeling is feeling purged of all cognitive and volitional elements. Each absolute is a pure experience, i.e., positively an actualization of the unique nature of each function, and negatively, a lack of confusion or mixture with other functions. For Bhattacharyya, the absolute is the alternation of these three functions. There are three alternative Absolutes, which cannot be synthesized into one.

Bhattacharyya's conception of the absolutes is a corollary of his logic of alternation that he advocates. It is a logic of choice, commitment and co-existence. In our everyday discourse we are presented with alternatives, and we must choose, not because one alternative is correct and the other false, but because we must choose, and having chosen, we must abide by our choice. Bhattacharyya rejects inclusive disjunction (either-or, perhaps both) and accepts exclusive disjunction (either-or, but not both). X may be true, Y may be true, however, the conjunction of X and Y is not true. Alternation, so important in practice, is equally important in theory. With the logic of alternation, Bhattacharyya rejects philosophies that claim that their philosophy is the only true philosophy. For him, there are different paths that lead to different goals, and each goal is absolute in itself. No absolute is superior to any other; the ways of the absolute diverge, but one is not preferable to the other. When one is accepted, the others are automatically rejected. These are genuine alternatives. The absolute is an alternative of truth, freedom, or value.

To sum up: Bhattacharyya provides three possibilities of encountering an Absolute: to encounter the absolute as positive being or truth, or to encounter the non-being as freedom, or "their positive indetermination" or value. In K. C. Bhattacharyya's reading of the tradition, the Advaita Vedānta takes the absolute in the first way, i.e., as positive truth; the Buddhism of the Mādhyamika school in the second way, i.e., the absolute as non-being or freedom; and the Hegelian Absolute, in the third way, i.e., as the identity of truth and freedom or value. Thus there are three irreducible Absolutes.[20]

It is interesting to compare the three Absolutes as they are presented in "The Concept of Philosophy" (CP) and the three Absolutes as they appear in "The concept of the absolute and Its Alternate Forms" (AAF).

	CP	AAF
Knowledge	Advaita Being	Truth
Willing	Mādhyamika Non-Being	Freedom
Feeling	Hegelian synthesis	Value

I find it strange that Bhattacharyya reads Hegelian absolute as value. In his interpretation of the Hegelian absolute as value, Bhattacharyya seems to misconstrue Hegel for whom the science of the absolute is logic.

Before concluding this discussion I would raise some questions about three crucial concepts that Bhattacharyya uses in the hope that these reflections might provide impetus for further research and dialogue about these important concepts. The concepts I have in mind are: "demand," "denial," and "alternation."

1 The concept of "demand" frequently appears in Bhattacharyya's writings. He informs his readers that philosophy begins in reflective consciousness in which there exists a distinction between content and consciousness and a "demand" for "supra-reflective consciousness," i.e., a consciousness in which the distinction between content and consciousness is clearly visible. One wonders what is this demand? What kind of a consciousness is it? Is this consciousness not conscious of either a known or a willed or a felt content?
2 Bhattacharyya speaks of grades of thought and corresponding grades of speakables and argues that the ascent from the lower to the higher, from the less perfect to the more perfect, is possible because it is possible to deny the lower. Each ascent is based on a series of denials. For example, objects are denied because of our belief in the subject, and the denial of the subject or the self is possible because of our belief in the absolute. All of us would agree that the denial of facts is possible, however, only particular facts can be denied. One particular fact may be denied in favor of another, yet how does one deny all facts? The ascent to the final stage is difficult to grasp in the absence of some philosophical position, e.g., Advaita Vedānta. I can possibly deny my ego only if I concede the reality of a non-subjective awareness that provides the basis for such a denial.
3 How does one move from one attitude of thought to the other? Bhattacharyya explains the mutual relation between truth, freedom, and value as alternation. He used the term "reality" to mean "freedom" and concludes his discussion of the alternative absolutes in the following words:

> . . . it appears to be meaningless to speak of truth as a value, of value as real, or of reality as true while we can significantly speak of value as not false, of reality as not valueless and of truth as not unreal, although we cannot positively assert value to be truth, reality to be value and truth to be reality. Each of them is absolute and they cannot be spoken

> of as one or many. In one direction their identity and difference are alike meaningless and in another direction their identity is intelligible though not assertable. Truth is unrelated to value, value to reality and reality to truth, while value may be truth, reality value and truth reality. The absolute may be regarded in this sense as an alternation of truth, value and reality.[21]

In what sense is Bhattacharyya using the concept of alternation? He informs his readers that truth, freedom, or value are not simply alternative descriptions of the Absolute. Is it simply epistemic? It does not appear to be so. Is alternation constitutive of the Absolute? If so, does it make sense to talk of the absolute as one or triple? It is not clear how the absolute, though of the alternative nature in the sense of "either-or," can at the same time remain as the Absolute.

These questions notwithstanding, Bhattacharyya's conception of "alternation" is unique; it is an original contribution to philosophy. He has made a genuine attempt to show that absolutism is not incompatible with pluralism. His philosophy goes a long way toward removing the popular Western misconception that Indian philosophy is only mystical, intuitive, and practical.

Śrī Aurobindo

In the concluding paragraph of his magnum opus, *The Life Divine,* Śrī Aurobindo presents his spiritual vision in the following words:

> If there is an evolution in material Nature and if it is an evolution of being with consciousness and life as its two key-terms and powers, this fullness of being, fullness of consciousness, fullness of life must be the goal of development towards which we are tending and which will manifest at an early or later stage of our destiny. The self, the spirit, the reality that is disclosing itself out of the first inconscience of life and matter, would evolve its complete truth of being and consciousness in that life and matter. It would return to itself—or, if its end as an individual is to return into its Absolute, it could make that return also,—not through a frustration of life but through a spiritual completeness of itself in life.[22]

Though the above quotation begins with a hypothetical, the preceding nine hundred forty-six pages of *The Life Divine* seek to demonstrate that the claims made in the above paragraph are indeed true.

Śrī Aurobindo's philosophy, taken as a whole, is Vedāntic. Śrī Aurobindo, drawing on the resources of the Vedas and the Upaniṣadic texts, asserts that the ultimate reality is *brahman*; it is existence-consciousness-bliss. An important part of this metaphysics is the account of evolution that he provides in his *Life Divine*. When compared to Western thought, in Indian thought evolution has not played a significant role, though the traces of it are found in the Vedas and the Upaniṣads; it, however, occurs more systematically in the Sāṃkhya system. Śrī Aurobindo gave evolution the place it was due. Indeed, Śrī Aurobindo's theory of evolution is key to understanding his entire philosophy. The goal of his theory of evolution is to show that the evolutionary structure of the world process is due to the creative force inherent in reality.

Aurobindo rejects Śaṃkara's *māyāvāda*, i.e., the falsity of the world, and develops a metaphysical position called "Integral Advaita." The world and the finite individuals are not false, but rather are manifestations of the *brahman*, and so real. The *brahman* is both transcendent and immanent in the world, and the finite individuals are self-manifestations of the *brahman* by its own infinite creative energy. He subscribes to a theory of emergent evolution, according to which evolution presupposes a prior involution. Matter, argues Aurobindo, develops through the stages of life, mind, and many other levels of consciousness just because the spirit had descended into matter and remained in it potentially. This is a form of the classical *satkāryavāda* (the effect preexists in the material cause), that allows for the emergence of new qualitative changes.

Fundamental questions and issues for any evolutionary philosophy are the following:

1 "Evolution" is a word which usually states the phenomena without explaining it. Is there any explanation of the phenomena?
2 Can reality augment itself?
3 What is the relation between evolution and the Absolute?

   a Is absolutism consistent with change?
   b Even if it is, is it consistent with ordered and progressive change?
   c Progress implies new creation: Does that imply that that there is some want in the Absolute?
   d Does the absolute itself evolve? Or, alternately, does it contain evolution within itself?

There is no doubt that Śrī Aurobindo was aware of most, possibly all, of these questions, and formulates both his conception of the absolute spirit and theory of evolution accordingly.

In this essay my discussion will revolve around the following question: Is a doctrine of evolution consistent with the thesis that the *brahman* alone is real? There are such philosophers as Whitehead and Charles Hartshorne who hold that God evolves, becomes more and more perfect, as he was less perfect in the beginning. Śrī Aurobindo being a Vedāntin would not subscribe to such a thesis. The *brahman* is perfect, yet it goes through the evolutionary process. Why, and how? Can Aurobindo's position—that the *brahman* though one becomes many—be justified from a philosophical standpoint? In order for us to answer these questions meaningfully, we would have to first lay down an exposition of his metaphysical position.

Aurobindo's Conception of the Absolute

In the very opening chapter of *The Life Divine*, Śrī Aurobindo reveals the task of his philosophy as well as the unique character of his own spiritual experience in the following words: "For all problems of existence are essentially problems of harmony."[23] The title of this chapter, "The Human Aspiration," clearly tells us that Aurobindo perceived humanity as a phase of evolution attempting to seek harmony within itself and in its relation to other levels of existence. He concedes that the history of Eastern and Western philosophy testifies to the difficulties entailed in realizing such a harmony, though the interpretations of disharmony vary in the East and the West. He refers to this disharmony as "the refusal of the ascetic" and "the denial of the materialist." Śrī Aurobindo identifies the ascetic with the spiritualist who takes the matter to be illusory and the materialist, on the other hand, takes the spirit to be illusory. Both positions are extreme and one-sided.

Throughout his writings, Śrī Aurobindo provides a variety of reasons to demonstrate that both matter and spirit are equally real, because matter is also *brahman*. Both are real constituents of *saccidānanda*, the divine reality. The conception of matter and spirit as equally real goes a long way toward explaining Śrī Aurobindo's conception of the world. "If One is pre-eminently real, 'the others,' the Many are not unreal."[24] The world is neither a figment of one's mind nor a deceptive play of *māyā*. Śrī Aurobindo's realistic streak would not allow him to surrender the reality of the world to the deceptive play of *māyā*, the theory accepted by Śaṃkara. Not unlike many of the older critics of Śaṃkara, Śrī Aurobindo asks: Is the *māyā* real or unreal? If it is real, there is a dualism between the *brahman* and *māyā*. If an appearance, then, we may ask, what is the nature of this apparent reality? Who perceives *māyā*? If it is the *brahman*, there is an obvious absurdity. If it is the *jīva*, we ask, isn't *jīva* itself unreal and due to *māyā*, in which case we would have an infinite regress? For Aurobindo, "*māyā*" means nothing more than the freedom of the *brahman* from the circumstances through which he expresses himself. *Māyā* is "not a blunder and a fall, but a purposeful descent, not a curse, but a divine opportunity."[25] *Saccidānanda*, as an infinite being, consciousness, and bliss, creates the universe, and unfolds itself into many. Spirit's involvement in matter, its manifestation in grades of consciousness is the significance of evolution. Evolution is the unfolding of consciousness in matter until the former becomes explicit, open, and perceptible. And, the act of transformation from matter to spirit is the reverse of involution—it is reunion, an evolution. Let me elaborate it further.

The Nature of Creation: Involution and Evolution

As energy, consciousness is not merely self-manifesting, it is capable of self-contraction and self-expansion, descent and ascent. Accordingly, in his theory of involution/evolution, Aurobindo argues that nature evolves on several levels because the *brahman* (*saccidānanda: sat* or existent being, *cit* or consciousness-force, and *ānanda* or bliss) has already involved itself at each level. From a logical perspective, prior to evolution there is involution through which the *brahman* seeks its own manifestation in the multilevel world. The order of involution, is as follows:

Existence ↓
Consciousness-Force
Bliss

Supermind

Mind
Psyche
Life
Matter

After plunging into the farthest limit, i.e., the lowest form, consciousness turns around in order to climb the steps it had earlier descended. Evolution, the inverse of involution, is a conscious movement. Thus, evolution presupposes involution; in fact, evolution is possible because involution has already occurred. Thus, the order of the evolutionary process is as follows:

Matter ↓
Life
Psyche
Mind

Supermind

Bliss
Consciousness-Force
Existence

The first four in the order of evolution constitute the lower hemisphere and the last four the upper hemisphere. Evolution from the lower to the higher, i.e., from matter to spirit, is possible because each level contains within it the potentiality to attain a higher status.

Uniqueness of Śrī Aurobindo's theory of evolution lies in its triple processes: of widening, heightening, and integration. Widening signifies extension of scope (incorporation of co-existent forms and the development and growth toward higher forms); heightening leads to the ascent from the lower to the higher grade; and integration means that the ascent from the lower to the higher is not simply the rejection of the lower but rather the transformation of the lower to the higher. In other words, when life emerges out of matter, it not only signifies an ascent to a higher grade but also a transformation of matter. The same characterizes the next two, i.e., psyche and mind. Thus life, psyche, and mind modify matter and in turn are modified by it.

This, however, is not enough, because the mind is essentially characterized by ignorance and error. Aurobindo was well aware that finite intellect has its limits and so is not able to grasp the integral view of reality. In Aurobindo's words: "The intellect is incapable of knowing the supreme truth, it can only range about seeking for truth, and catching fragmentary representations of it, not the thing itself."[26] Additionally, mind, for Aurobindo, is not a faculty of knowledge. "It is a faculty for the seeking of knowledge . . . [it] is that which does not know, which tries to know and never knows except in a glass darkly. . . ."[27] A creative consciousness is needed which is able to see unity as well as diversity, and is able to apprehend all relations in their totality. He terms this power of divine creative consciousness "supermind." Thus, mind is only a transitional term which points beyond itself to its perfection, its destiny, the supermind, which, in Aurobindo's words is "a power of Conscious-Force expressive of real being, born out of real being, and partaking of its nature and neither a child of the Void nor a weaver of fictions. It is conscious Reality throwing itself into mutable forms of its own imperishable and immutable substance."[28] It is the culmination or the consummation of mind.

The difference between supermind and mind is the difference in their way of looking at reality. Supermind has an integral outlook; it achieves a unitary picture of reality, but mind by its very nature has a piecemeal picture. The supermind is the link that connects the two horizons, lower and higher. Without the instrumentality of the supermind, there would neither be the descent of supramental consciousness into the mind nor the ascent to supramental consciousness.

There is continuity of growth between the mind and the supermind as we pass through different levels of consciousness. Aurobindo refers to these levels using such terms as "higher mind," "illumined mind," "intuition," and "overmind." A Western reader is at a loss in his attempt to understand this kind of speculation. It is difficult for him to agree with Aurobindo that the crisis of modern civilization reveals an essential weakness in the power of the human mind which can only be resolved by the emergence of something higher. Aurobindo gives us a truly teleological approach to the understanding of the nature of mind.

The ascent to the supermind is achieved through a triple transformation: psychic, spiritual, and supramental. The psychic change is the removal of the veil which hides our psyche or soul; the spiritual change gives us an abiding sense of the Infinite, the experience of the true nature of the self, the *Īsvara* and the Divine; and the supramental transformation, signifies a transformation into knowledge and the emergence of gnostic being, a divinized spirit, a perfect individual who personifies integration within and without. It views everything from the perspective of *saccidānanda* and follows the command of the will of the spirit in which the laws of freedom replace the empirical laws. It does not amount to rejecting the world, but rather recognizing that matter is also *brahman*. It is a full life—a life of perfect freedom. The gnostic being is the return of the spirit to itself; it is the summit of evolution.

Thus, the spirit is not only the source of creation but also the final end of realization. A divine perfection of the human being is Aurobindo's aim. Aurobindo articulates spiritual experience in terms of an evolution of individual in relation to the absolute being, the *brahman*. It is at once an experience of one spiritual reality as it is in itself and as it manifests itself in the creative becoming manifested in the universe. An individual contains within himself various powers of consciousness that are capable of an unlimited awareness and knowledge. These higher powers of consciousness must emerge, develop, and reach completion through an individual's mental, vital, and physical being in order for the spiritual evolution to be fulfilled. Descent is a necessary condition of evolution. It is an original force in the universe. In fact, ascent and integration are possible because of the descent of the consciousness

Concluding Reflections

From the One to the One via the Many

Aurobindo made no secret of the fact that he is first and foremost a Vedāntin, thus it is not surprising that he made the one being, the starting point of the origin, nature, and end of the universe. For a Vedāntin the problem of the one and the many is not, as for a scholastic philosopher, how to relate the two in an intelligible fashion, but rather how to make many appear out of the one. Aurobindo, on the one hand maintains that the being or *brahman* is pure existence, eternal, indefinable, and on the other hand attributes becoming to it. Can we rationally attribute becoming to being while maintaining it as pure existence, etc.? Can Śrī Aurobindo's thesis be justified from a philosophical standpoint?

Śrī Aurobindo attempts to reconcile the two by affirming that the many preexists in the one and makes the becoming the inherent power of the one. The one and the many co-exist eternally. In response to the questions: Why does the world arise? Why evolution? Śrī Aurobindo points out that creation is the sportive activity of the *brahman*. The *brahman* is self-sufficient; he does not create the world out of any desire or lack. The world for Śrī Aurobindo is in a perpetual movement, which "carries with it the potentiality of repose and betrays itself as an activity of some existence." The world is the result of the delight of the *brahman*. Śrī Aurobindo identifies the *brahman* with delight.

In order to substantiate his metaphysics, Śrī Aurobindo reinterprets the Advaitin concepts of *līlā* and *māyā* and establishes a positive relationship between his spiritual experience and metaphysics. He explains *līlā* on the model of the rare moments of human life when one experience joy at its maximum; each person must discover the joy of delight in one's own creation and self-manifestation.

The Advaitic account eventually comes to terms with the utter inexplicability of individuation by coming to regard the many as but a product of *avidyā*, ignorance. The many is said to be the *līlā*, i.e., the sport of the one; in saying this, the Advaitins emphasize that the one could not have any purpose in creating the many. So, by excluding all elements of purpose from the question about the many, the question may be modified to become an interrogation into the "how" of the many, rather than the "why" of the many. The one in Advaita does not give its being to the many; it is that which *is* there in the many, indivisible and yet *as if* divided. Thus, the Advaitin has no choice but to conclude that the one is the only reality, and the many is a false appearance of the one. The one and the many belong to two different levels which are ultimately incommensurable.

With his concept of "delight," Śrī Aurobindo provides a response to the Advaita conception that the world is *māyā* or simply an appearance. The world, for Śrī Aurobindo, is not an illusion but rather a manifestation of creative energy, the play, the joy of the *brahman*; it is real. The play begins with the involution, i.e., when the divine plunges into matter, inconscience, etc., and it continues in evolution until the mind evolves into the supermind. Thus, the entire theory of evolution falls into the general theory of the delight of *brahman*; it is there "only for the delight of the unfolding, the progressive execution, the objectless seried self-revelation."[29] This, in short, is the scheme and the direction of the play.

Śrī Aurobindo recognizes three aspects of the divine: the transcendental, cosmic, and individual. The transcendent aspect means that although the divine permeates the world, it is not exhausted by the world; the cosmic aspect signifies the reality of the world because it is the self-manifestation of the *brahman*; and the individual aspect is the awareness of *ānanda* in each individual. By emphasizing these three aspects individually and collectively, Śrī Aurobindo offers a solution to the problem of being and becoming, one and many. In Śrī Aurobindo words:

> It can be said of it that it would not be the infinite Oneness if it were not capable of an infinite multiplicity; but that does not mean that the One is plural or can be limited or described as the sum of the Many: on the contrary, it can be the infinite Many because it exceeds all limitation or description by multiplicity and exceeds at the same time all limitation by finite conceptual oneness. . . .[30]

He was well aware that the finite makes an opposition between the Infinite and the finite and associates finiteness with plurality and infinity with oneness; but in the logic of the Infinite there is no such opposition and the eternity of the many in the one is a thing that is perfectly natural and possible.

The absolute, the unconditioned, infinite spirit, the pure unity of being is also the creative energy which is the source of the conditioned many. There are two poises of the *brahman*, which Aurobindo compares to the "two poles of being," the stillness of reservoir" and "the coursing of the channels which flow from it."[31] He observes:

> When we perceive Its deployment of the conscious energy of Its being in the universal action, we speak of It as the mobile active Brahman; when we

> perceive Its simultaneous reservation of the conscious energy of its being, kept from the action, we speak of it as the immobile passive Brahman,—Saguna and Nirguna. . . ."[32]

Thus, the reality of the world is the result of the creative or dynamic aspect of the *brahman*.

The delight functions not only on the level of the divine, but also in the physical world insofar as the *brahman* in itself is pure *ānanda* or bliss, and it also bestows bliss on those who become united with it. Thus, with the help of the concept of "delight," Śrī Aurobindo explains the relationship that exists between the human and the divine creativity.

All creation, holds Śrī Aurobindo, is self-manifestation out of delight and by the *cit-śakti* or the inherent conscious force, and the goal of evolution is the emergence of the superman, i.e., a form of conscious being who is superior to the human in all respects. It is with the emergence of human that the evolutionary process finds its true goal. Up until this time, it seemed as though the emergence of any form of being—inorganic or organic—was determined by the initial, given conditions. But now human being is able consciously to guide the evolutionary process, there is a reversal of natural evolution. Human beings can entertain a goal and consciously pursue it. The individual, besides the transcendental and the universal, now becomes the means of evolutionary change. Here Śrī Aurobindo's conception of *yoga* makes an appearance. *Yoga* becomes the process by which the individual brings about transformation of the universal. Integral emergence becomes the goal of evolution.

Two processes go on simultaneously: evolution of the outward nature and evolution of the inner being. It is only through this double evolution that comprehensive change is possible. Evolution of nature becomes evolution of consciousness. Instead of a mechanical gradual and rigid process, evolution becomes conscious, supple, flexible, and constantly dramatic, leading to the evolution of the spiritual man.

Śrī Aurobindo became widely known for providing an account of evolution which explains what evolution has been as well as predicting where it is heading towards. The last is the emergence of a higher form of consciousness, the supramental consciousness, in the human body. Human being is destined to grow into a superman. This is both the *nisus* of the evolutionary process and the goal of human spirituality.

Thus in his writings, Aurobindo attempts to preserve not only the Upaniṣadic thesis of the unity of the *brahman*, but also the reality of the world. Whereas his Vedāntic predecessors, e.g., Śaṃkara and Rāmānuja, tried to exclude subordinate one and many, Aurobindo placed the many and the becoming in the very heart of the *brahman*, the Absolute. One, for him, was the basis as well as the source of the many—basis not in the sense of simply being the support of the many, but rather in the sense of being the essence of the many.

NOTES

1 Introduction

1 The term "*Hindu*" is of Persian origin. After conquering India in the twelfth century CE, the Muslims used it to describe the people of *Hind* or India. The term "*Hinduism*" literally means the "beliefs of the Hindus." "80.5% of all Indians are *Hindus*," according to the *Census of India: Census Data 2001: "India at a glance, Religious Composition*," the Government of India, Office of the Registrar General and Census Commissioner website (http://censusindia.gov.in/Census_Data_2001/India_at_glance/religion.aspx).
2 Dating is perilous in the Indian context; the Indian seers were more concerned with the content and chose to remain anonymous.
3 *Nyāya Bhāṣya* (NB), I.1.1.
4 "An absolute presupposition is one which stands, relatively to all questions to which it is related, as a presupposition, never as an answer." Collingwood further adds: "Absolute presuppositions are not verifiable. . . . the idea of verification is an idea that does not apply to them. . . ." R. G. Collingwood, *Essays in Metaphysics* (Oxford: Clarendon Press, 1998), pp. 31–32.
5 Immanuel Kant, *Critique of Pure Reason*, translated by Norman Kemp Smith (London: Macmillan, 1973) pp. 208–238. Henceforth this book will be cited as *Critique of Pure Reason.*
6 Eliot Deutsch, *Advaita Vedānta: As A Philosophical Reconstruction* (Honolulu, Hawaii: University of Hawaii Press, 1969), chapter V. Hereafter this work will be cited as *Advaita Vedānta as Philosophical Reconstruction.*
7 Michel Foucault, *The Order of Things: An Archaeology of the Human Sciences* (London: Routledge, 1994), p. 336.
8 Friedrich Schleiermacher, *Hermeneutik und Kritik* (Frankfurt/Main: Suhrkamp, 1977), p. 79.
9 *Critique of Pure Reason*, "Preface" to the second edition, Bxiii.

2 The Vedas

1 Interested students may read B. R. Modak *Sāyaṇa* (New Delhi: Sahitya Akademi, 1995).
2 Sarvepalli Radhakrishnan, *Indian Philosophy* (Bombay: Blackie & Son Publishers Private Ltd., 1977), Vol. I, Chapter 2. Henceforth this work will be cited as Radhakrishnan's *Indian Philosophy*.
3 Śrī Aurobindo, *The Hymns of the Mystic Fire* (Pondichery: Sri Aurobindo Ashram, 1991).

4 Martin Heidegger, *Was Heisst Denken?* (Tübingen: Max Niemeyer, 1954). Translated by Fred Wieck and Glenn Gray as *What Is Called Thinking?* (New York: Harper and Row, 1954), part II, lecture 11, pp. 229–244.
5 RV, X.190.
6 Ibid., I.24.
7 Ibid., X.121.
8 Ibid., IV.23.
9 Ibid., X.133.
10 The significance of these hymns must not be minimized; they underscore the fact that conceptions of time in the Indian context date back to the *Atharva Veda*, thereby refuting the general Western perception that Indian philosophy does not take time into account and that the conceptions of time are strictly limited to the Western context.

3 The Upaniṣads

1 *Muṇḍaka* (MU), III.2.11.
2 *Kaṭha*, III.17.
3 Arthur Schopenhauer, *Parerga and Paralipomena*, translated by E. F. J. Payne (Oxford: Clarendon Press, 1974), vol. II of 2, p. 397.
4 *Kaṭha Upaniṣad*, VI.3.
5 *Kena Upaniṣad*, IV. 1–2.
6 TU, III.1.1.
7 BU, III.9.1–10.
8 MU, I.1.30.
9 TU, III. 1–6.
10 *Kaṭha*, 1.2.20–22.
11 *Śvetā*, III. 19–20.
12 BU, II.1.1–20.
13 Ibid., II.1.19.
14 Ibid., II.1.20.
15 Yājñavalkya appears twice in BU: first in a verbal contest with other *brahmins* and subsequently in a dialogue with King Janaka of Videha.
16 BU., IV.3.19.
17 Ibid., VIII.12.1.
18 CU, VIII. 7–12.
19 Ibid., V.11.1.
20 Ibid., Chapter VI.
21 Ibid., VI.2.1; VI.8.6–7.
22 Ibid., VI.12.3.
23 Ibid., IV.3.30.
24 *Aitareya Upaniṣad*, III. 1.3.
25 BU, I.4.10.
26 MAU, I.2.
27 CU, III.14.2.
28 *Aitareya Upaniṣad*, III.1.3,
29 MU, III.2.5,
30 BU, III.8.8.
31 Ibid., II.3.6.
32 *Śvetā*, I.1.
33 BU, II.4.14.
34 MU I.1.4

35 Ibid., I.1.6.
36 Ibid., I.1.9.
37 Ibid., III.2.3.
38 *Kena* II.3.
39 TU, II.4.
40 MU, III.2.9.
41 *Kena*, II.3.
42 MU, III.1.8.
43 *Kaṭha*, I.3.3–8.
44 Ibid., II.2.23.

4 The Cārvāka *Darśana* and the *Śramaṇas*

1 S. Radhakrishnan, *History of Philosophy Eastern and Western* (London: George Allen and Unwin Ltd., 1952), vol. I, p. 133.
2 CU, VI.6.1.
3 Ibid., VIII.7.8.
4 *Digha Nikāya*, I. 2. See Thomas W. Rhys Davids (tr.), *Dialogues of the Buddha* (Delhi: Motilal Banarsidass, 2007), pp. 56–95. Henceforth this edition will be cited as *Digha Nikāya*.
5 *Kaṭha Upaniṣad*, 1. 1. 20; 1. 2. 5–6.
6 *Maitrī Upaniṣad*, VII, 8–9.
7 Ibid., VII, 9.
8 Madhva, *Sarvadarśanasaṁgraha*, translated by E. B. Cowell and A. E. Gouch (Varanasi: Chowkhamba Sanskrit Series, 1978), chapter I, p. 2. Henceforth this edition will be cited as SDS.
9 S. N. Dasgupta, *A History of Indian Philosophy* (Delhi: Motilal Banarsidass, 1975), vol. 3, pp. 512–550. Henceforth this work will be cited as Dasgupta's *History*.
10 Kṛṣṇa Miśra, *Prabodahcandrodayam* with Hindi commentary by Pandit Ramanath Tripathi Śāstri (Varannsi: Chaukhamba Amarabharati Prakashan, 1977), pp. 76–77.
11 Jayarāśi Bhāṭṭa, *Tattvopaplavsiṃha* (ed.), Pandit Sukhlalji Sanghvi and Rasiklal Parikh (Baroda; Gaekward Oriental Institute, 1940), No. 1, LXXXVII. Henceforth this edition will be referred as TPS. The editors place TPS and its author in the eighth century CE. See the editors' "Introduction," p. x.
12 G. Tucci, "A Sketch of Indian Materialism," *Proceedings of the Indian Philosophical Congress*, Vol. I, p. 516.
13 Dasgupta's *History*, Vol. 3, p. 531.
14 Ibid., p. xi.
15 Ibid., p. i.
16 SDS, pp. 2–11.
17 Ibid., p. 2.
18 Ibid.
19 Madhva states: "Now this invariable connection must be a relation destitute of any condition accepted or disputed; and this connection does not possess its power of causing inference by virtue of its *existence*, as the eye, &c., are the cause of perception, but by virtue of its being *known*. What then is the means of this connection's being known?" Ibid., p. 5.
20 Ibid., p. 6.
21 Ibid., p. 9.
22 Dasgupta's *History*, vol. 3, p. 536.
23 Eli Franco, *Perception, Knowledge, and Disbelief: A Study of Jayarāśi's Scepticism* (Delhi: Motilal Banarsidass, 1994), p. 73.

24 For additional criticisms of the Cārvāka view, see Śaṃkara's commentary on BS III.3.54.
25 Sadānanda Yogindra, *Vedāntasāra* (tr.), Swami Nikhilananda (Kolkata, Advaita Ashrama, 1990), verses 124–127. Henceforth this work will be cited as *Vedāntasāra*.
26 BU, IV.3.22.
27 *Digha Nikāya*, I. 2, pp. 56–95. Also see, B. M. Barua, *A History of Pre-Buddhistic Indian Philosophy* (Calcutta, India: University of Calcutta, 1921), Part III. Hereafter this work will be cited as *A History of Pre-Buddhistic Indian Philosophy*.
28 Ibid., p. 70.
29 *A History of Pre-Buddhistic Indian Philosophy*, p. 279.
30 Pāṇini, *Mahābhāṣya*, VI. 1. 154.
31 Ibid.
32 Ibid., p. 71.
33 B. M. Barua, *Ājīvikas* (Calcutta, India: University of Calcutta, 1920), p. 11.
34 Ibid., p. 74.
35 Ibid., p. 75.
36 A. L. Basham, *History and the Doctrine of the Ājīvikas* (Delhi: Motilal Banarsidass, 1981), p. 34.
37 Ibid., p. 17.
38 K. N. Jayatilleke, *Early Buddhist Theory of Knowledge* (Delhi: Motilal Banarsidass, 1981), p. 142.

5 The Jaina *Darśana*

1 Erich Frauwallner, *History of Indian Philosophy* (Delhi: Motilal Banarsidass, 1973) Vol. 1, p. 196.
2 "Substance is possessed of attributes and modifications." Umāsvāmi, *Tattvārthadhigama Sūtra*, translated by J. L. Jaini (Arrah, India: The Central Jaina Publishing House, 1927), V. 8, p. 122.
3 This position is much like that of the Nyāya school to be discussed later.
4 Umāsvāmi, *Tattvārthadhigama Sūtra*, V. 16.
5 Of the nine schools of Indian philosophy, the Cārvākas and the Mīmāṃsakas deny omniscience; the Nyāya, Vaiśeṣika, Sāmflkhya, Yoga, some schools of Vedānta and later Buddhists (e.g., Sāntaraksita) admit its possibility—if not for humans, for God.
6 Malliṣeṇa's *Syadmañjari with Anyayoga-vyavaccheda-dvātriṃtikā of Hemacandra*, edited by A. B. Dhruva (Bombay: S. K. Belvalkar, Bhandarkar Oriental Research Institute, 1933), XXIII.
7 We get the sixth judgment by successively combining the second and the fourth.
8 We get the seventh judgment by successively combining the third and the fifth.
9 Umāsvāmi, *Tattvārthadhigama Sūtra*, I.1.
10 For a concise account of the Jaina philosophy, readers may consult M. L. Mehta's *Outlines of Jaina Philosophy* (Bangalore: Jaina Misssion Society, 1954).

6 The Bauddha *Darśana*

1 In the past half century, German scholars have argued that the years c. 460–380 BCE may be a better estimate of when the Buddha lived.
2 From *The History and Literature of Buddhism*, T.W. Rhys Davids (Varanasi: Bhartiya Publishing House, 1896), p. 88. Henceforth this book has been cited as *The History and Literature of Buddhism*.
3 "*Anitya*" means "non-eternal," not "momentary." However, many Buddhist

scholars take the Buddha's use of the word "*anitya*" to mean not only non-eternality, but also momentariness.

4 Christmas Humphreys, *Buddhism* (Baltimore, Maryland: Penguin, 1974), pp. 81–82.
5 Ibid., p. 89.
6 Ibid.
7 Clarence H. Hamilton, *Buddhism* (Indianapolis: The Library of Liberal Arts, 1952), p. 55.
8 David Kalupahana, *Buddhist Philosophy: A Historical Analysis* (Honolulu, Hawaii: University Press of Hawaii, 1976), p. 36.
9 Henry Clark Warren, *Buddhism in Translations* (New York: Atheneum, 1963), p. 133. Henceforth this book will be cited as *Buddhism in Translations.*
10 Ananda K. Coomarswamy, *Buddha and the Gospel of Buddhism* (New York: Harper Torchbooks, 1916), pp. 106–107.
11 *Majjhima Nikāya*, I. 262–64.
12 *Saṃyutta-Nikāya*, xxii.9017. *Buddhism in Translations*, p. 166.
13 Ibid., p. 166.
14 There were two opposed perspectives regarding causality, both of which the Buddhists reject: *satkāryavāda* and *asatkāryavāda.* The first holds that the effect pre-exists in the material cause. There are two varieties of it: (a) the change from cause to effect is a real transformation (the Sāṁkhya view), and (b) the change from cause to effect is simply an appearance (the Advaita Vedānta view). The second holds that the effect is non-existent in the material cause; the effect is something new. Nyāya-Vaiśeṣika and Mīmāṃṣā hold this position.
15 Vaiśeṣika takes *mokṣa* to be cessation of pain and not a positive state of bliss.

7 The Mīmāṁsā *Darśana*

1 This topic has been discussed under the rubric of *loka vedādhikaraṇa.*
2 Jaimini's *Mīmāṁsā Sūtras*, I.1.1.
3 For a concise introduction to *Mīmāṁsā*, readers might wish to consult P. V. Kane, *A Brief Sketch of the Pūrva-Mīmāṁsā System* (Poona: Aryabhushan Press, 1924).
4 For an excellent discussion of the Bhāṭṭa theory of knowledge, readers might wish to consult Govardan P. Bhatt's *Epistemology of the Bhāṭṭa School of Mīmāṁsā School* (Banaras: Chowkhamba, 1962).
5 See Chapter I on Nyāya *Darśana* in this work.
6 In general, the Mīmāṁsā conception of inference is very similar to the Nyāya conception, and I will discuss it further in the chapter on Nyāya of this work.
7 Jaimini's *Mīmāṁsā Sūtras*, I.1.6–23.
8 Ibid, I.1.27–32.

8 The Sāṁkhya *Darśana*

1 *Sāṁkhya-kārikā* (SK),15.
2 It is worth noting at this juncture that there is another variety of *satkāryavāda* called "*vivartavāda*," upheld by Advaita Vedānta. Both *pariṇāmavāda* and *vivartavāda* hold that the effect pre-exists in the material cause prior to production; however, for the former the effect is a real manifestation of the cause, for the latter, it is simply an appearance of the cause.
3 SK 9.
4 This axiom is opposed to the Western idea of creation out of nothing.
5 *Gītā*, II.16.

6 For Śaṃkara's criticisms of Sāṃkhya position, see BSBh, 2.2.1–10.
7 B. N. Seal, *The Positive Sciences of the Ancient Hindus* (New Delhi: Motilal Banarsidass, 1991), pp. 3–4. Henceforth this book will be cited as *The Positive Sciences of the Ancient Hindus*.
8 This point of view is also found in the writings of K. C. Bhattacharyya. See the chapter on "Studies in Sāṃkhya Philosophy," in his *Studies in Philosophy* (New Delhi: Motilal Banarsidass, 1983), pp. 127–142.
9 SK, 19.
10 Ibid., 17.
11 Ibid., 21.
12 Ibid.
13 Ibid., 57. There are other striking examples. Kant's remarkable phrase "purposiveness without purpose" most aptly captures this idea of unconscious teleology.
14 It may be noted that the precise number of principles varies in different expositions. Twenty-five is the number given in SK.
15 SK, 36–37; *Sāṁkhya-Sūtras*, 2. 40–43.
16 See *Ṛg Veda*, X.129.
17 SK, 59.
18 Dasgupta's *History*, Vol. I, p. 260.
19 SK, 4.
20 See the chapter on Nyāya of this work.
21 Other systems, the Nyāya and Mīmāṃsakas, recognize additional *pramāṇas*, the Sāṁkhya only these three and reduces the remaining to these three.
22 SK, 5.
23 Ibid., 5.
24 See the chapter on Nyāya of this work.
25 SK, 7–8
26 Ibid., 8.

9 The Yoga *Darśana*

1 There exists some doubt among scholars if the author of the *Yoga Sūtras* is the same as the author of the great commentary on Pāṇini's grammar. The *Yoga Sūtras* is certainly after the time of the Buddha and before the rise of the Buddhist schools.
2 *Yoga Sūtras*, I.2.
3 For the concepts of "*guṇa*," "*prakṛti*," and "*puruṣa*," see Chapter 8 on Sāṁkhya *Darśana*.
4 *Yoga Sūtras*, I.5–6.
5 Ibid., I.6.
6 The Advaitins regard it as being due to the superimposition of one thing upon another.
7 *Studies in Philosophy*, p. 262.
8 The Advaita Vedānta regards this consciousness to be the witness of ignorance, while the Yoga takes it to be a *vṛtti*.
9 *Yoga Sūtras*, I.11.
10 *Studies in Philosophy*, p. 259
11 *Yoga Sūtras*, I.5.
12 Ibid., II.3.
13 Ibid., II.4.
14 A subtle point of difference between Sāṁkhya and Yoga understandings of ignorance is worth noting. For Sāṁkhya, ignorance is the failure to discriminate between the self and the not-self; however, for the Yoga, it is taking one to be the other.

15 Ibid., II.6.
16 Ibid., II.9.
17 Ibid., II.8.
18 Ibid., I.12.
19 Ibid., II 29–32.
20 *Studies in Philosophy*, p. 310.
21 *Yoga Sūtras*, II. 86–87.
22 Ibid., III. 4–5.
23 Ibid., III.3.
24 *Studies in Philosophy*, p. 284. Also see N. K. Brahma, *Philosophy of Hindu Sādhanā* (New Delhi: Motilal Banarasid as, 1993), esp. chapter VIII.
25 *Yoga Sūtras*, II. 24–25.
26 Ibid., IV.14.
27 Ibid., IV.12.
28 Ibid., IV.15.
29 Ibid., IV.16.

10 The Vaiśeṣika *Darśana*

1 Eric Frauwallner, *History of Indian Philosophy*, vol. II (Delhi: Motilal Banarsidass, 1973); *Dasgupta's History*, Vol. I (Delhi: Motilal Banarsidass, 1975).
2 Materialism reduces all entities to matter. Naturalism does not. But for naturalism every entity belongs to nature.
3 See *The Positive Sciences of the Ancient Hindus*, Chapter 1.
4 If there are other languages, where verbs are central to a sentence, then the ontology sustained by those languages may accord the same place of importance to verbs.
5 Some scholars such as Karl Potter object to translating "*guṇa*" as "quality." Qualities are universal-like, while a *guṇa* is a particular. He therefore prefers the word "trope." See "Are the Vaiśeṣika *guṇa*, qualities?" in *Philosophy East and West*, vol. 4, no. 1, 1954. Also, some of the *guṇas* in Vaiśeṣika are such relations as "conjunction," "difference," "non-difference." If A and B touch each other, then conjunction with B is a *guṇa* of A. A quantity (*pariṇāma*), such as size, is also a *guṇa*, a *guṇa* of an atom is atomic in size, while a *guṇa* of the self is all-pervasive in size. These are not qualities in the strict sense.
6 For a detailed account, see Raja Ram Dravid, *The Problem of Universals in Indian Philosophy* (Delhi: Motilal Banarsidass, 1972), p. 32.
7 *Tarka-Saṃgraha of Annaṃbhaṭṭa with Dīpīka and Govardhana's Nyāya-Bodhinī*, translated by Yashwant Vasudev Athalye (Poona: Bhandarkar Institute Press, 1963), sec. 8, p. 96 (Bombay Sanskrit and Prakrit Series edition, No. LV). Henceforth this work will be cited as TSDNB.
8 TSDNB, pp. 164–165. *Bhāṣā-Parriccheda* explains contact as follows: "The meeting of two things that are removed from each other is called conjunction. It is described as being of three kinds: The first is due to action in either of them . . . Similarly it may be due to action in both; and the third is due to contact. The conjunction of a falcon and a hill and so on is described as being of the first kind . . . The encounter of two rams is said to be of the second kind. The conjunction of a jar and a tree owing to the conjunction of one-half of the jar and the tree is of the third kind." *Bhāṣā-Parriccheda* with *Siddhānta-Muktavalī*, translated by Swāmī Mādhvānanda (Calcutta: Advaita Ashrama, 1977), 115–118, pp. 207–208. Hereafter this work will be cited as BP,
9 It is generally recognized by all scholars that such early Vaiśeṣika philosophers as

Kanāḍa and Praśastapāda did not explicitly recognize negation as an objective reality. The Naiyāyika, on the other hand, from the beginning recognized it as a category.

10 *Tarka-Saṃgraha of Annaṃbhaṭṭa with Dīpīka*, translated by Gopinath Bhattacharyya (Calcutta: Progressive Publishers, 1976), p. 374. Henceforth this work will be cited as TSD.

11 Ibid., p. 380.

11 The Nyāya *Darśana*

1 *Bhāṣya* on NS, I.1.1.
2 NS, I.1.3,
3 NS, I.1.4.
4 Ibid., III.1.1.
5 Ibid., I.1.14; III.1.2; III.1.58.
6 Ibid., I.1.10
7 See Uddyotakara's *Vārttika* on Nyāya *bhāṣya*, NS, I.1.2.
8 NS, I.1.5. Translation of I.1.5 and Vātsyāyana's commentary on it is included in Appendix IV.
9 Students should ask themselves: does this Nyāya theory involve an infinite regress?
10 The Vaiśeṣika list of *padārthas* however is different from Gautama's list.
11 See NS, 1.1.23.
12 See J. N. Mohanty's "Nyāya Theory of Doubt," *Phenomenology and Ontology* (The Hague: Nijhoff, 1970).
13 NS I.1.24.
14 Ibid., I.1.25.
15 Ibid., I.1.26.
16 Ibid., I.1.27.
17 Ibid., I.1.40.
18 Ibid., I.1.41.
19 Ibid., I.2.1.
20 Ibid., I.2.2.
21 Ibid., I.2.3.
22 Ibid., I.2.4.
23 Ibid., I.2.10.
24 Ibid., I.2.18.
25 Ibid., I.2.19.
26 See, Vātsyāyana's commentary on NS, I.1.9.
27 NS, I.1.9.
28 Ibid., I.1.10.

12 The Buddhist Schools

1 MMK 25.19–20.
2 Ibid., 24.19.
3 T. R. V. Murti, *The Central Philosophy of Buddhism* (London: George Allen and Unwin Ltd., 1960), p. 132.
4 *Thirty Verses*, 28.
5 Ibid., 29–30.
6 It was Asaṇga who first developed the notion of *tathatā* "suchness" as the identical property of all *dharmas*; the *buddhhood* is the universal sameness in all beings. It is in this sense that all things are called *Tathāgata garbha* (the womb of *Tathāgata*).

7 Asaṇga makes a distinction among three bodies of Buddha: (1) *dharmakāya* which is the real *Tathāgata*, the truth body or the essential body; (2) the *sambhogakāya* or enjoyment body which is still material, but subtle and leads *bodhisattvas* to their goal; and (3) *nirmāṇakāya*, which is the physical body in which the actual Buddha was born among men. With this body, the Buddha helps the *śrāvakas* to reach their goal.

13 The Vedānta *Darśana*

1 This is part of a *śloka* (stanza) that occurs in *Bālabodhinī*, a work attributed to Śaṃlkara.
The *śloka* reads as follows:
ślokārdhena pravakṣyāmi yad uktami granthakoṭibhiḥ
brahma satyam jagan mithyā jivo brahmaiva nāparaḥ
2 BSBh, II.1.6; II.1.11.
3 BSBh, II.1.16.
4 Śaṃkara's *"Adhyāsbhāṣya."*
5 This is a special kind of identity, which is not pure identity but that which tolerates "differences."
6 *Ṛg Veda*, VI.47.18. Also see, BU, II.5.19.
7 BSBh, I.1.1.
8 KUBh, III.1
9 BGBh, III.27 & 18.26.
10 BGBh, XIII.2.
11 Ibid., II.1.33.
12 BSBh, II.3.50.
13 See BU, IV.3.6: in BSBh, I.3.22, Śaṃlkara also quotes several BU texts to substantiate the claim, that *ātman* is self-luminous.
14 *Taittirīya Upaniṣadbhāṣya*, II.1.
15 In the introduction to his commentary on BS, Śaṃlkara defines superimposition as the "apparent presentation (to consciousness) in the form of remembrance of something previously experienced in something else." *"Adhyāsabhāṣya."*
16 Once ten young men were traveling together. On their way, they came across a brook which had overflowed its banks. The travelers had never seen such an expanse of water. After considerable debate, they decided to wade through the water. In order to make sure that all of them had crossed the brook safely, one of the young men counted the number in the party, leaving himself out, and asked: "Where is the tenth?" Each repeated the counting, leaving himself out and started crying. A passerby realized what had happened and said to each one of them: "you are the tenth man," "you are the tenth man."
17 Dharmarāja Adhvarīndra, *Vedānta Paribhāṣā*, translated by Swamī Mādhavānanda (Mayavati: Advaita Ashrama, 1983).
18 *Vedānta Paribhāṣā* states: Mental modes are of four kinds: doubt, certitude, egoism, and memory. Considering this division of the mental mode, the internal sense, although one, receives different appellations, namely, mind (*manas*), intellect (*buddhi*), ego-sense (*ahaṃkāra*), and memory (*citta*). [Accordingly], it has been said:"the internal instruments are *manas*, *buddhi*, *ahaṃkāra*, and *citta*, and the [their] contents [functions] respectively are: doubt, certitude, egoism, and retro-cognition." Bina Gupta, *Perceiving in Advaita Vedānta* (Lewisburgh, PA: Bucknell University Press, 1991), Chapter V.
19 The Advaitins argue that the inner sense is located within the body and is constituted of very fine transparent matter of predominantly *sattva* quality. The transparency of the *sattva guṇa* enables the inner sense to come in contact with empirical objects through the outer senses and assume their forms. The inner sense is divided

into three parts, so to speak. One part remains inside the body, the second part makes contact with the object, and the third part resides between these two making the whole a unit. The transparency of the inner sense allows pure consciousness to manifest in it and according to the three parts of the inner sense, consciousness is manifested in three different ways: as the cognizer, the cognitive operation, and the cognition.

20 Perceiving, pp. 167–68.

21 *Vedānta Paribhāṣā*, see the chapter on inference.

22 Madhusūdana in his *Advaitasiddhi* provides twenty-six inferential arguments to demonstrate that the world is illusory. To illustrate his reasoning, I will note three syllogisms: (1) The world is not real, because it is something other than the *brahman*, like shell-silver; (2) perceptuality cannot belong to the thing that is absolutely real, because it resides in nameable things, like shell-silver; and (3) the world is not real, because while not being the object of knowledge that leads to *mokṣa*, it is different from shell-silver. Madhusūdana, *Advaitasiddhi* (Delhi: Parimal Publications, 1988), pp. 417–422.

23 VP chapter on Verbal testimony.

24 For a discussion of three kinds of *sākṣī-pratyakṣa*, see Bina Gupta's, *Disinterested Witness: A Fragment of Advaita Vedānta Phenomenology* (Evanston, Illinois, Northwestern University Press, 1998), pp. 80–90.

25 *Akhaṇḍākāra vṛtti*, for the Advaitins, is the highest human achievement. *Vṛtti jñāna* obtained through a mental mode is fragmented in form. *Akhaṇḍākāra vṛtti*, on the other hand, has no fragmented form, because the *brahman* has no form.

26 *Kaṭha*, I.2.4.

27 *Īśā*, 9 and 11.

28 It plays the same role in Rāmānuja's system that inherence (*samavāya*) does in Nyāya-Vaiśeṣika.

29 *Śrī Bhāṣya*, II.2.29.

30 *saviśeṣa vastu viṣayatvātsarva pramāṇam*, Ibid., I.1.1.

14 The *Bhagavad Gītā*

1 Given the nature of this text, in this chapter I am including translations in the body of the text rather than in a separate appendix.

2 Ibid., IV.19.

3 Ibid., II.20.

4 Ibid., IX.3.

5 Ibid., X.2.

6 Ibid., III. 17–19.

7 Ibid., VIII.14.

8 Ibid., IX.15.

9 Ibid., IX.15; IV.23.

15 Modern Indian Thought

1 "*Kroḍapatra*" are unpublished handwritten manuscripts, usually palm leaves, which were circulated by the teachers to their own students; outsiders did not have access to these manuscripts.

2 K. C. Bhattacharyya's *Studies in Philosophy*, edited by Gopinath Bhattacharyya (Calcutta: Progressive Publisher, 1956 and 1958). The publisher Motilal Banarsidass brought out the two volumes in one edition, and references in this book are from that edition.

3 For a concise discussion of K. C. Bhattacharyya's philosophy, readers may wish to read Kalidas Bhattacharyya, *The Fundamentals of K. C. Bhattacharyya's Philosophy* (Calcutta: Saraswat Library, 1975).
4 Ibid., pp. 4–5.
5 Ibid., p. 36.
6 Ibid., p. 179.
7 *Studies in Philosophy*, p. 331.
8 Ibid.
9 Ibid., p. 342.
10 *Studies in Philosophy*, p. 590. Emphasis supplied.
11 Ibid., p. 385.
12 Ibid., p. 497.
13 Ibid., p. 490.
14 Ibid., p. 485.
15 Ibid., p. 494.
16 Ibid., pp. 463–469.
17 Ibid., p. 478.
18 Ibid., p. 500.
19 Ibid., p. 501.
20 Ibid. p. 479.
21 Ibid., p. 505.
22 Śrī Aurobindo, *The Life Divine* (New York: Dutton, 1951), p. 947.
23 Ibid., p. 4.
24 Śrī Aurobindo, *Isha Upaniṣad* (Calcutta: Arya Publishing Co., 1924), p. 26.
25 *The Life Divine*, p. 527.
26 Śrī Aurobindo, *The Riddle of This World* (Calcutta: Arya Publishing Co., 1933), p. 23.
27 *The Life Divine*, p. 110.
28 Ibid., p. 109.
29 Ibid., p. 743.
30 Ibid., p. 304.
31 Ibid., p. 512.
32 Ibid., p. 513.

GLOSSARY OF IMPORTANT SANSKRIT WORDS

abādhita	non-contradicted
abhāva	absence; negation
abhidhā	designative power
abhihitānvayavāda	the theory that the separate designata of words are conjoined together to form meanings of a sentence
abhyāsa	practice
ācārya	teacher; spiritual guide
adharma	demerit
adhyāsa	superimposition
adṛṣṭa	unseen; unseen power; *karmic* potencies
advaita	non-dual; non-dualism
advaitin	non-dualist
advaya	non-dual; one
āgama	a traditional doctrine or precept; collections of such doctrines
agni	fire; the fire deity
ahaṃkāra	egoness; I-ness
ahiṃsā	non-violence; non-injury
ājīvikas	a group of atheistic ascetics
ajñāna	ignorance
ajñāta	unknown
ākāṅkṣā	expectancy
ākāra	form
ākāśa	empty space; sky; ether
akhyāti	no false or invalid knowledge
akhyātivāda	the doctrine that illusion is the non-cognition of the difference between two cognitions: the seen and the remembered
ālayavijñāna	receptacle; storehouse of consciousness
anantam	infinite
anattā	no-self
anekāntavāda	the doctrine that a thing has infinite aspects

aṅgas	limbs
anirmokṣa	impossibility of *mokṣa*
anirvacanīya	indescribable
anirvacanīyakhyāti vāda	the doctrine that the object of illusion is indescribable in terms of being and non-being, reality and unreality, existence and non-existence
anitya	non-eternal
antaḥkaraṇa	inner sense
anubhava	experience
anumāna	inference (one of the means of true knowledge); syllogism
anumiti	inferential cognition
anupalabdhi	non-cognition; non-apprehension; non-perception
anuvyavasāya	cognition of an original cognition
ānvīkṣikī	examination using logical rules
anyathākhyāti vāda	the doctrine that illusion is the perception of an object which is not here but elsewhere
anyonyābhāva	mutual difference
aparāvidyā	lower knowledge
aparokṣa	direct; immediate
apauruṣeya	not created by a human being; authorless
apramā	untrue cognition
apūrva	supernatural; merit or demerit in the form of latent potencies
arhat	an enlightened person (in the Therāvāda Buddhism)
artha	meaning; object; wealth; purpose; aim
arthakriyā	purposive action
arthakriyākāritvā	the power to bring about successful practice
arthāpatti	postulation (one of the means of true knowledge)
asat	non-being; non-existence; unreal
asatkāryavāda	the doctrine that the effect is non-existent in the material cause prior to its production
asatkhyātivāda	the doctrine that the object of illusion is non-existent
asmitā	egoism
āśrama	a stage of life; a hermit's abode
āśrava	inflow of *karma* in Jainism
asteya	non-stealing
āstika	one who accepts the Vedic authority; one who believes in the existence of god
ātman	spirit; self; soul; consciousness
atyantābhāva	absolute non-existence
āvaraṇa	veil
avayava	member; parts of a whole; constituents of an argument
avidyā	same as *ajñāna;* nescience; ignorance

bādha	sublation; contradiction; cancellation
bhakti	devotion
bhakti yoga	the discipline of devotion
bhedābheda	identity-cum-difference; identity-in-difference
bhrama	error; illusion; hallucination
bodhisattva	an enlightened person (in the Mahāyāna Buddhism)
brahmacarya	celibacy
brahman	the absolute; the ultimate reality
buddhi	reason; intellect
catuṣkoti	quadrilemma; the four-cornered negation
cit	consciousness
citta	that which gathers and synthesizes knowledge; mind
cittavṛittis	modifications of the mind
darśana	view; vision; philosophy; school
devas	the shining ones
dharma	virtue; duty
dharma śāstras	treatises on *dharma*
dhyāna	meditation; concentration
dik	space; direction; see *ākāśa*
doṣa	defect
dravya	substance; thing
dukkha	pain; suffering; discontent; lack of harmony
dvaita	dual; dualism
dveṣa	hatred or jealousy
guṇa	quality; property
guru	teacher; preceptor
hetu	cause; reason; ground
hetvābhāsa	fallacy; pseudo-reason
Hīnayāna	the inferior vehicle
hotars	an ancient order of Aryan priests
indriya	sense organ
Īśvara	God
jaḍa	unconscious
jāti	genus; universal; caste
jīna	a victor
jīva	empirical individual
jivanmukti	freedom in this life
jñāna	consciousness; knowledge; cognition
jñāna kāṇḍa	the part of the Vedas that deals with knowledge (speculative issues)
jñāna yoga	the discipline of knowledge
jñātā	the knower
kaivalya	aloneness; salvation
kāla	time; to collect; to count

kāma	desire; passion
karaṇa	instrument
kāraṇa	cause; reason
karma	action; past actions in their potential forms
karmakāṇḍa	the part of the Vedas that discusses actions (in the ritualistic sense)
karmayoga	the discipline of action
kevala	alone; absolutely direct (knowledge) in Jainism
khyātivādas	theories of false cognition
kleśas	defects
kośas	sheaths
kṣana	instant; moment
kṣanikavāda	the doctrine of momentariness
lakṣaṇā	mark; characteristic; secondary power of designation
līlā	divine play; sport
Mahāyāna	the superior vehicle of Buddhism; a name for all the northern schools of Buddhism taken together
manana	reflective thinking
manas	mind
mārga	way; path
māyā	ignorance; a synonym for *avidyā; ajñāna;* etc.
mīmāṃśā	exegesis
Mīmāṃśā	one of the six *āstika* schools of Indian philosophy
mithyā	false
mokṣa	freedom; liberation
nāstika	one who denies the Vedic authority; one who does not believe in the existence of god
nididhyāsana	contemplative meditation
nigamana	drawing the conclusion
niḥsvabhāvatā	lack of inherent essence
niravayava	partless
nirguṇa	without qualities; without attributes
nirodha	cessation
nirvāṇa	freedom from suffering; peace
nirvikalpa	indeterminate (cognition)
nirviśeṣa	without any determinations
nirvṛtti	without any mental modifications; the life of inaction (renouncing worldly life)
padārtha	all reals or objects that belong to the world
pakṣa	the subject of the conclusion; "the minor term"
parā	the highest
parāmārśa	consideration
pāramārthika	pertaining to the highest reality
parārthānumāna	inference for others

parāvidyā	higher knowledge
parikalpita	imagined
pariṇāma	transformation
phala	result; fruit
pradhāna	nature; a synonym for *prakṛti; māyā; etc.*
Prajāpati	the deity *Brahmā*
prajñā	wisdom
prakāra	epistemic form
prakṛti	nature; a synonym for *māyā;* etc.
pramā	valid knowledge; valid cognition
pramāṇa	means of true or valid cognition
prāmāṇyavāda	the doctrine of the validity of knowledge
pramātṛ	subject
prameya	the object of true cognition or knowledge
prasaṅga	*reductio ad absurdum*
prātibhāsika	apparent; illusory
pratijñā	thesis; hypothesis; the proposition to be established
pratītyasamutpāda	dependent origination; dependent co-arising
pratyakṣa	sense-perception (one of the means of true knowledge)
pravāha	stream
pravṛtti	with mental modifications (the life of action); acting with a view to gain benefits
puruṣa	person; man; subject
rāga	attachment
rajas	one of the three *guṇas;* characterizes activity
ṛta	order; way; truth; an abstract principle
śabda	verbal testimony; sound; word
sādhya	what is to be established; the predicate of the conclusion "major term" (of a syllogism)
saguṇa	with qualities or characteristics
śākṣījñāna	witness-cognition (awareness)
śākṣin	witness-consciousness
śakti	denotative power; force
samādhi	meditation; concentration; absorption
sāmānya	universal
samavāya	inherence
saṁsāra	the world
saṁskāras	residual impressions
saṃskāras	impression; traces of past experience; residual impressions
samvāda	coherence
saṃyoga	conjunction
sannikarṣa	contact
sat	being; existence; reality

satkāryavāda	the doctrine that the effect pre-exists in the material cause
satkhyātivāda	the doctrine that the object of illusion is real or existent
satya	truth; reality
savikalpa	determinate (cognition)
skandha	aggregate
smṛti	memory; recollection
śravaṇa	hearing
śruti	what is heard; a synonym for the Veda
sukha	happiness; pleasure
śūnya	void; empty
śūnyatā	voidness; emptiness
suṣupti	deep or dreamless sleep
sūtra	thread; aphorism
svabhāva	one's own nature
svarga	heaven
svarthānumāna	inference for oneself
svataḥ prāmāṇya	intrinsic validity
svayaṃprakāśa	self-manifesting
syadvāda	the doctrine of conditioned predication
tādātmya	identity
tamas	one of the three *guṇas*; characterizes inertia; darkness
tarka	counter-factual conditional argument; hypothetical argument
tārkikas	one who argues for the sake of arguing
tathāgata	one who thus arrived; a name of the Buddha
tātparya	implied meaning
tīrthaṇkara	a person who has mastered all passions and attained omniscience
triloka	three horizontal levels (heaven, earth, and atmosphere)
tṛṣṇā	thirst; craving
turīya	the highest level of consciousness
udāharaṇa	example
upādhi	limiting adjunct; limiting condition
upamāna	comparison (one of the means of true knowledge)
vaidika	pertaining to the Veda
vairāgya	detachment
varṇa	color; caste
vāsanās	impressions; traces of past experiences
videhamukti	freedom after death
vidhi	injunction; imperative
vidyā	knowledge
vijñāna	consciousness
vikalpa	conceptual construction

vikṣepa	projection
viparyaya	false knowledge
viṣaya	object of cognition; content
viśeṣa	a distinguishing characteristic
viśeṣaṇa	qualificandum
Viṣṇu	a deity (worshipped as early as the Vedic times) taken to be the "preserver" of the universe
vivarta	apparent transformation
vṛtti	mental modification
vyāpti	universal concomitance of the *sādhya* ("major") and *hetu* ("middle") terms of a syllogism
vyavahārika	the empirical
yajña	worship; praise (especially in the context of sacrifice or fire oblations in the Vedic religion)
yama	the deity of death
Yoga	one of the six *āstika* schools of Indian philosophy
yoga	yoke; harness; bind
yogi	one who practices *yoga*
yogyatā	appropriateness; suitability

BIBLIOGRAPHY

Anacker, Stefan. *Seven Works of Vasubandhu*. Delhi: Motilal Banarsidass, 1984.

Bhatt, Govardan P. *Epistemology of the Bhāṭṭa* Mīmāṁsā *School*. Banaras: Chowkhamba, 1962.

Chatterjee, Satischandra, and Dhirendramohan Datta. *An Introduction to Indian Philosophy*. Calcutta: University of Calcutta, 1960.

Dasgupta, Surendranath. *A History of Indian Philosophy*. 5 vols. New Delhi: Motilal Banarsidass, 1975.

Datta, Dhirendra Mohan. *Six Ways of Knowing: A Critical Study of the Vedānta Theory of Knowledge*. 2d rev. ed. Calcutta: The University of Calcutta, 1960.

Devaraja, N. K. *An Introduction to Śaṅkara's Theory of Knowledge*. Delhi: Motilal Banarsidass, 1962.

Dīgha-Nikāya. In *Dialogues of the Buddha*. 3 Vols. Translated by Rhys Davids. New Delhi: Motilal Banarsidass, 2007.

Edgerton, Franklin. *The Beginnings of Indian Philosophy*. London: George Allen & Unwin, 1965.

Gambhirānanda, Swāmī *Eight Upaniṣads with the commentary of Śaṅkarācārya*. 2 vols. Calcutta: Advaita Ashrama, 1965.

Gautama. *Nyāya Sūtras*. With four commentaries including Uddyotakara's *Nyāyavārttika*. Calcutta: Calcutta Sanskrit Series, 1936–44. English translation of *Nyāya Sūtras* with *Bhāṣya* of Vātsyāyana in 4 Vols. Delhi: Motilal Banarsidass, 1974.

Gupta, Bina. *Cit (Consciousness)*. New Delhi: Oxford University Press, 2003.

——. *Disinterested Witness: A Phenomenological Analysis*. Evanston, Illinois: Northwestern University Press, 1998.

——. *Perceiving in Advaita Vedānta*. Lewisburg, Pennsylvania: Bucknell University Press, 1992.

Halbfass, W. *India and Europe*. New York: State University of New York Press, 1988.

——. *Tradition and Reflection: Explorations in Indian Thought*. New York: State University of New York Press, 1991.

Hiriyanna, Mysore. *Outlines of Indian Philosophy*. Bombay: George Allen & Unwin, 1973.

Jayatilleke, K. N. *Early Buddhist Theory of Knowledge*. New Delhi: Motilal Banarsidass, 1983.

Kalupahana, David. *Buddhist Philosophy: A Historical Analysis*. Honolulu: University Press of Hawaii, 1974.

Kane, P. V. *A Brief Sketch of Pūrva-Mīmāṁsā System*. Poona: Aryabhushan Press, 1924.

Kant, Immanuel. *Critique of Pure Reason.* Translated by Norman Kemp Smith. New York: Macmillan Press, 1973.

Kaviraj, Gopinath. "Introduction." In *Bauddha Dharma Darśana,* by Ācārya Narendra Dev. Delhi: Motilal Banarsidass, 1994.

Keith, A. B. *Karma* Mīmāṁsā. Oxford: Oxford University Press, 1921.

Kochumuttom, Thomas. *A Buddhist Doctrine of Experience: A New Translation and Interpretation of the Works of Vasubandhu the Yogacarin.* Delhi: Motilal Banarsidass, 1982.

Krishna, Daya. "Is Nyāya Realist or Idealist?" In *Discussions and Debates in Indian Philosophy,* edited by Daya Krishna. New Delhi: Indian Council of Philosophical Research, 2004.

——. "Three Myths about Indian Philosophy." In *Indian Philosophy: A Counter Perspective.* Delhi: Oxford University Press, 1991, pp. 3–15.

Kumārila. *Śloka-Vārtikā.* Trans. G. N. Jha. Calcutta: Asiatic Society of Bengal, 1908.

Majjhima Nikāya. In *Further Dialogues of the Buddha.* Vols. 5 and 6. Translated by Lord Chalmers, 121–122. London: Oxford University Press, 1927.

Matilal, B. K. *Epistemology, Logic, and Grammar in Indian Philosophical Analysis.* The Hague: Mouton, 1971.

——. *Perception.* Oxford: Clarendon Press, 1986.

Miśra, Keśava. *Tarkabhāṣā.* Translated by Badrinath Sukla. New Delhi: Motilal Banarsidass, 1996.

Mohanty, J. N. *Gangeśa's Theory of Truth.* rev. ed. Santiniketan: Center for Advanced Study in Philosophy, [1966] 1989.

——. "Indian Philosophy Between Tradition and Modernity." In *Indian Philosophy: Past and Present,* edited by Pappu S.S. Rama Rao and R. Puligandla. Delhi: Motilal Banarsidass, 1982.

——. "Nature of Indian Philosophy: Theory of *Pramāṇas.*" In *Explorations in Philosophy,* edited by Bina Gupta. New Delhi: Oxford University Press, 2000.

——. "Nyāya Theory of Doubt." *Phenomenology and Ontology.* The Hague: Nijhoff, 1970.

——. *Reason and Tradition: An Essay on the Nature of Indian Philosophical Thinking.* Oxford: Clarendon Press, 1992.

Moore, Charles A. "Philosophy as Distinct from Religion in India." *Philosophy East and West* XI (1961): 5–7.

Mukhopadhyaya, Pradyot. *Indian Realism: A Rigorous Descriptive Metaphysics.* Calcutta: K. P. Bagachi and Co., 1984.

Murty, K. Satchidananda. *Revelation and Reason in Advaita Vedānta.* New York: Columbia University Press, 1959.

Prasad, Rajendra. "The Concept of *Mokṣa.*" *Philosophy and Phenomenological Research* XXI, no. 3 (1971): 382–383.

Radhakrishnan, Sarvepalli. *The Hindu View of Life.* London: Allen and Unwin, 1964.

——. *Indian Philosophy.* 2 vols. London: George Allen & Unwin, 1923–1927.

——. *The Principal Upanishads.* Delhi: Oxford University Press, 1990.

Raju, P. T. "The Western and the Indian Philosophical Traditions." In *Indian Philosophy: Past and Present,* edited by Pappu S.S. Rama Rao and R. Puligandla. Delhi: Motilal Banarsidass, 1982.

Rambachan, Anantanand. "Response to Professor Arvind Sharma." *Philosophy East and West,* 1994: 721–724.

——. "Śaṃkara's Rationale for *śruti* as the Definitive Source of *Brahmajñāna*: A refutation of some contemporary views." *Philosophy East and West* 1996: 25–38.

Siderits, Mark. "The Sense-Reference Distinction in Indian Philosophy of Language." *Synthese* 69 (1986): 81–106.

Taber, John. "Reason, Revelation and Idealism in Śaṅkara's Vedanta." *Journal of Indian Philosophy* 9 (1981): 283–307.

Tantia, Nathmal. *Studies in Jaina Philosophy*. Benaras: P. V. Research Institute, 1951.

Umāsvāti. *Tattvārthādhigamsūtra*. Mysore: Superintendent Govt. Branch Press, 1944.

Upadhyaya, K. N. "Śaṅkara on Reason, Scriptural Authority, and Self-Knowledge." *Journal of Indian Philosophy* 19 (1991): 121–132.

von Oldenberg, Hermann. *Buddha, Sein Leben, Seine Lehre, Seine Gemeinde*. Stuttgart und Berlin: J. G. Cotta'sche Buchhandlung Nachfolger, 1923.

Warren, Henry Clark. *Buddhism in Translation*. New York: Atheneum, 1963.

Woodward, F. L., trans. *Aṅguttara Nikāya*. Vol. I. London: Luzac and Company, 1960.

INDEX

Taylor & Francis

eBooks

FOR LIBRARIES

ORDER YOUR FREE 30 DAY INSTITUTIONAL TRIAL TODAY!

Over 23,000 eBook titles in the Humanities, Social Sciences, STM and Law from some of the world's leading imprints.

Choose from a range of subject packages or create your own!

- Free MARC records
- COUNTER-compliant usage statistics
- Flexible purchase and pricing options

- Off-site, anytime access via Athens or referring URL
- Print or copy pages or chapters
- Full content search
- Bookmark, highlight and annotate text
- Access to thousands of pages of quality research at the click of a button

For more information, pricing enquiries or to order a free trial, contact your local online sales team.

UK and Rest of World: **online.sales@tandf.co.uk**

US, Canada and Latin America:
e-reference@taylorandfrancis.com

www.ebooksubscriptions.com

Taylor & Francis eBooks
Taylor & Francis Group

A flexible and dynamic resource for teaching, learning and research.

Printed by PGSTL